The United States continues to provide opportunities for travel and tourism to domestic and international travelers. This is the first book to offer students a comprehensive overview of tourism in this region, paying specific attention to the disciplines of geography, tourism studies and, more generally, social science.

Tourism in the USA explains the evolution of tourism, paying attention to the forces that shaped the product that exists today. The focus of the book includes the manner in which tourism has played out in various contexts; the role of federal, state, and local policy is also examined in terms of the effects it has had on the US travel industry and on destinations. The various elements of tourism demand and supply are discussed and the influence that transportation (especially Americans' high personal mobility rates and love affair with the automobile) has had on the sector is highlighted. The economics of tourism are fleshed out before focusing more narrowly on both the urban and rural settings where tourism occurs. A look into the manner in which the spatial structure of cities is transformed through tourism is also offered. Additionally, a brief examination of future issues in American tourism is presented along with explanations concerning the ascendancy of tourism as an economic development tool in various areas.

The book combines theory and practice, as well as integrates a range of useful student-oriented resources to aid understanding and spur further debate, which can be used for independent study or in class exercises. These include:

- 'Closer Look' case studies with reflective questions help show theory in practice and encourage critical thinking about tourism developments in this region
- 'Questions' for discussion at the end of each chapter encourage stimulating debates
- 'Further Reading' sections direct the readers to related book and web resources so that they can learn more about the topics covered in each chapter.

Written in an engaging style and supported with visual aids, this book will provide students around the world with an in-depth and essential understanding of the complexities of tourism and travel in the USA.

Dimitri Ioannides holds the Chair of Human Geography at Mittuniversitetet (Mid-Sweden University). He also is a Professor of Tourism Planning and Development at Missouri State University. Dr. Ioannides has published extensively on various facets of tourism, especially the economic geography of tourism and sustainable tourism development.

Dallen J. Timothy is Director of Tourism Development and Management, School of Community Resources and Development at Arizona State University. He is also Visiting Professor of Heritage Tourism at the University of Sunderland, England, and Editor of the *Journal of Heritage Tourism*. His primary research interests include tourism planning, borderlands and peripheral regions, heritage tourism, religious tourism, and tourism in developing countries. He has published widely on these and several other aspects of tourism studies.

Tourism in the USA

A spatial and social synthesis

Dimitri Ioannides and Dallen J. Timothy

Routledge
Taylor & Francis Group

LONDON AND NEW YORK

First published 2010
by Routledge
2 Park Square, Milton Park, Abingdon, Oxon, OX14 4RN

Simultaneously published in the USA and Canada
by Routledge
270 Madison Avenue, New York, NY 10016

Routledge is an imprint of the Taylor & Francis Group, an informa business

Typeset in TimesNewRoman by
Keystroke, Tettenhall, Wolverhampton
Printed and bound in Great Britain by
TJ International Ltd, Padstow, Cornwall

British Library Cataloguing in Publication Data
A catalogue record for this book is available from the British Library

Library of Congress Cataloguing in Publication Data
Ioannides, Dimitri, 1961–
    Tourism in the USA : a spatial and social synthesis / Dimitri Ioannides
    and Dallen Timothy.
        p. cm.
    1. Tourism — United States. I. Timothy, Dallen J. II. Title.
    G155.U6L63 2009
    338.4′79173—dc22   2009025277

ISBN 13: 978–0–415–95684–0 (hbk)
ISBN 13: 978–0–415–95685–7 (pbk)
ISBN 13: 978–0–203–86465–4 (ebk)

ISBN 10: 0–415–95684–6 (hbk)
ISBN 10: 0–415–95685–4 (pbk)
ISBN 10: 0–203–86465–4 (ebk)

● Contents

List of plates   *vii*
List of figures   *ix*
List of tables   *xi*
List of Closer Look Cases   *xiii*
Preface   *xv*
Acknowledgements   *xvii*

1   Introduction: The tourism phenomenon in the USA   1

2   American tourism: A study through time   12

3   The institutional setting for tourism in the United States   32

4   Demand for tourism in the United States   54

5   Tourist attractions, tourism types, accommodations, and intermediaries   72

6   The transportation system   102

7   Tourism's economic significance   125

8   Urban tourism in the USA   144

9   On the road to Small Town, USA: Rural tourism and its significance   165

10   Conclusions: Trends and futures of tourism in the USA   186

References   *194*
Index   *215*

Plates

1.1	Golden Gate Bridge, San Francisco	2
1.2	Coastal scenic route in California – A major attraction for motorists	6
2.1	El Tovar Hotel, Grand Canyon	20
2.2	Santa Cruz, California – Historic destination to surfers' paradise	23
2.3	Historic Route 66 sign, Needles, California	26
3.1	Seaside Florida, a planned community	35
4.1	US–Mexico border crossing at Nogales, Arizona	56
5.1	A Native American demonstrating her culture to tourists	74
5.2	Freedom Trail, Boston	77
5.3	Plimoth Plantation, Massachusetts	78
5.4	The Bellagio Resort and Casino, Las Vegas	85
5.5	Bed and Breakfast in Mendocino, California	94
6.1	Katy Trail, Missouri – A Rails-to-Trails attraction	106
6.2	Ready for take-off – Aircraft at Newark Airport	114
7.1	Tourism-dependent community: Calistoga, California	142
8.1	Finding New York City in Las Vegas?	148
8.2	Restoring history for tourists – Beale Street, Memphis	158
9.1	Lighthouse in coastal New England	170
9.2	Finding the unusual in rural North Dakota – Rugby, the geographic center of North America	174
9.3	The majestic American countryside – The Grand Canyon	176
10.1	Ethnic foods as a tourist attraction: Chinatown, San Francisco	190

Figures

1.1	The United States of America	5
2.1	The fashionable tour in upstate New York in the early 1800s	15
4.1	US domestic travel volumes, 1996–2006	59
4.2	Seasonal variations in demand in three popular destinations in 2007, as measured by occupancy rate	68
4.3	Seasonal variations in domestic tourism in the US, 2006	69
5.1	National Parks in the United States	84
6.1	Passenger rail network in the United States	104
6.2	Katy Trail, Missouri: a Rails-to-Trails project in the heartland	109
6.3	Major interstate highways in the United States	110
6.4	The hub-and-spoke transportation system	113
6.5	Airline hub-and-spoke system based on two fortress hubs	113
9.1	Tourism-dependent rural counties	180

Tables

4.1 Total tourist arrivals to the US from Canada, Mexico, and overseas, 2007   55
4.2 Top 20 inbound foreign tourist markets to the United States, 2007   57
4.3 Top destination states or territories in the United States among foreign visitors, 2007   58
4.4 US domestic business and leisure person-trips, 2000–2006   59
4.5 Air travel as proportion of total domestic travel, 2000–2006   60
4.6 Domestic demand for lodging types, 2006   60
4.7 Numbers of American overseas trips by year   61
4.8 Destination regions visited by outbound US residents, 2000–2007   62
4.9 Overseas outbound travel from the US by primary purpose of trip, 2007   64
4.10 US Department of State travel warnings and alerts, February 2009   66
5.1 Examples of open-air, living heritage museums in the United States   78
5.2 Examples of Civil War properties operated by the National Park Service   79
5.3 Examples of historic sites based on westward expansion themes   80
5.4 Cultural heritage-based National Park Service properties   82
5.5 Outdoor pursuits in the United States   83
5.6 Nature-based National Park Service properties   84
5.7 Top 15 amusement parks in the United States by number of visits, 2007   88
5.8 A selection of Catholic pilgrimage shrines in the United States   89
6.1 The ten busiest Amtrak train stations in the US, 2008   105
6.2 A selection of airlines in the United States   112
6.3 Low-cost airlines based in the United States   117
6.4 Annual cruise passenger growth in North America   120
6.5 Top ten cruise departure ports in the US, 2005–2007   121
7.1 Selected sectors of the NAICS that can be attributed directly to tourism   129
7.2 Rank of top 20 US cities according to visitor spending   138
7.3 Ranked location quotients (LQ) for the accommodation sector (NAICS 721), select large cities   140
7.4 Ranked location quotients (LQ) for the accommodation sector (NAICS 721), cities under 200,000 employees   140
7.5 Location quotients for various tourism-related sectors for Las Vegas and Orlando   140

Closer Look Cases

2.1 Eureka Springs, AR: a destination reinvented through time   16
2.2 The Grand Canyon   21
3.1 Development without public involvement: Walt Disney World, Florida   36
3.2 Helping a community develop its tourism potential   47
4.1 Americans are still loved abroad   63
4.2 Sundance, Utah, copes with seasonal demand   68
5.1 The Hopi Indians of Arizona protect their cultural heritage   75
5.2 New Age pilgrimage   91
5.3 Travel agents: the voice at the other end of the line   97
6.1 Corridors for trains no more: Rails-to-Trails and tourism   107
6.2 Southwest Airlines: "Often imitated, never duplicated"   117
7.1 Avoiding the straw that breaks the camel's back: balancing tourism's impacts   135
8.1 Ask me no questions   145
8.2 How can mid-sized cities compete for tourism?   153
9.1 Forks, Washington: Twilight zone   171
9.2 National parks and rural tourism   176

Preface

This book is the result of almost two decades of thinking about and researching tourism as a geographic phenomenon. We both have taught a variety of tourism-related courses at universities in the United States and elsewhere over the years and have benefited from witnessing first-hand how tourism evolves in urban and rural communities throughout this country and many others. We have observed with interest the effects of tourism on local economies as well as the natural and cultural environments and have studied its interaction with topics ranging from economic geography to sustainable development, and from cultural heritage to cross-border collaboration.

Both of us have regularly engaged in lively dialogues concerning many different facets of tourism with colleagues at meetings held in venues throughout the United States and in some of the most fascinating and remote parts of the world. We have been extremely fortunate to have been among a relatively small group of geographers in the United States who in the 1990s researched various aspects of travel and tourism, and have watched in silent amazement and with a hint of pride as more and more young academics have embraced this fascinating area of study. Indeed, the growth over the last few years in output of monographs, edited collections, research articles, dissertations and theses, and proceedings papers that relate to tourism, many of which have been prepared by geographers, has been truly astounding.

Nevertheless, we would both argue that it is in the context of developing our various university courses and in the actual interaction with our students that we have developed the most as tourism researchers. In-class discussions, not to mention our involvement in leading field courses directly related to the geography of tourism, have enabled both of us to mature as scholars and teachers. It is within this context, however, that we also recognize the various gaps in the literature when it comes to suitable textbooks for tourism courses. To be sure there exist quite a few textbooks engaging in comprehensive examinations of travel and tourism, but many of these have been written by scholars in business and marketing, and their focus is markedly non-spatial. There also exist various texts on topics such as the impacts of tourism, the interaction of tourism and sustainable development, tourism and heritage, and tourism and transportation.

One interesting characteristic about many publications on tourism is their tendency to be edited collections. While there is immense value in such endeavors in that they allow the reader to reflect on different perspectives relating to a particular theme, such books are not always the best tools for teaching purposes. In fact, in our respective teaching experiences we have often found it hard to identify a dominant textbook for a course, choosing instead to assign readings from a variety of texts or from journal publications. There is always value in such an approach to a large extent because it allows the students to draw material from numerous viewpoints. At the same time, however, it means that students and instructors lack a single dominant text that can form the basis of the course. And, remarkably, given the large number of courses taught in the United States that focus specifically on tourism, and despite the fact that many such courses are taught in geography departments, there is a marked absence of overviews of the working of tourism in any particular country or region. Indeed, surprisingly there is no text that provides an in-depth examination of various facets of tourism within the entire United States.

When we were originally approached by Routledge in March 2006 with an invitation to prepare this book, neither of us hesitated in making our decision to accept. We were particularly honored to be asked to undertake this project and at the same time we were extremely excited because of the challenges that lay ahead. There have been many twists and turns in preparing the text, and this explains to a major extent why the endeavor took longer than we anticipated. In fact just in the week leading up to the wrapping up of the project a new potential worldwide crisis reared its ugly head; this time it was Swine Influenza, or virus H1N1. It remains to be seen what impact that will have on travel both in the United States and internationally.

We wanted to ensure that the book provided a comprehensive overview of the travel and tourism phenomenon in the United States but also to make certain that the geography and social science were not lost in the text. Making a final decision on our approach has been a major challenge in itself.

While the book provides a geographic angle on tourism, it is not written only with students of geography in mind. Rather, we feel that instructors in any undergraduate course within the social sciences that relates to tourism can make use of such a text either as the principal resource or as supporting material. Further, while *Tourism in the USA* was written primarily with an American university audience in mind, it certainly could be a valuable resource for instructors in other parts of the world who wish to offer their students a glimpse of the workings of tourism in North America.

It is with these thoughts in our minds that this book is being launched. Some people would possibly contend that given the uncertain future of the travel industry both globally and within the USA, largely because of the ongoing economic crisis, the timing of the release is odd. Yet, we feel that this is precisely the best time to reflect on the state of the travel and tourism industry in the USA. This is an era when the future is perhaps more uncertain than ever before. In addition to the latest worldwide economic crisis, the events relating to the "war on terror" of the last few years, not to mention issues like the growing concern for global climate change and rapidly diminishing energy resources, mean that nothing about travel and tourism can be taken for granted. The whole shroud of uncertainty surrounding tourism's future both in the United States and worldwide makes it even more imperative to sharpen our understanding of this phenomenon. It is our sincere hope that the readers of this book will examine the encompassed material critically and use it as a launching pad for further in-depth analysis of a sector that is not yet fully understood.

Professor Dimitri Ioannides
Östersund, Sweden

Professor Dallen J. Timothy
Gilbert, Arizona

Acknowledgements

Though we have both toyed with the idea of preparing a book specifically on tourism within the United States, the principal instigator of this project was David McBride, the one-time senior editor for Routledge in New York. David was a key advocate of the book from the beginning. We truly are honored that he approached us to undertake this ambitious work because it gave us both the opportunity to collaborate on what has turned out to be an extremely exciting project.

We are also indebted to Andrew Mould, Senior Editor for Geography at Routledge (UK office), who chose to take over the project once David left the company. In particular Emma Travis and Michael P. Jones have been extremely helpful in guiding us through the publication process. Without their help it would be impossible to sort through the quagmire of requirements one has to follow when trying to convert a raw manuscript into the final product. Thanks to all three of you for your gentle task-mastering.

A huge thank you and verbal hug also has to go to Evangelia Petridou who has been a great help from the outset of this endeavor. Not only has she undertaken much of the primary research relating to various issues covered in the book, she has also written several of the boxed case studies covered in the chapters and has offered immense editorial assistance. Without her careful comments and suggestions we would have struggled to finish the text. Her insider's perspectives on the travel agency and airline industries were of immense value.

In addition we would like to extend a major thanks to Shuo Sheng (Derek) Wu who prepared all the wonderful maps included in this text. Derek, who works as the cartographer for the Department of Geography, Geology, and Planning and the Center for Resource Planning and Management at Missouri State University, took time from his extremely busy schedule to create these maps.

We must also acknowledge a number of people at our respective institutions. Specifically, Dimitri Ioannides would like to thank Tom Plymate, Department Head in the Geography, Geology, and Planning Department, and Tammy Jahnke, Dean of the College of Natural and Applied Sciences at Missouri State University for graciously making arrangements for a reduced teaching load during the fall 2008 semester to work on this book. Bo Svensson, Director of ETOUR at Mittuniversitetet in Sweden – where Dimitri moved in August 2008 – has patiently allowed him to finish the project before embarking on various other important projects. Bo was also very gracious to provide some of the pictures from his personal collection to be included in this text. Other colleagues at ETOUR have helped Dimitri maintain his sanity by offering opportunities for breaks at critical moments. Especially, Daniel Wolf-Watz should be thanked for the joining Dimitri in some training to "clear the mind."

A special thanks must be reserved for Dr. Kevin Evans of Missouri State University who has been a marvelous sounding board for Dimitri's ideas. Despite Kevin's training in the hard sciences – he is a geologist – he has amazing insights to offer about the United States and was instrumental in identifying issues to be covered in the book. Moreover,

Kevin has stayed up many a night with Dimitri just discussing the project and offering moral support. He has been a true friend.

Dallen would specifically like to thank all those with whom he has traveled throughout the United States – it has been an enjoyable journey. He considers his homeland a prized jewel and worthy of much more exploration. Dallen appreciates the support and understanding of Kathy Andereck, Director of the School of Community Resources and Development at Arizona State University for "cutting him some slack" in his administrative responsibilities as the Tourism Management and Development Program Director in the School. This added freedom was extremely instrumental in allowing the book to be completed. Dallen also wishes to extend a hand of appreciation to his colleagues in the Department of Geography at Brigham Young University, Provo, Utah, where he was a Professor for one year, during which time he carried out much of the research for this book.

Finally, we would each like to thank our respective families without whose support this project would never have been completed. For Dimitri, Evangelia has been a rock, while Michael (Mikie) has provided many instances of comic relief with his insightful comments about life in Sweden. Dimitri's daughter, Sasha, has been amazingly patient and good-hearted putting up with her father's prolonged absences. She was also a very patient co-traveler on his last trip to the American Southwest in March 2009, offering her own thoughts on the best perspectives for picture-taking. Dallen's wife, Carol, and children, Kendall, Aaron, Olivia and Spencer, have continued to support him in all his endeavors, including this book. Carol's pleasant attitude about having to make dinner alone during his late nights on the computer does not go unnoticed. To all of you, and many others, we owe a deep debt of gratitude.

➊ Introduction
The tourism phenomenon
in the USA

2008 will clearly go into the history books as a year of turbulence and contrasts. In the twelve months since UNWTO published its January 2008 edition of the *World Tourism Barometer*, including forecasts for the year ahead, the growth in international tourist arrivals has slowed drastically worldwide, under the influence of an extremely volatile and unfavorable global economy – due to factors such as the credit crunch, the widening financial crisis, commodity and oil price rises, and massive exchange rate fluctuations. All this has, inevitably, undermined both business and consumer confidence, contributing in turn to the current global recession.

(United Nations World Tourism Organization 2009: 1)

The quote above, from the most recent *UNWTO World Tourism Barometer* (2009), contextualizes the growing uncertainty on the part of tourism experts worldwide concerning the sector's future. Certainly, in the United States the public is inundated with stories on a daily basis about how the current global recession has affected Americans' travel patterns. It is said, for instance, that an increasing number of people are choosing a "staycation," when on leave, a far more affordable and stress-free approach to spending their holidays, allowing them either to explore the attractions of their home community or, simply, relax by the backyard pool (Alban 2008). Meanwhile, communities, large and small, report declining visitation, lower room occupancy rates, and reduced revenue. According to the Las Vegas Convention and Visitors Authority, the number of arrivals in the city during 2008 fell by 4.4 percent; room occupancy rates were also down, and the daily revenue per room was reduced by almost 10 percent from the previous year. Additionally, the city reported a decline in convention attendees and noted that revenue from gambling has also fallen substantially (Velotta 2009).

The travel industry in the USA is, of course, no stranger to crises, especially since the tragic events of September 11, 2001. In the immediate aftermath of that fateful day demand for travel fell astronomically and the tourism industry nationwide took a massive hit (Floyd *et al*. 2003; Goodrich 2002; Green *et al*. 2003). The airline industry was particularly hard hit and has since had to undergo major restructuring in order to survive. Importantly, much of the luster that used to be associated with the trip itself (especially air travel) has all but disappeared as travelers not only have to face arduous security checks at airports and harbors but also rapidly declining service quality, long delays, lost luggage, and other hardships, many of which travelers claim to be an invasion of their privacy but which the government argues are necessary for national security.

Nevertheless, despite the pitfalls associated with travel during the era of the "war on terror," the US tourism industry gradually rebounded as an increasing number of Americans quickly learned to adapt to the new realities in their travel pursuits. Regardless of the public outcry about having to remove their shoes for x-ray purposes at airports, having to put up with surly Transportation Security Administration (TSA) officers or airline personnel, or having to endure long traffic jams, and major road works during holidays, people have once again started traveling, in record numbers, that is until the latest economic downturn, which began in 2007. In other words, things may appear dire at present, and the most ardent pessimists would suggest that the sky is falling on America's travel industry. Nonetheless if history has a tendency to repeat itself, sooner or later the economic crisis will turn around. Furthermore, while the current recession may be far more severe than others in the past, it is likely that people will eventually adjust. We can already see that people are traveling less often than they did in the past as a coping mechanism. Maybe their choice of destination or their mode of travel will change, but truth be told, there will always be demand to visit places in the USA and abroad.

The United States is a vast country, with a remarkable range of attractions from unique natural formations to some of the most astonishing human-created spectacles on earth. The USA is home to instantly recognizable global symbols and emblems, including the Statue of Liberty, the Golden Gate Bridge (Plate 1.1), the Grand Canyon, and the Saint Louis Gateway Arch. It is the home of Hollywood and the birthplace of Coca-Cola and the "worlds" of Disney, powerful symbols that have been so influential in terms of "Americanizing" the world. Additionally, in the United States holidaymaking as a democratic phenomenon has a fairly long history ranging back to the nineteenth century, and Americans have long enjoyed a very high standard of living compared to most other countries which has for decades allowed many families to use discretionary income for vacation travel.

Plate 1.1 Golden Gate Bridge, San Francisco
(Dimitri Ioannides)

Communities throughout the United States have increasingly focused on tourism as the motor that is meant to engender economic growth and diversification, especially in the post-industrial era. Increasingly, places compete with each other on the basis of which one can offer the most dazzling aquarium, the best-designed and largest convention center, or the most up-to-date sports arena. It is not unusual for local governments to authorize enormous amounts of spending on infrastructure that underpins tourism from airport facilities to civic parks or from new sidewalks to baseball stadiums (Judd 2003).

Yet, despite all the fuss about tourism in the USA, it is more than clear that it is a misunderstood phenomenon. Civic leaders, for instance, often support major spending on projects they hope will entice a large number of visitors, without first undertaking a detailed feasibility study to see if the expenditure is indeed justified. Frequently they acknowledge that the project will cost far more than it was supposed to and that they expect the revenue to fall short of expectations. Nevertheless, they will often back the expenditure for a new stadium or museum regardless of whether the money can be recouped in a timely fashion, as long as the project serves to boost the community's image (Crompton 2004; Judd 1995). This failure to undertake a rigorous analysis of tourism's impacts in turn further fuels already existing debates concerning the sector's economic effects. On the one hand we regularly hear from analysts how tourism is a major sector in terms of contribution to employment generation and regional economic growth, while on the other hand critics lament that the jobs created are poorly paid, often part-time, and unskilled. The same critics also argue that reinventing an economy into one that is based on tourism services is an insult to a glorious past based on the production of tangible manufactured goods like steel or military equipment (Herzenberg *et al.* 1998; Ioannides and Debbage 1997, 1998).

To be sure, debates about the dynamics and effects of tourism extend well beyond economics. Discussions have been generated, many of them relating to the United States itself, exploring urban tourism as a modern phenomenon, and academics have, among others, adopted a political economy perspective to comprehend the workings of tourism and its effects within cities (Hoffman *et al.* 2004; Judd and Fainstein 1999). What are the ramifications, for instance, of the growth of tourism for the spatial structure of metropolitan regions? Who benefits from tourism's growth and who loses out? How do local populations react to the influx of visitors and can we, in the modern era, really discriminate between tourists and local residents who use the same facilities?

Discussions have also been produced examining the darker side of tourism development, especially from a socio-cultural perspective, in specific parts of the USA. In *Devil's Bargains*, for instance, Hal Rothman (1998) weaves a fascinating account of the history of the growth of tourism in the American west since the early part of the nineteenth century, while also warning that communities that embrace the sector as a means of growth are selling-out to outside interests and, consequently, become subject to neocolonialist, exploitative relationships.

The issues just highlighted reflect only a fraction of the interest that has been generated in tourism-related discourse. We are aware of these and many other discussions and, in fact, we touch upon a number of them throughout the text. Nevertheless, the principal objective of this book is not to launch into an in-depth analysis of these topics. Instead a choice was made to leave these for more specialized volumes. Our aim here is to provide an overview and detailed account of the workings of tourism as a modern-day phenomenon in the United States of America. We have approached this, conscious of the fact that there are no other texts that examine the breadth and depths of tourism in the United States as a whole. Further, there are several texts that examine the structure and composition of the American tourism business (e.g., travel retailers and wholesalers, airlines, and destination management organizations) but these tend to be non-geographical (e.g., Goeldner and Ritchie 2006). In other words they do not relate to any specific locality or region within the country.

While this book like many others deals with tourism, it does so specifically with reference to the United States and, as such, provides a geographic perspective of the phenomenon. We explore how tourism has evolved, the industry's structure and organization, and analyze the development of tourism in various contexts. The rest of this chapter briefly introduces the topic and provides a detailed outline of the rest of the book.

Factors affecting travel in the USA

On the surface, Americans' proclivity to travel reflects the extreme mobility which characterizes this society. Throughout the history of the United States people have moved in large numbers in constant search of more fertile land, a well-paying job, and a better life in general. Even today, Americans are extremely mobile, often traversing hundreds or even thousands of miles in pursuit of better employment or a change in lifestyle. Consider, for instance, the large numbers of highly educated people who are drawn to trendy cities like Portland, Oregon, and Seattle, Washington, or the vast number of retirees who escape the metropolitan areas of Chicago, Minneapolis, and New York for warmer climates in the south, like Arizona and Florida. Furthermore, on a daily basis Americans undertake numerous trips between their residences, work places, shopping centers, or the places where their children go to school and play.

Two major factors have historically enabled Americans to be as mobile as they are. The first has been a prevailing national psyche that epitomized the need to settle the frontier, to move west and constantly seek better living and work opportunities. More importantly, however, it was the exceptional transportation infrastructure that evolved over the last 150 years or so that enabled this increase in mobility . First, during the early nineteenth century, the elaborate system of canals enabled New Yorkers to explore the far reaches of their own state. Not much later, railroads linked the distant corners of the country with the already settled north and central eastern seaboards. With the advent of the automobile in the early part of the twentieth century and, most importantly, the growing affordability of personal cars from the 1920s onwards, Americans became the first society worldwide where people had the ability to travel a considerable distance to a destination of their own choosing without being shackled to network or timetable restrictions. This new-found liberty led to the growing desire to take road trips for the sole purpose of leisure and relaxation, including visits to the seaside or the countryside. Especially after the 1950s, with the development of a comprehensive Interstate Highway System and the enormous increase in living standards, more and more Americans sought to travel for the purpose of recreation or to visit friends and relatives. Indeed, as reflected in so many Hollywood movies of the 1960s and '70s, it was almost unthinkable for a middle-class American family not to embark in the ubiquitous station-wagon on the annual obligatory trip to discover the wonders the country had to offer.

The advent of jet passenger travel in the late 1950s and the introduction of safer and larger aircraft served to increase the popularity of air travel, and by the 1980s, following the deregulation of the airline industry and the emergence of cheaper fares, increasing numbers of Americans took to the skies. While business travel flourished because of superior air connections, the leisure market also grew. Importantly, new destinations further afield emerged and flourished because of air transportation, including Hawaii and southern Florida. Meanwhile, a growing number of Americans began to spend their holidays abroad, in places like the Caribbean and Europe while, concurrently, better global connections meant that more overseas visitors began coming to the United States.

The high degree of mobility is, of course, but one aspect of the story of travel and tourism within the United States. The transportation system has been a key enabling factor, allowing Americans to become increasingly mobile, but it is the rich supply of a wide range of attractions, both natural and human-built, that has stirred the imagination for travel in the first place. After all, the United States is a vast country, with a total land area exceeding nine million square kilometers. It is more than twice the size of the European Union and a little larger than China. Indeed, it is the third largest country in the world, after Russia and Canada. The vastness of the country means that certain parts encompass some of the remotest parts of the world while, concurrently, others have some of the most developed metropolitan regions. While the country's climate could be described mostly as temperate, it also encompasses an assortment of other climatic zones, including arctic (Alaska), tropical or sub-tropical (Hawaii and Florida), and arid (Southwest) (CIA 2009). In turn, the wide array of climatic zones means that different parts of the country have varying types of vegetation. In the Pacific Northwest there are large expanses of temperate rainforest; in places like western Kansas and Nebraska one can find vast expanses of prairieland, and in the southwest scrub vegetation is dominant (Rowntree *et al.* 2006). The contiguous part of the country, the lower 48 states, spans approximately 5,000 kilometers from the Pacific to the Atlantic Ocean (Figure 1.1). The northernmost coastline of the country (northern Alaska) is located on the Arctic Ocean, while farther south the Hawaiian Islands lie in the tropics.

Numerous landscapes exist throughout the United States from the fjords of Alaska to the sandy beaches of Hawaii, California and Florida and from the impressive mountain chains such as the Rockies, Cascades, and Sierra Nevada in the west to the far gentler Ozarks in the lower Midwest and the Piedmont and Appalachians in the east. Indeed, the

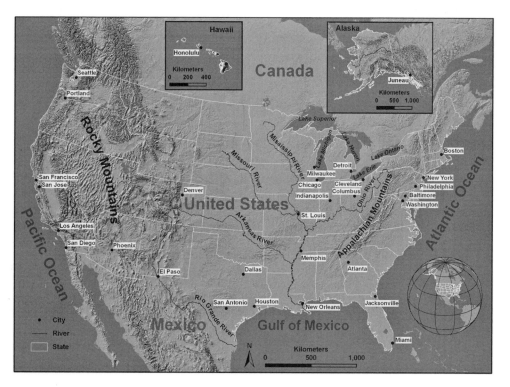

Figure 1.1 The United States of America

United States claims both the highest and lowest points in North America, Mount McKinley in Alaska, and Death Valley in California. In the northern part of the United States are the Great Lakes, while in many other parts of the country there are many smaller lakes, including a significant number of artificially constructed dams and reservoirs of varying sizes.

Places like the Grand Canyon, Yellowstone, the Florida Everglades, Niagara Falls, or the volcanic peaks of Hawaii are among the unique wonders of the world, high on the wish list of many aspiring travelers, Americans and foreigners. Raging rivers allow people to engage in white-water rafting or kayaking, while in many parts of the country the tradition of floating down a slow-moving river in a canoe is one of the most popular pastimes on a hot summer weekend. Scenic highways, such as Route 1 that hugs the California coastline, have become major attractions for motorists (Plate 1.2). Other travelers spend their holidays following the routes made popular in folklore (e.g., Route 66) or the paths of early explorers like Lewis and Clark who opened the way to the American West. In recent times, thousands of kilometers of abandoned canals and rail-roads have been converted into greenways – hiking paths, bicycle and horse trails, and riparian corridors – and they are enjoyed by millions of users on a daily basis.

Meanwhile, heritage and culture enthusiasts are spoiled for choice. They can, for instance, view sites of early European settlement along the Atlantic seaboard. People are able to visit battlegrounds marking the various wars fought on American soil from 1500 onwards or the homes of famous historical figures who played a key role in shaping the country's fortunes. Furthermore, many American cities have emerged as key global tourist destinations, given to their attainment of wide-scale global recognition through

Plate 1.2 Coastal scenic route in California – A major attraction for motorists
(Bo Svensson)

art, literature, and film. Then there are localities that have been created entirely for the pleasure of visitors, places that represent the epitome of mass tourism, such as Las Vegas and Disney World, catering to millions of tourists annually. There are also much smaller communities that have reinvented themselves as attractions for local and regional day visitors. In addition to all these attractions, communities throughout the USA constantly seek to draw visitors by hosting small-scale festivals and events, as well as mega events such as Olympic Games, the Super Bowl, major rock concerts, or air shows.

The population of the United States, which currently stands at 307 million (CIA 2009), is highly diverse compared to other western countries reflecting more than four centuries of migration from various parts of the world. Today, millions of migrants live in the country (Rowntree 2006). With its white population standing at about 80 percent, the USA also has sizeable ethnic groups (African-Americans – 12.85 percent; Asian-Americans – 4.43 percent). Hispanics who live in the USA, including people of different races who are of Latin American descent, amount to 15.1 percent of the population. More importantly, however, several parts of the country (especially many major metropolitan areas) have particularly high concentrations of ethnic groups, and many of these areas have developed a reputation as extremely popular visitor destinations. Consider, for instance, the "ethnic villages" in so many American cities, the "Little Italies," "Little Havanas," the "Chinatowns" and "Koreatowns," which draw domestic and international visitors. On any given day one can see throngs of tourists meandering their way through Boston's North End, one of the nation's most famous Italian ethnic villages. Many of them stop for a café espresso and a cannoli at Caffe dello Sport, or a pizza at Ernesto's. Others simply stroll through on their way to Boston's Old North Church, following the historic Freedom Trail, and along the way they have the opportunity to look at interesting buildings, or watch elderly men sitting on the sidewalk discussing the latest soccer results from Italy or simply chatting with their neighbors across the street.

Likewise, entire regions boast a unique cultural heritage like the Cajun towns along the Louisiana coastline. Lafayette, Louisiana, is an extremely popular destination and attracts many people who are in search of Creole and Cajun cuisine – an important part of that region's culinary heritage. Numerous small towns throughout the American heartland and hinterland boast an ethnic heritage tied to their original settlers. Though most would be hard pressed today to find many descendants of their original founding fathers, they have skillfully exploited their image as "Dutch" towns, "German" towns, or "Swedish" towns and developed a range of attractions to draw in visitors.

Finally, it is vital to mention that the United States has a rich cultural heritage tied to its Native American population. Though the number of Native Americans (including Alaska natives) comprises less than 1 percent of the total population, there are many sites throughout the country where visitors can see evidence of their settlement through history. The Southwest is the most popular destination region for people who are interested in Native American heritage. The Hopi and Zuni Pueblos, for instance, in New Mexico and Arizona draw a large number of visitors, and many people spend significant amounts of money on traditional and modern Indian art in these areas.

The rich cultural background of the country, which is tied to its extremely diverse population, the incredible natural wonders that are on offer in so many regions, and some of the most photogenic contemporary cities, not to mention certain truly astounding representations of, what Umberto Eco (1986) calls, "Hyperreality" (e.g., Las Vegas and Disney World) mean the United States has been established as a major player in international tourism. The World Tourism Organization has for several years listed the USA as one of the top five international destinations worldwide. In 2007 the country attracted 56 million visitors (US Department of Commerce 2008). Unsurprisingly, Canada was the single largest source of visitors; that year almost 18 million Canadians came to the USA, many of them on shopping and sightseeing trips in states bordering the southern Canadian provinces. Mexicans are also a major market for United States tourism, while the four most important overseas sources of visitors are the UK, Japan, Germany, and France respectively

Moreover, since the United States has such a large population and because of its vast size and diverse offering of regions, it means there is a substantial domestic population crisscrossing the country for the purpose of visiting various destinations. The majority of trips, especially those by car, are within an easy drive from home. For example, people will take short vacations or weekend trips to destinations within their own state or surrounding states. However, if they have time many Americans do not think much of driving considerable distances, sometimes a thousand kilometers or more to visit friends and relatives, to view a major event, or to participate in some specialized activity that they cannot undertake closer to home (e.g., skiing). And, of course, nowadays taking a plane to visit grandma in California or to take the kids to Disney World in Florida hardly raises an eyebrow. Neither is one too surprised if one's neighbors come back with a tan after a four-day absence; they may have just been on a mini-cruise to nowhere out of Miami or New Orleans.

Themes covered: outline of the book

Although this book primarily offers a comprehensive overview of tourism in the United States, certain themes should be highlighted at the outset. In discussing the forces leading to the manner in which tourism has evolved, attention is paid to the role of policy. It is not our contention that United States tourism is a result of targeted government policies but, rather that a variety of decisions and actions at all levels of government from federal to local have either directly or indirectly influenced the sector. Decisions relating to the development of transportation or actions that have had something to do with the establishment of national parks have undoubtedly had an influence on the manner in which tourism has evolved, regardless of the fact that tourism was not the primary concern of the policymakers when the parks were established or when the interstate highways were constructed. Also, the decision to build the Hoover Dam in the 1930s, to provide water to the parched Southwest, indisputably became a key factor behind the phenomenal development of Las Vegas as one of the world's premier destinations.

These issues are first highlighted in Chapter 2, which offers a historical account of the manner in which tourism has evolved since the early 1800s. It can also be seen that the development of tourism was very much tied to technological advancements, especially in the transportation sector. A growing sense of nationalism, especially during the latter part of the nineteenth century, fueled the industry's further growth as Americans became increasingly proud of what the country had to offer in its vast interior. Additionally, the growth of the national parks played a massive role in encouraging travel, especially in the western states, and later on programs such as the release of the American Guide Series during the 1930s played their part in promoting tourism throughout the country.

Chapter 3 offers perspectives on the institutional setup in the United States. The chapter stresses that the USA is quite unique in that it lacks a central tourism organization on a par with organizations that exist in so many other countries. Indeed, much of the responsibility for tourism promotion and marketing rests on state and local institutions while at the federal level the major body responsible for tourism-related matters is hidden within the Department of Commerce and plays little more than an advisory role. Having said that, the reader is again reminded that despite the absence of a focused tourism policy at the national level there exist various measures and actions emanating from various federal departments that have consequences for tourism's growth and evolution. Yet another issue discussed in Chapter 3 is the issue of tourism planning. In the majority of cases, tourism plans are essentially marketing documents geared to boost the image of tourism in a particular state or locality and increase arrival numbers. By contrast, physical planning guidelines that relate to the development of tourism facilities and infrastructure in a sustainable manner are far from commonplace.

Chapter 4 analyzes the demand for tourism in the United States. It discusses how the country compares to other nations as an international tourist destination and offers a brief insight into demand on the part of Americans for overseas travel. A discussion of domestic tourism is also included in this chapter given that this substantially exceeds international arrivals and because it is so important for the overall national economy. Additionally, the chapter explores various factors that influence changes in demand over time.

The following two chapters shift to the supply-side of tourism. Chapter 5 focuses on the tourism-related attractions that draw visitors to the country or initiate domestic travel. This detailed investigation also examines the lodging sector briefly and finishes with an overview of travel intermediaries, namely the actors who in the past have been significant in terms of arranging and selling holidays for travelers. Some speculation as to the future of these extremely volatile sectors is also provided. In Chapter 6 the focus turns to the transportation system as one of the most critical elements of tourism supply. Attention is drawn to various modes of transportation and the love affair that Americans have with their own personal automobiles. Indeed, in the United States there is a certain stigma often attached to public modes of transportation, especially bus transit and to a lesser extent rail travel, and as a result, these methods of travel have been de-popularized for a variety of uses, including vacation travel. By contrast, air travel has become increasingly popular, especially following the industry's deregulation in the late 1970s and early '80s, and even though airlines are currently facing a number of economic and structural problems, this mode of travel remains the most popular for long distances. Chapter 6 also examines cruise tourism, which has proved to be quite phenomenal over the last two decades. Indeed, it appears that cruise tourism still has considerable room for growth given that cruises cater to a substantial number of travelers who find the convenience associated with all-inclusive arrangements too hard to resist.

The next portion of the book (Chapters 7–9) shifts direction to highlight the economics of US tourism and the urban and rural contexts within which it occurs. In Chapter 7 we examine the economic significance of tourism. It begins with an overview of the theoretical conundrum that accompanies attempts to portray tourism as an industry, and seeks to identify simple ways to overcome this definitional problem. This conceptual debate is followed by an overview that seeks to shed some light on the size of the US travel and tourism sector at the national, regional, and local levels. The final portion of the chapter discusses how a relatively simple technique, which has long been available to economic geographers (namely the use of location quotients), can improve our understanding of the relative importance of tourism in metropolitan regions.

Chapters 8 and 9 depict the characteristics and growth of tourism in two distinct settings – urban areas and rural regions. Chapter 8 begins with a discussion of the study of urban tourism in general and explains how the topic has shifted from its peripheral position in academic discourse to more central discourses that have to do with themes like urban restructuring, the growth of the experience economy, and the effects that globalization may have on eliminating local differences. Among others, we see how regulation theory has been forwarded as a conceptual framework enabling a better understanding of the interplay between major pressures relating to globalization and local contingencies. For instance, the role of the state is paramount in understanding how tourism evolves in a particular locality; this is something that has not been explored in depth in the US context until now. Neither has the concept that geography actually does matter, a theme that must be stressed when explaining the differences between different locations and how tourism evolves and functions differently. Chapter 8 also examines why cities seek visitors in the first place and offers a description of different types of tourist cities. Finally, the chapter also looks at recent trends that see more and more visitors to cities venture beyond the touristified downtown enclaves into other parts of the city, including various residential neighborhoods and asks what this phenomenon ultimately means.

The focus of Chapter 9 shifts to rural settings, where the industry has emerged as a major lifeline for many smaller communities throughout the American countryside. In addition to defining what is meant by "rural America," the chapter exposes some of the most significant handicaps that non-metropolitan regions have to face on a daily basis in their efforts to grow tourism. Attention then turns to the significance of tourism as a strategy for economic survival and diversification in rural communities. It is obvious that regions where there is a wealth of natural amenities (e.g., access to lakes or rivers or snow-covered mountains for skiing) possess locational advantages to become successful visitor destinations. At the other extreme, many rural communities at first glance do not possess the balance of ingredients necessary to develop a successful visitor industry. What then do these places do? Beyond discussing the answer to this question Chapter 9 also offers a synopsis of the major positive and negative impacts associated with tourism development.

The final chapter of the book focuses on drawing out the main theories, concepts, and issues noted throughout the book, placing them in a broader context of what is known about the tourism phenomenon in the United States. It also provides a cursory overview of current issues and challenges facing the US tourism industries and highlights critical issues that must remain at the forefront of thought and action as government agencies, destination communities, entrepreneurs, and students of tourism plan, develop and research the intricacies of this vast sector in the United States of America.

Questions

1. In your opinion how important has the US auto-culture been for the type of tourism that has evolved in the USA?

2. The term "staycation" has recently become a popular word especially in the media. What factors have led to the growing tendency of Americans to take a "staycation"? Have you, or has anyone you know, chosen this form of activity instead of traveling during your time off?

Further reading

Goeldner, C.R. and Ritchie, J.R. (2006) *Tourism: Principles, Practices, Philosophies.* Hoboken, NJ: Wiley.

Rothman, H.K. (1998) *Devil's Bargains: Tourism in the Twentieth-Century American West*. Lawrence, KS: University Press of Kansas.

Useful Internet resources

CIA World Factbook: https://www.cia.gov/library/publications/the-world-factbook/
Transportation Security Administration: http://www.tsa.gov/
World Tourism Organization: http://www.unwto.org/

2 American tourism
A study through time

The inspiration for the growing popularity of Lake George in the 1820s would come not from James Caldwell but from the works of two famous visitors: James Fenimore Cooper and his acquaintance Thomas Cole, who both explored Lake George in the mid-1820s. Their artistic efforts gave natural wonders and historic sites in the United States the type of exposure that only European destinations had previously enjoyed.

(Corbett 2001: 45–46)

The railroad differed from any preceding form of travel. Not only did it comfortably convey larger numbers of people greater distances than ever before, but for the first time, people passed through a landscape yet did not necessarily engage it.

(Rothman 1998: 39)

Introduction

For decades, the image of Americans piling into the family car to undertake a cross-country road trip to see grandma, attend a ballgame, visit the seaside, national parks, civil war battlefields, historic neighborhoods or Disney World has become a way of life. By the same token, demand for cruise travel or for activities like gambling has risen continuously. Heavily overcrowded airports, especially during popular holiday periods, have become the norm and passengers seem increasingly resigned to expect long lines and delays.

Growing demand for tourist-related activities is, of course, tied to the fact that a growing number of households budget for leisure travel in the same manner they save money for consumer products like entertainment systems or household appliances. It is worth remembering that demand among the masses for leisure-time travel is very much a modern phenomenon and one which was virtually unknown 150 years ago. Indeed, tourism as an activity did not begin in the United States until the second decade of the nineteenth century and, at that time it was very much restricted to a small number of extremely affluent people. Moreover, during these early days, very few places had emerged that could truly be labeled "tourist destinations."

To a major extent the growth of tourism since the beginning of the nineteenth century has been a result of a sequence of innovations in transportation systems, which through time served to make travel over significant distances to what once were hard-to-reach places faster, affordable, and more comfortable. As the real cost of travel fell, an increasing number of people from many walks of life aspired to take a holiday some place that would be within their budget.

The introduction of the railroad in the early 1800s led to the rapid growth of communities throughout the country, many of which became commercial and industrial centers. In turn, this led to the growth of an increasingly affluent middle class, which was driven by a growing demand for consumer products; travel for leisure and relaxation became a direct outgrowth of this demand.

Through time the railroad has been eclipsed by other modes of transportation, which again have had a significant impact on Americans' travel patterns. During the 1920s and '30s an increasing number of Americans could afford private automobiles and the growth of this mode of transportation was quickly accompanied by the creation of a comprehensive interstate road system that by the 1950s made extensive cross-country travel a reality. Additionally, the growth of air travel over the last 50 years has meant that people are no longer restricted within a radius of a few hundred miles from their homes but can take affordable trips to far-off places like Hawaii and Florida. Airline deregulation in the late 1970s played a major role in democratizing air travel and making it affordable to the masses as in real terms the price of flying fell significantly between 1975 and 1995.

The chapter that follows provides a historical perspective of the dynamics of tourism evolution within the United States over the last 200 years. We show that beyond the innovation of transportation systems, the growth in demand for tourism and the resulting rise and fall of key destinations was tied to various factors including changes in public policy, the growth of consumer culture, and changing perceptions regarding the importance of leisure versus work (Shaffer 2001).

The early years

Before the beginning of the nineteenth century the concept of traveling for leisure was virtually unknown to the masses; it was the privilege of the wealthy. To be sure, by this time the tradition of the aristocratic Grand Tour, whereby young British nobility traveled through Europe, usually over an extended period of time, had been well established. Following the US War of Independence, North America became an extension of the Grand Tour for a small number of Europeans who were curious to explore the new country's people and culture. Likewise, because of growing wealth and leisure in North America, the emerging upper classes of Americans began to copy the lifestyles of European and British aristocracy (Bocock 1993). This encouraged those Americans who possessed the means to travel to visit Europe – especially the British Isles – since they believed it was there they could become refined and learn proper etiquette.

By the late 1700s, the famous English spa towns, including Bath, Cheltenham, Harrogate, and Tunbridge Wells, had been established. These were destinations where the upper classes could escape the routine and grime of the early industrial city and pursue pleasure for the purpose of healthy living. Americans who had visited these early British destinations were very much influenced by their experiences. This led to the appearance of spa communities, particularly in upstate New York. Ballston Spa, established in the 1790s, was one of the first. It was here in the early 1800s that the original full-service hotel, and the largest one in the nation at that time, was constructed (Corbett 2001).

It should be stressed that very few people made the cumbersome and time-consuming trip to Ballston Spa or the handful of other resort towns that had emerged during these early years. The unstable political climate of the young United States did not help matters and was certainly not conducive to the development of tourism, since this was a country where political strife and skirmishes remained common. Further, Sears (1998) argues that during the early nineteenth century there was a general lack of popular perception of places that could be classified as truly out of the ordinary compared to a person's normal place of residence, to no small extent perhaps because such places were simply too far away from major population centers or had simply not yet been "discovered."

All of this was about to change with the advent of a new transportation infrastructure, starting with Robert Fulton's invention of the steamship in the early 1800s, the construction of a comprehensive canal system, and eventually the introduction and subsequent rapid diffusion of the railroad by the late 1830s. Not only did these new modes of travel make it more convenient to reach distant places, but they also acted as attractions in their own right (Brown 1995). Importantly, these technological innovations in transportation were a reflection of a broader trend which was occurring during this time, namely the advent of the Industrial Revolution in North America that "helped spur the expansion of the capitalist market. A wider array of ready-made goods, changing notions of work and leisure, an expanding middle class, and increasing levels of expendable capital revealed a consumer-oriented society in the making" (Shaffer 2001: 13).

The Erie Canal, in particular, is credited with sparking an initial surge in recreational travel to places in upstate New York and beyond. This impressive project whose first section opened up in 1819 and which was completed in 1825 ran from the Hudson River in Albany, New York, through places like Syracuse and Rochester, eventually emptying into the Niagara River in Buffalo. Because of the canal, new settlements in the western part of New York State were established, and cities like Buffalo, Schenectady, and Syracuse boomed. Importantly, the opening of the canal and the introduction of steamships led to the establishment of the country's first tourist circuit, famously dubbed the "Fashionable Tour" (Shaffer 2001). By the early 1820s it was possible to travel in a steamship from New York City to Albany along the Hudson, and then from Albany westwards along the Erie Canal (Gassan 2005). Some of the stops on this "Fashionable Tour" included the Catskill and Adirondack Mountains, Saratoga and Ballston Springs in upstate New York, and Niagara Falls (Figure 2.1).

It was not only the new transportation technology that made travel faster and more convenient. Reduction in journey times also resulted from enhanced competition between rival steamship companies as they vied to increase their market share. In reality, this era marked the nascence of the commercialization of tourism, reflecting the reorganization of businesses seeking to meet the demands of emerging markets. This commercialization, which was particularly evident along the Hudson River Valley, was reflected through the proliferation of guidebooks and other tourist-related literature including maps and geography books (Gassan 2005).

It is worth mentioning that the growing interest during this time in ex-urban travel and the desire to gaze upon natural scenery was fueled by the Romantic Movement, which served to raise nature's importance *vis à vis* humankind. Michael Hall (1998a: 15) points out that "to the romantics the New World was perceived as a new Eden in which man could draw close to wild nature . . . Contact with wilderness was believed to give man great strength and hardiness and an innate moral superiority over his more civilised counterparts." Löfgren (1999) explains that the keen interest in natural settings Americans began showing in the early part of the nineteenth century reflected their reaction towards the leading intellectuals' perception that the new nation lacked the cultural assets that could be found in Europe. To make up for the absence of castles, cathedrals, and other monumental historic buildings, tourists in the United States turned their attention towards natural wonders (e.g., mountain chains, waterfalls, lakes). It was not surprising then, that by the 1820s there was increased demand for travel to scenic spots in reaction to authors' and artists' (especially the painter Thomas Cole's) glorification of American nature. In response to this demand, entrepreneurs began providing travel facilities like hotels and taverns in the areas where such attractions were located (Shaffer 2001).

Saratoga Springs in upstate New York is a perfect example of a pre-Civil War tourist destination. This popular stop on the "Fashionable Tour" gained prominence with the

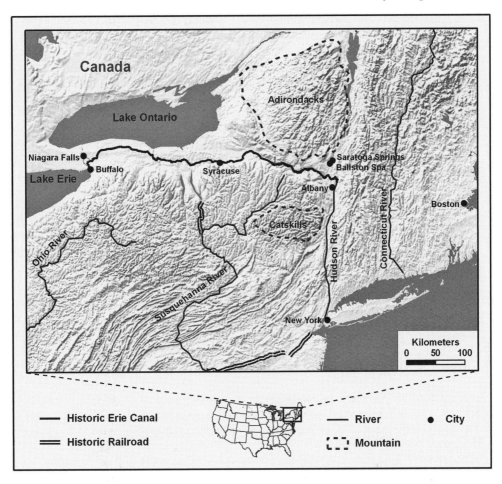

Figure 2.1 The Fashionable Tour in upstate New York in the early 1800s
Source: after New York State Canal Corporation; http://gis.fra.dot.gov;
and http://memory.loc.gov/ammem/gmdhtml/rrhtml/rrhome.html

opening of the Erie Canal and by 1822 it boasted four major hotels, two of which had a capacity over 100 beds each (Corbett 2001). Saratoga Springs was a well-planned community offering a number of amenities including open spaces, public buildings and parks; it even had a sophisticated water and sewage system making it one of the first places in North America to boast such infrastructure. Significantly, this town was one of the first communities, if not the first, following the Industrial Revolution to consciously reject economic growth based on manufacturing, focusing instead on creating a visitor-based environment (Sterngass 2001). While, as will be seen in later chapters, there is nothing remarkable about towns that boost their tourism image nowadays, the fact that Saratoga Springs, and indeed Newport, Rhode Island, did this more than 150 years ago before the onset of service-dependent economies, is truly astounding.

Places like Saratoga Springs, Newport in Rhode Island, Cape May in New Jersey, and the White Mountains of New Hampshire rapidly became key resorts for travelers in antebellum America. Arguably, though, it was Niagara Falls that established itself as the most popular destination on the Fashionable Tour by the 1830s, and at the end of the nineteenth century it was the premier resort in the United States (Sears 1998). Since

Niagara offered a truly unique natural setting, not only did Americans include it on their "to do" list, but also many early foreign travelers wanted to visit the falls (Dumych 1996).

Ironically, Niagara was one of the very first destinations to witness wide-scale commercialization when a variety of fee-based side-shows were established in an area surrounding the key natural attraction. The tacky nature of much of this development, not to mention the over-visitation of the area, led commentators at the time to voice their concern about the threat it posed to the principal attraction (Berton 1997; Sears 1998). This concern demonstrates that awareness regarding tourism's negative impacts on the environment is not something recent but very much pre-occupied the minds of certain observers more than 150 years ago. Importantly, as noted below, this concern also led to moves by the early 1870s to protect natural areas and was a main incentive behind the establishment of the National Park movement.

Eureka Springs, Arkansas, is one town that originally made use of its natural assets, namely the availability of hot springs in the vicinity to attract visitors beginning in the later part of the nineteenth century. Over time, the importance of the hot springs as a principal attraction for the town has waned, but Eureka Springs has reinvented its image and still remains a popular destination in the Midwest (see Closer Look Case 2.1).

CLOSER LOOK CASE 2.1

Eureka Springs, AR: a destination reinvented through time

Just south of the Missouri–Arkansas border and in the midst of the Ozarks is Eureka Springs. This is a place where one can get married, go to a spa, do some shopping, visit a gallery to browse the local art and eat in one of the best Italian restaurants in the area – though not necessarily in this order. The city was established in the 1870s in the vicinity of the thermal springs which had been discovered there a couple of decades earlier. In 1881 it became the fourth largest city in Arkansas and was named "City of the First Class" as visitors flocked to take advantage of the healing powers of its thermal springs. The Eureka Springs Improvement Company (formed in 1882) was instrumental in bringing the railroad to the city, which began operations in 1883 with six trainloads of visitors daily (Reserve Eureka). The Perry House and the Crescent Hotel were among many hotels constructed during the 1880s; the latter was built in 1886 and still operates today as a luxurious historic hotel and spa. Eureka Springs became less popular as interest for the springs faded, only to be revived by automobile tourism in the 1920s. It lost its luster again during the Great Depression and World War II, to regain it steadily thereafter (Eureka Springs Tourist Center).

Many wooden buildings were torn down for their lumber during the Great Depression. Because of this, and also because of several fires in the late 1800s, almost all the surviving buildings are made of limestone, giving Eureka Springs its distinctive nostalgic feel. The downtown area has an unmistakable air of authenticity which eludes many other surreal American towns that seem compelled to add an 'e' to the word 'town' to evoke a made-up past. There are no buildings here which are made to look old; they really *are* old. There are no fake façades, and no fake stones, and no building deceives the visitor by pretending it is something it is not. Eureka Springs is old, but she has aged quite well. The entire town is on the National Register of Historic Places, which means it is a place worthy of preservation. The National Register of Historic Places is administered by the National

Park Service and is part of a national program to protect and evaluate the nation's historical and archaeological resources (www.nps.gov).

Eureka Springs was in fact one of twelve distinctive destinations named by the National Trust for Historic Preservation. Its identity is inextricably bound to the fantastic link to the past that belies its building stock. The place is dotted with small bed-and-breakfasts promising Victorian charm, whereas hot tubs and spas have replaced the thermal springs of an erstwhile era.

Eureka Springs is a very diverse destination. It boasts an alternative art scene and a successful annual music festival; it is a place where one can get married Las Vegas-style in the heart of the Ozark Mountains, as well as a popular place for Harley Davidson riders and their fans. What is more, it is the venue of the Great Passion Play, a dramatized account of Christ's life, now on its 41st season. This is an outdoor event, taking place in the proximity of a sizeable statue of Christ, a miniature version of the one found on the Corcovado in Rio de Janeiro, Brazil. The play attracts the evangelical Christian crowd, and is big business for the town. Southwest Missouri and Northwest Arkansas with Branson and Eureka Springs respectively target evangelical Christians who abound in the area, partly due to the concentration of Bible Colleges and the fact that the Assemblies of God denomination headquarters office is in Springfield, Missouri, and also to its rural character.

Location remains one of Eureka Springs' most important assets. The community's proximity to waterways such as the Buffalo River and Beaver Lake draws outdoor enthusiasts every year.

Eureka Springs is an example of a successful destination that keeps re-inventing itself by using its natural and man-made assets in order to diversify its clientele and survive the changing times.

Sources

Eureka Tourist Center (2009) *Historical info*. Available from http://www.eurekasprings. com/ (accessed March 16, 2009).

National Park Service (2009) *National Register of Historic Places*. Available from http://www.nps.gov/nr/ (accessed March 18, 2009).

Reserve Eureka (2009) *History of Eureka Springs*. Available from http://www.reserve eureka.com/historic_eureka.htm (accessed March 22, 2009).

Questions

1. Consider Eureka Springs or another town like it that has been a long-term destination. How important is it for historic towns such as these to reinvent their tourism product periodically? How can they ensure that the new attractions that are introduced do not harm the community's historic character? Do you think some types of tourism are more suitable for historic destinations than others? If so, can you give examples?

2. You have inherited a historic home in a place like Eureka Springs. The three-story house is quite large (it has six bedrooms) and could be converted into a tourist business. What type of business would you like to convert it into? Considering there might be plenty of other similar businesses in the area how would you ensure that your establishment will be successful? In other words what would you focus on to give a unique twist to your business?

Evangelia Petridou

Era of expansion: 1850–early 1900s

The years leading up to the Civil War saw the proliferation of numerous tourist destinations, no doubt aided by the continued expansion of transportation networks. Although the White Mountains of New Hampshire were already quite popular in the 1820s, rapid development of the region did not occur until the 1850s when a railroad connection to the area was established. Suddenly, this destination received growing attention in popular guidebooks, and residents of Boston and other major cities of the northeast, including a growing number of blue collar people, began visiting (Brown 1995). Similarly, by 1850 Newport, Rhode Island, benefited substantially from a direct steamboat service from New York that made trips faster and more affordable (Sterngass 2001).

The expansion of new transportation infrastructure meant that over the years the real price of travel had progressively declined. Between 1820 and 1830 travel costs from New York City to Saratoga Springs fell dramatically, while the duration of the journey also declined (Brown 1995). During the 1840s, due to further reductions in fares, leisure-based tourism had become the privilege not only of the extremely wealthy; following the end of the Civil War, middle-class city folk, including clerks and others living on modest wages, were able to look forward to a holiday away from the grime of the industrial city. In response to this emerging demand, a growing number of destinations catering to various market niches based on household income, ethnicity, and other traits began emerging. In some cases, on the outskirts of resort settlements, tent cities emerged catering to poorer people, while it was not unusual for farmers to offer lodging to visitors seeking a few days in the countryside in exchange for some work (Brown 1995).

Until 1860, despite the rapid growth of arrivals in many destinations that effectively spelled the beginnings of mass-oriented visitation, tourism was largely regional in nature with people escaping their northeastern cities for a few weeks each year either to visit natural spots in surrounding areas (e.g., lakes, mountain resorts, and hot springs) or sightsee historical places like battlefields (Shaffer 2001). Localities that had already experienced severe economic malaise because of the decline of a traditional activity turned to tourism, viewing it as an alternative engine of economic growth. Following the collapse of its whaling industry, for example, Nantucket (Massachusetts) promoted a tourism product based on its heritage (Brown 1995). It was also not unheard of for some people to include places like prisons and asylums in their travel itineraries, partly because buildings like these were monumental in size akin to nothing else during that period, but more importantly, because these institutions were a new system for addressing societal or health problems (Sears 1998).

The end of the Civil War heralded a new age with the focus on travel within the US shifting from regional to national. The landscapes of the east were now considered too "tame," and for this reason "the American tour expanded westwards in search of 'real wilderness'" (Löfgren 1999: 38–9). Shaffer (2001) maintains that after 1865 there was a growth of a new form of nationalism with the emergent central federal government becoming an instrumental force behind the country's westward expansion. Simultaneously, people's perception of the nation's geography and vast resources grew substantially. For example, awareness about places like Yosemite Valley, which had been discovered a few years earlier, had increased, leading to more people wishing to experience this region's magnificence.

By the 1870s more people than ever before were traveling with new destinations constantly being "discovered" and opening up throughout the nation. Yosemite and Yellowstone became key destinations with urbanites (Gunn 2004), primarily from the eastern seaboard, beginning to display a hunger for "national icons and for places which symbolized the exotic of a region just beginning to be known" (Sears 1998: 123). Artists, in particular, became major promoters of Yosemite as an attraction for visitors to San Francisco. Painters first, and then photographers, captured many of the unique features of this natural area and fueled the public's awareness about what was on offer. Ironically, the increasing numbers of visitors to Yosemite rapidly led to complaints that these wealthy people were nothing more than spoiled and lazy sightseers who "demanded every modern convenience, touring the valley by horse and carriage" (Löfgren 1999: 57).

Growing concerns that the natural wonders of Yosemite and, eventually Yellowstone, would suffer from over-visitation and associated impacts in the manner Niagara and the White Mountains of New Hampshire (especially Mount Washington) had witnessed years earlier, soon led to the birth of the national park movement. Hall (1998a) points out that tourism bears much of the responsibility for initially creating the national parks in the United States, since it was an activity that gave value to areas originally considered worthless in terms of their economic potential for extractive industries or agriculture. Effectively, tourism became the reason for destinations like these with their abundance of natural wonders to be protected without anyone making the argument that their protection would lead to a loss of their potential economic value.

On returning from his expedition to Yellowstone during the early 1870s, the Head of the US Geological Survey, Thomas Hayden, presented a report to Congress where he vehemently argued for turning this area into a park. Subsequently, in 1872, the bill establishing Yellowstone as a national park was signed by President Grant (Shaffer 2001). Importantly, although this was a significant milestone for conservationists, in many ways it became a milestone in tourism's history within the United States. Sears (1998: 163) underscores Yellowstone's influence on the promotion of tourism within the US.

Educated Americans had increasingly recognized the cultural and economic importance of the nation's tourist attractions. They were not only objects of national pride in themselves, which matched the natural and architectural monuments of the Old World, but the subject of paintings which also became objects of admiration . . . The creation of the Yellowstone National Park recognized what was already a fact – that the nation's natural wonders were its sacred places and should be treated as such.

While the national park movement is in many ways synonymous with the nascence of tourism's development in the western states, the railway's role in facilitating travel to this part of the country must be underscored. From 1869 onwards, George Crofutt became a leading advocate of tourism's expansion throughout the USA because he recognized the opportunity provided through the growth of the railroad network. Being a publisher, he produced the *Great Trans-Continental Railroad Guide*, which included "train schedules, information on fares, and advice to travelers as well as a brief description of the region traversed" (Shaffer 2001: 18). This became the first guide of its kind and was followed by numerous publications during the next two decades, all of which sought to promote tourism in the western part of the country.

According to Shaffer, various railroad companies were influential in terms of promoting tourism to regions like Yellowstone and later on, the Grand Canyon. A financier of the Northern Pacific Railroad, Jay Cooke, became a firm advocate of marketing the geothermal wonders of Yellowstone. After the park was established, in the years between the early 1880s and 1915, Northern Pacific worked with various other stakeholders in an effort that consciously promoted tourism to the region. One outcome of the association was the Old Faithful Inn, completed in 1904, which became known as "a grand luxury hotel in the American wilderness" (Shaffer 2001: 47). More significantly, perhaps, this development marked just one of a series of actions that during the beginning of the twentieth century "transformed the Yellowstone landscape into a premiere wilderness resort" (Shaffer 2001: 48).

In a similar fashion to the development of Yellowstone, the Santa Fe Railroad together with the Fred Harvey Company played a key role in leading the development of tourism to the southwest. By the 1920s their partnership had led to the establishment of a number of hotels, including the famous El Tovar (Plate 2.1) on the southern rim of the Grand Canyon, and they had even created an Indian Department, through which they accumulated and sold Native American crafts (Limerick 1975; Weigle 1989). (See Closer Look Case 2.2.)

No doubt, the private railway companies' role in promoting famous landscapes, including many of the ones within the major national parks, was prompted by their need to attract riders on their system. By the second decade of the twentieth century, however, the individual national parks had come under the umbrella of an independent federal service (the National Park Service) and with this, the role of managing these sites as visitor attractions in a coordinated fashion became the function of central government. The establishment of the NPS epitomized the growth in strength of federal government machinery and, with that, the encouragement of various projects that, either directly or indirectly, had a bearing on the further development of American tourism (Shaffer 2001). These included the development of a nationwide transportation network, particularly the construction of thousands of miles of paved roads following the Federal Aid Road Act of 1916 and, later, the Federal Highway Act of 1921; the latter sought an interconnected system of highways throughout the nation. It is also important to add that various interests

Plate 2.1 El Tovar Hotel, Grand Canyon
(Dimitri Ioannides)

CLOSER LOOK CASE 2.2

The Grand Canyon

The Grand Canyon has been forming for the past 10 to 20 million years, with help from the Colorado River. The canyon is part of the much larger Colorado River Basin and Colorado Plateau system, which geologists believe date back nearly 70 million years. The river has cut through layers of sandstone and other rock substances to create one of the world's most recognizable natural features and among the most admired natural attractions in the United States.

The Grand Canyon has been known by Native Americans for thousands of years; some of the earliest human relics in this area date as far back as 12,000 years. The first Europeans to see this impressive sight were Spanish explorers in 1540. Since this earliest European sighting, other groups have subsequently "discovered" and explored the Grand Canyon, including John Wesley Powell in 1869.

The late 1800s saw growing numbers of adventurers wishing to explore the canyon and its surroundings, and by the beginning of the twentieth century the Grand Canyon had become a desirable attraction for adventuresome tourists. In 1903, President Theodore Roosevelt visited the canyon and was so impressed that he pushed legislation through Congress to protect the environment as a game preserve and national monument. In 1919 the monument became a national park under the administration of the brand new National Park Service.

Fred Harvey, the nineteenth-century railway developer, restaurateur, and hotelier, was instrumental in the popularization of the Grand Canyon as a tourist destination. By the close of the 1800s, his Santa Fe Railway gave rise to a string of hotels and restaurants on an east-west corridor in the United States. In northern Arizona, the Santa Fe Railway ran just south of the Grand Canyon, and one branch of the company, the Grand Canyon Railway, extended northward to the canyon. By doing this, Harvey made a business decision to capitalize on the natural appeal of the area and was able to monopolize a considerable portion of the tourism industry at the Grand Canyon, at least until the household automobile gained increased popularity in the 1920s and '30s. Under Harvey's direction a Santa Fe Railway resort (El Tovar Hotel) was designed, although it was not completed (1905) until after his death in 1901. Today, the El Tovar is a luxury hotel/lodge on the south rim of the canyon. It is a popular tourist getaway and has been listed as a National Historic Landmark on the National Register of Historic Places.

Every year Grand Canyon National Park draws between four and five million tourists from all over the world to appreciate its stunning vistas and natural features. Most tourists arrive via Las Vegas or Phoenix and visit the park on day trips. In addition to observing and admiring the natural landscape more passively, helicopter over-flights, hiking, camping, river rafting, and mule riding are among the most popular tourist activities at the canyon. The Hualapai Indians recently (March 2007) added a "skywalk" on their tribal land, outside the National Park, which for a fee allows visitors to the canyon an opportunity to stand on a transparent glass walkway to observe the canyon floor some 4,770 feet (1,450 meters) below. While some Native American groups and environmental advocates decry this new tourist attraction, the Hualapai people see it as an economic boost to their isolated community. This illustrates how new creations have been developed to supplement the natural and cultural heritage of the Grand Canyon in the name of tourism development.

Sources

Anderson, M.F. (1998) *Living at the Edge: Explorers, Exploiters and Settlers of the Grand Canyon Region*. Grand Canyon, AZ: Grand Canyon Association.

Pyne, S. (1998) *How the Canyon became Grand: A Short History*. New York: Viking Penguin.

Timothy, D.J. (2009) River-based tourism in the USA: tourism and recreation on the Colorado and Mississippi Rivers. In B. Prideaux and M. Cooper (eds) *River Tourism*, pp. 41–54. Wallingford, UK: CAB International.

US National Park Service (2009) *Grand Canyon National Park, Arizona*. Available from http://www.nps.gov/grca/ (accessed April 10, 2009).

Questions

1. What role did the trans-continental railways play in helping tourism grow in the western United States?
2. Is tourism at the Grand Canyon based only on the natural environment, or is the human history equally important?

that supported the national park idea, including the Far Western Travelers' Association in conjunction with the National Park Service became keen promoters of the concept of touring all parks as part of a concerted effort of encouraging Americans to see their country first because this would "help them to grow up better Americans" (Shaffer 2001: 116). The idea was that the park-to-park tour would become the Grand Tour of the twentieth century.

Fin de Siècle

The advent of national parks like Yellowstone, Yosemite, and the Grand Canyon, occurred in an age when travel for the purpose of leisure was becoming increasingly popular. By the last decade of the 1800s, numerous resort communities had already cropped up in various locations around the nation, many of which are still important tourist destinations to this day. Facilities for travelers also became more sophisticated, to no small extent to satisfy the increasing demands of visitors.

Already, by the late 1880s people from San Francisco and further inland had built summer cottages near the seaside in Santa Cruz, California, and by 1900 approximately 100,000 visitors visited this area, which was dubbed the "Riviera of America" during the summer months (Löfgren 1999) (Plate 2.2). A boardwalk was opened in 1907 while a few years later the resort Casa del Rey was established offering a hotel and 200 beach chalets. Similarly, by the late 1880s, resorts began popping up on the shores of Lake Michigan to cater to the recreational needs of the burgeoning population of nearby Chicago. These Michigan resorts, where mansions mingled with the humble cottages of poor immigrants, were known for beaches, amusement parks, mineral baths, and special events (Thomopoulos 2005).

This scene witnessed in Santa Cruz was repeated in hundreds of locales around the nation following the explosion in demand for leisure-based travel. By the beginning of the twentieth century, camping, which had previously been the privilege of only the very wealthy who could afford to embark on an expedition, became increasingly popular

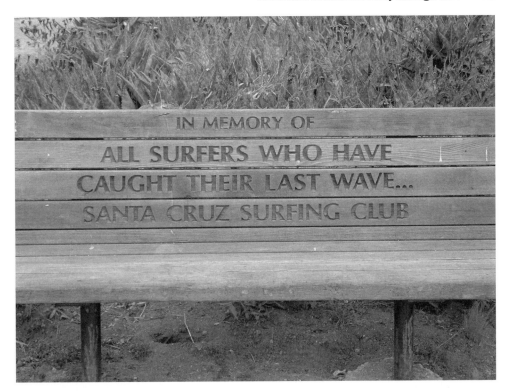

Plate 2.2 Santa Cruz, California – Historic destination to surfers' paradise
(Bo Svensson)

following the establishment of organized tent camps (Löfgren 1999). And, with the advent of the private automobile over the next two decades, touring the country and camping at various sites became an American institution.

One major revolution in the travel industry, which had begun towards the end of the nineteenth century, was the introduction of organized package tours. Borrowing a leaf from the practice of Thomas Cook – the inventor of the package tour – who had already arranged a tour of California in the 1870s, the Raymond and Whitcomb Company began offering organized trips by railway to various parts of the country (Cocks 2001; Shaffer 2001). The tourists were transported in luxury Pullman railroad cars to various places, including national parks, and along the way they would stop at the sites of major resort hotels, such as a luxury establishment located in Pasadena, California. The latter contributed to the making of southern California "as a tourist mecca" by the late 1880s (Cocks 2001: 113).

Another phenomenon, which emerged towards the end of the nineteenth century, was the growth of urban tourism. Whereas natural areas had rapidly become major destinations for Americans since the early 1800s, the nation's cities struggled initially to attract visitors, no doubt because they lacked the history of their European counterparts. To be sure, some people (including European visitors to the US) were extremely curious about these emergent cities since they offered the opportunity to view novel methods for dealing with the rising social problems of the time. Sears (1998) indicates that among the sites visitors to American cities wanted to see during the 1830s and '40s were institutions like asylums for the deaf or the blind, prisons, and cemeteries. He points out that when Alexis de Tocqueville visited the US, his primary aim was to view prisons while Charles

Dickens was interested in the manner in which the new institutions were meant to alleviate "human suffering" (Sears 1998: 88). Even guidebooks of the 1830s, '40s and '50s made a plea for visitors to come and see these institutions.

The interest in prisons and asylums waned by the late 1850s, mainly because there was a growing perception that these institutions had not lived up to their earlier promise of solving various social ills. But other developments within or close to urban areas began drawing visitors, including the newly introduced major public parks such as Central Park and Prospect Park in New York City. These vast open spaces in the midst of the otherwise dense urban jungle of the time were supposed to provide a respite to citizens from the problems of the day. Competing with these parks for visitors was Coney Island which, during the 1870s and 1880s, became a place of escape for New Yorkers from most walks of life. By the mid-1870s, up to 60,000 people visited on a daily basis, especially following the construction of the toll-supported Ocean Parkway (Sterngass 2001). Taking advantage of the newly introduced half-holiday movement for Saturdays, many city folk used the improved and cheap transportation systems to get to Coney Island where they enjoyed the range of amenities on offer. Visits to what became known as the world's largest amusement park were boosted because unions, business associations, and religious organizations began offering regular tours for their members (Sterngass 2001).

The ambivalence most Americans had shown towards their large cities as tourist destinations began dissipating towards the end of the nineteenth century, and over the following two decades visits to urban areas became more common, with a growing interest in "doing" the town (Cocks 2001: 107). Catherine Cocks explains that several factors led to this phenomenon, including the enhanced ease and comfort of travel and the fact that more and more people had growing disposable income and leisure time. Additionally, one of the major disincentives for travel to cities, namely the absence of hotels, was no longer a problem. By the 1890s, the advent of major luxury hotels, such as the grandiose Waldorf Astoria in New York City, became a major step in sending the message to the affluent that cities offered refined spaces far removed from the squalor associated at that time with tenements and factories.

The urban expositions, including the World's Fairs, which had become increasingly popular since the mid-1800s, provided additional impetus for the growth of urban tourism. The 1893 Chicago World's Fair (the World's Columbian Exposition) was a mega-event entirely staged in an effort to celebrate that particular city and the nation's history and industrial strength. Some 28 million visitors came to the Fair in 1893 (Bolotin and Laing 2002), and for this to occur, the city collaborated with railroad companies, accommodation establishments, and tour operators in an effort to secure discounted rates (Cocks 2001).

Beyond these events, the marketing of cities through package tour companies became increasingly commonplace by the beginning of the twentieth century. It was not unusual for these companies to promote mini-breaks to places like the nation's capital. Increasingly, sophisticated brochures and other advertising materials made their appearance both as a result of these companies' efforts to promote various destinations but also because by the early 1900s certain communities had enabled the appearance of bodies (e.g., tourism information bureaus) whose primary aim was to encourage tourists to visit.

During this era city leaders recognized the potential of promoting their cities as attractions and, in a boosterist effort, "argued that a city attractive to tourists would not only improve a city's economic outlook but also renew the civic loyalty and foster cordial class relations. Making money and strengthening the community would go hand in hand" (Cocks 2001: 126). Essentially, advocates of urban tourism quickly realized that attracting visitors to their city would necessitate various infrastructural improvements, many of which could be funded by taxing these visitors. In turn, these improvements would benefit local businesses, not to mention the host population.

One additional aspect of urban tourism during these early years was the opportunity to visit neighborhoods where ethnic minorities lived and worked (Conforti 1996; Takaki 1994; Timothy 2002). "Ethnic slumming," as it was called, was promoted in guidebooks as part of a tourist's itinerary when visiting places like San Francisco and New York. The claim was put forth that through visiting these ethnic neighborhoods, the tourists were able to see what a neighborhood was like in China or Italy (Cocks 2001).

> Ethnic entrepreneurs were quick to take advantage of the growing interest of white Americans in appropriating aspects of their cultures. The outstanding instance occurred in San Francisco's Chinatown. Destroyed along with most of the downtown in the earthquake and fire of April 1906, the neighborhood survived another of a series of efforts to force the Chinese out of the 'heart of the city.' . . . Drawing on Chinese and Chinese American capital, Look helped to finance the construction of two pagoda-topped bazaars in the center of Chinatown and the reconstruction of the pagoda-style telephone exchange.
>
> (Cocks 2001: 201)

In the case of San Francisco, these efforts convinced city leaders that to enhance the Chinese attributes of the neighborhood and not get rid of them would make solid financial sense, and over the next few years, conscious steps were taken to make the area look more Chinese, including the installation of "oriental" street lights. Visitors to the area had the opportunity to use local residents as guides and translators (Light 1974).

The interwar years: 1918–41

Just as the railway bears much of the responsibility for shaping the fortunes of tourism within the US during the nineteenth century, the automobile had much to do with the rise of numerous new destinations and the travel patterns of Americans during the twentieth century (Jakle and Sculle 2008). The advent of Henry Ford's affordable Model T in 1908 meant that for the first time Americans had the possibility of obtaining a personal mode of transportation, capable of traveling distances that a few years earlier would have been considered impossible. The car released travelers from the rigidity of the railway network and its time schedule, allowing them to explore areas flexibly and to stay in a whole range of accommodations, including roadside inns. The flexibility of the auto also meant that visits no longer had to be as lengthy as they were during the railway era; instead travelers could motor from place to place, staying in one destination for only a limited amount of time.

The concept of motor touring was introduced as early as 1907 in New England when motoring guides encouraged people to witness the wealth of landscapes and historical assets the region had to offer (Ewald 2003). In 1912 the Raymond and Whitcomb Company together with the American Automobile Association (AAA) organized a tour from New York to Los Angeles. The trip, which was meant to last about 45 days, cost just under $1,000 dollars per participant and included a side-trip from Phoenix to the Grand Canyon (Shaffer 2001). While only a few wealthy people were able to participate on this trip, its significance was that it proved the boundless opportunities of travel by automobile.

By the end of the second decade of the century, following a substantial decline in the original price of the Model T, there were more than seven million cars on American

Plate 2.3 Historic Route 66 sign, Needles, California
(Dallen Timothy)

roads, meaning there was increasing pressure to improve the road infrastructure. It was not surprising, therefore, that the federal government moved to introduce legislation enabling the development of a comprehensive nationwide roadway system. We have already mentioned the Federal Aid Road Act of 1916 and its successor the Federal Highway Act of 1921, which resulted in thousands of miles of paved roadway criss-crossing the country. In the 1920s the concept of numbered federal and state roads was introduced and each of these highways (including the famous Route 66) was promoted for the "historical, scenic, and educational value" it offered (Shaffer 2001: 164) (see Plate 2.3).

During the Depression, a few years later, the American Guide Series, a program initiated by the Works Progress Administration (WPA), became a major advocate of motor touring around the country. This guide series was created under one of President Roosevelt's many New Deal programs, namely the Federal Writers' Project in 1935. While the major aim of this project was to create jobs for unemployed writers, its effect was to generate what became the most comprehensive collection of guidebooks that had ever been published up to that time. In all, more than six million dollars were set aside by Congress to hire 6,500 writers to work on this project. By the time the project had come to its end in the early 1940s, it had witnessed the participation of approximately 10,000 writers, including John Steinbeck and Conrad Aiken (Bold 1999; Fox 1961).

Each guidebook followed a standard format and included essays about a state's culture, economy, physical characteristics, and history. The major cities were described in some detail and the books included numerous photographs. Scenic routes for motoring were also designated and other tours suggested. So influential was the American Guide Series that the historian Lewis Mumford wrote that the books constituted "the first attempt, on a comprehensive scale, to make the country itself worthily known to Americans" (quoted in Shaffer 2001: 202).

The WPA and the umbrella program under which it functioned (namely Federal One) were remarkable projects given it was the first time the national government had provided monies to fund writers and other artists. The underlying objective may have been job creation for writers but, in reality, the outcome of the WPA and, especially its principal product – the American Guide Series – was to engender a feeling of national pride, at a time of rising international tensions. This was achieved because the American Guide Series successfully highlighted the accomplishments and cultural heritage of the US. Coupled with the fact that for the first time in its history travel through the country was facilitated by the miles upon miles of newly paved roads, this led to a realization that the American Guide Series would significantly boost travel for leisure purposes. Indeed, even in the midst of the Great Depression in 1935 a total of 35 million Americans embarked on a trip within the country. And, significantly, "the guides would serve the rapidly growing number of visitors to national parks, as well as the newly emerging youth hostel movement, the American Camping Association, and the Scouts" (Findley and Bing 1998).

Shaffer (2001: 219) argues that overall the WPA series did much to promote tourism nationally, but it achieved even more than that. Ultimately, its intent was to "legitimize America as a united nation . . . [and] . . . in seeing America, in experiencing the nation firsthand, tourists could reaffirm their identity as Americans."

Postwar–Present

It is obvious from the preceding sections that the seeds for the take-off of American tourism were set during the first part of the twentieth century. The advent of the private automobile and the massive growth of the interstate road infrastructure played a huge part in this development since they served to make remote places more accessible to population centers (Jakle and Sculle 2008). It is, however, the last five decades or so that have seen an astounding growth in tourism both from the demand and supply sides. A number of factors have played a part in this.

The years following the Second World War witnessed an impressive growth of the American economy since, for the first time, the country sought to assert its position as a world power. By the early 1960s incomes had risen significantly and more and more Americans had become home-owners thanks to governmental programs like VA (Veterans Administration) and FHA (Federal Housing Administration) loans that enabled citizens to acquire mortgages. A growing mass of people joined the ranks of the middle class and, as a result, they had access to an increasing discretionary income with which they could acquire all sorts of gadgets for their homes. In short, by the early 1960s Americans probably had the highest level of disposable income on the planet. Additionally, more and more people obtained jobs that guaranteed at least a modicum of paid vacations and, because of this, the annual vacation away from home became the norm for the middle classes throughout the country.

Following the passage of the Federal Highway Act of 1956 during Eisenhower's presidency, a brand new system of interstate highways was quickly developed making travel throughout the country more convenient than ever before. The interstate system, which eventually grew to cover 46,876 miles, has drastically transformed the manner in which Americans travel, especially given the phenomenal increase in automobile ownership and usage, but also the way Americans live and work (US Department of Transportation 2008). The highway system essentially caused small towns and cities to be bypassed by motorists, with many small businesses being negatively affected and popular rural routes, such as Route 66, nearly becoming obsolete (Gunn 2004).

One of the major outcomes of the interstate system is that it has made what were once distant vacation spots easily accessible by car. In a matter of less than 24 hours one can drive from the New York region to southern Florida. Also, places such as Las Vegas are within easy reach from major population centers like Los Angeles and Phoenix. On a grand scale, the advent of the 1956 Act rapidly accelerated the phenomenon of suburbanization as millions of predominantly white Americans fled the inner cities and settled in what had up to then been open countryside. By the 1970s America truly became a suburban nation as employers, following the lead of their workers, fled the inner cities and retail malls on green-field sites replaced entire downtown shopping areas. As this ex-urban form of living became the norm, too many places around the nation developed an aura of anonymity, characterized by endless subdivisions of uniform housing in treeless farmland, and box-style retail developments.

This uniformity and sterility of landscape provided the extra impetus for suburbanites to seek places offering out-of-the-ordinary sights and, ironically, many of the downtown areas they had once shunned were suddenly transformed into places for visitors (Beauregard 1998). As will be demonstrated later in this book, many forces have been in place since the mid-1970s to transform the downtown areas of American cities drastically, with places like Boston, San Francisco, and New York, as well as hundreds of smaller communities, emerging as "places to play" for millions of domestic and foreign visitors (Judd 1999).

While the automobile and its associated infrastructure have undoubtedly been catalysts in terms of the phenomenal growth of tourism within the US over the last five decades, the advent of airplane travel has also had an immense impact on travel flows throughout the country. Before 1960 few people had ever been on a plane for the purposes of leisure travel and, if they had, they probably were wealthy. With the advent of the passenger jet age in the 1950s (especially the introduction of the Boeing 707), the cost of air travel gradually began to fall and a growing number of Americans began flying. Suddenly, distant destinations like southern Florida, California, and even Hawaii, became far easier to access, much more quickly, and at more affordable rates; thus, some of the traditional destinations like Atlantic City, New Jersey, which were much older and closer to major population centers, entered a period of major decline (Stansfield 2004; Stansfield and Rickert 1970).

Deregulation in the late 1970s and early 1980s allowed enhanced competition in the airline industry and resulted in the creation of many new entrants and the expansion of regional carriers like Mesaba Airlines, Skywest, and United Express. This led to a significant reduction in the cost of air transportation in real terms. Consequently, millions of Americans took to the skies. The introduction of the hub and spoke system allowed airlines to increase their aircraft load factors significantly and operate in a far more efficient manner than ever before since more and more places around the nation became accessible by air.

Even though by the 1990s a number of major airlines had been driven into bankruptcy and some of them had ceased to exist because of deregulation and other factors, other carriers were able to consolidate their hold of the market (by the mid-1990s the big three (United, American, and Delta) controlled over 47 percent of the market) and, for a while, they competed with each other on the basis of price (Air Transport Association 2008). However, the September 11, 2001, terrorist attacks in the United States have led to a slump in the airline industry, and owing to rising operational costs, especially for fuel, nearly all carriers have faced hard times in recent years. Unfortunately, the price of air transportation has also been creeping upwards, although this trend so far appears not to have reduced the appetite of Americans for air travel.

Conclusion

Today, thousands of travel destinations exist within the United States. The country's wealth of astonishing natural wonders ensures millions of travelers flock to its shores, mountains, canyons, and deserts. Birthplaces of national heroes, authors, and artists, sites where famous battles took place and locales where other important moments in history were recorded also entice numerous visitors. The national, state, and county parks that have been established throughout the nation to celebrate many of its treasures attest to the significance of such attractions. In 2006, some 438.4 million visits were recorded at National Park Service properties alone.

By the same token, many people travel to major metropolitan areas as well as other communities, large and small, situated outside their own home towns. Often, the principal purpose of the trip is business. Others, however, travel because they seek leisure and relaxation away from the drudgery of their everyday lives. That they choose to undertake these trips in ever-increasing numbers reflects the enhanced drawing power numerous localities throughout the country have following substantial investments in tourism-related infrastructure. Billions of dollars are spent annually on tourist-specific venues, including airport terminals, ballparks, aquaria, convention centers and museums. Furthermore, the epitome of America's destinations appears in the form of tourism industrial complexes like Las Vegas and, of course, the agglomerations of theme parks, including the queen of them all: Disney World and its sister parks in Orlando, Florida.

The story of how America has become a nation where tourism is now well and truly entrenched as a key social and economic phenomenon is an intricate one. We have seen that the growth of tourism is recent, certainly spanning less than two centuries. This evolution has resulted from various forces including the innovation of transportation systems, a series of government policies, and a growing sense of nationalism. To no small extent, a long tradition of civic boosterism/place promotion has also ensured that in many communities throughout the country tourism has become a major sector of the economy.

Much of the responsibility for the fortunes of the tourism industry during the nineteenth century is borne by the advent and diffusion of the railroad. By contrast, during the twentieth century it was first the private automobile and eventually air travel that shaped the evolutionary pattern of American tourism. Obviously, these transportation systems alone could not have had the impact they did, had the federal government not taken various actions that provided the impetus for the phenomenal growth of these transportation modes and which, by association, determined how the tourism industry in this country ultimately evolved

Government actions have not only been instrumental in shaping the country's transportation patterns. The establishment of Yellowstone as the world's very first national park and the eventual creation of the National Park Service have been major catalysts in the development of travel and tourism. The effort of President Roosevelt's administration to create employment, including jobs for thousands of unemployed writers during the 1930s led to the creation of the American Guide Series, whose ultimate aim was to enhance the profile of American places as destinations. Additionally, had the investment in massive infrastructure projects, most notably the Hoover Dam, not taken place, it is highly unlikely that a place such as Las Vegas would have become one of the world's leading tourism-industry complexes.

The impact of nationalism on America's tourism sector must not be underestimated. Especially during the post-Civil War era the enormous growth of tourism within the country's interior had much to do with the pride Americans felt for their country and what it had to offer. Realizing that the US could not compete with Europe as a destination based on its built heritage, a strong emphasis was placed on the country's unique natural treasures. Initiatives like "see America first" (Shaffer 2001) introduced during the late 1880s and again after the beginning of the First World War (Jakle and Sculle 2008) were specifically designed with the aim of enticing Americans to discover their own country before embarking on foreign travels. By the 1960s, a similar program had again been put into place, namely President Johnson's "see the USA" initiative, which was aimed at encouraging Americans to feel pride for their country and spend their dollars at home, thus boosting the balance of payments. The travel industry itself played a major role in encouraging Americans to travel within their own country as one of their civic duties. "Tourist interests insisted that by seeing the sights and scenes that embodied the essence of America, by consuming the nation through touring, tourists would become better Americans" (Shaffer 2001: 4).

Finally, numerous places around the country would not have become major destinations had it not been for the ingrained culture of boosterism that characterizes American promotional politics at the local level. The leaders of communities like Saratoga Springs and Newport realized early on that by promoting tourism, they could inspire economic growth. And, major events like the Chicago World's Fair in 1893 were aimed not only at enticing millions of visitors but, more importantly, at elevating the status of that particular metropolis as a global city.

Questions

1. In what way did the development of the canal system in the United States during the early part of the nineteenth century influence the growth of tourism?

2. What influence, if any, did artists and writers have on the development of tourism in the early 1800s?

3. Briefly explain how the railroads became a key force behind the growth of tourism, especially in the West.

4. During the Great Depression the American Guide Series was developed as a means to create employment for writers. Try to find a book about a state you are most familiar with that was published in this series during the 1930s or early '40s and see what attractions are highlighted. Based on what you know about this state has there been a substantial change in its tourism product since that book was published? To what extent could you rely on that early publication if you wanted to take a trip now?

Further reading

Harrison, B.A. (2006) *The View from Vermont: Tourism and the Making of an American Rural Landscape*. Lebanon, NH: University of Vermont Press.

Norkunas, M.K. (1993) *The Politics of Public Memory: Tourism, History and Ethnicity in Monterey, California*. Albany, NY: State University of New York Press.

Sears, J.F. (1998) *Sacred Places: American Tourist Attractions in the Nineteenth Century*. Amherst: University of Massachusetts Press.

Shaffer, M.S. (2001) *See America First: Tourism and National Identity, 1880–1940.* Washington, DC: Smithsonian Institution Press.

Useful Internet resources

Coney Island USA: http://www.coneyisland.com/
Erie Canal Museum: http://www.eriecanalmuseum.org/
National Amusement Park Historical Association: http://www.napha.org/nnn/
National Historic Route 66 Federation: http://www.national66.com/
National Trust for Historic Preservation: http://www.preservationnation.org/
Saratoga Springs History Museum: http://www.saratogahistory.org/
Ohio's Historic Canals: http://my.ohio.voyager.net/~lstevens/canal/
US National Park Service: http://www.nps.gov
http://en.wikipedia.org/wiki/Tourism_in_the_United_States – cite_ref-1850s_1–3

③ The institutional setting for tourism in the United States

At a time when other countries have become better funded, more coordinated and sophisticated in their efforts to attract international visitors, the USA still lacks a national strategy to compete. This situation puts the USA in a distinct competitive disadvantage in efforts to attract world travel . . . The consequences of this competitive gap have already materialized. A close analysis of key indicators and trend lines reveals that beneath the surface of seemingly good news, the USA has been steadily losing market share for years, at a cost of hundreds of billions of dollars and millions of jobs.

(US Travel and Tourism Advisory Board 2006: 4)

Introduction

In the previous chapter we stressed the point that over the last one hundred years or so numerous forces have shaped to varying degrees the evolutionary path of tourism in the USA. These include federal policies relating to issues like transportation, environmental protection and wildlife management, and national parks. Admittedly, many of these measures have not been directly aimed at tourism – indeed many of them do not even refer to the word tourism – but we cannot neglect their broad repercussions on the manner of the sector's eventual development.

Undoubtedly, within any country, government at various levels – from national to regional to local – is an important player in tourism, to a large extent because it coordinates what is a highly fragmented sector involving numerous actors at various points in space who represent both the private and public spheres. In brief, government can play multiple roles, including those of entrepreneur, promoter, regulator, and planner (Hall 1998b, 2008). Interestingly, however, the United States has never really had the strong presence of an organization at the federal level dealing directly with tourism matters. In other words, what is a common phenomenon in most countries, namely a national tourism organization (NTO) effectively does not exist in the USA (Timothy 2005a, 2006b). Instead, the task of dealing with travel and tourism matters at the national level has either been centered on bodies with minimal clout and negligible budgets or has been scattered throughout various federal entities which, more often than not, do not coordinate their actions in a beneficial manner for the industry. In fact, much of the responsibility for marketing places as tourism destinations has fallen on either state entities or local agencies. The problem with this approach, of course, is that there is a noticeable absence of coordination when marketing the United States as an entire destination. This results, effectively, in the various states and localities competing with each other to attract visitors.

This chapter begins by exploring the role of government overall within tourism. Our central premise is that governmental intervention in the management and marketing of tourism is a necessity because the extremely fragmented nature of the industry at any destination, consisting of numerous businesses of different sizes and representing various interests, means that each one of these players is primarily concerned more with its own slice of the pie than with the broader picture, namely the benefit of the entire destination. We also discuss the various roles that government plays when it comes to tourism. This is followed by a focused investigation of the situation within the USA where, as we conclude, there is a lack of a clear-cut national tourism organization at the federal government level on par with NTOs found in most other countries. The chapter then focuses on state and local level involvement in tourism development and promotion and ends with some thoughts about tourism planning. Specifically, we seek to answer the question why tourism as a sector normally does not feature clearly in comprehensive land-use plans in most communities around the country.

The role of government in the tourism industry

In any given destination tourism is an extremely fragmented sector. It involves an amorphous conglomeration of businesses, attractions, agencies, organizations, and individuals all of whom are primarily concerned about their own respective activities. In the case of a hotel, for instance, the operator's priority is to maximize profitability and market penetration, whereas for the inhabitants of the destination a major objective may be the generation of employment and an overall improvement in quality of life. In this respect, then, tourism differs from a more traditional economic sector such as an industry that manufactures computers, furniture, or motorcycles. In the case of these mainstream industries, the firm assumes a major role for the design, development, marketing, and distribution of the product. By contrast, when it comes to tourism, what essentially is on offer is the destination itself, including both private and public domains, and so there arises a need for an overarching entity that can plan, develop, and market the locality as a complete unit. After all, the owner of a major hotel wants to ensure that the room occupancy rates are high, while the operator of an attraction wishes to draw as many visitors as possible in order to make a profit. Though in both cases, these players will undoubtedly benefit from increased visitation to the area their underlying concern is their own individual enterprises.

Thus, it is usually up to a government or quasi-governmental organization – both at national and sub-national levels – to ensure the destination as a whole is promoted and marketed to potential visitors (Jeffries 2001). Its principal purpose is not to draw tourists to any single particular attraction or lodging facility, but rather to ensure that the entire destination attracts as many visitors as possible to maximize economic benefits, while seeking to avoid potential pitfalls associated with the sector's growth. Pearce (1989) argues that beyond the promotion of economic objectives the state also becomes involved in tourism for reasons such as protecting the well-being of the consumers (the tourists) and the local residents and safeguarding the key cultural and environmental assets of the destination. He points out, further, that through the active promotion of tourism, national governments have sometimes managed to "further their political objectives" (Pearce 1989: 41) as was the case in Spain in the 1950s and 1960s when the Franco regime used the sector to enhance its legitimacy. Similarly, during the late 1960s, the military junta in Greece played a vital role as a driver of that country's tourism development with the aim of making international public opinion more favorable towards that regime.

The level of government involvement varies, depending on the sector's degree of importance within the overall economy. Holloway and Taylor (2006: 423) maintain that at the national level, the higher the dependence on tourism "whether domestic, inbound or outbound, the more likely it is that the government will intervene in the industry's activities." This explains why in many countries where the economies are heavily reliant on tourism, there exist governmental bodies (e.g., ministries) dealing directly with tourism affairs, whereas this is rarely the case in countries with highly diversified economies. It also seems that countries where tourism has revealed its ugly side by causing a number of adverse social and ecological impacts that in turn threaten their competitiveness as tourist destinations, are far more willing to enact policies to rectify or avoid such problems.

Holloway and Taylor go on to argue that the type of government existing within a specific country very much influences the manner in which the state will intervene. In a centrally planned economy one may expect a high degree of top–down control from the central government, as was the case in the ex-Soviet bloc. Today, this type of rigid control is exceedingly rare in tourism because even centrally planned countries such as China and Cuba have allowed a considerable degree of latitude to private firms to operate there. In mixed economies there is a considerable degree of public–private interaction determining the manner in which tourism evolves, though admittedly the "balance of public versus private involvement will vary" (Holloway and Taylor 2006: 424). It appears that within developing countries government involvement in tourism can be strong, at least at an early stage of tourism's development, since private investors may show initial reluctance to invest in what they see as a risky region. Finally, the phenomenon of government-owned airlines, despite an overall trend towards the privatization of carriers, can be explained by the amount of perceived prestige the national carrier can bestow on a country (Wheatcroft 1998; Bowen 2002).

Michael Hall (1994, 1998b, and 2008b; see also Hall and Jenkins 1995) has written extensively on the role of government organizations in tourism development. He argues that government (from the national to the local level) has a major say in the evolution of tourism in any particular destination. There are, according to Hall (2008b), several ways in which government influences tourism. For example, it can influence, plan, and coordinate the sector's development, but it can also introduce legislation and regulations that either directly or indirectly have an effect on the travel industry. When it comes to tourism, government has also assumed the tasks of place promoter, entrepreneur, and protector of public interests.

To begin with, a governmental or quasi-governmental entity like a destination management organization (DMO) is in a position to play a key part in ensuring that the actions of various businesses and bodies relating to tourism development – whether directly or indirectly – are synchronized. It is vital, for instance, to guarantee for the sake of effective tourism development that the policies arising from various governmental bodies are not contradictory from the tourism industry's point of view, and to guarantee there is no duplication of efforts (Hall 2008). By assuming the role of coordinator, government authorities can also monitor the growth in supply of tourist facilities and make certain this is not out of tandem with existing patterns of demand (Holloway and Taylor 2006).

Governments often assume a major role as tourism planners and developers. In the case of France the massive development of the Lanquedoc-Roussillon coastline during the 1960s resulted from a top–down central government effort, which sought to bring economic development to a depressed region (Pearce 1989). In a similar manner, the Mexican resort of Cancun resulted from federal government efforts to promote various types of development through the construction of growth poles in underdeveloped regions (Torres and Momsen 2005). Much more recently, the South Korean government has taken an active role in the construction of Tourism Leisure Cities (TLCs) with the goal of decentralizing development, which has thus far focused heavily on Seoul and

Plate 3.1 Seaside, Florida, a planned community
(Dimitri Ioannides)

the Seoul–Pusan axis. These "instant" cities aim at fulfilling the residential and amenity requirements of South Korea's burgeoning middle class that is no longer satisfied with the existing densely inhabited cities, including the capital Seoul. The growing demand for domestic tourism, which has arisen from a phenomenal growth in per capita income as well as the recent reduction of the work week from six to five days, plus the proximity of potential markets, especially China, are also key factors that have propelled this government-led initiative.

In the United States there has never been a tradition of public-led initiatives such as the ones witnessed in Mexico or South Korea whereby the aim is to build brand new towns specializing in activities like tourism. This has very much to do with the obvious hands-off way of governance in this country, which essentially gives much more leeway to the private sector to become engaged in new developments. This does not mean to say that new communities specializing in tourism and recreation do not exist in the United States. On the contrary, there are literally hundreds of privately built communities all around the country, many of which have become attractive as second home destinations or places for retirees (see Plate 3.1). A number of these places are based on amenities such as golf. Many new towns are run privately by community associations, and a significant number of them are gated, meaning that they are spatially segregated from the surrounding community. An investigation into the role played by the Disney Corporation in developing a whole range of facilities, including a brand new town, in central Florida is discussed in Closer Look Case 3.1. The problems associated with private-led initiatives, a phenomenon that is quite common throughout America, are discussed there.

CLOSER LOOK CASE 3.1

Development without public involvement: Walt Disney World, Florida

When looking down from an airplane on the central part of Florida one can notice a truly astounding phenomenon. Lying below, just on the outskirts of Orlando, is an industrial complex, except one would be hard pressed to pinpoint a manufacturing plant anywhere in the vicinity. This agglomeration of activities is based entirely on tourism. The center of this development is Walt Disney World (WDW), a vast expanse of land encompassing the following attractions: the Magic Kingdom, Animal Kingdom, and Hollywood Studios theme parks; the Typhoon Lagoon and Blizzard Beach Water Parks; Disney's Boardwalk Area; Disney's Wide World of Sports Complex; Disney Resort hotels; and Downtown Disney Area. More than 50,000 workers are employed here, while the hotels of the resort cater to tens of thousands of visitors daily. In Downtown Disney one can find a wide selection in terms of shopping and eating out. There are also plenty of things to do for an evening's entertainment, such as visiting the House of Blues or the Cirque du Soleil. These developments associated directly with Disney have also spawned numerous additional attractions, lodging establishments, and eateries all of which have helped transform this region into a massive development whose economy relies overwhelmingly on tourism.

In addition to this massive ensemble of recreational facilities, the Walt Disney Corporation has built Celebration, a private new town on 4,900 acres which will eventually house 20,000 people. This community, which follows the tenets of New Urbanism, is surrounded by a substantial green belt, meaning it cannot be encroached on by surrounding development. The privately run community, which has been developed as a place to live where the automobile is kept at bay and walking or biking is encouraged, includes a mix of land uses, housing types, and development densities. It has a traditional-style downtown with shops and a central post office and boasts several buildings designed by world famous architects, including Michael Graves and Philip Johnson. Celebration is a town run by a Homeowners' Association and lacks a publicly elected government. However, despite the lack of public involvement in managing the community's growth it is important to stress that certain pundits have lauded Celebration and the overall WDW as one of the best examples of city planning. The noted NBC reporter David Brinkley even went as far to suggest that the master plan of the entire WDW is so impressive that other cities throughout the nation should hire the Disney Corporation to manage their growth (Foglesong 1999).

The entire region administered by the Disney Corporation covers approximately the same area as San Francisco. In addition to enforcing strict regulations relating to design of the buildings and landscaping, even controlling the color of the drapes one can hang in one's home, Disney is in charge of providing fire protection and security. When Disney first took control of the land in central Florida back in the 1960s it made sure to acquire more land than it originally needed so that it would not run the risk of being restricted for future development should the need arise.

Foglesong points out that effectively the form of "government" found in WDW, meaning the public is kept at bay, has ensured that problems commonly associated with a pluralist democratic society, such as the difficulty of getting different groups of stakeholders to agree, are avoided. No one is in a position to challenge the decisions of the private government. Foglesong argues that, at first glance, the order that reigns inside the privately administered region suggests the private form of governance works better compared to the unruly development that exists on the publicly run I-Drive (just outside the WDW).

Yet, at the same time the lack of citizen participation in a privately-run domain such as WDW is deeply problematic. Harvey (2000) views the attempt by companies like Disney to create a utopia as nothing more than a veiled attempt to exclude those who do not belong (e.g., ethnic minorities and people of lower socioeconomic status). In fact, multiculturalism cannot thrive in places like this. Housing for the poorly paid tourism workers is hardly ever provided and, if it is, it is not adequate to satisfy demand. When the state of Florida tried to force Disney to provide affordable housing, the Corporation fought against this since it did not want additional residents with voting rights on its premises. Meanwhile, the impacts Disney has on the surrounding community (e.g., rapidly increasing land values and housing prices, and increasing traffic congestion) become externalities that the Corporation fails to cover. In fact the burden of development falls squarely on the inhabitants of surrounding areas.

WDW is the poster child of a development form that has become increasingly common in the United States, particularly in communities that stress leisure and recreation. It demonstrates a tendency on behalf of developers to exert enormous power and concurrently restrict government intervention because this is often seen as antithetical to the motives of profitmaking and efficiency. On a broader basis it reflects Americans' deeply ingrained suspicion of government. Yet, not all things can be left to free market forces, especially when it comes to dealing with the externalities of private-led projects such as these. In the case of tourism-dependent communities, which often experience rapid change, it remains to be seen whether local residents can avoid the negative effects associated with the sector without any help from a democratically elected government.

Sources

Foglesong, R. (1999) Walt Disney World and Orlando: Deregulation as a strategy for tourism. In D.R. Judd and S.S. Fainstein (eds) *The Tourist City*, pp. 89–106. New Haven: Yale University Press.
Harvey, D. (2000) *Spaces of Hope*. Berkeley: University of California Press.

Questions

1. There are many communities around the United States, but also in other countries, that like Celebration, Florida, are planned, privately managed, and often gated. What are some of the advantages of such communities and what are some of the negatives associated with them? Would you like to live in such a community, or at least have a second home there?
2. Look up the term "new-urbanism." To what extent does a community like Celebration meet the description of a new-urbanist community?
3. One of the major problems in many tourism communities is that they are unplanned and display an image of haphazard development. Do you believe that a privately designed, developed, and administered tourism community can function more sustainably than a locality that is run by a public government? Try to think of examples of both types of communities and use these to justify your answer.

Various forms of plans exist relating to tourism. These are developed by a number of public or quasi-public entities at the national, regional, and local levels (Hall 2008). However, Hall stresses that it is rare to find a single public body (for instance, such as a regional planning department) making plans that focus "exclusively" on tourism. "Instead, planning for tourism tends to be an amalgam of economic, social, political and environmental considerations that reflect the diversity of factors which influence tourism development" (Hall 2008: 14). In the case of a community's comprehensive master plan, it is possible that tourism may feature as one of numerous sectors discussed in the plan, perhaps as a part of the economic development strategy, but it is unlikely that the planning authority will prepare plans dealing solely with tourism.

Hawaii was one of the first places to include tourism within its overall 1959 State Plan (Inskeep 1991). During the 1960s and '70s, plans relating at least partly to tourism were also developed especially in different parts of Asia, including Nepal, Bali, Fiji, and French Polynesia, while later plans for Hawaii included "the preparation of more detailed land use plans for resort areas" (Inskeep 1991: 17). Hall (2008) mentions that developing countries and several island states where tourism is a mainstay of the economy have often developed detailed national or regional tourism development plans. These include several Caribbean islands and the island states of Malta and Cyprus.

In most advanced economies, however, tourism development plans, especially ones focusing on the sector's land-use implications, are rare. It is more usual to see, as in the case of Australia, a national tourism strategy emphasizing the role of public–private partnerships. Moreover, what is often described as a tourism development plan by a DMO is in reality a marketing plan which fails to deal with the sector in a comprehensive manner, and certainly does not refer to issues such as impact mitigation. Hall (2008) warns that one of the problems with both tourism plans and strategies is that they often have only an indicative role since the tools for implementing these documents are either absent or weak. Also, if the plan arises from an organization like a quasi-governmental NTO it is unlikely to have much clout, given the notoriously weak political status of such entities.

Regulations and legislation are yet another way through which government affects the tourism sector both directly and indirectly. For example, regulations relating to environmental protection influence the manner in which tourism evolves in a particular locale. Then, we must consider the plethora of controls issued by immigration authorities or bodies dealing with safety and security (e.g., visa regulations and travel restrictions). If a certain country has draconian visa requirements, then this is likely to act as a disincentive to visitors from other countries. If, by contrast, visa requirements are eradicated, at least for travelers from certain countries, this measure is likely to lead to enhanced visitation. Additionally, countries have instituted regulatory frameworks addressing the quality of their accommodation sector or stipulating requirements relating to the labor force. Some places may even have land-use regulations relating directly to the location of key tourist facilities. Rules concerning building height, acceptable color schemes, appropriate signage, and view-scapes have also been adopted in certain instances.

Beyond the roles that have been described, governmental or quasi-governmental entities function as providers of the key infrastructure necessary for tourism development, including transportation systems (e.g., airports, highways, marinas), solid waste or sewage disposal facilities, and sporting venues and conference halls (Judd 2003a, 2004). To attract private tourism-related investment, it has become increasingly common for local governments to offer incentives in the form of tax breaks, low interest loans, and cheap or free land, all of which are meant to stimulate further development (Hall 2008).

Place marketing has become a leading activity, especially at the local government level (Ashworth and Voogd 1990; Britton 1991; Coles 2003; Hall 1998b, c). This is because many places throughout the world have witnessed a massive transformation from production-based (e.g., manufacturing and warehousing) to consumer-oriented service activities, including tourism. The bodies responsible for tourism's development, including national, regional, and local organizations regularly spend substantial amounts of money on the development of websites and promotional brochures, as well as television, radio, and newspaper advertisements (Holcomb 1999). These organizations often undertake research to identify the key existing and potential markets and invest heavily in terms of opening and operating bureaus in important origin areas. Hall points out that the irony of place-making efforts on behalf of government organizations is that despite the vast amounts of money they spend, "the most unusual features of tourism promotion by government tourism organisations is that they have only limited control over the product they are marketing, with very few governments actually owning the goods, facilities, and services that make up the tourism product" (Hall 2008: 168). This, in Hall's mind, provides evidence of the excessive powers the tourism industry and the various organizations that lobby for it can exert in the public sphere, supposedly in the name of the broader good of the entire community.

Government bodies also have the role of protectors of the broader public interest, especially given that the profit-driven actions of private companies do not necessarily meet the equity concerns within any given community. This, of course, not only happens in the case of tourism. Rather, bodies such as urban planning departments regularly have to deal with finding a balance between economic growth and environmental and social objectives, and, at least in theory, they are there to protect the interests of the least powerful groups (Campbell 1996). Hall (2008: 169) maintains that specifically in the case of tourism planning where there are numerous sector-specific interests, a need arises for a dedicated public body to intervene as "arbiter between competing interests." However, he admits that today in many locations the tendency to create private–public partnerships and to hand virtually limitless powers to such institutions while removing any opportunities for citizen participation appears to have become a growing problem.

The question that arises within the context of this chapter relates to the role of the US federal government in relation to tourism. To what extent is the US government similar to or how does it differ from other countries when it comes to various tourism-related functions such as marketing, data gathering, and regulation? These issues are explored in the next section.

NTO and the USA

In September 2008 the US House of Representatives passed the Travel Promotion Act of 2008 (also known as H.R. 3232) (US Congress 2008: 1). If the Senate eventually approves this Act and the President signs it, it will constitute a significant step towards the creation of "a non-profit corporation to communicate United States entry policies and otherwise promote tourist, business, and scholarly travel to the United States" (US Congress 2008: 2). The proposed Act clearly states that the non-profit corporation shall not be "an agency or establishment of the United States Government" (US Congress 2008: 2). Instead, it shall be run by a board of directors appointed by the Secretary of Commerce in consultation with the Secretaries of Homeland Security, State, and Education. The Undersecretary of Commerce will function as the liaison to the corporation. Each member of the board of directors should have an extensive background in each of the sectors that relates either directly or indirectly to the travel industry (e.g., lodging, restaurants, retail, and attractions). The proposed legislation underlines that federal employees are barred from serving on the board. Additionally, a position on the board is strictly non-political and non-salaried. The tourism corporation will be accountable to Congress and has to submit a comprehensive report of its activities and expenditures on an annual basis.

The corporation's primary responsibilities are to develop an effective communications channel to inform potential visitors to the USA about the country's security and entry policies and to strive to alleviate fears or misunderstandings concerning existing travel policies. It will also promote the entire country as an international destination, including regions that may not normally have a popular image in the global arena. In this respect the corporation should perform, at least in part, the functions of a national tourism office, like those in so many competing nations (Hotel News Resource 2008). However, one thing that sets this organization aside from a regular NTO is that its funding will come entirely from the private sector and a special fee charged to travelers from Visa Waiver countries; no resident taxpayer dollars will be used to operate the corporation.

This proposed travel bill was initiated because policymakers had become increasingly alarmed by the dramatic decline in international arrivals to the USA in the aftermath of September 11, 2001; 2 million fewer international visitors came to the USA in 2007 compared to 2000 – this despite the US dollar, at that time, being exceedingly low compared to most other currencies. According to the Travel Industry Association (TIA), this trend has cost $94 billion in visitor spending, $16 billion in tax receipts and almost 200,000 jobs.

The pending adoption of the Travel Promotion Act constitutes the latest in a series of moves over the decades to create an organization responsible for marketing the USA on a par with the NTOs seen in nearly all other countries throughout the world. At the same time, however, it reflects a deep-seated ambivalence on the part of legislators toward the tourism industry and especially a definite ill-will towards any move perceived to involve the expenditure of substantial amounts of taxpayer money to benefit what many people see only as private corporations. This bias against a federal government entity (equivalent to an NTO) responsible for promoting the USA as a tourist destination was highlighted in 1996 when Representative John Dingell (1996: 1) vehemently argued that no proof exists that such an organization would draw into the United States "more than what it cost American taxpayers to fund it." Given that this seems to be the prevailing attitude towards the travel and tourism sector, it is not surprising, therefore, that the responsibility for dealing with tourism at the federal level has historically been shared among a number of departments as well as non-profit private-public corporations while officials have repeatedly stressed that no taxpayer dollars whatsoever will be used for marketing purposes.

In essence, Dingell's criticism was against the closest thing the USA had ever had to an NTO, the United States Travel and Tourism Administration (USTTA), which had recently been shut down because of budget shortfalls. Effectively, the USTTA, which between 1961 and 1981 was known as the US Travel Service, operated under the umbrella of the Department of Commerce and had been responsible for marketing the USA abroad to foreign travel agents and tour operators, while it also conducted research and coordinated with various government agencies to make international travel easier overall.

Since 1996, however, the responsibility for the industry has been fragmented into the hands of numerous bodies, both government and non-profit and, indeed, there exists a considerable amount of duplication of responsibilities between these entities while at the same time coordination appears to be minimal. In fact little has changed since the early 1970s when the Department of Commerce concluded that tourism was spread through 100 programs within 50 agencies, a phenomenon that led to "confusion and disarray" (Brewton and Witham 1998: 7). Today, the Office of Travel and Tourism Industries, located within the Department of Commerce (in the International Trade Administration, Manufacturing and Services Bureau), "fulfills the inherent role of expanding travel and tourism business opportunities for employment and economic growth" (OTTI 2009). The OTTI was an outgrowth of a previous law, the National Tourism Organization Act of 1996, which stipulated that the Secretary of Commerce should undertake "critical tourism functions such as to collect and publish comprehensive international travel and tourism statistics and other marketing information, facilitate in the reduction of barriers to travel . . . and maintain the US participation in international travel and tourism trade shows." While on the surface it appears that the OTTI performs similar functions to those of other NTOs, and although it has retained many of the functions of the disbanded USTTA, it is important to point out that it does so with a minuscule operational budget and approximately 12 employees compared to its predecessor, which had close to 100 (Harreld 1996). Additionally, unlike the USTTA, the OTTI lacks a marketing arm; instead, marketing efforts are now under the auspices of non-profit groups, with representatives from the private sector.

Other bodies that have varying responsibilities with regard to tourism include the Travel Industry Association (TIA), a non-profit organization with more than 1,000 members (companies but also government agencies) that, among others, undertakes research, marketing, training, and lobbying. The one downside of the TIA is that its research (as opposed to the research conducted by the OTTI) is only provided to its members for a substantial fee. The lobbying arm of the TIA is the Travel and Tourism Government Affairs Council, which in 2006 pushed for an "open borders" mentality for travel between all nations (Harris 2006). The US Travel Data Center is yet another non-profit, privately supported agency that conducts research concerning the travel industry and its economic impacts. Finally, the Tourism Policy Council, an interagency committee, involves the leaders of nine federal agencies who aim to coordinate federal decisions and policies that may either directly or indirectly affect the sector's development (Office of Travel and Tourism Industries 2009).

The existing institutional structure at the federal level with regard to tourism leads to a key question: Does a comprehensive US tourism policy actually exist? The answer to this is far from clear. First, as we have already shown, policymakers themselves, including a number of US presidents, have often regarded tourism as a marginal matter and, as a result, a tourism policy has not been high on their agenda. While there are numerous organizations and agencies that somehow relate to travel and tourism, and although there exists the Tourism Policy Council, in reality tourism policy within the USA "has been characterized by weak and limited authority, little regulatory ability, inconsistent direction, and unreliable [in fact negligible] government support" (Brewton and Witham 1998: 7). In fact, Brewton and Witham lament that US tourism policy is exceedingly weak and narrow, a problem they interpret as arising from the "distance between the policy makers (legislators) and policy implementers (the industry)" (p. 2). Additionally, much of what constitutes tourism policy within the USA relates to promotion and marketing, which in fact is just a small slice of what a comprehensive tourism policy is meant to cover.

US tourism policy displays enormous gaps in numerous areas including those relating to licensing and certification. No federal hotel quality measure exists akin to the systems in place in many countries. A plethora of federal, state, and local agencies oversee standards in transportation, fire safety, and food quality, all of which relate to tourism, but there is no specific directive from a tourism agency concerning these issues. Additionally, no policies explicitly address employment and labor training, nor are there programs at the federal level to promote domestic destinations throughout the country. When it comes to the protection of tourism-related resources, especially natural environments, this task belongs to the Environmental Protection Agency, the Bureau of Land Management, the National Park Service, or various state entities that deal with natural or cultural resources. In spite of this important role, however, many national-level land management agencies reject the idea that they are part of the tourism system and are stewards over tourism resources, arguing instead that they facilitate visitors but are not the gatekeepers of tourist attractions (Timothy and Boyd 2006b). Finally, the federal government entirely ignores tourism's interrelationship to land use, a matter that is hardly surprising given that this country lacks a national land use policy to begin with (Cullingworth 2007).

Another non-profit group, the US Travel and Tourism Advisory Board, has also highlighted the lack of a clear-cut strategy or policy relating to tourism at the national level within the USA in its 2006 report *Restoring America's Brand*. Adopting an extremely critical tone, the report laments that the USA had become the only country among its competitors to have suffered a decline in its market share of world travel since 9/11.

> When government officials and agencies speak for security, who in government is charged with speaking for travel and tourism? It is clear that other countries that compete with the USA have coordinated visa/entry/exit, air service, regulatory, tax and other policies that favor travel and tourism as well as meaningful budgets for traditional promotional campaigns to attract these visitors. Countries that are competitive for tourism also ordinarily have ministries for tourism or other governmental entities that help coordinate policy decisions that impact this sector. The USA, by contrast, has no specific Ministry of Tourism or Office high enough to advocate these issues at the highest policy levels in support of this vital, growing sector.
>
> (USTTAB 2006: 18)

Evidence of the discordance between various national legislation initiatives and the tourism industry's interests was highlighted following the passage of the Intelligence Reform and Terrorism Prevention Act of 2004 (Hedrich 2008). Specifically, Section 7209 – the Western Hemisphere Travel Initiative – of this act, could serve to make international travel to and from the USA much harder than it already is. In simple terms, Section 7209 specifies that US citizens and certain categories of non-immigrant aliens (specifically from Canada and Mexico) who travel into the USA from countries within the western hemisphere must now (see Chapter 4) *always* present a valid passport at their point of entry. In the past, Canadians did not have to produce a passport when entering the USA; instead, they merely had to provide proof of legal residency or citizenship like a birth certificate, a green card, or a driver's license. The same was the case for US citizens traveling to and from Mexico and Canada, although Mexicans have always been required to show a passport when traveling into the USA, unless they lived within a 25-mile frontier radius in which case they could use an electronic visa. Other new immigration laws also affect transit passengers. As of 2003, the US Department of Homeland Security requires all transit and connecting passengers, even if they do not leave the airport, to possess a transit visa. This has been especially difficult for people from Latin America, who have traditionally flown via cities like Miami, Dallas, and Los Angeles to make connections to Europe and Asia. US visas are not easy or inexpensive to acquire. Industry observers suggest that this requirement has slowed the growth of international arrivals and caused bad feelings among some of the United States' South and Central American allies.

Section 7209 and other new legislation could, at least in the short term, have an adverse impact on international tourism to and from the USA. In 2004 a significant portion of travel expenditure by US travelers (59 percent) was incurred in Canada, while Canadian travelers in the USA accounted for 55.8 percent of that country's total travel expenditure. Hedrich (2008) argued that the requirement for passports would deter, to an extent, travel between the two countries. He cited evidence from businesses in the Niagara Falls area and Windsor, Ontario, that had already experienced a decline in spending because of the new measures. He sees the new measures as counterproductive from the tourism industry's point of view, especially at a time when in other parts of the world travel restrictions have actually been reduced or are non-existent (e.g., within Europe's Schengen Area). Rather cynically, Hedrich maintains that the main beneficiaries of Section 7209 are the private companies in the security industry who have been developing the new US e-passport. On a more optimistic note, he argues that over the long term, the need to obtain a passport even for travel to Canada or Mexico may lead to increased outbound travel from the USA to other parts of the world since one of the deterrents for overseas travel – the lack of a passport – will have been removed.

Regardless of what the effects of Section 7209 may turn out to be, it is obvious that the passage of the Terrorism Prevention Act, an outgrowth of Homeland Security, was not implemented with an eye on facilitating tourism flows to and from the USA. In fact, this legislation has quite the opposite impact since it makes the USA appear less than welcoming to overseas visitors. The transit visa requirement noted above is evidence of this problem. The authors of *Restoring America's Travel Brand* clearly had this legislation in mind, as well as a number of other measures which had been instituted in the post-9/11 era, when they prepared their report, which in essence constitutes an attempt to spread the seeds for a comprehensive national tourism strategy (USTTAB 2006). They argue that a comprehensive tourism strategy is a necessity and must include at least the following elements: (a) first, it has to reverse the feeling that has emerged among many foreigners that the USA is an unfriendly place to visit due to the draconian safety and security measures that have been enforced since 9/11; (b) it has to include a marketing campaign that is coordinated for the entire nation; and (c) it must ensure that the nation's competitiveness *vis à vis* other countries is constantly monitored. The report stresses that for a fraction of the $800 million spent by the State Department on programs that "communicate America's values to other countries and cultures, through exchange, information programs and other public relations activities" (2006: 7) the travel and tourism industry can contribute considerably to the same effort by "ASKING people to visit us."

To make it easier for people to visit the USA the barriers to travel should be significantly reduced. Visitors to the USA should find themselves in a position to gain a good first impression of the country upon their arrival and the different taxes, fees and regulations that are inappropriate for the travel sector must be removed. The report recommends, for example, that the wait for visas be reduced by hiring additional well-trained staff in overseas embassies. It also mentions that visa requirements for legitimate travelers should be either eradicated or reduced and that the Visa Waiver program should be expanded to cover more countries.

The states and tourism

What the USA lacks at the federal level, namely an umbrella organization with the functions of a National Tourism Organization, exists in all states, albeit under various guises. In other words, there are state agencies that perform many, if not all, of the tasks that in other countries come under the jurisdiction of national entities. There are no precise rules as to what the structure and organization of these entities should be, nor are there any national directives that mandate their responsibilities. Rather, it is up to each state to determine the set-up of its bodies responsible for tourism.

Nevertheless, a glance at the websites of these state tourism organizations reveals several similarities in their structure and organization as well as the functions they perform. Invariably, all these organizations exist to protect the interests of their respective state's tourism industry. For instance, the Missouri Division of Tourism (2007) sets as its overriding mission the growth of the state's tourism sector as a means of generating jobs and economic development, and of increasing tax revenues. Similarly, the "statutory mission of the Oregon Tourism Commission is to encourage economic growth and to enhance the quality of life in Oregon through strengthening the economic impact of tourism throughout the state" (Oregon Tourism Commission 2005). The New Jersey Division of Tourism (State of New Jersey 2009) also aims to encourage higher rates of visitation and expenditure as a means to economic growth, although it also highlights the importance of protecting its natural and cultural resources, which are valuable assets for the tourism industry.

The statewide bodies responsible for tourism are either stand-alone departments within the overall structure of their respective state government or are housed within a broader entity such as a department of economic development. In Texas, for instance, tourism in handled by the Office of the Governor, Economic Development and Tourism. In the state of Washington it sits within the Department of Community, Trade and Economic Development (under international trade and economic development). The Missouri Division of Tourism is located in the Department of Economic Development. The overseeing body for tourism in this state is the Missouri Tourism Commission, a ten-member organization created following the passage of a state law and headed by the Lieutenant Governor of the state. In Oregon, the Oregon Tourism Commission, which functions as Travel Oregon, is a semi-autonomous body set up in 2003. The Tourism Commission, which is appointed by the Governor, effectively oversees the staff and programs of Travel Oregon. The tourism departments in both Florida and Nevada are stand-alone entities. The latter is run by a director who is directly appointed by the governor. Again, there is a commission comprising 11 members that advises the tourism department. The Lieutenant Governor heads this Commission, while its members, who are appointed by the Governor, have to have experience in the travel and tourism industry; the chief administrators from the Las Vegas and Reno-Sparks Convention and Visitors Authorities also serve on the Commission.

In California, the Division of Tourism is housed in the Business, Transportation, and Housing Agency, which is part of that state's executive branch (under the Governor's office) and collaborates with the California Travel and Tourism Commission (CTTC), a not-for-profit organization, to promote the state as a tourist destination. The CTTC has 37 members representing each of California's 12 regions. These members must reflect all components of the tourism industry, namely accommodation, restaurant and retail, attractions and recreation, transportation and travel services, and the passenger car rental sectors. Of these members, 24 are elected by 5,000 member businesses. Another 12 are directly appointed by the Governor while the 37th member is the Secretary of the Business, Transportation and Housing Agency. Although the CTTC and Division of

Tourism are legally separate, collectively they are named "California Tourism." Between 1998, when CTTC was formed, and 2003 "California Tourism consisted of the originally conceived private–public joint marketing venture partnership of the CTTC and the State of California. The sole source of California's tourism marketing budget is now directly derived from assessed businesses in the travel and tourism industry" (California Travel and Tourism Commission 2009: n.p.).

California is not alone in seeking to avoid burdening taxpayers when it comes to funding the operations of state tourism offices. Missouri passed legislation in 1993 (House Bill 188), requiring that a certain percentage of tourism-related tax revenue has to go into tourism promotion (Missouri Division of Tourism n.d.). This ensures that resident taxes do not have to be increased for the purposes of the tourism sector. The legislation targets businesses representing 17 categories (according to the Standard Industrial Classification system), which either directly or indirectly relate to travel and tourism, and requests that part of their tax revenue is annually invested in tourism marketing. The sectors include eating and drinking establishments, hotels, public golf courses, and botanical and zoological gardens. Oregon has a similar procedure in place, whereby it uses the revenues from a statewide 1 percent lodging tax to fund its branding and marketing campaigns. Additionally, Nevada uses 80 percent of its hotel and motel tax for financing its marketing operations while its publication operations derive from the sales of advertising space and subscriptions. Most states in the USA follow a similar pattern where tourism taxes are used to fund tourism promotion and marketing.

The functions performed by the various state tourism offices appear to be quite similar, and they match to a large extent the efforts of national tourism organizations in other countries. In all cases, marketing seems to be the primary responsibility of the state tourism offices. The Missouri Division of Tourism, which in 2007 maintained an operating budget of almost $18 million, allocated 54.7 percent of this to domestic marketing, 22 percent to cooperative marketing, and a further 1.4 percent to international promotion efforts. Unsurprisingly, California has a considerably larger budget (annually it comes to $50 million through to 2013), a major part of which is again used for marketing the state both home and abroad. During the budget year 2005–6 California ranked sixth among all states in terms of its tourism office budget. The same year, Hawaii was first (California Travel and Tourism Commission 2007). California's budget derives from a 60/40 split between the state and the CTTC and businesses provide 60 percent of the marketing budget.

An important product of every state tourism organization's work is a strategic marketing plan. This document, which is normally produced either annually or every second year, concentrates mostly on prescribed future marketing and promotion actions in order to strengthen tourism's position. For example, in its five-year strategic marketing plan, the CTTC adopts three components: the marketing plan for the next five years, domestic annual work plans, and international country plans. One of the primary aims of the marketing plan is to identify actions to increase California's market share as a tourist destination. The annual work plans reveal "in detail how and where $50 million in tourism program funds will be spent each year to reach CTTC's goal of increasing travel spending and tourism employment in California" (CTTC 2007: 5). Additionally, given the importance of international markets to California, the strategic marketing plan reveals actions to be taken to strengthen the state's position as a destination for foreign visitors. For instance, California has established a tourism office in London, since the UK is such a major source of its international visitors. States with more meager budgets may not be in a position to set up overseas offices, but they still collaborate with public relations firms in their main international markets. It is also quite common for states to concentrate much of their marketing effort in neighboring/contiguous states, given their relative proximity. For example, the Oklahoma State Tourism Office regularly airs television commercials in southwest Missouri and northwest Arkansas, while Arkansas has for years aired its "Natural State" commercials in Missouri.

The implementation of a state's tourism marketing plan requires coordination with, among others, industry associations, local visitor and convention bureaus, local chambers of commerce, government agencies, and private sector businesses, a phenomenon, which is repeated in many states, including Oregon, Washington, and Maryland. Additionally, state tourism organizations commonly develop and distribute media kits for tourism publications.

While marketing is a major function within state tourism organizations, it is certainly not their only responsibility. These entities also engage, albeit to varying degrees, in other activities, including research and public relations. Research is regularly performed in-house, but it appears that many of the reports that assess, for instance, tourism's economic impact, are prepared either by university researchers or national consulting companies. The state tourism agencies may also be engaged in educational and professional development programs and will sometimes host an annual "governor's tourism conference," as in the case of Oregon and Arizona. States that are predominantly rural, such as Kansas, may develop workshops for rural tourism development (see Closer Look Case 3.2). Finally, another function of the state tourism organizations is to fund and oversee their welcome centers, which are often located along major thoroughfares leading into each state. California, for example, strives to ensure that each of the state's 12 regions has a welcome center that is strategically located to accommodate as many visitors as possible. Some states, like Oregon, also oversee their scenic byways.

Tourism at the local level

Undoubtedly, state tourism organizations in the USA are key actors, especially in tourism marketing, but also in travel research endeavors, serving to fill in the gaps created by a weak federal tourism set-up. To be sure, as a result of the lack of a national directive and the absence of federal funds for these state organizations, their effectiveness varies. While, on the one hand, some states have major budgets and are able to perform a variety of tasks, on the other hand, there are states whose tourism organizations have limited functions. For example, although all state organizations engage to some extent in marketing endeavors, only some organizations undertake research on travel and tourism in-house, while others sub-contract these activities to private consultants.

It is clear that it is impossible for a state to provide every locality equal weighting in its marketing efforts. Communities with a wealth of tourism resources (existing or potential) are more likely to receive attention in promotional materials, while other localities may be all but neglected. This means that municipalities wishing to develop and promote their tourism sector must also rely on local bodies for their marketing efforts.

The most common type of local tourism promotion organization in the USA is the Convention and Visitors Bureau (CVB). Although the concept of the CVB is not new – the first one was established in Detroit in 1896 – in more recent years their number has exploded. In the 1990s it was estimated that there were more than 900 such organizations around the USA (Morrison *et al*. 1998). CVBs can represent a small city, a metropolitan area, or in some cases a collection of cities. According to Morrison *et al*. (1998), CVBs can either be independent non-profit organizations or they can be public, quasi-public or even private entities. Most CVBs are independent non-profit organizations while a number of others are either located within a city's chamber of commerce or can be part of a city's government structure.

CLOSER LOOK CASE 3.2

Helping a community develop its tourism potential

In the United States, government at all levels from federal to state and local can have an effect, both directly and indirectly, on the manner in which tourism evolves. A major share of the responsibility for promoting and marketing places as tourist destinations comes at the state level, with Destination Management Organizations (DMOs) playing the same role as national tourism offices in other countries. However, beyond the state DMOs other agencies can also influence the manner in which tourism will grow and the shape it will adopt. A state that puts considerable emphasis on tourism development as a tool for economic development, especially in rural regions, is Alaska. Here the state's Division of Community and Economic Development has released a manual that guides communities throughout Alaska on the ways in which they can develop their tourism industry. Alaska is not the only state to produce such a manual; other states also have "how to develop your tourism" guidelines, though in many cases these are developed by their state university extension services.

The *Alaska Community Tourism Handbook* is quite basic and functions as a layperson's guide for developing and running localities as tourist destinations. The manual discusses the pros and cons of tourism, warning community leaders not to expect a quick fix to their economic woes if they choose to introduce tourism. The manual also explains why tourism can be a good thing from an economic standpoint and how it can help improve the community's image. It stresses that there are five factors (the 5 As) for creating a successful destination, which in turn are: attitude, access, accommodations, attractions, and advertising.

To ensure that locals have a good attitude towards tourism, the handbook suggests that the host community must perceive tourism as a business about people. Thus, locals must do their best to make visitors welcome. In terms of access, the report stresses the importance of dependability. In other words, the frequency of services between the destination and the main markets is less important than ensuring that visitors can depend on the schedules. For accommodations, the *Alaska Community Tourism Handbook* indicates the importance of ensuring that the destination offers comfortable places to stay as well as a variety of restaurants and other eating establishments and a range of quality shops. It also should have good and clean services like public restrooms and beach facilities and must ensure that choices for local public transportation are more than adequate. The handbook urges communities to identify their unique selling proposition, namely the attraction(s) that will draw the visitors in the first place. Finally, it underlines the point that no one will visit a community if its attractions are not advertised. It explains to civic leaders that they must work diligently to promote their community.

Yet another area where Alaska's Division of Community and Economic Development feels communities can benefit substantially in terms of building their tourism industries is on the topic of package businesses. Stressing that a significant number of arrivals (over 40 percent to the state come on pre-arranged package tours), it urges communities to strive to include themselves on the itineraries of tour operators and cruise companies. The handbook even offers a very basic tutorial on how the tourism industry works from the point of sale through a retailer to the consumer all the way to the actual consumption of all the services and attractions. It projects the concept of market segments and finally offers advice on where civic leaders and businesses who are interested in promoting tourism can find assistance at the state and federal levels. In addition, through a different publication, the same state institution offers a detailed listing of funding opportunities for communities or businesses that are serious about starting up in tourism. This is a valuable resource with useful advice for people who are unsure of what grants exist to initiate projects.

Alaska is hardly unique in seeking to offer a top-down "tutorial" on how to develop and manage tourism. Indeed, it represents a phenomenon witnessed in many states that have a heavy dominance of smaller communities, many of them remote. In the absence of local resources that can support the development of a visitor industry, state agencies can play a critical role in determining whether or not communities succeed in their quest to draw visitors.

Sources

State of Alaska Division of Community and Economic Development (n.d.) *Alaska Community Tourism Handbook: How to Develop Tourism in Your Community.* Juneau: Division of Community and Business Development.
State of Alaska Division of Community and Economic Development (n.d.) *Tourism Funding Programs.* Juneau: Division of Community and Economic Development.

Questions

1. Think about a small rural community close to where you live. Preferably this should be one that is not yet a major visitor destination. If you were asked to be a consultant for this community what advice would you offer to the locals about developing their community for tourism? What would be the three most important things you would tell them to concentrate on?
2. One of the problems for many smaller communities when it comes to developing their tourism product is that there are no clear sources of funding to initiate product development or marketing. Can you think of any innovative ways to collect funds that can be used for such endeavors? Try to be as specific as possible.

The CVB in a mid-sized metropolitan area like Springfield, Missouri, is a non-profit organization working on the basis of an annual contract with the city with the aim of promoting economic development through tourism (Springfield, Missouri CVB 2007). Fundamentally, the major role of this and other similar organizations is to act as a destination marketing organization, as they work to attract conventions of various sizes, leisure-oriented travel groups, as well as independent travelers. For instance, the Denver Metro Convention and Visitors Bureau (DMCVB) is a DMO promoting Denver and the rest of Colorado as a destination for meeting attendants and general vacationers (Denver CVB 2009).

The board of directors of this CVB, as indeed that of most non-profit CVBs, is made up of volunteers representing both the public and private sectors. In the case of Springfield, Missouri, the Board of Directors includes persons working for major businesses in the area (both travel-related and other), representatives from the chamber of commerce, and a local baseball team. Additionally, there are a number of paid employees (either full-time or part-time).

Many CVBs, including that of Las Vegas, have very large budgets, certainly larger than that of any federal government entity responsible for tourism (Morrison *et al.* 1998). The budget of a CVB is often supported through a motel/hotel tax and state cooperative marketing funds (Gartner 2004); any shortfall in the budget may be filled through private funds, including fees charged to businesses that decide to join as members. Other sources of funding include government matching grants and restaurant taxes. In recent years, it has also become clearer that funds generated through the organization of special events also help subsidize the activities of CVBs (Weber 2001). If one examines the CVBs for mid-sized cities, it is evident that almost half their budget goes into sales and marketing efforts, while the rest funds mostly personnel and administrative costs. Additionally, smaller CVBs are far more dependent on room taxes for their budget than larger CVBs, which are able to diversify their funding better (Morrison *et al.* 1998; Gartner 2004).

Morrison *et al.* (1998) give a clear picture of the functions performed by a typical CVB. In addition to their marketing tasks, these organizations work as "a 'one-stop shopping center' for visitors. As an example of this latter function, for the convention meeting planner, the CVB can check hotel availability, distribute meeting specifications to hotels, solicit bid proposals, conduct personalized site inspections, suggest spouse programs and other activities, and provide transportation and other logistical assistance" (p. 2). Typically, a CVB will not favor one hotel over another when making a recommendation to a visitor.

Because CVBs seek to attract meetings and conventions they must ensure their relationship with meeting planners is good. Thus, they try to provide them with a steady stream of information about the destination and host familiarization trips to demonstrate what is on offer. In addition to providing such services, most CVBs, if not all, maintain a website. This is largely because there is a growing realization that Internet-based marketing plays a major if not "a determining, part of their overall marketing endeavor" (Wang and Fesenmaier 2006: 239). However, Yuan *et al.* (2003) have strongly argued that the Internet applications used by most CVBs have, until recently, remained relatively unsophisticated, revealing little understanding of the technology involved. Wang and Fesenmaier (2006) have concluded that most CVBs in the USA are still in the early stages of technology adoption, acting mostly like on-line glorified brochures but lacking sophisticated e-commerce capabilities.

At a very minimum on a CVB's website one can find information about attractions, places to eat and stay, as well as access to a calendar of events. However, things may be changing. In an increasing number of cities, CVBs have begun offering transportation and/or hotel (online) booking facilities plus the ability to purchase event tickets. Sometimes, it is also possible to book a package of activities. For example, on the St. Louis CVB website one can book a variety of stay-over packages, all of which can be customized (St. Louis Convention and Visitors Commission 2009). In this manner the CVB acts like an inbound tour operator (Litvin and Alderson 2003).

A word on tourism and planning

Much of this chapter has focused on marketing/promotion efforts relating to the travel industry within the USA. But what about planning for tourism? Tourism planning is much more than promoting a place or marketing a tourism product. It is typically done at varying scales, ranging from national-level planning to individual sites and attractions. Regional tourism planning aims to develop the industry in a way that benefits the destination economically without exacting the environmental and social costs so often associated with unplanned mass tourism. An important part of systematic tourism planning is physical development – infrastructure, transportation systems, attractions and lodging properties, green space, and so on. Unfortunately, blind promotional efforts in the United States regularly cause deterioration in physical landscapes and residents' attitudes towards tourism and tourists. Proponents of sustainable growth understand the importance of looking at tourism holistically in planning and development efforts, and realize that marketing and place promotion are only a small part. This background leads us to ask questions such as: What about the physical aspects of tourism planning? Who is responsible for regulating the design elements of tourist facilities? What body ensures that tourism-related developments do not cause serious adverse impacts on natural or historical resources? In any community, whose job is it to monitor tourism's growth in a comprehensive manner in order to avoid problems in other sectors such as transportation, the labor market, or housing? Or, alternatively, is tourism's growth in American communities better left to market forces?

Certainly, many states and municipalities produce documents labeled "tourism development plan" or "strategic plan for tourism" but most of these documents are detailed marketing plans and rarely, if ever, examine the land-use and or design/physical planning implications. The California Tourism and Travel Commission has a five-year strategic marketing plan, concentrating heavily on the central theme of making this state one of the main travel destinations in the world (CTTC 2007). Similarly, the Oregon Tourism Commission's Strategic *Marketing Plan and Budget* (2005: 2) aims to expand "economic growth and enhance the quality of life" in the state by ensuring that the economic effects of tourism are increased. A glance at this plan's table of contents reveals that its entire focus is on issues like marketing, tourism product development, and building recognition for the industry.

It certainly appears that state tourism agencies within the USA rarely engage in the physical aspects of tourism planning and development. One notable exception is the Hawaii Tourism Authority, whose tourism strategic plans are prepared in accordance with the overall 1978 Hawaii State Planning Act, Chapter 226, which requires every state agency to have a functional plan to "guide the implementation of State programs in their respective areas (e.g., health care, tourism)" (Hawaii Tourism Authority 2005: 1). Hawaii is one of only a handful of American states that has comprehensive planning at the state level and perhaps is the only one dealing with tourism in depth. The latest plan for 2005–15 is a comprehensive and inclusive document, prepared according to the tenets of sustainable development. This is a far more all-encompassing document than that for California, Oregon, and many other states, since beyond marketing it addresses a number of issues including transportation to and from the islands as well as within the islands; safety and security; stakeholder interaction, including resident participation; the need to safeguard Hawaiian culture, protect the islands' natural resources and ensure that built resources do not damage natural environs; the need for county tourism plans; and the need to ensure that the workforce is highly qualified. In addition to the state-wide plan for tourism, Hawaii has a series of county-wide tourism strategic plans which more closely recognize the uniqueness of each part of the state. Each of these plans is prepared in accordance with the state-wide plan, but at the same time its level of detail is far greater.

The current situation in Hawaii with regard to tourism planning reflects that state's long tradition in comprehensive planning that spans almost five decades. Indeed, the very first plan for the state, the 1959 State Plan for Hawaii, "included tourism as a major component and was quite progressive for its time in integrating tourism planning into the total regional development plan" (Inskeep 1991: 17).

Hawaii is very much an exception when it comes to tourism planning and the reader must realize that in the vast majority of cases there is a shortage of agencies in this country that clearly and systematically recognize tourism as an agent of adverse environmental and socio-cultural change. Even at the local level, in municipalities that traditionally have been the most common geographical scale in which comprehensive land-use planning is practiced in the USA, it is exceedingly rare to find a section within the master plan (comprehensive land-use plan) specifically dealing with tourism. If tourism is mentioned at all in such a document it will normally be within the economic development segment; by contrast it is uncommon to find detailed discussions in master plans relating to the physical aspects of tourism development. Similarly, in zoning and subdivision documents, which in the USA are major implementation tools for comprehensive plans, no reference is made explicitly to tourism uses; rather tourism developments are influenced by rules and regulations that apply to more general land uses such as commercial activities. Also if a community that depends heavily on tourism has detailed and strict signage, landscaping, or historical preservation ordinances, the quality of its tourism product can be influenced indirectly, while in places where such regulations are lax, something which is more common than not, the result is often an extremely haphazard development pattern.

The obvious explanation as to why tourism does not feature prominently within physical planning documents is that it is multifaceted, involving a large variety of businesses of varying sizes, some of which are totally dependent on tourists while others rely only partially on them. In addition, tourism is made up both of public and private sector entities, so creating a blanket policy relating to the land-use aspects of the sector is not an easy task. Finally, tourism-related development normally occurs over a lengthy span of time and, thus, it is hard to coordinate. The cumulative effects of the sector are rarely foreseen, especially at the early stages, given the large number of players involved, and it is often only after excessive periods of rapid and uncontrolled development that a local authority may decide to introduce mechanisms to curb the sector's further growth. In that respect, then, planning as it relates to tourism within the USA is often a reactive rather than a proactive process.

Conclusions

This chapter has explored the institutional set-up of the travel and tourism industry within the United States. We have shown that at the federal level there is a weak mechanism for tourism marketing, since this country lacks a powerful entity filling the role of a national tourism organization such as those found in many other countries throughout the world. We have also stressed that national policies relating to tourism either directly or indirectly can be contradictory and thus have a negative impact on the sector. For example, the introduction of measures following 9/11 in an effort to beef up safety and security has had the negative side-effect of making the USA an unwelcoming destination in the eyes of numerous international travelers. Efforts have been made in recent times to improve this situation, including the ongoing process of adopting new legislation (Tourism Promotion Act of 2008), but the feeling remains that there is still a lack of motivation at the national level to create a stronger body to deal exclusively with tourism.

Therefore, the major task for tourism promotion and marketing has become the responsibility of state tourism agencies that operate as destination management organizations. In addition to being responsible for marketing the states as tourist destinations, these organizations frequently engage in travel-related research and may also be responsible for conducting workshops relating to issues such as rural-based tourism and labor training. At the local level, underlying these organizations are the so-called convention and visitors bureaus (CVBs), which are charged with place-promotion through the organization of conferences and special events. These entities, many of which are non-profit organizations, act as tourist information bureaus and work closely with local authorities to meet the goal of economic growth through tourism.

Without a doubt, the state and local destination management organizations in the USA play an important role in tourism marketing and place promotion and, indeed, they are engaged, albeit to varying degrees, in the preparation of strategic plans. However, the vast majority of these strategic plans tend to be detailed marketing strategies and rarely deal with aspects like the land-use planning for tourism development. Additionally, city planning departments with responsibilities for physical planning, almost never have dedicated tourism plans, nor do they incorporate tourism explicitly within their comprehensive land-use documents, with the possible exception of referring to the sector within the context of overall economic development. This generally means that tourism development is often left to the whims of the market and that any planning intervention that is made to minimize the sector's negative effects occurs in a reactive fashion, after problems have occurred.

Of course, planning for tourism, which is, after all, such a multifarious activity – especially when it comes to mitigating the sector's negative effects – is not an easy task. One has to understand that while there may not be one document dealing with tourism explicitly, a number of policies, directives, and plans that relate to various issues may have important repercussions for tourism and its ultimate development form in any destination. The following three chapters explore in depth the heterogeneous nature of the tourism system, first examining the demand for travel and tourism within the United States and then focusing specifically on the numerous attractions and sectors that make up this complex industry.

Questions

1. The USA does not have a national tourism office like many other countries. Instead, most of the marketing for tourism is left to state and local organizations. What are the major disadvantages of not having a national office?

2. To what extent has the campaign against terrorism influenced inbound tourism to the United States?

3. Can you think of any federal policies arising from any department that may have a direct or indirect effect on tourism? Please give examples.

4. What are the typical functions of a state tourism office? Are there any significant differences between different states in the manner in which they market tourism?

Further reading

Crompton, J.L. and Richardson, S.L. (1986) The tourism connection: when public and private leisure services merge. *Parks and Recreation*, 21(10): 38–44.

Maguire, P.A. and Uysal, M. (1990) Tourism supply: a US perspective. *Revue de Tourisme*, 45(3): 2–6.

McGehee, N.G., Meng, F. and Tepanon, Y. (2006) Understanding legislators and their perceptions of the tourism industry: the case of North Carolina, USA, 1990 and 2003. *Tourism Management*, 27(4): 684–94.

Morrison, A.M. (1987) Selling the USA, Part 1: International Promotion. *Travel and Tourism Analyst*, 2: 3–12.

Owen, C. (1992) Building a relationship between government and tourism. *Tourism Management*, 13(4): 358–62.

Shafer, E.L. and Choi, Y.S. (2006) Forging nature-based tourism policy issues: a case study in Pennsylvania. *Tourism Management*, 27(4): 615–28.

Smith, R.V. (1990) Tourism and tourism planning in Ohio. *Tourism Recreation Research*, 15(2): 22–9.

Stein, T.V., Clark, J.K., Rickards, J.L. (2003) Assessing nature's role in ecotourism development in Florida: perspectives of tourism professionals and government decision makers. *Journal of Ecotourism*, 2(3): 155–72.

Useful Internet resources

American Planning Association: http://www.planning.org/
Greater Boston Convention and Visitors Bureau: http://www.bostonusa.com/
Hawaii Tourism Authority: http://www.hawaiitourismauthority.org/
Office of Travel and Tourism Industries: http://tinet.ita.doc.gov/
Travel Industry Association of America: http://www.tia.org/index.html
US Department of Commerce: http://www.commerce.gov/

4 ▶ Demand for tourism in the United States

> Americans fancy themselves grand innovators. But when it comes to vacation preferences, the same destinations pop up with the regularity of midwinter flight delays in Chicago.
>
> (Clark 2006: n.p.)

> More than 75 percent of Americans in a recent consumer poll said they like to make all their travel arrangements themselves. Only 10 percent said they mostly buy independent tours (an itinerary you can do on your own), and 5 percent said they buy vacation packages (separate elements bundled together). Yet the U.S. Tour Operators Association has found that travelers save an average 20–30 percent when buying the same arrangements in a vacation package or tour rather than on their own.
>
> (United States Tour Operators Association n.d.)

Introduction

As noted in earlier chapters, the United States of America is a vast country with a multitude of natural and cultural resources that appeal to a wide tourism audience. It is one of the most desirable destinations for global travelers and has been included consistently for many years in the World Tourism Organization's list of top five destination countries as measured by international arrivals. Tourists from all around the globe arrive daily at airports, border crossings, and ship ports to visit relatives, to see America's vast network of national parks, relax at a beachfront resort, shop, or tour the country's mega-amusement parks.

From the perspective of domestic travel, the USA is also a world leader. Demographically the United States is the third largest country in the world, following China and India, with an approximate population of 307 million. By all economic measures, the US population is one of the most affluent in the world with a mean per capita income of some $46,000. In addition, the US population is highly mobile; the average American household owns between two and three vehicles, and more Americans are traveling longer distances by air than ever before in history. These demographics notwithstanding, a relatively small proportion of the American population ever travels outside the country's borders, with observers often citing the fact that there is so much to see and do at home in such a large and diverse country that there is little reason to travel abroad. In addition, there is a deep-seated fear among many Americans related to the increased risk of terror attacks abroad, concerns over economic uncertainties everywhere, and for some people, a neophobic trepidation about visiting places that are poorer or much different from home. These demographic characteristics and trends, combined with the fact that most Americans love to travel in their homeland, create a situation wherein domestic tourism flourishes.

This chapter examines the demand for tourism in the United States from global and domestic perspectives. General patterns are described along with their broader socio-political implications. There is a notable lack of data available for public perusal regarding tourism in the USA, so some of the data available and presented in this chapter are dated by a few years. Nonetheless, patterns and trends are elucidated from the available data, and it is the patterns that are of most concern in this book.

International travel to the United States

Foreign tourists are fond of the United States, and visitors come from all over the world to experience the types of attractions and services described already in Chapter 3 and later in Chapter 5. The USA has consistently been listed on the World Tourism Organization's top five most visited countries for several decades and will most likely continue on this trajectory into the future. The single largest foreign source of tourists to the United States is Canada, accounting for nearly 18 million cross-border arrivals in 2007 (Table 4.1). There has been a long tradition of economic cooperation, commerce, and travel between the USA and Canada, which continues to this day. These close relations resulted in the 1988 enactment of the Canada–US Free Trade Agreement, which was replaced by the North American Free Trade Agreement in 1992 to include Mexico and to solidify economic relations between the three member states (Clausing 2001; Schott 2004). From a tourism perspective, the flow of Canadians to the USA has been disproportionately larger than Americans traveling to Canada. This has traditionally been seen to be a result of exchange rates between the two countries' currencies; the fact that most of Canada's population lives relatively near the international border, while the US population is not concentrated near the border; and economies of scale have driven Canadians to shop south of the international boundary for household goods, clothing, shoes, gasoline and even supermarket items, which are less expensive, often of higher quality, and part of a larger selection of products (Di Matteo and Di Matteo 1996; Kreck 1985; Timothy 1999a; 1999b; Timothy and Butler 1995).

Most Canadian tourists come from Ontario, Quebec, British Columbia, and Alberta, with other provinces representing secondary markets. Approximately one-third of Canadians arrive by air, and New York and Florida are the most important destinations for Canadians. The border states with substantial Canadian populations nearby (e.g., Washington, Montana, Maine, Vermont, and Michigan) also fare well with Canadian visitors, most of whom come by car to shop, sightsee, and visit friends.

Mexico is the USA's second most important international market, with 14.3 million arrivals in 2007 (Table 4.1). Some of the tourism-related activities undertaken by Mexicans in the United States resemble those of Canadians – namely shopping for items that are less expensive than at home (e.g., toys, clothing, household items, and some food products) (Gibbons and Fish 1987; Timothy and Canally 2008), but they are also marked by frequent northward trips to visit family members.

Table 4.1 Total tourist arrivals to the US from Canada, Mexico, and overseas, 2007

Arrivals from Canada	Arrivals from Mexico	Arrivals from overseas	Total international arrivals
17,746,000	14,333,000	23,921,000	56 million

Source: US Department of Commerce (2008a)

The construction and spread of *maquiladoras* – foreign-owned factories and assembly plants near the US border that produce cars, electronics, and other assembled products – as a result of Mexico's 1960s–2000s border development program, have increased affluence and created relatively wealthy border communities on the Mexican side. Because of this, and the growing prosperity throughout the country in general, increasing numbers of better-off Mexicans are able to travel to the USA to shop, visit relatives or experience attractions such as theme parks or historic sites. Familial connectivity is extremely important in Mexican culture, so there is a strong network of linkages between Mexican-Americans and their kin in Mexico (Williams 1990), which entails considerable numbers of Mexicans traveling northward to visit their relatives in the United States. The most important US destination for Mexican tourists is California, followed by Texas, Arizona, Nevada, and Florida (see Plate 4.1).

If cross-border day trips were counted in tourism statistics, which they are not (just overnight stays are counted), the number of arrivals from Canada and Mexico would be much higher. In most years, 20–30 million same-day trips are taken to the USA from Canada with similar numbers of Mexicans visiting on same-day excursions, primarily for shopping purposes.

Arrivals from the UK and Germany account for more than half of all European arrivals to the USA, although several other European countries are important sources of tourists as well (Table 4.2). There are frequent and widespread air connections between Europe and the United States. British Airways, for example, serves 19 US cities, and Lufthansa a number of others (US Department of Commerce 2008a). The Japanese are an important

Plate 4.1 US–Mexico border crossing at Nogales, Arizona
(Dimitri Ioannides)

Table 4.2 Top 20 inbound foreign tourist markets to the United States, 2007

Rank	Country	Number of arrivals
1	Canada	17,746,000
2	Mexico	14,333,000
3	United Kingdom	4,497,858
4	Japan	3,531,489
5	Germany	1,524,151
6	France	997,506
7	South Korea	806,175
8	Australia	669,536
9	Brazil	639,431
10	Italy	634,152
11	India	567,045
12	China and Hong Kong	539,824
13	Spain	516,471
14	Netherlands	506,852
15	Ireland	491,055
16	Venezuela	458,678
17	Colombia	389,752
18	Sweden	337,474
19	Israel	313,077
20	Taiwan	311,020
	Total top twenty	49,810,546

Source: US Department of Commerce (2008a)

foreign market as well, with 3.5 million Japanese trips to the USA in 2007. The most important destinations for Japanese tourists are Hawaii, Guam, California and New York. Guam and Hawaii are especially important short-haul American destinations for the lucrative Japanese market, which sees these two island destinations as shopping paradises. Japanese tourists are prone to spend thousands of dollars on shopping during each trip; Guam and Hawaii benefit significantly from the Japanese market (Timothy 2005b).

Arrivals from China and Hong Kong ranked twelfth in the top-twenty list, but China's position has the potential to climb dramatically over the next few years because the United States was branded with China's coveted Approved Destination Status in December 2007. Chinese leisure travel to the USA was scheduled to begin in the second half of 2008, so future data will be important to watch in determining the effects of this designation on Chinese arrivals.

Another important aspect of demand of interest to geographers and other social scientists is where tourists go once they arrive at their destination. Table 4.3 illustrates the 15 most significant destination states or territories in the USA for foreign tourists. New York is hardly surprising as the primary destination for foreign tourists with nearly a third of all international visitors arriving and/or planning to spend time there. New York City is an important gateway with three international airports: John F. Kennedy International Airport, La Guardia Airport, and Newark Liberty International Airport. Although the Newark airport is in New Jersey, it is counted as one of the New York City airports and is located in the greater New York metropolitan area just a few miles outside Manhattan. In addition to the gateway status of New York City, it is one of the largest and best-known cities in the world, and it is often viewed abroad as the embodiment of America.

Table 4.3 Top destination states or territories in the United States among foreign visitors, 2007

Rank	Destination state or territory	2007 market share (%)	2007 visitation ('000s)
1	New York	33.1	7,908
2	California	21.7	5,185
3	Florida	19.6	4,683
4	Hawaii	7.8	1,864
5	Nevada	7.4	1,768
6/7	Massachusetts	4.9	1,171
6/7	Illinois	4.9	1,171
8	Guam	4.6	1,099
9	Texas	4.2	1,003
10	New Jersey	4.0	956
11	Pennsylvania	3.4	812
12	Arizona	2.4	573
13	Georgia	2.2	526
14	Washington	1.9	454
15	North Carolina	1.5	358

Source: US Department of Commerce (2008b)

California and Florida are ranked second and third, largely because of their entertainment value, being home to some of the largest theme parks in the world, including Walt Disney World, Disneyland, Knott's Berry Farm, Sea World, and Universal Studios. Both states are also home to attractive beachfront resorts and sites made famous in Hollywood movies. In addition, California and Florida, like New York, are home to sizeable immigrant populations from Asia, the Caribbean, Latin America, and Africa, who have many ties to their ancestral homelands. Travel to these states by relatives of immigrants is an important part of the tourist appeal.

As already noted, Guam and Hawaii rank highly primarily because of their Japanese connection and shopping opportunities, but they are also known as tropical paradises for many people besides the Japanese. Nevada, the fifth most visited state for international tourists, is obviously popular because of the entertainment and gaming value associated with Las Vegas and Reno, and Arizona ranks highly because of the Grand Canyon, which many foreigners visit in conjunction with trips to Las Vegas, as well as the resorts and warm winter weather of the Phoenix area.

Domestic travel in the United States

In 2007, 903 million international trips were recorded around the world, reflecting a two-fold increase since 1990, when 457 million international trips were taken (UNWTO 2008). Both the World Tourism Organization and the World Travel and Tourism Council do a good job of estimating international arrivals. Domestic travel, by contrast, is much harder to tabulate because people do not cross international boundaries and are, therefore, not counted at points of arrival. In some countries, domestic tourism is almost negligible; in the USA it is massive.

The US Department of Commerce defines a domestic trip as traveling away from home a distance of more than 50 miles (Smith and Timothy 2006). At the local level, domestic travel estimates are calculated using lodging records, which is a grossly inaccurate measure of tourism, given that many people stay in private homes, and the numbers reported by hundreds of thousands of accommodation facilities are notoriously

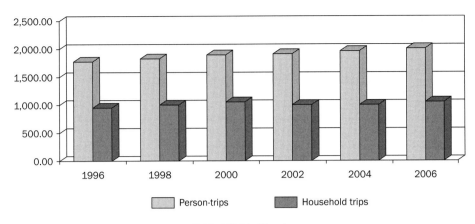

Figure 4.1 US domestic travel volumes, 1996–2006 (millions)

inexact. At the national level in the United States, projections are usually made via random household surveys on an annual basis. Despite their pitfalls, these measures do provide some indications of trends and patterns.

Industry estimates suggest that domestic tourism figures exceed global tourism totals by several times. This is certainly the case in the United States. In 2006, 2.001 billion domestic person-trips were generated in the USA and 1.034 billion household trips were taken, reflecting the largest extent of domestic travel in recorded history (Figure 4.1). More than one quarter (26 percent) of all US domestic travel was for business purposes, including conventions, seminars, training, meetings and general business. Since 2000, business-related travel has seen a notable decline in the United States (Table 4.4). This is largely a result of improved telecommunications technologies that allow virtual meetings and telecommuting, with the effect of reducing physical travel for business, saving companies and public agencies millions of dollars in travel expenditures. Leisure trips in 2006 accounted for nearly three quarters (74 percent) of all domestic travel with some 1.5 billion person-trips taken for vacation and pleasure purposes. While business travel has declined, domestic leisure travel among Americans has grown in response to increased affluence between 2000 and 2006, combined with a widespread apprehension about traveling abroad (Table 4.4).

Table 4.4 US domestic business and leisure person-trips, 2000–2006 (in millions)

	2000	*2001*	*2002*	*2003*	*2004*	*2005*	*2006*
Business Trips	566.6	545.3	512.0	502.1	513.0	510.0	508.7
Leisure Trips	1,325.4	1324.6	1407.1	1,388.2	1,440.4	1,482.5	1,491.8

Source: Adapted from TIA (2007)

California, Texas, New York, Florida, Ohio, Pennsylvania, Illinois, Michigan, North Carolina, and Virginia are the top origin states of domestic US travelers. The top ten destination states are California, Texas, Florida, New York, Pennsylvania, Michigan, Ohio, North Carolina, Illinois, and Missouri. Most domestic travel is still undertaken by automobile (84 percent), followed by air (8 percent) (Table 4.5), and other modes (8 percent) including trains, coaches/buses, and watercraft (TIA 2007).

Table 4.5 Air travel as proportion of total domestic travel, 2000–2006

Person-Trips	2000	2001	2002	2003	2004	2005	2006
Number in millions	187.5	179.9	175.1	163.3	165.1	164.6	156.8
Share of total	10%	9%	9%	9%	9%	9%	8%

Source: From TIA (2007)

Demand for lodging also shows some interesting patterns. For instance, some 44 percent of lodging nights in the United States were spent by business tourists, while 56 percent were spent by leisure travelers. The high level of business travelers' demand for lodging despite their accounting for only 26 percent of all domestic travel and the relatively low level of lodging demand by leisure tourists in spite of their 84 percent share reflects the latter group's propensity to stay in the homes of friends and family members. Conversely, business travelers nearly always spend their nights away in hotels and other public accommodation facilities (American Hotel and Lodging Association 2008). As Table 4.6 denotes, more than half of all domestic travelers stay in hotels, motels, bed and breakfasts, or similar commercial establishment. The next most important sleeping venue is someone else's home, while campgrounds, recreational second homes, and timeshares are also important lodging venues.

Table 4.6 Domestic demand for lodging types, 2006 (in millions)

	Hotel/ Motel/ B&B	Someone's home	RV/tent	Second home	Condo or timeshare	Other
Volume in person-trips	501.0	330.1	43.2	15.9	16.8	75.2
Share of total	52%	34%	4%	2%	2%	8%

Source: Adapted from TIA (2007)

Outbound travel by US residents

Another perspective on demand is outbound travel by US residents to other countries. Evidently, in terms of the percentage of traveling population to total population Americans do not travel abroad to the same extent as their European and Canadian counterparts. Indeed, roughly 27 percent of Americans possess a valid passport – that is just about 82 million people. Yet, foreign travel by US residents has seen considerable growth during the past 15 years (Table 4.7). In 1995, 19 million overseas trips were taken by residents of the United States. By 2007 the number had grown to approximately 31.3 million overseas trips. As Table 4.7 indicates, despite the notable growth since the mid 1990s, there have been times of decline. The most obvious occurred in 2001 and 2002 in response to the terrorist attacks of September 11, 2001. During that time there was a widespread apprehension about flying, and because of economic uncertainties, many efforts were made to reduce family expenditures. Despite this short-lived regression, outbound travel has recovered substantially so that 2004 saw levels of travel higher than

Table 4.7 Numbers of American overseas trips by year (millions)*

1995	2000	2001	2002	2003	2004	2005	2006	2007
19.059	26.853	25.249	23.397	24.452	27.351	28.787	30.148	31.228

* Does not include travel to Canada and Mexico

Source: US Department of Commerce (2008c)

those prior to 2001. These types of occurrences will be discussed in greater detail later in this chapter.

The most popular foreign destinations for Americans are Mexico, Canada, and the United Kingdom followed by Italy, France, Germany, and Japan (Table 4.8). Closer Look Case 4.1 discusses destinations that more than others are particularly welcoming to Americans these days, especially when the label "ugly American" has gained prominence in recent years. Obviously the proximity of Mexico and Canada is their primary advantage, and they have long been favored destinations for Americans. The beach resorts of the Pacific and Caribbean coasts of Mexico exude a particular appeal for Americans for a variety of reasons. First, a foreign experience can be gained without having to travel great distances. Most flights to Mexico from the USA are of a relatively short duration. Second, these destinations tend to be a good value, especially with regard to cruises and all-inclusive resorts. Third, Mexico has a reputation of being a popular and enjoyable vacation destination. Mexico is adept at promoting itself in key market regions in the USA using geographical marketing tactics that appeal to the American audience. Finally, Mexico is seen as a winter destination; when the weather in much of the United States is cold, the warm sunshine, beaches, and ocean waters of its southern neighbor convey an irresistible appeal for many people.

Canada is also a popular destination for a variety of reasons. One salient reason is its cultural similarity to the United States, and the fact that the two countries share many elements of a common history. With the exception of Quebec and a few communities in New Brunswick, Americans can travel to Canada and not be concerned about a foreign language. Another reason is Canada's natural beauty, which many see as being equal or superior to the natural environments of the United States. Niagara Falls is an important gateway into Canada from the United States, and many Americans visit the Canadian side of the falls and nearby Toronto. In the early 2000s, exchange rates between US and Canadian dollars were such that it became economically advantageous for Americans to shop in Canada, which they did by dining out, purchasing goods and services, and even buying second homes in places such as British Columbia and Ontario.

Another important statistic related to outbound American travel concerns the reason for taking a trip in the first place. Table 4.9 shows the primary purpose of travel among outbound Americans in 2007. While some of these purposes overlap (e.g., leisure and visiting friends), these figures are important in understanding why people travel and what activities they undertake while away from home. Some 38 percent of all US residents traveling overseas claimed leisure vacations as their primary purpose for traveling. Visiting friends and relatives constitutes another extremely important motivation and might be the most significant reason for traveling in the domestic context. Approximately 20 percent of trips were taken for business purposes, including research, sales, and meetings. It is interesting to note that 2 percent of overseas trips were for religious reasons. Religious tourism is an important form of heritage tourism in many parts of the world. In the US outbound context it reflects the growth of the evangelical Christian movement, whose adherents are avid travelers to the Holy Land and other parts of the

Table 4.8 Destination regions visited by outbound US residents, 2000–2007

Region	2000 ('000)	2001 ('000)	2002 ('000)	2003 ('000)	2004 ('000)	2005 ('000)	2006 ('000)	2007 ('000)
Mexico	19,285	18,623	18,501	17,566	19,370	20,325	19,659	19,453
Canada	15,189	15,570	16,167	14,232	15,088	14,391	13,855	13,371
Western Europe	12,916	10,983	9,640	9,781	11,022	11,227	11,336	11,523
Eastern Europe	806	959	796	929	1,149	1,209	1,266	1,343
Caribbean	3,867	4,141	4,258	5,306	4,868	5,182	6,150	5,184
South America	2,095	2,247	1,755	1,981	2,352	2,361	2,442	2,811
Central America	886	1,414	1,521	1,663	1,778	1,756	1,538	2,248
Africa	483	505	421	465	629	576	663	874
Middle East	1,370	1,010	819	685	1,039	1,094	1,115	1,312
Asia	4,914	4,318	4,492	3,937	5,087	6,074	6,271	6,714
Oceania	1,047	1,187	819	831	821	835	874	874

Source: US Department of Commerce (2008c)

CLOSER LOOK CASE 4.1

Americans are still loved abroad

With many people and countries in the world frustrated with American foreign policies, a perceived cultural arrogance on the part of American tourists abroad, and American ignorance about the world around them, the old term "the Ugly American" has gained new ground during the past decade or so in the international tourism context. Some destinations have even downplayed the importance of their American markets.

In response to a heightened anti-American sentiment in many parts of the world, particularly in Europe and the Middle East, AOL's travel website recently published a list of countries that are still friendly towards the United States and which welcome American tourists with open arms. With hints that the number of Americans applying for passports has grown during the past few years and some initial promise of a partial economic recovery by 2011, these American-friendly countries will reap the financial benefits of encouraging American arrivals and treating their American guests with respect.

According to the article, Albania is the most USA-friendly country in Europe and welcomes American guests with great enthusiasm. Tanzania is next on the list, largely, according to AOL Travel, because the US never attempted to colonize sub-Saharan Africa in the same way that several European powers did. India is also known for its largely pro-American stance, especially among the educated youth. Vietnam attempts to lure Americans to its shores, including former Vietnam War veterans. Overall, American tourists are well cared for and accepted with welcoming arms in the United Kingdom. Some observers suggest this is because of the many similarities between the two countries. The Japanese are avid fans of American popular culture and US-based consumer products, which translates into a degree of fondness for American visitors. The Irish, according to AOL, welcome Americans because of the well-known Irish hospitality, where almost everyone is friendly and jovial. Poland is another European country that has, since the collapse of communism there in the early 1990s, become a close ally of the United States. Ghana, another of the United States' allies in Africa, is a popular destination for African-Americans seeking their African roots. This, together with several other familial and economic connections, has created a staunch US tourism ally in Ghana. Finally, but not least, Canada is the USA's nearest and dearest friend. In spite of a fairly active anti-American movement, the neighbor to the north has been a constant friend and confidant throughout history, and Americans are generally welcomed as one friendly neighbor would welcome another friendly neighbor.

Source

AOL Travel (2009) *10 countries that love Americans*. Available from http://travel.aol.com/travel-ideas/international/galleries/countries-that-love-americans (accessed April 25, 2009).

Questions

1. What are some of the reasons outbound American tourists are sometimes disliked in some parts of the world?
2. Why do some countries "love" American tourists while others do not?

Table 4.9 Overseas outbound travel from the US by primary purpose of trip, 2007

Main purpose of trip	% of total*
Leisure/Recreation/Holidays	38
Visiting Friends/Relatives	34
Business	20
Study/Teaching	3
Convention/Conference	2
Religion/Pilgrimage	2

* Does not equal 100% as some purposes overlap
Source: US Department of Commerce (2008c)

Mediterranean to walk in the footsteps of the apostles in Italy, Greece, Turkey and Cyprus (Belhassen and Santos 2006; Collins-Kreiner *et al.* 2006). In addition, there is a strong contingent of Roman Catholics who travel to Rome and other sacred sites in Europe (e.g., Medjugorje, Lourdes, Fatima, and Santiago de Compostela) to commune with the deity and strengthen their faith. There is also a strong connection between the large American Jewish community and Israel, which entails considerable travel between the two countries (Ioannides and Cohen Ioannides 2002, 2004).

Demand shifters

This chapter has so far described patterns of demand for international, domestic, and outbound tourism to, in, and from the United States. It is important to note, though, that demand for tourism in this country is not uniform among travelers, destinations, or products and experiences. Tourism is highly unpredictable; it fluctuates rapidly and errat-ically with every social, political, environmental, or economic occurrence in the tourist destination and point of origin. Forces that cause demand for tourism to fluctuate up or down are sometimes referred to as demand shifters, and they can be identified in any number of forms, including demographic trends, the staging of special events, economic challenges, political unrest and security threats, or natural disasters, to name but a few. All of these individually or in tandem affect changes in demand for tourist destinations and products.

One of the most significant demand shifters in the United States in recent years has been safety and security concerns (mentioned in greater detail in Chapter 10). The United States has long been a target of terrorist attacks, largely a reaction to its foreign policies in the Middle East and the spread of American lifestyles to much of the world, where imposed Americanization of cultures, cuisines, social mores, morality, dress codes, behaviors, television programs and movies, music, and politics is seen as undermining traditional values, cultural foundations, and religiosity (Destler 2005; Sobek and Braithwaite 2005). The September 11, 2001, terrorist attacks on US soil, however, were a salient turning point for the way in which the United States views its role in the world and how it treats national security. The data in Table 4.7 denote a decline in Americans traveling abroad in 2001 and 2002, immediately after 9/11. Americans were very wary of flying and traveling overseas in general for some time after the 2001 attacks, as is reflected in outbound travel statistics and in the destinations US residents chose to visit. Departures in 2003 were also lower than pre-9/11 numbers, although they showed growth over 2002 departures. By 2004 outbound travel had recovered enough to set a new record for overseas travel by residents of the United States. As Table 4.8 demonstrates, Americans avoided the Middle East following the 2001 incident, with trips to that region declining by 50 percent between 2000 and 2003. Only Canada, the Caribbean, and Central America realized growth in American arrivals in the year or two after the terrorist attacks, underscoring public perceptions that these regions were much safer alternatives to Europe, Africa, Asia, and the Middle East. Unfortunately, terror attacks and warfare are becoming a more salient part of life in the modern world and are a good example of demand shifters.

In response to the events of 9/11, security steps at border crossings, airports, and sea ports are perhaps the most visible safety measures in the tourism landscape. The United States has adopted significant procedures to defend its national security and the safety of its citizens. One such action is the use of biometrics, such as eye scanning and electronic fingerprinting, to record all incoming travelers by air and to identify those who might pose a security threat to the country. Similarly, the new passport and visa require-ments mentioned in Chapter 3 will have necessitated the possession by all incoming travelers of a passport by the end of June 2009; the regulations already require citizens of non-Visa Waiver countries to have a transit visa even when their only time in the USA is during an airport transfer, which in some cases lasts only a few hours. Immigration requirements have overall become more stringent, which some observers and organiza-tions believe will deter many potential tourists, including Canadians, from traveling to the United States.

Related to this are other political factors that influence demand. One of the most obvious is the various State Department travel warnings and travel alerts (Table 4.10). Travel warnings are issued to describe long-term conditions that render a country dangerous or unstable, or when the US government's ability to aid American citizens is constrained. Travel alerts are issued to notify Americans of short-term circumstances that might affect their personal safety while traveling to individual countries. These warnings and alerts are known to decrease demand for tourism to the countries on the list (Sönmez 1998; Thapa 2003). As some Americans feel especially targeted for crime and terrorism, government travel warnings play an important role in many Americans' travel decision-making (Nwanna 2004).

Currency exchange rates are another prominent demand shifter in the context of the United States. Correlation studies have highlighted a direct relationship between exchange rates and travel. When the Canadian dollar is strong, Canadians travel more frequently to the United States. When the Mexican peso is strong, Mexicans visit the USA more often and in larger numbers. The same is true when the US dollar is strong in relation to other world currencies (Chadee and Mieczkowski 1987; Di Matteo and Di Matteo 1996; Diehl 1983; Timothy 1999b). However, a weak dollar compared to many world currencies, including the euro, has not acted in the last few years as the major incentive for foreign visitors – especially those from countries outside the Americas – that one might have expected given the extremely draconian security measures that the US adopted in the post-9/11 era.

Related to exchange rates are economic hardships, such as the current (2009) reces-sion in the United States and other countries. As unemployment rates increase, inflation soars, taxes rise, personal and business bankruptcies escalate, and home foreclosures mount, demand for travel inevitably declines. The 2007–9 economic crisis in the USA and other countries has had a noticeable effect on international arrivals to the USA and outbound travel by Americans. In fact, the recent rise in the value of the dollar compared to many other currencies has not seemed to inspire Americans to travel abroad. According to the US Department of Commerce (2009), inbound travel from abroad during the fourth quarter of 2008 dropped by 5.5 percent over the same period in 2007.

Table 4.10 US Department of State travel warnings and alerts, February 2009

Country/Region travel warnings	Purpose of warning
Afghanistan	War, violence, kidnappings, violent crime
Algeria	Civil war, terrorism
Burundi	Rebel warfare, crime
Central African Republic	Rebel warfare, crime, banditry
Chad	Banditry, clashes between government and rebel forces
Colombia	Drug-related terrorism, kidnappings
Cote d'Ivoire	Rebel warfare, coup situation
Democratic Rep of the Congo	Guerilla warfare, violent crime
Eritrea	Acute political tensions along the borders of Ethiopia and Djibouti
Georgia	Unexploded ordnances, tensions in breakaway regions of Abkhazia and South Ossetia
Haiti	Violent crime, kidnappings, natural disasters, public protests
Iran	Anti-American sentiments, unsafe conditions near the Iraqi border
Iraq	War, general violence, terrorism, crime, kidnappings
Israel, West Bank and Gaza	War, threat of terrorism
Kenya	Threat of terrorism, carjackings, violent crimes
Lebanon	Threat of terrorism, violence in the city of Tripoli
Nepal	Armed robberies, rival party clashes
Nigeria	Kidnappings, violence, armed attacks
Pakistan	Threat of terrorism, other violence
Philippines	Kidnappings, terror attacks, rebel warfare on Mindanao and other southern islands
Saudi Arabia	Threat of terrorism, anti-western violence
Somalia	Terrorism, kidnappings, crime, banditry, general lawlessness
Sri Lanka	Civil war, terrorist attacks
Sudan	Terrorism, armed conflict, anti-western demonstrations
Syria	Threat of terrorism, anti-Israel and anti-American demonstrations
Uzbekistan	Terrorism, anti-US sentiments
Yemen	Terrorism
Zimbabwe	Disease, public riots, collapse of government services

Travel alerts	
Arabian Peninsula and Persian Gulf	Terrorist threats against specific targets and American interests
French West Indies	Labor strikes and riots in Guadeloupe and Martinique
Comoros	Public demonstrations and civil unrest owing to fuel shortages
Madagascar	Violent clashes and public riots as a result of a political rift between parties and candidates
Mali	Kidnapping threat against westerners who attend the Festival in the Desert at Essakane near Timbuktu in January 2009
Mexico	Increasing crime and violence throughout the country, but especially along the US border

Source: US Department of State (2009)

In addition, American outbound travel has seen a dramatic plunge since June 2008; September 2008 saw a plummet of 7 percent in outbound travel from the USA, and the figures are expected to worsen drastically over 2009 and 2010.

A changing demographic environment also transforms demand for tourism in the United States. Immigration, particularly illegal immigration, from Mexico has received a great deal of attention in public forums and the media in recent years. Every year, thousands of people immigrate across the southern US border in search of work or to be reunited with family members. According to the US Census Bureau (2009b), there are approximately 28.3 million Americans of Mexican descent, comprising some 9 percent of the US population, mostly concentrated in the southwestern states of California, Arizona, New Mexico and Texas but with significant cohorts throughout the United States. As noted earlier, Mexicans and Mexican Americans are family-oriented, and their connections to Mexico are strong. This has the effect of masses of Mexican immigrants and their posterity traveling to Mexico each year to visit friends and family members. African-Americans comprise more than 10 percent of the US population, with 2004 data showing a total black population of 36.12 million. African-Americans, like other races and ethnicities, often have unique travel demands and interests, such as a focus on urban areas and a desire to visit the African homeland (Bruner 1996; Goodrich 1985; Polzin *et al*. 1999).

There is a similar demographic change occurring among retirees, who are part of the baby boomer generation. This population cohort is relatively affluent and healthier than previous generations, living longer than their parents did. These characteristics combine to create demand for more expansive global travel, more active lifestyles, and more exotic destinations. The baby boomers' longevity and affluence have in part brought about an increase in certain types of travel, including adventure tours, ecotourism, genealogical journeys, other forms of heritage and cultural tourism, and educational travel.

Seasonality

A concept that overlaps somewhat with demand shifters is seasonality. Every destination in the United States experiences some degree of seasonal variation in demand; some localities experience seasonal changes more noticeably than others. Two sorts of seasonality can be identified: institutional (or human-induced) and natural seasonality. In the United States both causes of seasonal demand are evident and deal primarily with weather or climatic conditions (natural), and school breaks or public holidays (institutional).

The enormous size of the USA has enabled tourism to develop in various parts of the country to suit all seasons. For example, Figure 4.2 illustrates seasonality in three important tourist destinations: Chicago (Illinois), Scottsdale (Arizona), and San Diego (California). The data show that the season of lowest demand in Scottsdale is May to September, which is indicative of the prohibitively high summer temperatures in that part of Arizona. January to April, however, is considered a pleasant-weather period, making Scottsdale a suitable winter golf and resort destination. Chicago experiences opposite trends, with its bitter winters being a deterrent to would-be travelers between December and March, though it is a popular destination in the summer. San Diego on the Pacific coast of California has a more steady demand for tourism, owing to its beaches and the cooling effect of the ocean winds during the summer and warming effect during the winter months.

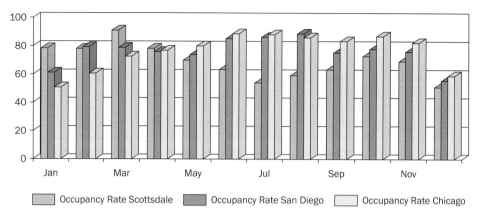

Figure 4.2 Seasonal variations in demand in three popular destinations in 2007, as measured by occupancy rate

Successful winter destinations have developed as either cold- or warm-climate destinations. For the people of the northern states, where winters can be bitterly cold, the warmth of the southern states is extremely appealing between November and April. The annual migration of "snowbirds" (retirees from the north) to California, Nevada, Arizona, Texas, and Florida is a momentous tourism phenomenon (Mings and McHugh 1995; McHugh and Mings 1992; Smith and House 2006). The number of inhabitants of some communities in Arizona doubles or triples each winter as influxes of retirees from Canada, Minnesota, Iowa, Michigan, Montana and Wisconsin cause a swell in the local populations. Other winter destinations thrive as a result of their cold climates. The ski resorts of Utah, Colorado, Montana, Idaho, Vermont, and New Hampshire are examples of popular attractions in winter, and many of them make efforts to offset low season (summer) by hosting special events or changing their product orientation (e.g., to hiking and camping) (see Closer Look Case 4.2).

CLOSER LOOK CASE 4.2

Sundance, Utah, copes with seasonal demand

Sundance Resort in the Wasatch Mountains of Utah was purchased by movie actor Robert Redford in 1969 and has since become a world-renowned ski resort and year-round vacation destination. Although skiing was the original and primary tourist activity in the area between November and March of each year, since the 1970s Redford and his company have been instrumental in extending seasonal demand from the winter season by offering a wide range of activities and attractions that go far beyond the short snow season of the mountains. In addition, one of the resort's proudest accomplishments is its environmentally friendly approach to natural resource-based tourism development.

Sundance considers itself a boutique resort, offering world-class skiing and snowboarding in the winter, as well as snowshoeing and cross-country ski trails. Given that snow skiing was already popular at Sundance, and with the realization that business could be extended beyond the heavy snow season particularly because of the resort's scenic location in a region of high amenity, the resort's efforts moved to attracting visitors during non-ski periods.

Resort managers have established a wide assortment of summer activities that appeal to many market segments, some of which have little interest in skiing. Night-time ski lift rides are a popular activity on clear starry nights. The resort also offers a wide selection of outdoors-oriented activities, including hiking trails, horseback riding, flyfishing, mountain biking, river rafting, and children's day camps. Food and wine festivals, guest lectures by well-known authors, summer theater, and concerts are planned as special events to draw local Utah day-trippers to the mountains during "off-season" and to attract people from further afield, making low-season Sundance nearly as popular as the winter ski season. Additionally, world-class and award-winning dining facilities and lodging options are highlighted during the summer season to attract "local tourists" for a chance to enjoy fresh mountain air away from the crowds and pollution of Salt Lake City or other urban areas in the country.

Sources

Hudson, S. (2006) Ski resorts: enjoyment versus environmental responsibility – does there have to be a choice? In I.M. Herremans (ed.), *Cases in Sustainable Tourism: An Experiential Approach to Making Decisions*, pp. 123–44. New York: Haworth.

Sundance Resort (2009) *Sundance Resort*. Available from http://www.sundanceresort. com/ (accessed April 27, 2009).

Questions

1. What are some things seasonal tourist attractions or destinations can do to lessen the negative implications of low season?
2. Why do you think it is important for destinations to try to stretch demand beyond the traditional high season?

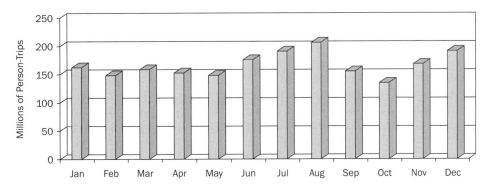

Figure 4.3 Seasonal variations in domestic tourism in the US, 2006 (millions of person-trips)

Conclusion

This chapter has highlighted some of the most prominent patterns of demand for tourism in the United States. The USA is one of the most visited countries in the world, and arrivals from Europe, Canada, Mexico and other parts of the world continue to increase with each passing year. It currently ranks as the third most visited nation on earth (after France and Spain) and first in terms of total earnings from tourism. This popularity no doubt reflects the vast country's wide range of cultural and natural attractions, its physical and demographic size, but also an increased global awareness about the USA as a tourist destination helped by its prominence gained from factors like the media and Hollywood movies.

Domestic tourism exceeds international arrivals by several times and is extremely important in the tourism economy. Most Americans travel in their own country by car and more than a third stay in the homes of friends or relatives, making the collection of data relating to domestic travel extremely difficult. The most popular domestic destinations tend to correspond with locations where large-scale theme parks, beaches, large cities, and colonial American heritage dominate the tourism offering.

Outbound travel by Americans, while continuing to grow, is hampered by their wariness about being outside the security of their homeland. The events of 9/11 and its follow-up have hardly helped the situation. Most international travel today targets Mexico and Canada owing to geographical proximity and cultural similarity (in the case of Canada), but this could be impeded in the near future when, after June 2009, passports will be required for all international travel, even to Canada and Mexico. Only one quarter of the US population possesses a valid passport and there is a general reluctance on the part of many to apply for one. Nevertheless, on a more optimistic note, the fact that more Americans may acquire passports due to the new requirements would mean that they could have more incentive to travel further afield to countries outside North America, a point that was touched upon in Chapter 3.

New passport and visa requirements are good examples of demand shifters, or socio-political, economic, and cultural variables and occurrences that transform tourist demand for a destination. Political incidents and pressures are among the most influential demand shifters in the USA today, together with changing demographic trends and economic challenges. These problems notwithstanding, the United States of America still has some of the most scenic natural areas and fascinating cultural heritage, not to mention some of the most remarkable theme parks that make it one of the most visited nations on earth. Despite the challenges currently facing the USA and the rest of the world, it is likely that demand for the US experience will continue to grow among foreign and domestic tourists. As we shall describe later, for instance, many urban areas, which have always been major destinations in this country are undergoing significant transformations that will likely lead to increased visitation of various market segments. Similarly, numerous rural communities have also benefited from increased visitation and, as we shall discuss in Chapter 9, places in the countryside, close to major domestic markets, are likely to become even more popular for short-term visitors.

Questions

1. What are some of the most important demand shifters that affect tourism? List as many as possible and explain how they affect demand for travel.
2. What short-term effects can an event like the international outbreak of swine flu in April 2009 have on demand for tourism? Do you think that such an event has a

uniform impact on demand throughout the world or are some markets more affected than others?

3. If you were a small-scale tour specialist and you were asked to create tour packages for American students on a spring break how would you determine different market niches?

4. How may the requirement for all Americans to use passports for all international travel, even across the border to Canada and Mexico, affect demand for travel to other regions? Explain your answer with examples.

Further reading

Gut, P. and Jarrell, S. (2007) Silver lining on a dark cloud: the impact of 9/11 on a regional tourist destination. *Journal of Travel Research*, 46(2): 147–53.

Haden, L. (2008) US outbound. *Travel and Tourism Analyst*, 6: 1–41.

Hwang, Y.H. and Fesenmaier, D.R. (2003) Multidestination pleasure travel patterns: empirical evidence from the American travel survey. *Journal of Travel Research*, 42(2): 166–71.

Hwang, Y.H., Gretzel, U. and Fesenmaier, D.R. (2006) Multicity trip patterns: tourists to the United States. *Annals of Tourism Research*, 33: 1057–78.

Khan, M. (2008) The growth and potential of multicultural meeting market: a case study. *Journal of Quality Assurance in Hospitality and Tourism*, 9(2): 159–83.

Kim, K.Y. (2007) Understanding differences in tourist motivation between domestic and international travel: the university student market. *Tourism Analysis*, 12(1/2): 65–75.

Kuentzel, W.F. and Ramaswamy, V.M. (2005) Tourism and amenity migration: a longitudinal analysis. *Annals of Tourism Research*, 32: 419–38.

Nyaupane, G.P. and Andereck, K.L. (2008) Understanding travel constraints: applications and extension of a leisure constraints model. *Journal of Travel Research*, 46(4): 433–39.

Shih, C., Nicholls, S. and Holecek, D.F. (2009) Impact of weather on downhill ski lift ticket sales. *Journal of Travel Research*, 47(3): 359–72.

Uysal, M., Fesenmaier, D.R. and O'Leary, J.T. (1994) Geographic and seasonal variation in the concentration of travel in the United States. *Journal of Travel Research*, 32(3): 61–64.

Useful Internet resources

Travel Industry Association of America: http://www.tia.org/index.html

Travel Weekly, The National Newspaper of the Travel Industry: http://www.travel weekly.com/

US Department of Commerce: http://www.commerce.gov/

World Tourism Organization: http://www.unwto.org/index.php

World Travel and Tourism Council: http://www.wttc.org/

⑤ Tourist attractions, tourism types, accommodations, and intermediaries

. . . a "first class" hostelry was "a strong presumption of social availability." Where the traveler "stopped" while in the city signaled his or her social status to the local elite, many of whom resided semipermanently at such fine hotels in the mid-nineteenth century.

(Cocks 2001: 71)

Introduction

The fundamental element of tourism is its attractions. The United States has no shortage of human-made and natural attractions that draw hundreds of millions of visitors each year. The diversity of its cultural and natural landscapes creates a condition where nearly every type of attraction can be found. Fundamentally, three types of attractions exist in the USA: cultural, natural, and entertainment-oriented. The country's native peoples and later immigrants created landscapes and communities that exude significant appeal among tourists. The immigrant landscapes of urban America (e.g., Chinatowns and Little Italies) maintain their footprint and provide an important element of the attractiveness of cities.

America's vast array of natural landscapes provides numerous backdrops for tourism rivaled by only a few other regions of the world. The country is endowed with a wide range of natural environments, including interesting topography, a wide range of climatic and vegetative zones, and ecosystems. Permanent glaciers in Alaska and in the mountains of Montana and Colorado are important attractions for many types of tourists, including cruise passengers in Alaska and car travelers in the Rocky Mountains. At the other extreme are the warm climatic zones that vary little in temperature between seasons, such as the tropical and subtropical areas of Hawaii and southern Florida, which draw winter tourists from around the country and the world. Between these two extremes are a multitude of other more temperate climates that appeal to a wide range of tourists. The USA is home to extremely high mountains, and one of the lowest valleys on earth (e.g., Death Valley at 282 feet below sea level). Flat prairies and coastal plains also give way to foothills and high mountains – all contributing to the allure of nature in America.

Additionally, there has been a rapid growth of entertainment-type tourist attractions since the mid-1800s: amusement parks, golf courses, spas, and beach resorts. The Disney parks alone, in southern California and central Florida, have made these regions global tourist magnets. All these facilities are a salient part of the tourism landscape of the USA and compete for tourist attention throughout the country. Given the great size and diversity of the United States with its huge selection of existing and potential tourism resources, it is little wonder that it is one of the most visited countries in the world.

This chapter describes some of the most common tourist attractions and tourism types in the United States, examining elements from all three categories noted above. The chapter first investigates cultural heritage and the tourism associated with it. It then highlights nature-based tourism, followed by gambling, amusement parks, seaside resorts, and religious tourism. It concludes with an examination of the development and current situation of the accommodation sector and other tourism service providers (intermediaries).

Heritage and cultural tourism

Heritage is most commonly defined as the modern-day use of the past, including its tangible and intangible elements (Graham *et al.* 2000; Timothy and Boyd 2003). Thus, it encompasses archeological sites, ancient monuments, museums, art, music and dance, religious traditions, battlefields, cultural landscapes, historic homes and buildings, cemeteries, cuisine and foodways, folklore, and many other aspects of the inherited human past. Some observers have distinguished between heritage tourism and cultural tourism by suggesting that cultural tourism is based more on the arts and travelers' own needs for cultural fulfillment. Despite subtle differences, both terms refer to similar products and experiences and will be used interchangeably in this section.

Heritage sites in the USA can be categorized into five primary groups: indigenous; colonial and nationalistic; immigrant; frontier and westward settlement; and industrial. These are not mutually exclusive.

Indigenous heritage

The indigenous heritage of the United States is rich and diverse. While scientists are unable to quantify the number of Native American tribes prior to the European arrival, most estimates suggest there were at least ten-million inhabitants and hundreds of distinct ethno-linguistic groups, which have been variously divided between the Eastern Woodlands Indians, the Plains Indians, the Southwest Indians, the Northwest Coastal Indians, the Great Basin and California Indians, the Athabascan Indians, and the Inuits and Aleuts, or Arctic peoples.

Each of these broad groups and its sub-groups had unique architectural styles and utilized whatever building materials were available. Like aboriginal people elsewhere, Native Americans built homes and shelters from materials that biodegraded easily over the centuries and millennia since their construction. Longhouses, wikiups, hogans, thatched-roof shelters, earthen lodges and pit houses were built of animal skins, plant leaves and tree branches, tree bark, and soil. Very little evidence of these original dwellings is still discernible in the landscape (Nabokov and Easton 1989). The primary exceptions to this generalization are archeological sites associated with the remains of pit houses and the grand pueblos built by the Southwest Pueblo Natives in Colorado, Arizona, New Mexico and Utah. Rather than living in individual, detached dwellings, the Pueblo Indians (the Anasazi) built multi-roomed, multi-story communal homes of adobe and/or stone with relative precision. Often these were built in caves and on cliff faces to provide the most protection for their inhabitants. Many remnants of these original pueblos still exist in the southwestern states and have become popular heritage attractions. Among the best known of these ancient sites are at Aztec Ruins National Monument (New Mexico), El Morro National Monument (New Mexico), Mesa Verde National Park (Colorado), Canyon de Chelly National Monument (Arizona), Montezuma Castle National Monument (Arizona), Tuzigoot National Monument (Arizona), and

Hovenweep National Monument (Utah) (Budruk *et al.* 2008; Nyaupane *et al.* 2006; White *et al.* 2005).

In addition to these pueblo ruins, there are several living pueblos in New Mexico and Arizona, which were established several hundred years ago and are still inhabited by Native Americans. A few of these have become significant tourist attractions, including Taos Pueblo (New Mexico), Zuni Pueblo (New Mexico), and the Hopi Reservation (Arizona), while several others have shunned tourism as a way of protecting their cultural heritage (Jett 1990; Mallari and Enote 1996). Although most images of Native American archaeological sites depict the southwestern locations, there are also important indigenous sites in the eastern and Midwestern states as well. The Great Serpent Mound in Ohio and the Etowah Indian Mounds in Georgia are two prominent examples of important Indian archaeological sites that attest to the dominance of native cultures throughout the entire United States prior to the European arrivals (King 2003; Randall 2003).

Contemporary Native Americans also play an important role in cultural tourism. They commonly share their cultural past with tourists through indigenous festivals and ceremonies (e.g., powwows), food, music and dance (Lew 1996; Lew and van Otten 1998; Sweet 2007; Turco 1999) (see Plate 5.1). Cultural interpretive centers are also located on several of the largest native reservations today, and cultural demonstrations are common. Throughout the world there has been widespread criticism of tourism as a culturally destructive force that commodifies cultural traditions and exploits native peoples (Johnston 2006). The same has been argued in the context of Native Americans (Laxson 1991; Hollinshead 1992). This issue has been at the forefront of much Indian tourism

Plate 5.1 A Native American demonstrating her culture to tourists
(Dallen Timothy)

development since the 1970s with concepts such as authenticity, cultural integrity, and participatory community development being at the core of such debates.

These notions have led many Native American groups to approach tourism with considerable caution and establish boundaries between their sacred space and ceremonies and the "profane" space of tourists. The Hopis of Arizona, for instance, have spatially segregated tourism away from the core of their dwelling area and from their holiest spaces and ceremonies (see Closer Look Case 5.1); some places are completely off limits to all outsiders. In addition, photographing certain places, people and events is forbidden (Lew and Kennedy 2002). Likewise, the Taos Indians of Taos Pueblo, New Mexico, close their community to outsiders for a period of time each year during which they perform sacred rituals and renew their kindred ties (Lujan 1993; Sweet 2007). Handicraft cooperatives have also been established to assure economic benefits to the community and some degree of authenticity of products being sold as Indian crafts. These and other methods have been adopted by Native Americans as a way of empowering their communities against the forces of tourism and to ensure that their cultural property rights are respected (Johnston 2006).

CLOSER LOOK CASE 5.1

The Hopi Indians of Arizona protect their cultural heritage

Indigenous peoples have lived in what eventually became the United States for thousands of years. They had many unique social characteristics, languages and belief systems, and they all lived off the land by hunting and fishing, gathering, and growing crops. One of the most unique Native American tribes is the Hopi tribe of northern Arizona, who have withstood much of the outside European influence, even until today, primarily by their own choice to protect their sacred traditions and unique culture. The Hopi Reservation comprises 2,532 square miles with a population of nearly 7,000. Geographically it lies in the southwest desert and is entirely surrounded by the much larger Navajo Reservation.

Hopis have lived in their current location for hundreds of years and established pueblo-style villages on the tops of three mesas, known as First Mesa, Second Mesa and Third Mesa. Old Oraibi, established in 1150 AD, is often cited as the oldest continuously inhabited village in the United States.

Tourism is an important part of the Hopi Nation economy. More than 50 percent of tribal jobs are in tourism (e.g., motels, food services, gas stations, and souvenirs), with the majority of the remaining jobs consisting of tribal and federal government employment. Scenic pueblo villages perched high on the edges of the desert mesas, cultural performances, art galleries, and handicrafts are the most popular tourist attractions. Unlike many other US tribes, the Hopis have not yet established a casino. While non-Hopi outsiders are welcome to visit the indigenous communities, there are several strict prohibitions that have been established in order to protect the native culture from being exploited or diluted. First, religious ceremonies and Kachina dances are off limits to non-Hopi outsiders. Such celebrations are considered so sacred that non-adherents would not appreciate or respect the devotion and gravity associated with the ceremonies. Second, photography, video recording, audio recording, sketching, or any other form of recording is prohibited at all villages and at all ceremonies. The Hopi claim ownership of their sacred sites, villages, and ceremonies; publishing or selling images of this nature is considered stealing and therefore immoral and in some cases illegal, according to tribal law. Third, visitors must dress appropriately (modestly) for all Hopi ceremonies and events. Tourists should dress respectfully, as they would for rites and rituals in their own communities. Fourth, tourists must not touch anything in the villages and are required to stay in prescribed areas. It is considered very disrespectful to touch sacred relics or monuments that honor the dead, for example. Finally, visitors may not interrupt any ongoing ceremonies. This would be considered as rude as disrupting a wedding ceremony or religious service on non-Native lands.

Sources

Arizona Department of Commerce (2008) *Hopi Indian Reservation: Community Profile.* Phoenix, AZ: Arizona Department of Commerce.

Hopi Cultural Preservation Office (2007) *Hopi Visitor Information.* Available from http://www.nau.edu/~hcpo-p/visit/index.html (accessed April 20, 2009).

Questions

1. What measures have the Hopis taken to ensure that their culture will not be exploited or altered by tourists?
2. What are the primary tourist attractions associated with the Hopi Nation and other indigenous American groups?

Colonial and nationalistic heritage

Colonial/revolutionary and nationalistic heritage is the second main form of cultural tourism in the United States. The American infatuation with its colonial past is rooted in the struggle for religious freedom and other liberties, such as economic freedom (i.e., capitalism) by the earliest European colonists, many of whom departed England to escape the heavy-handed dictates of the monarchs. This notion of freedom and personal liberty is at the very core of the American psyche and was established more than 400 years ago. The earliest colonists are seen as hard-working, righteous and God-fearing, and destined to inhabit a land that was divinely appointed to be settled (and subdued) as a land of freedom, a concept often referred to as "Manifest Destiny." These principles have been taught in American schools since colonial times – unfortunately often to the exclusion and peripheralization of the pre-Columbian indigenous heritage of America (Boniface and Fowler 1993; Kehoe 1990; Timothy and Boyd 2003). This idealized heritage and other forces, including religious and family traditions, have created an overwhelming sense of patriotism in the United States that overshadows the nationalism exhibited in many other countries (Li and Brewer 2004; O'Leary 1999). This context is important in understanding the role of nationalist and colonial heritage in the landscape of American tourism.

Most colonial heritage-based tourism takes place in cities of the mid-Atlantic and northeast regions, such as Boston and Philadelphia, but can also flourish throughout the region's small towns and rural areas. The revolutionary history associated with Boston is experienced by millions of visitors along Boston's Freedom Trail each year (Timothy and Boyd 2006a). In 2008, 2,232,495 people visited the US National Park Service properties that are part of the Freedom Trail (US National Park Service 2009) (See Plate 5.2). The

Plate 5.2 Freedom Trail, Boston
(Dimitri Ioannides)

2.5-mile trail links 16 historic sites (churches, meeting halls, museums, parks, harbor, cemeteries, and historic markers) in the old city, all of which have important colonial/ revolutionary heritage connotations. In Philadelphia, the first capital of the United States, tourists visit Independence Hall, which is a National Park Service property and a UNESCO World Heritage Site (since 1979); the Liberty Bell, made famous as the bell that called the citizens of Philadelphia for the public reading of the Declaration of Independence; the grave of revolutionary hero Benjamin Franklin; and the homes of famous revolutionary characters such as Betsy Ross, who is believed to have sewed the first American flag. Rural areas also host many important colonial and revolutionary sites, such as Valley Forge, where the Continental Army led by George Washington spent the winter of 1777–78. There are many other battlefields, homes of national heroes, public buildings, and cemeteries associated with the colonial and revolutionary period, which are visited by millions of tourists each year.

Among the most prominent heritage attractions related to the colonial period, however, are those variously known as open-air museums, folk museums, folk-life museums, living museums, or historic theme parks. These museums are staffed by real-life characters dressed in period and ethnic costumes, and demonstrations are made to tourists about everyday life at a given period of time. These living museums originated in Europe in the 1800s but spread to the United States as a response to rapid industrialization and a perceived need to preserve some degree of the American past. Today there are dozens of these folk museums throughout the USA (Table 5.1), primarily in the east, and a few are particularly pertinent to the context of colonial heritage, namely: Colonial Williamsburg,

Table 5.1 Examples of open-air, living heritage museums in the United States

Museum	Location
The Historic Village at Allaire	New Jersey
Colonial Williamsburg	Virginia
Old Nauvoo	Illinois
Conner Prairie	Indiana
Hale Farm and Village	Ohio
Jamestown Settlement	Virginia
Old Salem	North Carolina
Old Sturbridge Village	Massachusetts
Shaker Village of Pleasant Hill	Kentucky
This is the Place Heritage Village	Utah
South Park City	Colorado
Old World Wisconsin	Wisconsin
Westville	Georgia
Plimoth Plantation	Massachusetts

Source: National Conference of Catholic Bishops (1998); Catholicshrines.net (2009)

an eighteenth-century colonial town in Virginia; Plimoth Plantation, a 1627 colonial village in Massachusetts (Plate 5.3); Old Sturbridge Village, a 1790–1840 New England village in Massachusetts; and Mystic Seaport, an 1800s seaport and ship-building maritime village in Connecticut.

Plate 5.3 Plimoth Plantation, Massachusetts
(Dallen Timothy)

Another category of colonial and nationalist heritage site is Civil War battlefields and memorials, which are the primary remnants of the approximately 10,000 skirmishes or battles between the northern and southern states between 1861 and 1865. These abound throughout the southeast (Alabama, Arkansas, Florida, Georgia, Louisiana, Mississippi, North Carolina, and South Carolina), and especially in the Union and Confederacy border states, which were the front line in the war (e.g., Virginia, Kentucky, West Virginia, Maryland, Missouri, and Tennessee). However, a few battles were fought even in the upper Midwest states (e.g., Ohio and Indiana) and as far west as Arizona and New Mexico (Kennedy 1998). Many of these have become important tourist attractions and have been designated National Battlefields or Military Parks by the National Park Service or state parks by the various states where they are located (Table 5.2).

Modern political heritage tourism in its most common form involves visiting government sites in Washington, DC, and individual state capitals (Maitland and Ritchie 2007). All Americans grow up with images in mind of the White House, the Capitol Building, the Lincoln Memorial, and other well-known structures that symbolize the prominence of the United States in the world and illustrate the functions of the US government. Embassy hunting is another popular pastime in the capital city (Kummer 2003), and several important places are located within a reasonable proximity to the District of Columbia, such as Thomas Jefferson's Monticello, George Washington's Mount Vernon, the Pentagon, and Arlington National Cemetery, where US soldiers and dignitaries are interred.

Frontier and westward settlement

A third category of heritage is frontier and westward settlement. Nearly all of the colonial, nationalistic, and political tourist attractions are located east of the Mississippi

Table 5.2 Examples of Civil War properties operated by the National Park Service

Property	Location
Antiem National Battlefield	Maryland
Brices Cross Roads National Battlefield Site	Mississippi
Chickamauga and Chattanooga National Military Park	Georgia/Tennessee
Fort Donelson National Battlefield	Tennessee/Kentucky
Fort Pulaski National Monument	Georgia
Fort Sumter National Monument	South Carolina
Fort Washington Park	Maryland
Fredericksburg & Spotsylvania National Military Park	Virginia
Gettysburg National Military Park	Pennsylvania
Governors Island National Monument	New York
Harpers Ferry National Historical Park	Maryland/Virginia/West Virginia
Kennesaw Mountain National Battlefield Park	Georgia
Manassas National Battlefield Park	Virginia
Monocacy National Battlefield	Maryland
Pea Ridge National Military Park	Arkansas
Pecos National Historical Park	New Mexico
Petersburg National Battlefield	Virginia
Richmond National Battlefield Park	Virginia
Shiloh National Military Park	Mississippi/Tennessee
Stones River National Battlefield	Tennessee
Tupelo National Battlefield	Mississippi
Vicksburg National Military Park	Mississippi
Wilson's Creek National Battlefield	Missouri

Table 5.3 Examples of historic sites based on westward expansion themes

Property	Location
Fort Laramie	Wyoming
Sand Creek Massacre National Historic Site	Colorado
Salinas Pueblo Missions	New Mexico
Hubbell Trading Post	Arizona
Pipe Spring National Monument	Arizona
Golden Spike National Historic Site	Utah
Fort Vancouver	Oregon/Washington
Klondike Gold Rush National Historical Park	Washington & Alaska
Little Bighorn Battlefield	Montana
Fort Scott	Kansas
Mormon Pioneer Trail	Multiple states
Lewis and Clark Trail	Multiple states
Pony Express Trail	Multiple states
Cabrillo National Monument	California
Washita Battlefield	Oklahoma
Grant-Kohrs Ranch	Montana

River. Frontier settlement characterizes most of the country's heritage sites west of the Mississippi. Most of this genre of heritage focuses on conflict between Native Americans and white European settlers, the fur trade, the Gold Rush, railways, cattle ranching, mining, pioneer trails, and early Spanish explorers. Forts in the Midwest and western states attest to the expansionist heritage of the European colonizers as they encroached upon Indigenous lands. Ranches and farmsteads exemplify the agricultural heritage of a relatively inhospitable south-western desert region. Old mines, Gold Rush monuments, fur trading posts, and railway memorials commemorate the untapped economic potential of the far west for easterners struggling to survive. Pioneer and explorer trails are indicative of people's desires to have lands of their own where they could homestead, worship freely, and, in the case of the Spanish, claim lands for the king of Spain and Christianize the indigenous Americans (Table 5.3).

Immigrant heritage

Immigrant heritage is the fourth main type being considered here. The United States has been a destination for millions of émigrés from every corner of the world. The first to come were settlers from countries like Sweden, Spain, Britain, France and the Netherlands during the sixteenth and seventeenth centuries. In the mid-part of the nineteenth century a huge wave of Irish immigrants arrived following the potato famine. Germans and Scandinavians also arrived at roughly the same time. The latter part of the nineteenth and the early twentieth centuries saw massive waves of immigration of people such as Jews, Greeks, and Italians. In more recent years the large immigrant groups have come from Asia and Latin America. The USA is often referred to in popular lexicon as a melting pot of cultures, where a multiplicity of cultures meld together to form a unique American identity. Immigrants have been instrumental in bringing cultural diversity to the USA and have contributed many elements of modern-day tourism, including ethnic festivals, urban and rural enclaves, foodways and cuisines, religious traditions, cultural landscapes, music, and folklore.

Festivals are now commonplace in the United States, commemorating agricultural heritage, significant historical events, anniversaries of community founders, and immigrant heritage. Aside from the ubiquitous agricultural festivals associated with the Midwest harvests (e.g., Pickle Fest, Strawberry Days, Great Wisconsin Cheese Festival, and North Ridgeville Corn Festival), there is an abundance of ethnic and cultural festivals throughout the United States that draw many thousands of people into small or large communities each year. The primary focus of these immigrant/ethnic events is food, dress, music, artworks, and dance. Parades are usually an important part of the milieu, as are cook-offs, awards ceremonies, and language recitations. Hundreds of annual festivals exist in large cities and small towns to commemorate the immigration of the Irish, Swedes, Finns, Germans, Czechs, Chinese, Vietnamese, Dutch, Mexicans, Basques, Danes, Icelanders, Norwegians, Italians, Poles, Russians, Ukrainians, Cubans, Africans, and many more.

Not all immigrants departed for the shores of America of their own free will and choice. The slave trade, one of the world's most shameful misappropriations of humanity, forced millions of Africans from their homelands to unfamiliar places far across the sea. While Africans were sold into slavery in many different parts of the world, including the Caribbean, Central and South America, and Europe, the United States was among the worst perpetrators of this human atrocity, and slavery became the root of the country's Civil War. Under slavery, people of African lineage were bought and sold as property, much like cattle. They were abused, beaten, locked up, raped, and murdered, at the whim of their owners (Eltis 2000; Horton 2006).

Until recently, the heritage of African Americans was disguised, overlooked, and in some ways systematically written out of the heritage narrative in the United States. Since the abolition of slavery in the USA in 1865, slavery has been a point of contention and embarrassment for the country, and powerful elites have continued to keep the heritage of slavery at arm's length. Fortunately, today white and black Americans have begun to realize the need to rectify this aspect of "collective amnesia" (Timothy and Boyd 2003), resulting in more attention being directed to researching, preserving, and interpreting the heritage of African-Americans, including sites and events associated with slavery and human rights movements (Hayes 1997). The recent development of black heritage attractions (e.g., slave cabins, homes of prominent African-Americans, museums, and public memorials) attests to changing power structures and race relations in the country (Boniface and Fowler 1993). There are many efforts now to do away with the Euro-centric view of the American past, to present a more realistic and holistic view of the African and indigenous heritage in America. While there is still a long way to go in achieving equity in heritage representation in the United States, significant and laudable efforts are being made (Bartlett 2001; Smith 2000; Timothy and Teye 2004).

Industrial heritage

The final aspect of heritage tourism in this section is industrial heritage, which refers to the use of industrial sites and areas (e.g., factories, mines, railroads, quarries, dockyards, and processing plants) as tourist attractions. As we describe later on in Chapter 8, these have become increasingly popular in the United States following the substitution of manufacturing with post-Fordist, service-oriented sectors, including tourism. The decline of traditional manufacturing industries that have rushed in the new service-oriented economic era has brought about the dereliction of many former industrial buildings and zones. These outdated resources have begun to be reinterpreted and marketed as a new heritage resource (Alfrey and Putnam 1992; Xie 2006). In light of these de-industrializing trends, many rural and urban communities in the USA have attempted to reinvent themselves from centers of heavy industry to tourist destinations (Kerstetter *et al.* 1998; Leary and Sholes 2000; Rudd and Davis 1998; Timothy and Boyd 2003; Xie 2006). Mine tours,

Table 5.4 Cultural heritage-based National Park Service properties

Property type	Number of park properties	Number of visitors, 2008
National Battlefield	10	1,528,532
National Battlefield Park	3	2,231,732
National Historic Park	40	27,051,062
National Historic Site	77	9,639,416
National Memorial	27	29,507,434
National Military Park	9	4,564,033

Source: National Park Service (2009)

railway museums, factory tours, and heritage parks are only a few of the new trends in industrial heritage that have received tourist attention in the United States.

Many of the types of heritage attractions discussed in this section are owned, managed, and operated by various public lands trusts in the USA, including the National Park Service, the Bureau of Land Management, and the National Trust for Historic Preservation. The National Park Service also maintains the National Register of Historic Places, which includes thousands of properties, such as homes, monuments, libraries, schools, ships, and other important historic structures and places. The majority of properties on the list are privately owned, but some are owned and managed by the National Park Service and other public agencies. Table 5.4 demonstrates the categories and numbers of National Park Service properties whose primary focus is cultural heritage. Several other types of park properties also include heritage sites (e.g., national monuments), but these are listed in the next section as their primary focus is on nature.

In addition to federal agencies and programs to assist in preserving the nation's heritage, each individual state (and many counties and cities as well) has its own state parks system, which may also include cultural heritage properties. For example, Arizona's State Parks owns nine cultural heritage properties.

Nature-based tourism and outdoor recreation

Outdoor activities away from home have long been an important part of the tourism product in the United States. The country's varying natural landscapes and ecosystems have given rise to much demand for outdoor recreation and nature-based travel and tourism since the earliest European settlements.

With the Industrial Revolution and the subsequent mechanization of everyday tasks (e.g., weaving, travel, farming), Americans have undergone a transformation from a society that works to survive to a leisure society where people work hard so that they can enjoy leisure time and recreation. These and other trends – dissatisfaction with a rapidly modernizing world and the fast-pace of life today – are causing Americans to feel overstressed and pressured for time. One response to this frenetic pace of life in modern America has been an increase in nature-based pursuits, such as camping, rafting, boating, hiking, fishing and hunting (Lengfelder and Timothy 2000).

Americans are very recreation-oriented and spend much time outdoors. The activities listed above have achieved a great deal of prominence during the past 50 years, which is reflected in the growth of recreational equipment sales and participation in outdoor activities. According to the National Sporting Goods Association (2008), outdoor recreation pursuits have remained fairly steady during the past ten years, although some sports and activities have seen tremendous growth (Table 5.5). Cross-country skiing, hiking, and

Table 5.5 Outdoor pursuits in the United States

Activity	1997 Participation (millions)	2007 Participation (millions)
Backpacking/wilderness camping	12.0	13.0
Vacation Camping	46.6	47.5
Fishing	44.7	35.3
Hiking	28.4	28.6
Hunting (with firearms)	17.0	19.5
Mountain Biking (offroad)	8.1	7.4
Skiing (cross-country)	2.5	1.7

Source: National Sporting Goods Association (2008)

camping have all remained steady between 1997 and 2007. Wilderness camping grew from 12 million participants in 1997 to 13 million in 2007. Cross-country skiing and hiking have experienced minor declines since 1997, but they are still important outdoor pursuits. Hiking and hunting have also seen an increase, while several others have experienced a decline.

Ecotourism is an idealistic form of nature-based tourism that is purported not to degrade the natural environment and which, in fact, can benefit ecosystems and local communities through economic development and conservation (Fennell 2008). Most research on ecotourism focuses on countries of the less-developed world, primarily because there is a tendency for people to think of rainforests and other tropical ecosystems as the natural venue for this type of activity (Fennell 2008; Weaver 1998). This is a false assumption, however, and recent research shows that ecotourism can take place anywhere in any natural environment. Although most ecotourism studies have been carried out in places such as Latin America, Southeast Asia, and Central Africa, attention is now being paid to the deserts, mountains, rainforests, swamps, plains, taiga forests, coastal zones, and arctic regions of the United States (Che 2006; Fritsch and Johannsen 2004; Solomon *et al.* 2004).

Wildlife viewing is especially popular in some locations. Whale watching, for instance, has become a much-sought tourist pursuit in the Pacific Northwest, Hawaii, and Florida (Andersen and Miller 2005). Bird watching has emerged as a trendy recreational activity in many parts of the country, and people often visit parks, such as Yellowstone National Park, in hopes of seeing deer, bison, elk, moose, bears or wolves (Montag *et al.* 2005). Desert safaris in the southwestern United States (e.g., Arizona, Nevada, and California) have also become popular in the past two decades. These activities involve people traveling in small groups in 4-wheel drive vehicles in off-road conditions, enjoying nature and cultural relics (e.g., abandoned mines) along the way. Some trips include desert camping, while others utilize hotels and towns as their bases of operations for day visits into the wilderness. Likewise, climbing, hiking and wilderness camping in mountain areas are extremely popular tourist activities. These are only a few of the multitudinous nature-based activities that are popular among tourists in the United States.

Many of these activities and more, such as auto-based sightseeing, take place in the country's vast system of national parks (Figure 5.1). Table 5.4 earlier in the chapter highlighted the primary culture-based National Park Service properties. However, the foundational element of many of the NPS properties is the natural realm (Table 5.6), and, in fact, the National Park Service was established in 1916 as a national government body mandated to protect the natural environment. It was only later, in the 1930s and '40s that the NPS began acquiring and designating sites of a cultural heritage nature. As was

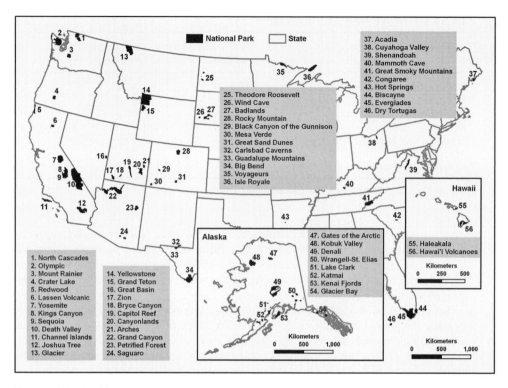

Figure 5.1 National Parks in the United States

shown in Chapter 2, the first national park in the world was Yellowstone National Park, established in 1872 under the auspices of the Department of the Interior. From this initial start, many other national park properties have been designated. The world soon caught on to this trend, and other countries also began preserving areas of natural beauty as national parks (Nelson 2000). The national park system was highly instrumental during

Table 5.6 Nature-based National Park Service properties*

Property	Number of park properties	Number of visitors, 2008
National Lakeshore	4	3,403,376
National Monument	69	21,610,296
National Park	58	61,159,714
National Parkway	4	30,165,232
National Preserve	9	2,790,473
National Recreation Area	17	49,584,382
National Reserve	1	85,893
National River	4	4,538,091
National Seashore	10	15,909,135
National Wild and Scenic River	7	1,281,000
Parks (Other)	11	9,903,148

* National Monuments and National Parks include cultural elements and foci. National Parkways, National Seashores, and Other Parks are a combination of natural and cultural properties

Source: National Park Service (2009)

the early 1900s in establishing tourism in the American west and in bringing people from the east to the west, where most of the national parks are located (Gunn 2004).

Casinos and gambling

Gaming has become a popular pastime in the United States and is a prominent form of tourism. Gambling is legal in the USA, but each state has the right to regulate it and decide whether or not to allow it. At the time of writing (2009), Utah is the only state in the USA that prohibits all forms of gambling, including lotteries. Gambling was first legalized in Nevada in 1931; subsequently, Las Vegas has become one of the best known gaming destinations in the world and is synonymous with casinos and entertainment. Other towns in Nevada also have liberal gaming laws and have become well established "casino resort" destinations (see Plate 5.4).

Atlantic City, New Jersey, was a popular seaside destination in the 1800s and early 1900s, because of its rail connections to eastern seaboard cities. However, it began to decline in popularity with the widespread ownership of private automobiles and the expansion of air travel, which allowed more freedom for people to travel to other destinations. In an effort to revitalize the local economy, the city petitioned the New Jersey state legislature in the early 1970s to legalize gambling in the same way the Nevada legislature had done a few decades earlier. Permission was finally granted to the city to establish casinos in 1976, with the first casino opening its doors in 1978 (Braunlich

Plate 5.4 The Bellagio Resort and Casino, Las Vegas
(Dimitri Ioannides)

1996; Meyer-Arendt and Hartmann 1998; Rubenstein 1984). Since that time only a small handful of states have allowed the establishment of casinos and high-stakes gaming off Native reservations.

Several interesting trends are observable on the American gambling scene. Perhaps the one receiving most attention these days relates to Indian casinos (Baron 1998; Chhabra 2007; Davis and Hudman 1998; Pfaffenberg and Costello 2001). In 1988, the US Congress passed the Indian Gaming Regulatory Act (IGRA), which governs the establishment and functions of casinos on federal Indian reservations. Because Native reservations are considered "sovereign nations" in the United States, they fall outside each state's jurisdiction in many practical areas, such as law enforcement, taxation, and so on, and are, therefore, able to establish high-stakes casinos, even in states where casino gaming is prohibited. The IGRA is a complicated piece of legislation. In short, however, it allows Native Americans to establish high-stakes and other gambling establishments in states where any other form of gaming is permitted, so that even in states with legal lotteries, Native Americans, owing to their sovereign nation status, are able to establish casinos. Today, hundreds of Indian casinos have been developed throughout the United States; two of the world's largest casinos are located on small Native reservations in the state of Connecticut (the Mohegan Sun and Foxwoods) (Carmichael and Peppard 1998; Dense and Barrow 2003).

Criticism of Indian gaming has grown considerably since the 1990s. Some observers suggest that Native Americans continue to be dependent on outsiders in a neocolonialist fashion. Similar criticisms indicate that this form of tourism is a continuation of the exploitation by white Americans of indigenous people in the same way it has carried on for centuries. Additionally, and perhaps more commonplace in the general public domain, is the fear of corruption, organized crime, and cultural and familial deterioration that often accompany this "tourism of vice" (Janes and Collison 2004; Moufakkir 2005; Stitt *et al.* 2005).

Another important gaming trend is riverboat gambling. As noted in Chapter 6 there are several cruise companies in the southeastern United States offering "cruises to nowhere." Their purpose is to take customers beyond American territorial waters, where they operate onboard casinos. A similar situation exists on some of the great rivers of the east and Midwest. The notion behind riverboat gaming is that while gambling is not allowed on shore (or on state territory), it can be permitted on adjacent boundary waters. Iowa was the first state to permit riverboat gambling in 1991 on the Mississippi River. Several other states followed suit shortly thereafter (e.g., Mississippi, Missouri, Louisiana, Illinois, and Indiana). Although legislators in several of these states would have preferred not to have any casino gambling, many felt they had little choice – either keep the money at home, or residents would cross state lines to gamble (Truitt 1996).

The riverfront states permitted river casinos for their promised economic benefits in societies where Fordist industrialization had begun to give way to post-Fordist service economies. With the early 1980s recession, accompanied by the rapid decline in agriculture, manufacturing, oil refining, and mining in the upper Midwest and Gulf states, states along the Mississippi River turned to gambling tourism as a viable economic alternative for much-needed jobs and tax revenue (Timothy 2009). A declining oil industry wrought havoc in Louisiana and Mississippi – large refining states – so that in 1992, Louisiana passed a law to allow 15 riverboat casinos to cruise its Mississippi waters (Dimanche and Speyrer 1996; Hsu 1999).

Amusement parks

Americans love amusement parks, and many people spend their vacations with theme parks at the core of the experience. Amusement parks are large complexes of rides, games, eating establishments and other attractions, which developed out of large fairs and expositions (e.g., World's Fairs) that offered activities for children, as well as "trolley parks" established by railway companies to keep passengers occupied at train and tram stations and along routes (Clavé 2007; Shaw 1986). Among the earliest amusement parks in the United States was Sea Lion Park on Coney Island, which developed in 1895 around a maritime theme (Adams 1991). The park no longer exists, but others have been developed on Coney Island to replace it, such as Steeplechase Park (est. 1897), Luna Land (est. 1902), and Dreamland (est. 1911) (Clavé 2007).

Knott's Berry Farm, one of America's oldest amusement parks, had its beginnings in 1940 when Walter Knott built a ghost town with railway and began charging admission. The "park" continued to develop between the 1960s and 1980s into one of the country's most popular amusement park attractions (Davis 1999). Likewise, Disneyland was one of the earliest large-scale theme parks to develop in the United States. It opened in 1955 with five themed areas and has continued to expand since that time. In 2001, Disney's California Adventure Park was opened adjacent to Disneyland, with the two parks together being rebranded as the "Disneyland Resort." The Walt Disney World Resort with its Magic Kingdom was opened in 1971 in Florida and has subsequently undergone expansion with new parks added in the 1980s (Epcot and Disney's Hollywood Studios) and 1990s (Disney's Animal Kingdom) (Bryman 1995; Clavé 2007). Today, it is the largest resort in the world with four theme parks, two water parks, and a large number of hotels and restaurants.

Today there are many theme parks throughout the USA (more than 400), and most experience their highest levels of demand during school breaks (e.g., summer vacation, spring and fall breaks) and during the winter holidays. In 2006, US amusement parks hosted 335 million guests, who took more than 1.5 billion rides (International Association of Amusement Parks and Attractions 2009). Most of the largest and most visited parks are located in Florida and California, although as Table 5.7 illustrates, there are popular theme parks in other states as well.

Most of the largest US amusement parks are owned and operated by a handful of park chains. Walt Disney Parks and Resorts, Six Flags, Universal Studios, Cedar Fair, Anheuser Busch, and Palace Entertainment are among the largest and widespread theme park operators. There are only a few independent amusement parks remaining, and they tend to be smaller in scale and utilized more by a local or regional market (Clavé 2007).

Critics of the amusement park movement in the United States suggest that the parks are simply manifestations of the mass consumption and materialism that have become so pervasive in American society, providing artificial experiences and places that superficially titillate the senses more so than traditional natural and cultural attractions and experiences (Clavé 2007; Johnson 1981; King 1981a, 1981b; Samuelson and Yegoiants 2001). In honor of the great American amusement park developer, the terms Disneyfication and McDisneyization were coined in the late 1970s and in the 1990s to refer to experiences that are based on contrived attractions and inauthentic places (Relph 1979; Ritzer and Liska 1997).

Table 5.7 Top 15 amusement parks in the United States by number of visits, 2007

Rank	Park	Location	Park attendance, 2007
1	Magic Kingdom at Walt Disney World	Lake Buena Vista, Florida	17,060,000
2	Disneyland	Anaheim, California	14,870,000
3	Epcot at Walt Disney World	Lake Buena Vista, Florida	10,930,000
4	Disney's Hollywood Studios	Lake Buena Vista, Florida	9,510,000
5	Disney's Animal Kingdom	Lake Buena Vista, Florida	9,490,000
6	Universal Studios at Universal	Orlando, Florida	6,200,000
7	Seaworld Florida	Orlando, Florida	5,800,000
8	Disney's California Adventure	Anaheim, California	5,680,000
9	Islands of Adventure at Universal	Orlando, Florida	5,430,000
10	Universal Studios Hollywood	Universal City, California	4,700,000
11	Busch Gardens Tampa Bay	Tampa, Florida	4,400,000
12	Seaworld California	San Diego, California	4,260,000
13	Knott's Berry Farm	Buena Park, California	3,630,000
14	Busch Gardens Europe	Williamsburg, Virginia	3,157,000
15	Cedar Point	Sandusky, Ohio	3,120,000

Source: Themed Entertainment Association (2008)

Seaside resorts/beach-based tourism

As noted elsewhere in this book, with the development of railway lines and highways, coastal resorts became popular destinations for urban Americans. Ocean City, Maryland, and Atlantic City, New Jersey, were popularized in the mid- and late 1800s. Since that time, however, the most favored locations for seaside development have become the tropical and subtropical environments of Hawaii and Florida. Nonetheless, coastal areas of the Pacific Northwest (e.g., San Juan Islands, Washington) and the eastern seaboard (e.g., Myrtle Beach, South Carolina) have remained popular family destinations.

Hawaii became a favored tourist destination, but hard to reach, during the nineteenth century with media coverage of famous Americans such as Mark Twain and Jack London visiting. Once Hawaii was annexed by the United States in 1898, and later became a state in 1959, its popularity among American tourists increased dramatically, as it offered an opportunity to travel overseas without the need to travel abroad. With the popularization of air travel during the 1950s, travel to Hawaii grew even more. Today, Hawaii is seen as the epitome of tropical paradise in the United States, and many Americans have a lingering desire to visit the islands (Farrell 1982; Sheldon *et al.* 2005).

Because of growing demand for Hawaii's tourism product, hundreds of beachfront hotels and resorts have developed since the 1950s, and airlines have offered special prices in conjunction with hotels for tourists from the mainland. The rapid development of beach tourism in Hawaii has received considerable criticism, particularly by many Hawaiians themselves, citing a degraded Hawaiian culture, rampant crime, crowded cities, and a commodified, inauthentic portrayal of the state's culture and environment (Douglas and Douglas 1991; Liu and Var 1986).

Religious tourism

Religious tourism, or pilgrimage as it is commonly known, is a form of heritage tourism wherein people travel in search of spiritual enlightenment, to get closer to deity, gain blessings, learn about religious traditions, or fulfill a religious obligation. While this form of tourism is not as widespread in the United States as it is in other parts of the world, such as Italy, Saudi Arabia, India, or Jerusalem, it does exist and is very important for several groups of people.

While not required for their religion, Roman Catholics undertake pilgrimages to all corners of the globe, with the most well-known pilgrimage destinations located in Italy, France, Spain, Portugal, Israel, and Bosnia Herzegovina. However, there are also significant numbers of Catholic destinations, such as shrines, churches, cathedrals, and grottos, in the USA (Table 5.8) (Rinschede 1990). Although not a comprehensive list, Table 5.8 does illustrate some of the shrines and their locations, which have become important Catholic pilgrimage destinations in the USA. In addition to these shrines dedicated to saints and the Virgin Mary, there are basilicas and churches throughout the country that have also become important Catholic religious attractions in their own right (e.g., the Basilica of the National Shrine of the Immaculate Conception in Washington, DC).

Table 5.8 A selection of Catholic pilgrimage shrines in the United States

State	Shrines
Alabama	* Shrine of the Blessed Sacrament (Birmingham)
Alaska	* Shrine of Saint Therese Lisieux (Juneau)
Arizona	* Shrine of Saint Joseph of the Mountain (Yarnell)
California	* Basilica of San Carlos Borromeo (Carmel)
	* National Shrine of St Francis of Assisi (San Francisco)
Colorado	* Mother Cabrini Shrine (San Louis)
Connecticut	* Shrine to Our Lady of Lourdes (Litchfield)
Florida	* Mary, Queen of the Universe Shrine (Orlando)
	* Shrine of Our Lady of Charity (Miami)
	* Shrine of Our Lady of LaLeche (St Augustine)
Georgia	* The Shrine of the Immaculate Conception (Atlanta)
Illinois	* National Shrine of Our Lady of the Snows (Belleville)
	* Dominican Shrine of St Jude (Chicago)
	* National Shrine of St. Maximilian Kolbe (Marytown)
Indiana	* Monte Casino Shrine (St Meinrad)
	* National Shrine of Our Lady of Providence (St Mary)
	* Seven Dolors Shrine (Valparaiso)
Iowa	* The Grotto of the Redemption (West Bend)
Kansas	* Shrine of Saint Philippine Duchesne (Mound City)
Kentucky	* Lourdes Rosary Shrine (Louisville)
	* Shrine of the Little Flower (Southgate)
	* Shrine of Our Lady of Guadalupe (Carlisle)
Louisiana	* Saint Anne National Shrine (Metairie)
	* Shrine of Our Lady of Prompt Succor (New Orleans)
	* International Shrine of Saint Jude (New Orleans)
Maryland	* Basilica and Shrine of the Assumption of the Blessed Virgin Mary (Baltimore)
	* National Shrine Grotto of Lourdes (Emmitsburg)
	* St. Francis Xavier Shrine (Warwick)
Massachusetts	* Madonna, Queen of the Universe National Shrine (Boston)
	* St. Joseph the Worker Shrine (Lowell)
	* Basilica and Shrine of Our Lady of Perpetual Help (Roxbury)
Michigan	* Shrine of Saint Anne (Detroit)
	* Shrine of St Jude (Detroit)
	* National Shrine of the Little Flower (Detroit)
Minnesota	* National Shrine of Saint Odilia (Onamia)
Missouri	* National Shrine of Our Lady of the Miraculous Medal (Perryville)

Table 5.8 continued

State	Shrines
	* Shrine of Saint Philippine Duchesne (St. Charles)
	* Shrine of Saint Joseph (St. Louis)
New Hampshire	* Shrine of Our Lady of Grace (Colebrook)
	* Shrine of Our Lady of La Salette (Enfield)
New Jersey	* National Shrine of Saint Gerard (Newark)
	* Saint Joseph Shrine (Sterling)
	* Shrine of the Immaculate Heart of Mary (Washington)
New Mexico	* Shrine of Our Lord of Esquipulas (Chimayo)
New York	* Our Lady of Victory Basilica and National Shrine (Lackawanna)
	* Holy Infant Jesus Shrine (North Tonawanda)
	* Saint Francis Cabrini Chapel (New York City)
Ohio	* Shrine of St. Anthony (Cincinnati)
	* Shrine of the Holy Relics (Maria Stein)
	* Saint Paul Shrine (Cleveland)
Oklahoma	* National Shrine of the Infant Jesus (Prague)
Oregon	* National Sanctuary of Our Sorrowful Mother (Portland)
Pennsylvania	* Shrine of the Sacred Hearth (Harleigh)
	* Saint Maria Goretti Shrine (Laflin)
	* Basilica of the National Shrine of Saint Anne (Scranton)
Rhode Island	* The Shrine of the Little Flower (Nasonville)
South Dakota	* Mid-America's Fatima Family Shrine (Alexandria)
Tennessee	* Shrine of Our Lady Virgin of the Poor (New Hope)
Texas	* The National Shrine of the Little Flower (San Antonio)
Vermont	* Saint Anne's Shrine (Isle La Motte)
Wisconsin	* Holy Hill Mary Help of Christians (Hubertus)
	* National Shrine of Saint Joseph (DePere)
	* Shrine of Our Lady of Guadalupe (La Crosse)

Source: National Conference of Catholic Bishops (1998); Catholicshrines.net (2009)

Other Christian groups demonstrate a remarkable tendency to visit sacred sites in much the same way Catholics do. For instance, members of the Church of Jesus Christ of Latter-day Saints (Mormons or LDS) commonly undertake journeys of a religious nature, even though pilgrimage does not constitute part of the church's official tenets. In most cases, Mormons travel to experience key locations in the development of their faith in New York, Ohio, Missouri, Illinois, Iowa, Nebraska, Wyoming, and Utah – places corresponding to the establishment of the LDS Church and its westward movement (Hudman and Jackson 1992; Olsen 2006). Like other Christians, Mormons are avid travelers to the Holy Land, but these experiences are more doctrinal in nature dealing with the life and teachings of Jesus. LDS travel in the United States is less doctrinal in nature, focusing more on the history of the church and the sacred events that occurred in various places in the east, Midwest, and western states. Perhaps the most significant Mormon religious destination today is Salt Lake City, the current headquarters of the LDS Church. Every year millions of people, primarily Mormons but many people of other faiths as well, visit Temple Square – home of the famed Salt Lake Temple and the Mormon Tabernacle. Also in close proximity are the Church Office Building, the well-known Family History Library, the Conference Center, and several other historic sites associated with the early Mormon settlement of the Great Salt Lake Valley (Olsen 2006; Otterstrom 2008).

Approximately four million people visit Temple Square each year (Olsen 2008). Many of these are LDS tourists who visit Temple Square to feel "the spirit" of the place, admire the temple, and undertake family history (genealogy) research in the Family History Library. Tens of thousands of Mormons also come from around the world to attend the semi-annual general conference located in the Conference Center near the temple. Additionally, non-Mormons visit Temple Square, typically out of curiosity about the faith, because of the historical significance of the church, and to view the interesting architecture of the temple, Tabernacle, and Assembly Hall (Hudman and Jackson 1992; Olsen 2006).

Jewish Americans are yet another group of people who undertake pilgrimage-like travel, even though their faith does not require it. In fact, outside of Jerusalem, few places, if any, are considered holy in the Jewish faith. Unlike churches, synagogues are not considered holy spaces – in fact, most holy ceremonies and celebrations take place at home (Ioannides and Cohen Ioannides 2004). Nonetheless, there is a significant amount of Jewish travel within the United States for heritage/remembrance reasons, some of which have a religious component. Historic synagogues, graves of famous rabbis, homes of well-known Jews, and museums and exhibits displaying important Judaica are examples of such places of remembrance that are popular among American Jews. One other type of Jewish travel is Jewish youth camps, especially in the eastern states. Jewish youth from all over the United States (and other parts of the world) travel to these summer camps to associate with like-minded children, to learn music and history, to read holy writings, and to reaffirm their Jewish identity through informal education (Chazan 1991; Cohen 2006).

In Closer Look Case 5.2 a short discussion on a different form of pilgrimage, namely New Age travel, is presented. The importance of Sedona, Arizona, as destination for these "new agers" is highlighted.

CLOSER LOOK CASE 5.2

New Age pilgrimage

Certain religions and denominations encourage the faithful to embark on long journeys, symbolizing perhaps the long leap of faith one has to take in order to believe in any god. For example, the ancient Greeks traveled to Delphi, which was thought to be the center of the earth; the Greek Orthodox today travel to Tinos, often making the long ascent to the church of the Virgin Mary on their knees. The church is known among the faithful for miracles and it is generally believed that the greater the suffering the more marvelous the miracle.

A non-traditional form of pilgrimage also exists in the US and centers on the New Age movement, which emphasizes the sacredness of nature, harmony of the cosmos, ancient spiritual traditions, past life regression, and self-improvement in terms of mind, body, and spirit. The New Age movement began during the 1950s and '60s in the United States and has spread rapidly throughout the developed parts of the world, most notably North America, Western Europe, the United Kingdom and Japan. New Ageism is not a formal religion in the organizational sense and has no central authority that establishes or interprets doctrine. Instead, it is a personal spiritual pursuit of well-being and oneness with the universe and utilizes beliefs related to extra-terrestrial life, indigenous knowledge and practices, and ancient mystico-spiritual systems such as druidism and other forms of paganism.

The movement is growing as more people are becoming dissatisfied with traditional religion and as people begin to realize the need to adopt a more relaxed and less harried lifestyle. This translates into significant numbers of persons traveling for health and spiritual reasons. New Agers are avid travelers, and their most sought-after destinations are those that reveal the powers of Gaia, or Mother Earth – places, or vortexes, that exhibit the highest concentrations of earth's powers. Health retreats are also extremely important and often go hand in hand with places associated with earth power. Sedona, Arizona, is informally known among New Agers as the New Age capital of the world. Sedona received this distinction because it is believed to be located at the convergence point of major vortexes, and the sacredness of the location among Native Americans attests to this assertion. Each year the community receives approximately four million tourists, many of whom fit into the category of New Age tourist. In addition, New Agers comprise one of Sedona's largest population cohorts as they move to the town to be close to their spiritual center, and much of the local economy is dependent upon this form of spiritual tourism.

The development of New Age tourism in Sedona and other parts of the world is not without controversy. The two most critical points of contention are conflict with Native Americans and environmental degradation. The American Indians believe the movement's adherents are misappropriating their cultural heritage (e.g., dances, music, smoke ceremonies, medicine men (shamans), and sweat lodges) without due credit and without permission. Environmental agencies in the vicinity of Sedona (e.g., National Forest Service) cite fires, prayer circles (made of arranged stones), breaking and collecting pieces of stones, and ritual litter as some of the most objectionable environmental abuses that scar the landscape and disturb the natural ecosystem of the surrounding desert.

Sources

Aldred, L. (2000) Plastic shamans and Astroturf sun dances: New Age commercialization of Native American spirituality. *American Indian Quarterly*, 24(3): 329–52.

Attix, S.A. (2002) New Age-oriented special interest travel: an exploratory study. *Tourism Recreation Research*, 27(2): 51–58.

Ivakhiv, A. (2003) Nature and self in New Age pilgrimage. *Culture and Religion*, 4(1): 93–118.

O'Neil, D.J. (2001) The New Age movement and its societal implications. *International Journal of Social Economics*, 28(5): 456–75.

Rountree, K. (2002) Goddess pilgrims as tourists: inscribing the body through sacred travel. *Sociology of Religion*, 63(4): 475–96.

Timothy, D.J. and Conover, P.J. (2006) Nature religion, self spirituality and New Age tourism. In D.J. Timothy and D.H. Olsen (eds), *Tourism, Religion and Spiritual Journeys*, pp. 139–55. London: Routledge.

Questions

1. Why is Sedona, Arizona, considered the New Age capital of the world?
2. How does New Age spiritual tourism differ from traditional religious pilgrimages?

Supporting services: accommodations

So far in this chapter discussion has centered on the sites and attractions that lure visitors. But, of course, when these visitors arrive they must also have access to a variety of supporting services, the most important of which are accommodation facilities but also eating establishments, places of entertainment (e.g., nightclubs and bars), and a variety of shops. Indeed, if a destination fails to offer a good mix of lodging facilities and places to eat, the overall quality of the visitor experience will be dampened considerably, regardless of how important the main attraction may be. Consider, for instance, a major destination like a colonial heritage village that seeks to attract a growing number of tourists. If the area where this facility is located does not have a large number of accommodation facilities, preferably catering to a broad range of market needs, or the available hotels are out of the price range of most visitors, then it is likely the destination will not flourish as well as its operators would like it to. By the same token one of the major reasons that St. Louis has never managed to be a key convention destination, despite the fact it offers a major meeting facility downtown, is that it lacks adequate accommodation capacity within its central business district and certainly does not have one major convention-oriented hotel to accommodate a high number of attendants. In other words, lodging facilities and other supporting services such as restaurants, bars, and cafes, are key ingredients to the overall survival and success of tourism within an area. This section focuses briefly on the background and current issues within the realm of tourist accommodations in the United States.

The custom of opening one's home to weary travelers dates back to the earliest colonial times in America. During the 1700s, lodging facilities were few and far between, so travelers depended on the kindness of strangers to provide a bed and breakfast for the night. During the eighteenth and nineteenth centuries, there were a limited number of stagecoach inns (some of which still survive today as inns, see Plate 5.5), which provided lodging for wayfarers along regular coach routes. They were most commonly associated with taverns and other places to eat. Following the advent of steam trains and the widespread construction of railway lines, inns and hotels became more commonplace. As cross-country railway lines were built, mega-hotels were constructed in cities and scenic areas that became important stopover points on cross-country trips.

With the arrival of the automobile, lodging facilities became even more prevalent, and most towns had at least one hotel. The use of trains and cars brought about the establishment of national park lodges – rustic cabin-like accommodations that allow visitors to be immersed in the natural environment of the place. Automobiles are to blame for the development of motels, which are truly an American phenomenon. Motel units usually have exits and direct access to the outside; motels have large parking lots, are typically organized in linear rows or L or U shapes facing a central parking area or courtyard, are rarely more than two or three stories in height, and have fewer rooms than hotels.

Motels appeared in the 1920s as long-distance highways began to develop. Their numbers grew quickly in the 1950s and '60s with the expansion of the Interstate Highway System. The motel, a shortened form of "motor hotel," was constructed along major roadways in rural areas or urban outskirts as a convenient lodging option for road-based travelers. The forerunner to today's motel was a set of separated or connected roadside cabins or tents typically referred to as a tourist camp, motor camp, auto camp, or cabin camp (Belasco 1979; Jakle *et al.* 1996). Most of these cabins were eventually connected and renamed motels. Some of these original set-ups continue to operate as roadside motels and can still be seen along the country's major highways. While thousands of these small-scale motels still remain along America's roadways and many of them continue to be operated by independent owners, a major expansion of large-scale motel

Plate 5.5 Bed and Breakfast in Mendocino, California
(Dimitri Ioannides)

chains has occurred since the 1960s. Two prominent examples are Motel 6 (part of the French-owned Accor group) and Super 8 (part of the international Wyndham group of hotels).

Today, the hotel landscape in the United States is dominated by just a handful of extremely large chain establishments, a number of which are also major players and highly visible on the global scene (Go and Pine 1995). However, it is fair to say that chain-based hotels are, overall, far more common in North America, including the USA, than in any other part of the world. These chains operate in a variety of ways, including franchise agreements and contract management (Piccoli *et al.* 2003). Though the rankings of the top fifty chains do shift somewhat from year to year, and indeed some of them are taken over by other companies on a regular basis, it is obvious that, invariably, the largest players – measured in terms of room capacity – are chains like Best Western, Choice Hotels International, and the Hilton Corporation. A relatively new hotel chain, America's Best Value Inn, has shown dramatic growth since it was first established in 1999. Between then and 2005 this company went from just five properties nationwide to 500 hotels, with more than 30,000 rooms (Watkins 2005).

Resorts constitute one of the most important modern-day lodging phenomena. Several different types of resort exist in the United States, including beach resorts, ski resorts, golf resorts, mountain resorts, theme park resorts, casino resorts, and health spa resorts. Not all of these will be examined here. In the USA, beach resorts typically include guest rooms and suites, recreational services, swimming pools, spas, game rooms, theaters, golf courses, exercise rooms, restaurants, gift shops, hairdressers, sports equipment rentals, and conference centers. Properties that provide these activities, rooms, and all meals are known as all-inclusive resorts. These are popular in places such as Florida and Hawaii. Disney Resorts (mentioned earlier) are a good example of a theme park resort, where lodging and food services are connected to amusement parks, and the parks themselves are the reason for the resorts' existence. Ski resorts are extremely popular in the Rocky Mountain states like Colorado, Utah, Wyoming, Idaho, and Montana, as well as in the Pacific Northwest (Oregon and Washington), and in the Green and White Mountains of New England (Vermont and New Hampshire). Several locations have developed into important golf resorts owing to their favorable climates. Scottsdale, Arizona, is a good example, where mild winter temperatures draw people from all around the country for golfing and good weather.

Timeshares, or vacation properties or interval ownership, are another important form of lodging in the United States and are located in resort and hotel properties all over the country. They are essentially properties of fractional ownership, wherein purchasers buy a set period of time at a given location. Although the notion of timeshares originated in Europe in the 1960s, it was incubated and developed in the United States, especially in Florida during the 1960s and in Hawaii in the 1970s. Timeshares are located in areas of high amenity, such as beaches and mountains, and each unit is self-contained with appliances, bedding, cooking and eating utensils, and many leisure accoutrements.

Since the early days of timeshares, there has been an evolution in ownership programs. The traditional one-week deeded ownership at a specific property has given way to various other programs, whereby consumers purchase a floating week or points, not attached to a single property. This allows more freedom to choose a vacation destination as points are accrued and spent, depending on time and location. According to the American Resort Development Association (2008), in 2008 6.5 million timeshare intervals and 180,158 units were owned throughout the USA. The top three timeshare destinations are Florida, California and South Carolina.

Recreational second homes have long been an important part of culture in some parts of the world (e.g., the Nordic countries) and exist in the domain of common folks. In the United States, however, second homes have traditionally been the domain of the wealthy and still are to a degree. Nonetheless, more sectors of the population have gained access to recreational homes during the past quarter century as property costs have remained relatively low, as family incomes have grown with more disposal income, and interest payments on second homes can even be used as a tax deduction. These and other factors have brought about more widespread ownership of second home properties in the USA. Like timeshares, which many see as a form of second home, recreational second homes are usually located in areas of high amenity, such as lakeshores, oceanfronts, or mountains (see Chapter 9). According to the US Census Bureau (2008) there were nearly 4.4 million seasonal/recreational homes in the United States in 2007.

Another aspect of this phenomenon is the seasonal migration of "snowbirds," or retirees, from the north to the southern states during the winter months. Cities such as Mesa, Arizona, where dozens of mobile home parks and retirement communities swell, often doubling or tripling in population during the winter, are economically highly dependent upon the seasonal second home owners who come from Canada and the northern states to enjoy the warm southern winters. Florida, Texas, Arizona, and California are among the most favored snowbird destinations (McHugh 2006).

Of all forms of accommodation in the United States, timeshares and second homes have seen the most controversy. During the 1960s and 1970s, second home developers took advantage of consumers by selling low-quality properties on land that was not properly surveyed or deeded, or to which utilities could not readily be extended. Fortunately, most municipality and state governments have cracked down on these types of dishonest dealings by improving zoning ordinances and subdividing more thoroughly (Timothy 2004).

Additionally, unscrupulous and high-pressure sales tactics have long plagued the time-share sector, particularly during the late 1970s and 1980s. Problematic management approaches and negative media exposure have tarnished the image of timeshares. This is particularly well illustrated in the false sales claims, which indicated that timeshares were guaranteed to appreciate in value as a real estate investment. In fact, this rarely happened. Other questionable claims were made by salespeople. For instance, they maintained that through renting out the timeshare the pay-off period could be shortened considerably. This, however, was not substantiated. As a result of public outcry and negative media exposure, federal and state governments enacted laws to crack down on dishonesty and overblown claims in the timeshare sector (Timothy 2004).

A word about travel intermediaries

A significant aspect of the travel and tourism industry are the so-called intermediaries, namely companies responsible for distributing the products of various travel providers (e.g., airlines, hotels, and the cruise industry) to consumers. These intermediaries include tour wholesalers, "brick-and-mortar" travel agencies, and Global Distribution Systems. Additionally, the advent of new information technologies, including the Internet but also other platforms such as mobile devices, has meant that online agencies and various other electronic distribution channels have appeared that allow consumers to by-pass the traditional intermediaries.

Generally speaking, tour wholesalers in the United States are not the giant companies seen in Europe (Ioannides 1998). Indeed, Ioannides and Daughtrey (2006) reveal that of the 3,200 tour operating companies listed in the *County Business Patterns* (US Census Bureau 2004) only two had more than 1,000 employees. This phenomenon can be partially explained by the fact that within the United States the demand by Americans for package tours, where all the components of travel (e.g., flight, accommodations, and tours) are placed in to a single product is far less common than it has been in other parts of the world (Lenhart 2004).

Nevertheless, there are several companies throughout the country that organize tours (many of them guided) both to other countries and also within various parts of the United States. A glance at the United States Tour Operators' Association website reveals several companies (46 full members) that collectively carry about 11 million passengers per year and account for $9 billion in annual revenues (USTOA website 2009). Some of these companies aim towards the luxury market; for instance, Tauck World Discovery offers organized tours to places like Cape Cod, the southern United States, Hawaii, and Alaska in addition to arranging trips to various other parts of the world. A trip for eight days to Michigan's lakes and Mackinac Island runs at about $2,400 per person. Though no detailed examinations of the share of the market that is accounted for domestic travel by American tour operators appear to exist, it is obvious that only a tiny portion of US citizens take advantage of such organized tours. Many of these people are retirees, most of whom appear to be fairly well off.

Even though Americans do not make major use of tour operators, especially in comparison to Europeans or the Japanese, in the past a very large number of people did rely on travel agencies to take care of their trip arrangements. In essence, while the tour operators function as wholesalers, packaging the various aspects of the trip into one product, the travel agencies are the retailers, where one can purchase airline tickets but also tour packages and other elements associated with travel (e.g., travel insurance and car rental). According to the Bureau of Labor Statistics (2009: n.p.) among others,

> travel agents help travelers sort through vast amounts of information to help them make the best possible travel arrangement. They offer advice on destinations and make arrangements for transportation, hotel accommodations, car rentals, and tours for their clients. They are also the primary source of bookings for most of the major cruise lines.

Yet, in the last few years this sector has undergone massive transformation for numerous reasons, the most important one being the appearance of the Internet. Additionally, the reduction and eventual loss of commissions from airlines that began occurring during the 1990s effectively removed one of the major if not the only sources of income for these companies and essentially signified economic ruin for many. Most agencies that survived were also forced to institute fees for their services to their clients and this was a hard pill to swallow for many consumers who had become used to what had been effectively in the past a free service. Thus, not surprisingly, many people – especially leisure-oriented travelers – have now turned to the Internet to make their travel arrangements (Ioannides and Daughtrey 2006) (see Closer Look Case 5.3 for a closer glimpse into the fate on travel agents).

CLOSER LOOK CASE 5.3

Travel agents: the voice at the other end of the line (an insider's perspective)

I was a travel agent in the late nineties. It was fairly easy to get a job working for a travel agency then. At the time, I had neither a university degree nor had I been to travel college. My previous employer was an airline company and that was the extent of my training in travel. I was hired by the local outfit and became a corporate travel consultant, meaning I booked neither Caribbean cruises, nor packages to Cancun. Instead, my mandate was to book air, car, and hotel for business travelers. Effectively, this meant I had to be a genius at reading my clients' minds, constantly seeking to book them into the hotel they wanted even when this was sold out, obtaining upgrades when none could be found and generally trying to surpass their secretary in making them happy.

Most of my colleagues were women, like me. Our boss was male. This was very much a feminized profession due to its low entry barriers and glamorized image based on erstwhile times. Though women did own small and medium-sized travel agencies and, occasionally, even big ones, and were represented in the higher strata of large travel companies, the norm was that the front-line workers were women whereas higher management was male-dominated.

Some of my colleagues were paid on commission. I was an hourly worker, not well paid at that – a consequence of feminized professions. Things got more difficult for the travel agencies when airlines lowered and capped the commissions they offered to travel agents for issuing their tickets. In 1994, commissions dropped from the 10 percent uncapped arrangement, which had been the norm for a long time, to 8 percent. These commissions were then capped to $100 for international tickets and $50 for domestic in 1997. By 2002 commissions had been reduced to zero. The fax announcing the cuts would always come to the office at 5 p.m. or later and the changes would be effective as of the following morning. One airline would take the lead (they would take turns) and then the rest would follow. In 2002 all the carriers blamed 9/11, but the truth is they had started the campaign to eradicate travel agencies long before that. The joke was that in the end the airlines would charge travel agents for selling their tickets. In 2004 that joke became almost a reality when Northwest tried to institute a per-ticket-issued fee to the travel agents. Northwest's attempt failed, but it illustrates the lengths the carriers were willing to go to push the consumers to book online by eliminating travel agencies altogether.

A lot of small, brick-and-mortar agencies were indeed eliminated. They could not keep up with the larger agencies which were still getting back-end commissions based on large sales volume. This meant fewer choices for the consumer and a lot of agents without a job. Additionally, Global Distributions Systems (GDSs) started moving to a point-and-click format. This made it easy for big travel companies to hire unskilled workers and pay them very little and for airlines to outsource their reservations function overseas, also hiring unskilled workers and paying minimal rates.

The company I worked for was one of the agencies which did not make it. We closed our doors in 2004. I found a job with an Internet company selling mostly hotels, but I was laid off after six months because they could no longer afford me. If I wanted to stay in the travel business my choices were limited: I could (a) become an "independent contractor" meaning I would have to pay the only travel agency in town left standing to have access to a GDS; it also meant I had to have had a loyal and broad client base; (b) take a considerable pay cut to go with an equally considerable demotion and work for that same agency; or (c) move in search of job.

I chose to leave travel for good. As far as I was concerned the airlines had won the war and I was not interested in the aftermath. Some of my friends and former colleagues still sell travel, occasionally to me. I still prefer to talk to (or e-mail) a knowledgeable and experienced person to arrange my often complicated tickets than go to a mega site and deal with its biases and preferred airlines. Even after all these years I still think travel agents are the human side of travel retail and don't mind paying a booking fee for their service.

Questions

1. Have you ever used a travel agent for your travel arrangements? Why or why not? Have your parents done so? Do you believe that different generations may have different attitudes towards the use of technology as it relates to making travel arrangements?
2. Is there any type of travel arrangement that you think would benefit from the knowledge of a travel agent? Consider, for example, a simple round trip flight to see your friends versus a cruise or a package tour.

Evangelia Petridou

One outcome of these phenomena has been the disappearance of thousands of small-scale travel agencies, while at the other end of the spectrum there has been phenomenal concentration with the largest companies (especially those with more than $100 million per annum) accounting for a major portion of the market. According to Ioannides and Daughtrey (2006), a few years ago the top thirteen travel agencies in the USA had incomes of over $1 billion each while the industry constantly experiences a series of mergers and acquisitions. The Bureau of Labor Statistics (2009) maintains that in the near future, employment in the travel agency sector is unlikely to show any major shifts. The travel agents who will survive, according to the BLS, will be those offering complex transactions that the average travelers cannot easily solve themselves. Additionally, the BLS also suggests that travel agencies that emerge as specialists offering unique travel experiences both domestically and abroad are likely to be the ones that flourish.

Concluding remarks

America's large size and its expansive resource base have allowed it to rise to prominence as one of the pre-eminent destinations in the world. This chapter has highlighted several of the main types of tourism that have developed since the country's foundation in the late 1700s and early 1800s. By a long way, cultural heritage and nature are the primary resource bases for tourism, although it is probably safe to suggest that the most common form of tourism is visiting friends and relatives (VFR). Of course, this type of tourism is practically impossible to measure since people typically stay with acquaintances and not in official accommodation establishments; nevertheless its apparent importance in economic terms should not be underestimated. For instance, one has to take into account the money that goes into the trip whether this is by air or by car and, of course, the spending en-route on food, gasoline, and other items.

The limitations of space have not allowed an expansive examination of all major forms of tourism in the United States in this chapter, although several important ones have been highlighted. Other extremely important forms of tourism, including business travel and convention attendance, have not been covered, but this does not mean their significance should be underestimated. Indeed, business-related tourism constitutes a very important segment of the travel market, and airlines would be in an even more dire economic condition than they currently are (see Chapter 6) if it were not for this form of travel. Additionally, especially for many major metropolitan regions, business tourism constitutes a significant portion of their tourism economy and it is no wonder, as seen in Chapter 8, that these localities invest heavily in the construction of convention centers and exhibition halls.

Another form of tourism that is also enormously important but has not been discussed is retail-oriented travel. Consider, for instance, the enormous number of people who shop when they are on holiday in cities like Boston, Chicago, and San Francisco. Even though they could probably find much of the merchandise available in their hometown mall there is an added experiential element that comes with buying items from a department store on Michigan Avenue in Chicago or Macy's in New York. Also, there are places like the Mall of America near Minneapolis, which draws more visitors than Disney World (Timothy 2005b). These visitors include Americans but also numerous foreigners (e.g., Canadians, Japanese, and Britons), many of whom travel specifically for the purpose of shopping at the Mall of America and the outlet malls scattered throughout the country.

Additional reasons for travel that have not been explored in detail here include the wish to attend a sports event or a rock concert. One only has to look at the impact that the American football Super Bowl has annually on the host city. Even college sports can be very important for certain communities. For instance, it is common for cities to compete to become the venue for the final playoffs in college basketball given the enormous draw these events have.

Beyond the attractions that bring the visitors to particular places in the first place, this chapter has also investigated some of the forms of lodging that are available for them.

Significantly, the point has been made that without a good range of accommodations, catering to a variety of market niches, many tourist destinations would suffer. However, it should also be borne in mind that the accommodations are a supporting service, playing a secondary role to the main reason for the trip. In some cases, especially when the accommodation is within the setting of a resort offering the possibility to enjoy many amenities on-site, then it can become the central reason for the trip.

The final portion of the chapter looked at travel intermediaries, highlighting the role they can play in distributing the various elements that make up the travel experience. Today, most Americans do not make much use of tour operators, preferring instead to arrange the various portions of the trip themselves. Certainly the rise of the use of the Internet and the appearance of popular publications like *Lonely Planet*, have helped them in this endeavor. Having said this, however, what about travel agencies that once provided an extremely useful service in terms of booking airline tickets and/or accommodations? It is evident that this sector has also undergone massive transformation in the last few years, and yet there are signs that certain agencies will linger on for a while to come, especially if they start to offer specialized services or make complicated travel arrangements, while making use themselves of online packaging and distribution tools (Ioannides and Daughtrey 2006).

Questions

1. How important is heritage tourism in the United States? What types of heritage tourism exist throughout the country?
2. In what ways has the Native American culture of the United States been portrayed as a tourism product? What are some of the most important controversies associated with tourism in Native American lands?
3. How do several communities throughout the United States celebrate their ethnic heritage? Give examples.
4. What are the pros and cons of casinos as an economic development tool?
5. Given that the American lodging industry is dominated by major chains, how can an independent hotel of medium size survive? In other words, what strategies are at the disposal of the owner of such a hotel to ensure that it does not go out of business?

Further reading

Christodoulidou, N., Brewer, P. and Countryman, C.C. (2007) Travel intermediaries and metasites: a comparison of customer perception. *Information Technology and Tourism*, 9(3/4): 227–43.

Davis, J., Jackson, M. and Jackson, R. (2009) Heritage tourism and group identity: Polynesians in the American west. *Journal of Heritage Tourism*, 4(1): 3–17.

Gallardo, J.H. and Stein, T.V. (2007) Participation, power and racial representation: negotiating nature-based and heritage tourism development in the rural south. *Society and Natural Resources*, 20(7): 597–611.

Hazen, H. (2009) Valuing natural heritage: park visitors' values related to world heritage sites in the USA. *Current Issues in Tourism*, 12(2): 165–81.

Piner, J.M. and Paradis, T.W. (2004) Beyond the casino: sustainable tourism and cultural development on Native American lands. *Tourism Geographies*, 6(1): 80–98.

Scarinci, J. and Richins, H. (2008) Specialist lodging in the USA: motivations of bed and breakfast accommodation guests. *Tourism*, 56(3): 271–82.

Vallen, G., Cothran, C.C. and Combrink, T.E. (1998) Indian gaming – are tribal employees being promoted to management positions in Arizona casinos? *Cornell Hotel and Restaurant Administration Quarterly*, 39(4): 56–63.

Weaver, D.B. and Lawton, L.J. (2008) Not just surviving, but thriving: perceived strengths of successful US-based travel agencies. *International Journal of Tourism Research*, 10(1): 41–53.

Wolfe, K., Kang, S.K. and Hsu, C.H.C. (2005) Identifying travel agent user segments. *Journal of Hospitality and Leisure Marketing*, 12(4): 73–92.

World Tourism Organization (2002) *The US Ecotourism Market*. Madrid: UNWTO.

Useful Internet resources

American Hotel and Lodging Association: www.ahla.com/
American Society of Travel Agents: http://www.asta.org/
Bureau of Land Management: http://www.blm.gov/wo/st/en.html
Indian Casinos: http://www.indiancasinos.com/
International Association of Amusement Parks and Attractions: http://www.iaapa.org/
International Ecotourism Society: http://www.ecotourism.org
Institute for Theme Park Studies: http://www.themeparkcity.com/itps/index.htm
Museums Association: http://www.museumsassociation.org/ma/10295
National Indian Gaming Commission: http://www.nigc.gov/
National Restaurant Association: http://www.restaurant.org/
Riverboat Casinos: http://www.riverboatcasinos.com/
United States Tour Operators Association: http://www.ustoa.com/index.cfm
US Forest Service: http://www.fs.fed.us/
US National Park Service: http://www.nps.gov/
World Religious Travel Association: http://www.religioustravelassociation.com/

6 The transportation system

> Motoring at first suggested a wanderlust where grass always seemed greener over the distant hill, a kind of independence, a freedom to get to places not only quickly but essentially under one's own direction. Motoring spoke of mobility not just geographical in nature but social as well. Motoring became the travel response not only to what Americans called the open road, a place of important opportunity.
>
> (Jakle and Sculle 2008: 2)

Introduction

Tourism in the United States has been successful largely because of the accessibility of its natural and cultural resources. The country's transportation network is among the best in the world, but it differs from other countries in a variety of ways. Despite being a vast country there are relatively few places within the United States, with the exception of large portions of Alaska, that remain entirely inaccessible to motorized traffic. This is unlike the countries of Europe, which are on the whole small compared to the USA, and Asia, Africa and Latin America where large regions are inaccessible to the masses owing to impenetrable natural landscapes and vegetation, or government-imposed restrictions. In many parts of the world the physical isolation of large areas (e.g., the Amazon rainforest of Brazil; the arctic regions of Canada; the mountains of South and Southeast Asia; and the deserts of North Africa) precludes the development of roadways, railway lines, and other travel infrastructure. These conditions tend to be less consequential in the United States.

The USA differs from other countries also in that the majority of Americans rely on their own transportation (i.e., private cars) to get from place to place; public transportation is much less popular than in other parts of the world and is sometimes stigmatized as the preferred transport mode of the less affluent social classes or overly green-conscious individuals (Glaeser *et al.* 2008; Jones and Rice 1979; Steel 1996). In spite of these traditional connotations, commuter buses and trains in large urban areas have become popular modes of inner-urban transportation. However, comparatively few places outside the major metropolitan regions are serviced by passenger trains or long-distance coaches, and many Americans prefer it to remain that way. While air travel is an increasingly popular mode of long-distance transportation, private vehicles remain an important part of the mix and are still the favored method of getting around.

The previous chapter highlighted the wide array of salient resources, destinations, attractions, and tourism types in the US today. However, it is obvious that successful tourism cannot exist without appropriate transportation to and from the destination. Therefore, this chapter argues that transportation has been vital to the development of tourism in the United States. Additionally, innovations in transportation have at times been a key factor in determining the rise of new destinations and, in certain instances, the fall of others.

The chapter examines accessibility through transportation as a critical element of the supply-side of tourism. It first highlights rail transport, followed by road-based transportation, air travel, and water-based travel, including cruises. Each of these is examined within the broader historical and socio-economic context that affects the forms and functions of transportation in the USA today.

Rail

Earlier, in Chapter 2, we discussed how the arrival of the railroad during the 1830s and its large-scale diffusion throughout the rest of the nineteenth century played a major role in opening up new destinations around the United States and encouraging an increasing number of people to go on holiday to various places including the newly established national parks. To be sure, the railroad was a key force that fueled the early growth of American tourism. Even though today the importance of railway travel for holidays has been eclipsed dramatically by air and motorcar travel, it is still important to offer some discussion about this mode of transportation.

The use of trains for transporting coal and limestone began in the 1790s in the United Kingdom. Originally, trains were pulled on their tracks by horses, but after James Watt invented a steam engine in 1782 that was capable of turning wheels, the first steam-powered locomotive was put into use in 1804, and in 1807 the first official steam-powered rail passenger service began in Wales and was known as the Mumbles Train (Rogers 1995). These breakthroughs facilitated faster travel that could cover longer distances. After the turn of the nineteenth century, trains became an increasingly popular method of transporting minerals from the mines to the smelting operations, and several passenger services were initiated in the UK and Continental Europe in the early 1800s.

In the United States, rail transportation essentially began in 1827, with the establishment of the Baltimore and Ohio Railroad (B&O), which connected Baltimore and Washington, DC. While earlier "gravity railroads" were used intermittently for transporting coal and ore, the B&O is usually regarded as the first steam-powered passenger service in the US. During the 1830s, additional passenger lines were added in the eastern portions of the country in states such as Alabama, New York, Pennsylvania, and New Jersey (Jensen 1993; Poor 1970). On May 10, 1869, the railway systems of the Union Pacific and the Central Pacific railroad companies were joined at Promontory Summit, Utah, linking the railway lines of the east to California in the west. This created the first coast-to-coast transcontinental railway line, which was extremely pivotal in the settlement and development of the American West (Williams 1996). The continued development of railroads throughout the late nineteenth and early twentieth century was a key factor in the development of cities on the east and west coasts (Duval 2007; Jenks 1944) and was crucial to the growth of famous coastal resorts such as Atlantic City, New Jersey, and Ocean City, Maryland (Stansfield 1978, 2004). Trains made these shoreline areas more accessible to the bourgeoning cities of the northeast, including Baltimore, New York City, Washington, and Philadelphia, where growing urban populations sought reprieves from the crowds via weekend getaways and longer vacations to the coast.

Train travel remained popular until the mid-1900s. However, its popularity waned considerably with the increase of private automobile ownership by American families, beginning from the 1920s onwards, and the advent of the Eisenhower Interstate Highway System, which developed during the 1950s and '60s. Likewise, larger, more efficient

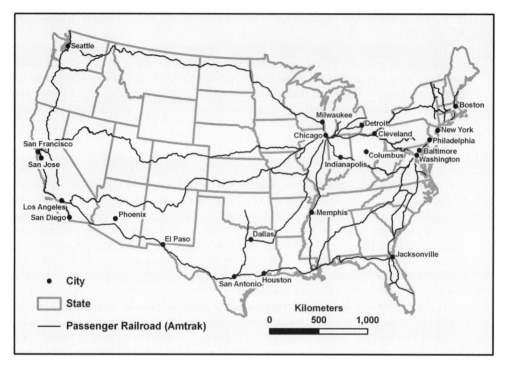

Figure 6.1 Passenger rail network in the United States
Source: after Federal Railroad Administration

airliners were also put into use following the Second World War, reducing time and cost for medium- and long-distance travel, which effectively popularized air travel.

These factors contributed to the wide-scale demise of rail-based travel in the United States during the twentieth century while, at the same time, it was growing in many other parts of the world. Consequently, between 1947 and 1971, the number of train passenger-miles had decreased by nearly ten times, from 40 billion to 4.4 billion (Baron 1990). In an effort to salvage passenger railway service, the federal government in 1970 enacted the Rail Passenger Service Act, which established the National Railroad Passenger Corporation (Amtrak) to oversee and subsidize the railroad sector. Amtrak, a government-owned company that provides the only transcontinental passenger rail service in the United States, serves a modest 21,000 miles of railroad in 46 of the 48 contiguous states (see Figure 6.1). Around 530 communities in all are serviced by this network, including 180 destinations in non-metropolitan (rural) counties (Brown 1998). Brown argues that "in many of these smaller towns, especially those without commercial air service, passenger rail is the only mode of public transportation available other than intercity buses" (1998: 13). Of course, most of the busiest train stations are in densely populated urban regions, including parts of the northeast and the upper Midwest, most notably the Chicago area. Table 6.1 shows the ten busiest train stations in the United States. Approximately 78,000 people utilize Amtrak links each day; during the fiscal year 2008, 28.7 million passenger trips were taken on Amtrak-operated trains (Amtrak 2008). This represents an increase over the 2007 fiscal year and the sixth consecutive year of growth. This growth likely reflects people's choice to ride the train owing to the enormous rising cost of gasoline and operating personal vehicles during the past few years and increasing expenses associated with airplane travel.

Table 6.1 The ten busiest Amtrak train stations in the US, 2008

Station	Tickets from	Tickets to	Total passengers
New York, NY	4,384,803	4,354,542	8,739,345
Washington, DC	2,258,113	2,231,842	4,489,955
Philadelphia, PA	1,984,998	1,983,280	3,968,278
Chicago, IL	1,548,101	1,556,050	3,104,151
Los Angeles, CA	787,707	794,657	1,582,364
Boston, MA	693,281	700,410	1,393,691
Sacramento, CA	578,957	567,351	1,146,308
Baltimore, MD	507,929	512,375	1,020,304
San Diego, CA	466,448	445,648	912,096
Albany-Rensselaer, NY	416,711	414,029	830,740

Source: Amtrak (2008)

Amtrak has undergone significant scrutiny and criticism since its founding in 1970. One of the most persistent complaints has been that the company operates annually at a significant monetary loss, and in fact it has not once generated a profit in all the years it has been operating (Baron 1990; Timothy 2006b). In 2008, Amtrak earned $2.45 billion in revenue, but its expenditures in the same year were $3.38 billion. The heavy subsidization, which began in the early 1970s, continues to this day. Many persons, who do not utilize the trains, complain that Amtrak is a waste of taxpayer dollars, which could be put to better use on other public programs rather than accruing additional public debt for a transportation option that relatively few Americans utilize.

Currently, most rail travel occurs in the northeastern megalopolitan region (Boston, New York, Baltimore, Washington, Philadelphia), where some 2,600 commuter trains operate every day. More than one third of Amtrak's passenger trips occur in the northeast region. Long distance rail travel in the United States is popular among some groups of people, although Amtrak argues that its customers are not just the less affluent who cannot afford air tickets. Instead, these passengers represent a wide range of people, including business travelers seeking other options besides air and automobile. In addition, many cross-country trips are seen by the public as a complete vacation experience. It is not uncommon for people from the east coast or vice versa to purchase a coast-to-coast ticket and return to their origin by air. These types of trips allow people to experience pristine parts of the country, particularly the mountains, which few car-based travelers are able to access (Stover 1997).

There has also been a significant growth of heritage railways catering specifically to tourists/recreationists and hobbyists. In most cases, these use old and well-known rail routes that have been resurrected to become heritage attractions and heritage experiences in their own right. Often heritage railways are associated with mining operations, the settlement of certain parts of the country, or well-established historic routes in areas of high natural or cultural amenity. One such historic railroad is the Grand Canyon Railway, which was originally established in 1901 to carry ore from mines to processors. However, the Topeka & Santa Fe Railway Company realized the potential for tourism to supplement their mining income, so they began hauling passengers from Flagstaff to the canyon for a small fee of $3.95. The Grand Canyon Railway was instrumental in the development of tourism at Grand Canyon National Park and in northern Arizona in general. The train ceased operating in 1968 owing to decreased demand as passengers wanted to experience the "road trip" in their own automobiles. In 1989, however, entrepreneurs purchased the railway and began offering passenger services once again. The Grand Canyon Railway is popular as a way of experiencing nature and seeing the canyon in comfort.

Plate 6.1 Katy Trail, Missouri – A Rails-to-Trails attraction
(Dimitri Ioannides)

Today, Grand Canyon Railway provides a historic and fun journey to the canyon with the help of authentic western characters who bring the Old West to life. Moreover, the train whose fate seemed sealed when it was shut down due to the popularity of automobiles, is now responsible for keeping approximately 50,000 cars outside of the national treasure.

(Grand Canyon Railway 2009: n.p.)

While the significance of rail travel in the United States has waned considerably over the last six decades, it is interesting to note that the abandoned rail corridors throughout many parts of the country are now often re-utilized as greenways, or recreational paths that have become popular with hikers, cyclists, cross-country skiers, and in some instances horseback riders. The piece of legislation that has allowed this change in use of rail-corridors to greenways is known as the Rails-to-Trails Act, which was passed in 1983. The actual Rails-to-Trails program has been in existence since 1986 (Brown 1998, 1999). According to Allen (2003), thousands of miles of recreational trails have resulted from this legislation, and these resources are used by millions of people each year. Closer Look Case 6.1 offers a glimpse into the manner in which trails resulting from the Rails-to-Trails Act have benefited regional communities (see Plate 6.1) (also Figure 6.2).

CLOSER LOOK CASE 6.1

Corridors for trains no more: Rails-to-Trails and tourism

The Rails-to-Trails program is a kind of adaptive recycling for defunct railroad tracks. Essentially this law (also known as the Rail-banking Act), which was passed in the early 1980s, allows states to take over abandoned rail corridors and put them into greenway (recreational trail) use. The idea is that effectively the railroad maintains the right of way and if it ever wishes to reintroduce rail service it can easily retake the corridor and put it back into use. In other words, utilizing the right of way for recreational purposes could be temporary (Ferster 2006).

One of the linear parks created by this act, the Katy Trail, is one of the longest recreational corridors in the United States. It covers 225 miles (362 kilometers) and runs from Clinton, Missouri, in the west to Saint Charles, Missouri, in the east. Much of the trail follows the Missouri River and crosses through several communities, including Jefferson City, the state capital. Over the years numerous communities that are on or close to the Katy Trail have taken advantage of this facility to promote their tourism industry. Essentially, small towns like Boonville and Augusta, Missouri, have witnessed the conversion of buildings into bed and breakfast establishments, while local entrepreneurs have opened cafés and restaurants, and have established bicycle repair and rental shops. These businesses cater to hundreds of visitors, many of whom are on a multi-day cycling trip along the trail.

A typical trip for the more adventurous rider is to begin from Sedalia, Missouri, and ride all the way to Saint Charles, a trip that for the average rider takes several days to complete. Along the way, one can eat and sleep at many of the dedicated establishments. One can even stop at one of the various wineries and sample the local fare while catching a glimpse of a glorious sunset. Once the entire trip is completed, the rider can then hop on an Amtrak train with her bike in Kirkwood and return to Sedalia to retrieve her parked car. Other less ambitious riders may only use a section of the trail for a shorter period of time. In the meantime many locals also take full advantage of the trail for bike rides, walks, or for jogging.

The Katy Trail is far from unique. Throughout the United States numerous recreational corridors have been created on the site of abandoned railroads. The agency responsible for overseeing rails-to-trails corridors like the Katy Trail indicated that there were almost 1,400 such trails nationwide, covering a total of approximately 15,000 miles.

Trails such as the Katy Trail have become wonderful recreational amenities for millions of Americans around the nation. First, residents in thousands of communities can take advantage of being close to such corridors and can use them daily for exercise and/or relaxation. Meanwhile, a number of these linear parks offer people the chance to cycle safely from community to community, sometimes for tens or even hundreds of miles and this has had an enormous effect in boosting cycling tourism nationwide. In turn, many communities, many of them smaller towns that lie on or close to such trails, find themselves in a position to capitalize on these linear parks by stimulating a tourism trade based on the users of the trails.

It is rather ironic, then, that although there has been a major decline in passenger rail transportation in the United States over the last several decades, many people are making use of trails that run exactly where railway tracks used to be. In the old days, trains transported millions of Americans, many of whom were traveling for recreational purposes. Today, the mode of transportation is far slower and much quieter than in the past and most riders cover only a fraction of the distance their ancestors did. The purpose of the trip has also likely changed. Nowadays it is more about the actual activity of cycling or walking, and the destinations serve mostly as places for rest and relaxation after a hard day's travel. In the past the route was a means to get to the destination, although the experience of riding the train, especially for the novice, undoubtedly held a lot of charm.

It remains to be seen whether the railroad will ever make a comeback as a major means of transporting tourists throughout the country. Certainly, the advent of high-speed rail in some countries has initiated some proposals to introduce updated rail systems in the United States, though this initiative is still at a very early stage. If it ever does take root it is likely that at least some of the trails that have been created courtesy of the Rails-to-Trails program will be turned back to the railroad once more.

Sources

Ferster, A.C. (2006) Commentary: Rails-to-Trails conversions: A review of legal issues. *American Planning Association – Planning and Environmental Law* 58(9): 3–9.
BikeKatyTrail.com (2009) Katy Trail Missouri: Maps, Services, Events, Towns and More. Available from www.bikekatytrail.com (accessed April 22, 2009).

Questions

1. There has been increasing news coverage about the possibility of introducing high-speed rail for travel, at least in certain regions of the United States. If this were to happen it would likely mean that a number of trails that have been created through the Rails-to-Trails legislation will have to revert to the railways. What would be the outcome of such a move? Do you think there would be a lot of opposition? If so, what would the opponents of the project say? How would you convince these opponents that the introduction of high-speed rail service would be a positive move despite the loss of a recreational amenity?
2. Look up the term "Greenway Corridor." How many different types of greenways are there? What do you think their main value is for the communities they pass through?

Road-based travel

Despite all the other modes of transportation that exist in the United States, road travel is fundamentally the most popular method of getting around. In fact, as Jakle and Sculle maintain, it is "the taking of trips [that] first made motoring an American obsession . . . The intrigue of adventure, the pleasure of being liberated from normal routines, and the sense of being in command of one's vehicle conspired to endear Americans to motoring" (2008: 24). Importantly, most Americans will drive to their holiday destination, especially when this is no more than 500 miles from home. However, if the traffic during holiday seasons such as Thanksgiving, Memorial and Labor Days, and the 4th of July is anything to go by, many people choose to drive long-distance (e.g., cross-country or from the Northeast to Florida) when the opportunity arises.

As of 2006, there were 4.017 million miles of paved roads in the USA and 135.4 million passenger cars; the average American household owned between two and three

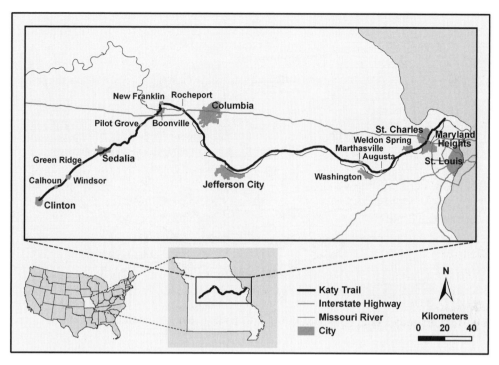

Figure 6.2 Katy Trail, Missouri: a Rails-to-Trails project in the heartland
Sources: after Missouri Department of Natural Resources. http://www.msdis.missouri.edu and US Census Bureau

automobiles, and 1.68 trillion miles were driven in passenger cars. In addition to private cars, there were 6.69 million motorcycles and 822,000 buses on America's highways in 2006 (Bureau of Transportation Statistics 2008).

This preponderance of road-based travel can be attributed to several influential factors, three of which are described here. First, American society has become extremely affluent over the past five decades, compared to other parts of the world. The exception to this has been the financial crisis of 2007–9 (which, at the time of writing, is ongoing), which has brought about the repossession of many people's homes and automobiles. Related to this is an increasing level of materialism in the USA, as personal vehicles become a sign of prestige and social standing. Relative affluence and materialism have resulted in millions of families purchasing multiple vehicles, increasing numbers of miles traveled each year, and the growth of drive tourism.

A second influential factor is an extensive highway system that has grown pervasively since the 1950s with the development of the Eisenhower Interstate Highway System. This was approved for construction by US Congress in 1956 and started shortly thereafter. The interstate highways are part of America's four million miles of paved roads. These major motorways total some 46,876 miles in 49 of the 50 states (see Figure 6.3). Until the 1950s, the road system in the United States was a network of a few well-paved roads but many more poorly paved back roads, country lanes, and gravel tracks (Gunn 2004). The freeways and highways proposed in the 1956 Federal Aid Highway Act and built between the 1960s and 2000s have improved the transportation of goods, strengthened the supply chain system, and made Americans one of the most mobile populations on earth (Lewis 1999).

A third influential variable is Americans' sense of personal independence. As noted in the introduction, there has traditionally been an underlying prejudice against utilizing

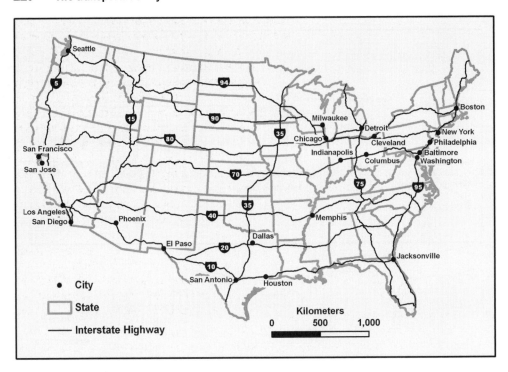

Figure 6.3 Major interstate highways in the United States

public transportation. This derives from several origins, one being that public transport is seen as the poor person's way of getting around. But perhaps even more influential is the idea that personal vehicles increase personal freedom – individuals can go wherever they want, they can make refreshment or meal stops whenever they desire, they are not required to live up to someone else's schedule or itinerary, and they can customize their vehicles according to their own tastes and comfort levels. In the minds of many Americans, personal vehicles are the epitome of personal liberty.

The development of America's pervasive highway network has spurred the designation of long-distance routes and scenic byways throughout the country (Jakle and Sculle 2008). Among the most famous are the Oregon Trail, the Lewis and Clark Heritage Trail, and the Trail of Tears National Historic Trail. These trails pass through multiple natural and human landscapes and are often designated and promoted by various heritage trusts or stewardship agencies including, in some cases, the National Park Service. In 1991, the National Scenic Byways Program was established within the US Department of Transportation in an effort to recognize, preserve and enhance scenic roadways throughout the United States. Today there are 98 designated National Scenic Byways that represent distinctive American roads, their stories and their "treasured places." The Program's mission is to "provide resources to the byway community in creating a unique travel experience and enhanced quality of life through efforts to preserve, protect, interpret, and promote the intrinsic qualities of designated Byways" (US Department of Transportation 2008: 1). Efforts such as these have been instrumental in reiterating the importance of road trips in the United States and stress the notion of enjoying what the country has to offer.

Air transportation

The first incident of scheduled air travel in the US was recorded in Florida in 1914 when Tony Jannus flew 21 miles (34 km) from St. Petersburg to Tampa in a two-seater machine at an altitude of merely 50 feet (15 m). The first trans-Atlantic flight took place a few years later in 1919 when Albert Read flew a US Curtiss Flying Boat from Rockaway, New York, to Plymouth, England, via numerous intermediate stops. In 1927, Juan Trippe founded Pan American World Airways, America's first international airline, which began regular global service with flights between Florida and Cuba. During the 1930s, this airline also began to offer regular service between the United States and China and the United States and England respectively. In 1928, Northwest Airways initiated regular service flights to Canada (Heppenheimer 1995).

The First and Second World Wars helped advance airplane technology considerably (Holloway and Taylor 2006). By 1945, at the end of the Second World War, the opportunities for air transportation between different cities had expanded due to a combination of factors including: a large stock of surplus military transporter airplanes, like the DC-3 and DC-4 that were easily converted into civilian aircraft; numerous well-trained fighter and bomber pilots who entered the civilian labor force after their war service ended; the advent of radar that significantly enabled high-altitude and poor weather flying; and thousands of airstrips worldwide that had been developed in support of the war effort and had now been demilitarized. Indeed, in 1945 American Overseas Airlines used a DC-4 to offer a service between New York and Bournemouth via Boston, Gander, and Shannon (Holloway and Taylor 2006).

By the 1950s the introduction of larger and more efficient passenger aircraft – especially the advent of jet passenger planes – meant that a growing number of cohorts of American society were able to travel both overseas but also within their own country. According to Holloway and Taylor, the major catalyst behind this turning point was the introduction in 1958 of the extremely popular and successful Boeing 707 jet, which truly heralded the new era in international passenger transportation, rapidly eclipsing the need for ocean liners. Also, within the US, people began demonstrating a growing preference for air travel over other modes of travel including, in particular, train but also private automobile, especially for medium and long distances (over 500 miles or 800 km) (Theobald 2005). One consequence of the growing popularity of air transportation was that it led to the emergence and rapid growth of new destinations within the country, including a number of places in central and southern Florida which became popular, among others, for the large northeastern market. Concurrently, certain more traditional destinations including seaside communities in places like New Jersey (e.g., Atlantic City), which relied on ground transportation from main markets like Philadelphia and New York, experienced a decline since people could now afford to travel conveniently by air to warmer coastal destinations within the country (Stansfield 1978).

While more and more Americans began flying to further-off destinations both within the USA but also to places in the Caribbean and Europe during the 1960s, the major turning point that truly led to an explosion in air travel occurred after 1978 following the deregulation of the airline industry (Jakle and Sculle 2008). Prior to this event the airline sector had been heavily regulated by the US federal government through the Civil Aeronautics Board (CAB), which was created during the 1930s. An underlying reason for regulation had been to promote safety, but the government also controlled routes, schedules, fares, and the market entry of new airlines (Page 2005; Pucher *et al.* 1993). This had the effect of dictating which airlines would service which routes and which airlines could monopolize certain markets and destinations (Kole and Lehn 1999). Also, as Page (2005: 207) points out, certain carriers were subsidized "so that small communities could be connected to the emerging inter-urban trunk network of air routes, to achieve social equity in access to air travel."

The actual act of deregulating the US-based airlines lasted until the mid 1980s but its effects are still being felt today. Importantly, the implementation of the Airline Deregulation Act resulted in several interesting and remarkable changes to the airline sector during the 1980s and into the 1990s and 2000s (Kahn 1988; Liu and Lynk 1999). First, airline deregulation meant that by 1984 the CAB had been abolished and the responsibilities of this body were taken over by the US Department of Transportation and the Federal Aviation Administration. Another outcome was increased competition between airlines, which lowered the price of air travel significantly. A related result was the ability of airlines to utilize their larger and more efficient aircraft on longer-haul routes, thus allowing more passengers to travel, which in turn increased efficiency levels, thereby also contributing to lower travel costs. Fourth, many airlines dropped their most unprofitable routes, which had originally been assigned to them by the CAB. This allowed the major airlines to focus more on the profitable routes and improve service on these mainstream itineraries. Fifth, these actions, aimed at dropping certain routes, resulted in the establishment of commuter/feeder airlines, some of which were sub-sidiaries of larger carriers that could operate on a smaller scale and realize profits from serving the larger airlines' less-profitable routes (Table 6.2).

The network which permits the smaller carriers (commuter or feeder airlines) to serve routes that are less lucrative for larger airlines, while the latter concentrate on major city pairs is known as the hub-and-spoke system (see Figures 6.4 and 6.5). In the USA this system emerged in the aftermath of deregulation and the abolition of the CAB as more freedom was granted to airlines to negotiate their own routing networks. The hub-and-spoke system is a network in which air traffic flows along spokes, or linear routes, to hubs, or major airports where passengers are transferred to connecting flights to other airports (Duval 2007). This set-up requires fewer non-stop flights and is more economical and efficient, especially because it enables airplanes to maximize their load factors. Duval explains that the central airline hub that exists in the hub-and-spoke system permits major carriers to centralize their operations since "passengers from the spokes would ultimately be routed at the hub, thus providing an increase in the potential market for the other spokes" (158).

Table 6.2 A selection of airlines in the United States

Regional airlines	Major carriers
Air Wisconsin	Alaskan Airlines
American Eagle Airlines	American Airlines
Atlantic Southeast Airlines	Continental Airlines
Colgan Air	Delta Airlines
Comair	Frontier Airlines
Compass Airlines	Hawaiian Airlines
Great Lakes Aviation	JetBlue
Horizon Air	Northwest Airlines
Mesaba Aviation	Southwest Airlines
Piedmont Airlines	United Air Lines
Pinnacle Airlines	US Airways
Republic Airlines	Virgin America
SkyWest Airlines	
US Airways Express	

Source: Regional Airline Association (2009)

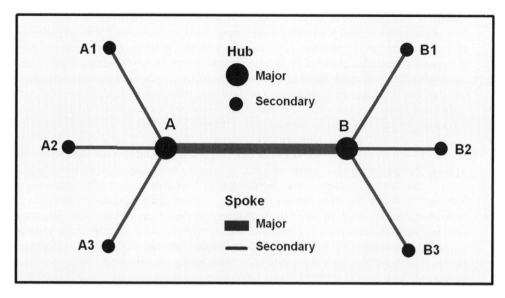

Figure 6.4 The hub-and-spoke transportation system

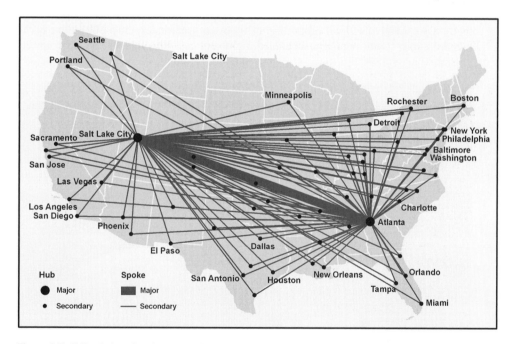

Figure 6.5 Airline hub-and-spoke system based on two fortress hubs
Source: This map is based in part on the hub-and-spoke system of Delta Airlines; http://www.airlineroutemaps.com

For passengers the effects of airline "hubbing" are twofold. On the plus side passengers are able to fly to many more destinations than they could under the traditional point-to-point network which dominated prior to deregulation. Consider for example, the person who wants to fly from a small town, for example College Station, Texas, to Syracuse, New York. In the old days this would be a harrowing trip, which may include numerous changes, not to mention the price would have been close to prohibitive. Nowadays, however, this person could quite easily fly with American Eagle (a subsidiary of American Airlines) to the hub city of Dallas-Fort Worth where he or she would then change to an American Airlines flight to another hub city, namely Chicago. Then he/she would transfer to an American Eagle flight to Syracuse. The advantage to passengers is that they can fly quite seamlessly from one smaller community to another.

On the downside, however, if a particular hub is a "fortress hub," like Dallas or Chicago (Duval 2007: 159), meaning that it is dominated by one or two key airlines (for example American and/or United) then customers may not benefit too much from discounted fares since there is limited competition in such instances. Debbage (2002) has warned that the power that dominant carriers exercise at certain fortress hub airports, namely their immense control over the number of available landing slots, means it is frequently not easy for other carriers, including discount airlines, to gain a foothold in these destinations. This, in turn means that tourist flows can be adversely impacted between particular city pairs in cases where the possibility of finding low cost fares is rare or does not exist. By association "resort destinations that are highly dependent on air-based tourist arrivals are especially vulnerable, particularly if the demand originates in markets that depend on gridlocked international airport gateways (such as JFK)" (Debbage 2002: 947) (see Plate 6.2).

Today, there are approximately 20,341 airports in the United States (Bureau of Transportation Statistics 2008). This means the USA has more airports than any other country in the world (Central Intelligence Agency 2008). Not all of these airports – in fact, only a relatively small proportion of them (approximately 500–600) – are commercial airports with regularly scheduled flight services. Nonetheless, the USA has an

Plate 6.2 Ready for take-off – Aircraft at Newark Airport
(Dallen Timothy)

excellent network of flights to and from local, regional, national and international airports. From a global perspective, there has been a significant growth in international gateway cities in the United States since the 1960s. While most international flights departed from and arrived at only the largest US cities during the 1950s and 1960s (e.g., New York, Chicago, and Los Angeles), the 1970s, '80s and '90s saw an increase in other international gateway cities as the hub-and-spoke system developed. Charlotte and Cincinnati are examples of metropolitan regions that have emerged as important gateway cities in the last few years. The primary international gateways into the USA include the following airports:

- Baltimore-Washington International Airport
- Charlotte/Douglas International Airport
- Chicago O'Hare Airport
- Cincinnati-Northern Kentucky International Airport
- Cleveland Hopkins International Airport
- Dallas-Fort Worth International Airport
- Denver International Airport
- Detroit Metro Airport
- George Bush Intercontinental Airport (Houston, Texas)
- Hartsfield Atlanta International Airport
- Honolulu International Airport
- John F. Kennedy International Airport (New York City)
- La Guardia Airport (New York City)
- Lambert-St Louis International Airport
- Logan International Airport (Boston)
- Los Angeles International Airport
- Louis Armstrong New Orleans International Airport
- McCarran International Airport (Las Vegas)
- Memphis International Airport
- Miami International Airport
- Minneapolis-St. Paul International Airport
- Newark Liberty International Airport (New York City and New Jersey)
- Philadelphia International Airport
- Phoenix Sky Harbor International Airport
- Pittsburgh International Airport
- Ronald Reagan Washington National Airport
- Salt Lake City International Airport
- San Francisco International Airport
- Seattle/Tacoma International Airport
- Washington Dulles International Airport

Many of these airports as well as several others are now major hub airports. By way of examples, American Airlines has adopted Dallas-Fort Worth, Chicago, and Miami as its primary hubs. The hub cities for US Airways include Phoenix, Charlotte, and Philadelphia, while those for Northwest Airlines include Detroit, Minneapolis, and Memphis.

Following deregulation the number of airlines increased impressively, especially during the early 1980s. At the time of writing (2009), there were approximately 154 airlines based in the US, including scheduled commercial passenger service, charter airlines, and cargo airlines. Regional and commuter airlines are plentiful in the United States with concentrations of commuter flights in the northeast, southeast, and west coast.

Nevertheless, it has to be stressed, that many new entrant carriers that had been established in the '80s, but also a number of the older more established companies, have over the years gone bankrupt and disappeared (e.g., Eastern Airlines, Pan Am, and Western Airlines) (Kahn 1988; Page 2005). A notable example of a short-lived new entrant company was that of People Express Airlines, a low cost airline that operated between 1981 and 1987. In addition, more recent years have seen the bankruptcy claims of several major airlines (e.g., America West, Continental, TWA, and Northwest) and their mergers with other airlines to create larger and more competitive corporations. Today American Airlines remains the only one of the original large players that has not yet filed Chapter 11 bankruptcy or merged with another airline.

Page (2004; see also Debbage 1990 and Goetz and Sutton 1997) argued that, in spite of deregulation, by the early 1990s the US airline industry had become increasingly oligopolistic with a major portion of the market share controlled by a few major companies. In fact, by the mid-1990s just eight carriers controlled more than nine-tenths of the market. This situation is ironic considering that one of the fundamental reasons for promoting airline deregulation in the first place was to reduce barriers to entry and allow new entrants to flourish.

Today, regardless of the structure of the airline industry, competition remains a significant outcome of deregulation, and naturally airlines continue to battle for travelers' dollars. During the early years of deregulation and through the 1990s airlines often competed on the basis of price discounts and various bonus programs, most notably frequent flier schemes aimed at building up customer loyalty. However, the years following 9/11 have been far from kind to the airline industry, and the recent economic downturn, not to mention the huge increase in fuel prices during 2007 and 2008, has taken its toll, a fact that has made it very difficult for carriers to maintain a competitive edge. If anything, US airlines have had to take a number of cost-saving measures in an effort to stave off catastrophic losses. These measures include shutting down more and more routes, reducing their fleets, laying-off personnel, and substantially cutting salaries and benefits packages. This climate has undoubtedly had an adverse impact on the airlines' ability to reduce their fees. In fact, overall, the price of airline travel has risen alarmingly as the carriers keep on adding new taxes and extra charges, and they are doing this while concurrently reducing or eliminating various perks and services that were once taken for granted (e.g., through the elimination of free on-board snacks and drinks, making passengers pay for checked luggage, or reducing frequent flier benefits).

What the final consequence of these developments will be for airline travelers, especially those who travel for leisure purposes, is still hard to envision. For the moment, if the crowds seen at most airports are anything to go by, it seems that most consumers are willing to put up with the increasing hardships, including overall declining service quality, associated with air travel. Whether this remains the case given the economic recession that is continually strengthening its grip remains to be seen.

In terms of recent developments, the new *laissez faire* approach (deregulation) of the US government has opened up possibilities for the emergence of several "discount" airlines that provide a no-frills service and offer highly competitive routes and prices (Table 6.3). With the exception of Southwest Airlines that has been in existence since the early 1970s (see Closer Look Case 6.2 for a more detailed discussion on Southwest Airlines and its unique way of doing business) the rest are new entrants. While these low-cost airlines based in the USA are a bit more expensive than their European counterparts, such as EasyJet and Ryanair, they do offer, in some cases, lower-priced alternatives to the standard mainstream airlines. But once more, their future is unclear given the current economic climate, also considering the fate of several "new" entrant airlines that failed to survive in the early years of deregulation.

Table 6.3 Low-cost airlines based in the United States

Airline	Extent of service
AirTran Airways	Domestic and international. Primarily eastern and midwestern routes. Also serves Cancun, Mexico.
Allegiant Air	Domestic only. Concentrates on northern states and upper Midwest.
Frontier Airlines	Domestic and international. Provides flights nationwide, as well as to Mexico and Costa Rica.
go!	Domestic only. Provides flights between the Hawaiian islands.
Horizon Air	Domestic and international. Serves primarily west coast states in the US, British Columbia and Alberta (Canada), and Loreto and La Paz, Mexico.
Island Air	Domestic only. Provides flights between the Hawaiian islands.
jetBlue	Domestic and international. Serves primarily California, the northeast and southeast. Also serves the Caribbean, Bermuda, Mexico, and Colombia.
Southwest Airlines	Domestic only. Provides flights nationwide.
Spirit Airlines	Domestic and international. Domestic flights are concentrated in the east and southeast. Also services Mexico, Central America, South America, and Caribbean.
Sun Country Airlines	Domestic and international. Most domestic flights focus on southeastern and southwestern states. Service also to Mexico and the Caribbean.
USA3000	Domestic and international. Domestic flights focus on Midwestern and eastern states. Also serves Mexico and Caribbean.
Virgin America	Domestic only. Concentrated on west coast and east coast.

CLOSER LOOK CASE 6.2

Southwest Airlines: "Often imitated, never duplicated"

Any employee of Southwest Airlines (SWA) in the mid-1990s would be familiar with this motto. SWA was so proud to be the underdog maverick that the company built an entire corporate culture on this premise. Legend has it that the carrier started with a drawing of a triangle on a cocktail napkin over drinks. The triangle depicted service between Houston, Dallas, and San Antonio, and the need for such a commuter service was the reason the airline began operating back in 1971.

SWA has always done things differently than other carriers. First of all, its routes have always been point-to-point instead of hub-and-spoke. This means that SWA has no hub cities as such. Instead it runs its planes as buses with intermediate stops on the way from city A to city B, specializing in short-haul, high-frequency routes. Second, the company uses only Boeing 737s. By doing this SWA saves money and improves the quality of training and maintenance. For many years the airline bought fuel in large quantities in advance, thus skirting oil price increases. In fact, in 2004 Southwest announced its 31st profitable year, a fact in stark contrast with other airlines which had been laying employees off, filing bankruptcy, and/or going out of business. Third, SWA has not been part of any Global Distribution System (GDS), though it allowed limited functionality on Sabre, one of the largest GDSs. This meant that a travel agent could "see" and book the Southwest flights on the Sabre system, but availability of seats was not always real-time and, thus, one had to contact the carrier before ticketing. Also, itinerary changes had to be handled with SWA directly.

The company uses its own proprietary software, a version of which it makes available to travel agents. SWA did not want to pay the per-segment fee to be a part of any GDS; however, since the deregulation of global distribution systems it has signed a ten-year contract with Galileo. Fourth, SWA was the only carrier to have open seating (meaning that seats are not pre-assigned but rather "first-come first-served") and one of very few not to offer first or business class. Passengers were given a plastic boarding pass corresponding with a boarding group. Quite simply, the earlier one got to check in, the earlier one could board. The reusable boarding pass made of plastic saved the company on card stock. Notably, with the prevalence of home computer check-in, SWA has changed its seating policy in recent years. Sixth, SWA has a policy of flying into smaller, often more convenient airports. Large airports are dominated by big carriers, charge high landing fees and are often far from the city. Southwest flies into smaller, cheaper airports which are closer to the cities' commercial center (e.g., Chicago Midway rather than O'Hare, Dallas Love Field instead of Fort Worth, and Oakland instead of San Francisco).

This policy and SWA's choice of headquarters (Dallas Love Field) sparked an astonishing act of protectionism, the Wright Amendment. This was federal legislation enacted in 1979 prohibiting air transportation by aircraft with a seating capacity larger than 50 in and out of Love Field to any state which does not border Texas with the exception of Mississippi and Alabama. Though this legislation specifically targeted Southwest, the airline managed to overcome the restriction very successfully and flourish thereafter.

SWA has been the only "no frills" carrier to withstand the changing times and continuous crises. It is an honest airline that has had a clear vision from the beginning; almost four decades later it is still a maverick, successfully and rightfully so.

Questions

1. Southwest Airlines has a very distinct organizational culture. Look up information about the company at www.southwest.com and consider the implications of a strong and distinct organizational culture on job satisfaction and employee retention. How might the airline's approach influence its profitability?
2. Do you agree that the Southwest Airlines model has never been fully duplicated by other carriers? Consider both US carriers and international airlines.

Evangelia Petridou

Water-based travel

Water-based travel has a long history in the USA, beginning with the ancient inhabitants of North America many hundreds of years ago. It was not uncommon for indigenous Americans to travel long distances by canoe or raft along coastlines and inland via well-established river routes. Also, as we have seen in Chapter 2, much of the very early tourism destination development in the northeast had to do with the development of the canal system during the first two decades of the nineteenth century. Today, water travel is an important part of commuter and tourist transportation in several regions of the country, including the Great Lakes, the Pacific Northwest, the northeast, along the great inland rivers (Mississippi, Missouri, Ohio), and along the east coast. Although cruises are perhaps the best known example of water travel today, this section examines what Duval (2007) refers to as "functional marine transport" and Douglas and Douglas (2001) call "line voyages," or modes of sea travel that transport people from point to point without providing the recreational benefits of cruises.

The ferry services in New York City between the islands (Staten Island, Long Island, Liberty Island, and Ellis Island) and the mainland have long been an important way of getting around the greater New York City area and are still widely used by local commuters and tourists alike (Weisbrod and Lawson 2003). A similar reliance on ferry transportation in the Pacific Northwest in the region of Seattle and the Puget Sound has played an important role in the development of tourism in that region (Dehghani *et al.* 1997). There are approximately 209 domestic ferry services in 35 states, with transport services across lakes, rivers, sea passages, ocean straights and along coastlines (Howder's Site 2009). In addition, several international ferry services travel between the USA and Canada on a daily basis, primarily between Washington and British Columbia, but also between Maine and the Canadian provinces of New Brunswick and Nova Scotia. In the past there were also ferry services between the USA and Mexico and the USA and the Bahamas, but these are now obsolete.

Cruises

Cruises are quite different than the functional marine services noted above. Instead of operating solely as a mode of transportation, cruises provide a complete vacation experience and are sought after for their all-inclusiveness, the interesting ports of call, and the variety of food and onboard entertainment. They are sometimes referred to as floating resorts. According to most research studies about motives for cruising, the ports of call and the all-inclusive nature of the experience (food, lodging, transportation, recreation, and entertainment) are the most appealing aspects of cruises (Miller and Grazer 2006).

While the earliest cruise ships were developed in the early 1900s, they were few and far between. The modern-day notion of cruises began with the normalization of transoceanic flights, which stole demand for trans-Pacific and trans-Atlantic transport from passenger ships. By 1960, approximately 70 percent of transatlantic travel was done by jet; by 1970 the figure was 96 percent (Stansfield 1977). Between 1960 and 1975, ship passenger service across the Atlantic from New York declined from 500,000 to 50,000 passengers a year (Hobson 1993). With declining demand for passage, the ships' owners had to reinvent their product in order to remain economically viable. From this change in travel demand, the idea of pleasure cruises originated and continues to grow today.

Throughout the world, cruising is becoming a more popular holiday option, but cruises are becoming especially popular among American tourists and have been since the 1970s. Passenger numbers grew by 190 percent between 1970 and 1980 and experienced nearly 9 percent annual growth throughout the 1980s (Hobson 1993). Table 6.4 illustrates the steady growth of cruise passengers in North America between 1990 and 2007. During the 1990s, cruises saw a significant growth, with a 90 percent occupancy rate, while hotels during the same period were having difficulties attaining 60 percent occupancy (Hobson 1993). Although the figures in Table 6.4 include all cruise passengers in North America, Americans and others, they are indicative of the rapid and constant growth of the cruise sector. Even the tragic terrorist events of 2001 did not affect the growth of cruise tourism the way they affected many other forms of tourism. More than 92 percent (92.25 percent) of all North American cruise passengers are US residents, comprising just fewer than 9.5 million of the 10.25 million total North American cruise trips taken. Canadians comprised 6.6 percent of North American cruise passengers in 2007. Not surprisingly, the home states of the largest cohorts of American cruisers are Florida and California, which

Table 6.4 Annual cruise passenger growth in North America ('000)

1990	1995	2000	2001	2002	2003	2004	2005	2006	2007
3,496	4,223	6,546	6,637	7,472	7,990	8,870	9,671	10,078	10,247

Source: CLIA (2008a)

is where most Mexican and Caribbean cruises originate. Still, only some 15 percent of the American public has ever taken a cruise (Miller and Grazer 2006).

Motion pictures and television shows (e.g., *The Love Boat*) that glamorized and romanticized the cruise were behind much of the sector's growing popularity in the 1970s and 1980s. Hobson (1993: 455) identified several other factors that influenced the growth and popularity of cruises in the United States. First, the Cruise Lines International Association (CLIA) was created in 1975 to oversee the development and promotion of cruising as an important sector of tourism. CLIA aims to collect cruise-related data and educate the public about and promote the importance of the cruise product. As of 2009, nearly all cruise companies in North America are members of CLIA, representing some 97 percent of the cruise capacity marketed from North America. Second, successful relationships were built between cruise companies and travel agents, who became the most important channel of distribution for cruises. Today, approximately 90 percent of all cruises are still purchased through travel agents; some cruise companies report as much as 97 percent of sales coming via travel agents (CLIA 2009). The third reason for rapid growth is the tapping of the cruise product into new market segments and changing perceptions of what cruises have to offer. Several new markets have been targeted by cruise companies since the 1990s, including families with young children, gay and lesbian couples, and singles. Fourth, new types of cruises have been initiated for different budgets and personal requirements. One good example is the growth of one or two night cruises closer to home. Two-night sailings from southern California that stop in Catalina Island (California) and Ensenada, Mexico, for instance, have become popular for budget-conscious travelers who want to try a cruise but feel they are unable to afford a more extensive experience. Finally, the sector has changed how it packages and offers its products. Collaborative efforts between the cruise companies, hotels, airlines, and tour operators have resulted in more inclusive packages, such as air and cruise combinations, post-cruise tours and extended stays, and a multiplicity of shore excursions.

The most popular cruise destination in the United States, and second most popular cruise destination overall for Americans (after the Caribbean), is Alaska (CLIA 2009; Munro and Gill 2006). Most Alaska cruises depart from Seattle, Vancouver (British Columbia, Canada), San Francisco, Los Angeles, and Seward and Whittier (Alaska). Demand for Alaskan cruises is seasonal, from May to September with a limited set of primary itineraries (Marti 2007; Ringer 2006). Alaskan cruises, unlike the slightly more popular Caribbean region, focus more on ecotourism, history and natural scenery. In the minds of many Americans, who comprise some 80 percent of Alaskan cruise passengers, Alaska is "the 'last frontier' and rings with the call of the wild, the rambunctiousness of gold rushes and the mysteries of native peoples" (Munro and Gill 2006: 147). Other important US cruises include inter-island voyages in Hawaii and east coast cruises, for example those from New York City into the New England States. Additional US locations are considered important ports of call on long-distance cruises, including inter-island voyages in Hawaii, Key West, Florida, on some western Caribbean cruises, and San Diego or Catalina Island on Los Angeles to Mexico cruises. Puerto Rico and the US Virgin Islands, which are not part of the 50 states but are US territories, are also important cruise destinations in the Caribbean. In addition to destinations in North America, Americans are avid cruisers in Europe, Mexico, and the Panama Canal.

While Alaska, Hawaii, and the northeastern United States are significant ports of call on regular cruise itineraries, there are many ports of embarkation located in the US, which serve as international ports of departure for cruises further afield. Table 6.5 shows the top ten embarkation ports in the United States and provides 2005 and 2007 passenger departure figures. With the transition from point-to-point ship travel to cruise tourism during the 1970s, the focus of ship passage moved from New York City to Florida (Stansfield 1977). This repositioning of departure ports saved time and cost for the cruise companies as the orientation moved from transatlantic passenger services to pleasure cruises to the Caribbean. Not surprisingly, Miami is the most popular cruise departure port in the country. Four of the top ten ports are located in Florida, and in fact ports in the state of Florida accounted for 54.2 percent of all cruise passenger departures in the USA. In the words of Pennington-Gray (2006: 291), "undoubtedly, Florida is the heart of the cruise industry in the USA." The top ten ports saw 83.4 percent of all embarkation traffic in the country in 2007.

In addition to the normative forms of cruising discussed so far in this section, other types of cruising also exist that have become popular in the USA in recent years. Smith (2006) describes several of these forms of cruising that are becoming more popular on the American tourism scene. Nostalgic cruising is a form of heritage tourism that takes passengers on heritage vessels or along historic routes. This form includes steamboats, many propelled by paddlewheels, on the Mississippi River. These are an important heritage product that focuses on the American frontier, Mark Twain's famous Tom Sawyer and Huckleberry Finn characters, and the romanticized image associated with the Mississippi River in the American psyche. Several steamboats continue to glide up and down the river in areas where the river is wide and deep. Tours operate between cities including the popular dinner cruises "to nowhere" (Timothy 2009).

Another of the adventure cruises described by Smith (2006) is yachting, which involves relatively small watercraft used for pleasure boating. These vessels are typically the domain of the wealthy in American society and are concentrated in Florida, California, New England, and the Pacific Northwest. Expedition cruises are another modern-day phenomenon that is a uniquely American product. These facilitate travelers'

Table 6.5 Top ten cruise departure ports in the US, 2005–2007

Port of embarkation	Embarkations 2005	Embarkations 2007
Miami	1,803,000	1,893,000
Port Canaveral	1,234,000	1,298,000
Port Everglades	1,283,000	1,289,000
Los Angeles	615,000	581,000
New York	370,000	575,000
Galveston	531,000	523,000
Seattle	337,000	386,000
Honolulu	236,000	382,000
Long Beach	363,000	370,000
Tampa	408,000	367,000
All remaining ports	1,476,000	1,520,000

Source: CLIA (2008b)

Note: This table is not comprehensive but merely reflects key sectors in the NAICS that either directly or indirectly serve tourists. Only sectors that in most communities depend heavily on tourists are shown. Other activities like restaurants, which may in some communities be heavily dependent on visitors, have been left out in this table. For a more concrete listing, please consult Roehl (1998).

desires to explore and learn rather than simply to relax in the sun. These cruises usually have a specific purpose (e.g., to have an encounter with certain migratory animal species) and are often associated with off-the-beaten path tourist destinations, such as the far north of Alaska and Canada, or other remote or pristine areas of North America (e.g., the Great Lakes area). Adventure Life Voyages is one such company that operates explorer-oriented cruises to Alaska and international destinations. Top of the World Tours offers adventure and learning cruises through the Great Lakes of the Upper Midwest.

Other contemporary cruise patterns exist in the USA that should be highlighted. One of the most salient of these is day-cruises, which take on several forms but among the most important are gaming cruises. These are very popular in Florida, Georgia, Texas and Massachusetts, where ships (small and large) depart for the open seas of the Atlantic or Gulf of Mexico. Once outside of America's territorial waters, they open their casinos and spend several hours floating while their passengers play slots, blackjack, craps, videopoker, and roulette. These "cruises to nowhere" literally have no destination, except the maritime boundary of the USA. Because they are stationed outside territorial waters they can set their own gambling age, which for most ships is 18 or 21 (Christensen 1998; Pennington-Gray 2006).

Conclusion

The story of tourism's evolution in the United States cannot be understood in the absence of an in-depth examination of the country's transportation system and the manner in which it developed. This has been examined earlier in the book. In this chapter a detailed picture of the various facets of the American transportation system has been presented. The obvious conclusion from this analysis is that the rise and fall of various destinations throughout this vast country is strongly connected with the manner in which Americans choose to travel.

On the one hand, Americans' excessive love affair with the automobile and the extremely high car ownership that exists in this country has meant that millions of people think nothing of getting on the road to travel to visit historic or natural sites and friends and family. To be sure, the vast majority of car trips relating to tourism purposes cover a fairly short distance from one's home and rarely exceed 500 miles (800 km). This is about the maximum one could drive in a car on any particular day given the current road infrastructure. But what is also evident is that numerous Americans do not think much of taking car trips that involve many days of driving and cover thousands of miles. Thus, it is not a surprise to see streams of cars flowing towards Florida during the Christmas season or spring break, and millions of Americans can recall childhood car trips with their parents to visit some of the nation's outstanding national parks.

On the other hand, the most popular form of mass transportation for the purposes of tourism in the United States is now air travel. This travel mode has grown by leaps and bounds since the late 1950s due mainly to the advent of new technologies, but the key turning point that has encouraged millions of Americans to take to the skies arrived with deregulation in the late 1970s. Airplane transportation and especially the advent of the hub-and-spoke system has meant that most Americans – even those living in smaller metro areas – can now quite easily choose to travel from their homes to literally anywhere in the country and beyond. Air travel has enabled new destinations to flourish and has been a key ingredient in the growing attraction of Florida and also Hawaii as key destinations. Even during these times of economic and political turmoil Americans still choose to fly, especially when their trip is over a long distance and for a fairly short time.

The one mode of transportation that has gradually almost disappeared, despite its enormous importance in shaping the country's early tourism development, is train travel. Considering that this nation's development owes a lot to the expansion and diffusion of the railroad, it is sad indeed to note that today the great American railroad has been reduced to only a few commuter corridors in the country's most densely populated regions. While the citizens of other countries (especially a number of European nations but also Japan and, increasingly China) have the ability to travel for the purposes of vacation by rail, in the United States only a very small number of rail aficionados appear to opt for this mode. Matters have not been helped by the failure of the USA to move towards a new era of high-speed rail on par with those systems seen in France, Germany, Japan, and China. To this date, any suggestion to introduce high-speed corridors in the USA appears to be dismissed as the notion of eccentric, tree huggers, who have little understanding for the true way of American travel – namely the open road. Thus, the last vestiges of rail travel in the USA are most often either provided along historic rail links, often using antiquated equipment, or represented in the transformation of abandoned rail corridors into recreational corridors for hikers and cyclists.

One quite remarkable revolution in the American transportation system that has created an entirely novel tourism product is the advent of cruise ships. Whereas these vessels are undoubtedly modes of transportation in their own right they have helped transform the trip itself into the entire tourist experience. The concept of a "cruise to nowhere," for instance, where the ship leaves a port like Miami for one or a few days and cruises around before returning has gained massive popularity since tourists can find all the leisure commodities they need on board. It is also worth mentioning that the importance of air travel for the cruise industry should not be underestimated. After all, it is because of the better links between key cruise port cities and the rest of the country that many Americans, regardless of where they live, can have access to a cruise, and this type of tourism is likely to continue to grow over the next few years.

Questions

1. Given the success that train travel (including high-speed rail) in many parts of the world has had, why is it that in the United States the number of rail passengers has fallen dramatically and many lines have gone out of existence?
2. What effect did airline deregulation in 1978 have on domestic and international travel by Americans?
3. Explain the concept of hub-and-spoke in the airline transportation system. Why is hub-and-spoke considered more efficient than other forms of networks and what are some of the most serious negatives associated with this type of network?
4. Have you been on a cruise? Do you agree with the label often given to cruise ships that describes them as floating resorts?

Further reading

Brown, G. (2003) A method for assessing highway qualities to integrate values in highway planning. *Journal of Transport Geography*, 11(4): 271–83.

Chang, Y.C., Hsu, Y.J., Williams, G. and Pan, M.L. (2008) Low cost carriers' destination selection using a Delphi method. *Tourism Management*, 29(5): 898–908.

Gayle, P.G. (2008) An empirical analysis of the competitive effects of the Delta/Continental/Northwest code-share alliance. *Journal of Law and Economics*, 51(4): 743–66.

Genc, I.H., Miller, J.R. and Gursoy, D. (2007) The macroeconomic environment and airline profitability: a study of US regional airlines. *Tourism Analysis*, 11(6): 381–95.

Ito, H. and Lee, D. (2007) Domestic code sharing, alliances, and airfares in the US airline industry. *Journal of Law and Economics*, 50(2): 355–80.

Liu, Z. and Lynk, E.L. (1999) Evidence on market structure of the deregulated US airline industry. *Applied Economics*, 31(9): 1083–92.

Loverseed, H. (1994) Rail travel in North America. *Travel and Tourism Analyst*, 1: 4–18.

McNichol, D. (2006) *The Roads that Built America: The Incredible Story of the U.S. Interstate System*. New York: Sterling.

Useful Internet resources

Air Line Pilots Association: http://www.alpa.org/
Air Transport Association: http://www.airlines.org/
Amtrak: www.amtrak.com
Association of American Railroads: http://www.aar.org/Homepage.aspx
Cruise Lines International Association: http://www.cruising.org/
Federal Aviation Administration: http://www.faa.gov/
Federal Railroad Administration: http://www.fra.dot.gov/
Florida-Caribbean Cruise Association: http://www.f-cca.com/
International Air Transport Association: http://www.iata.org/index.htm
National Association of Railroad Passengers: http://www.narprail.org/cms/index.php
National Highway System: http://www.fhwa.dot.gov/planning/nhs/
Regional Airline Association: http://www.raa.org/
Transportation Security Administration: http://www.tsa.gov/
US Department of Transportation: http://www.dot.gov/new/index.htm

7 Tourism's economic significance

Total direct travel spending in California in 2006 was 93.8 billion, while tourism supported jobs for approximately 929,000 people, up 2 percent from 2005. Travel and tourism generated $5.6 billion in state and local tax revenue in 2006.

(California Travel and Tourism Commission 2007: 14)

Introduction

It is not unusual for commentaries concerning tourism's impacts, whether in academic monographs, newspaper articles, government reports, or statements issued by industry associations, to overplay tourism's economic significance for destination areas. More often than not, these reports highlight how large the tourism sector is and how it dominates national, regional, and local economies. We are reminded that tourism is the largest or second largest industry (whether or not it is, is still a point of debate), based on measures such as employment generation or the sector's contribution to gross regional product and balance of payments. For instance, one of the major proponents of the tourism industry, the World Travel and Tourism Council (WTTC), regularly issues statements touting the sector's importance as the "one of the world's largest generators of wealth and jobs" (WTTC 2003).

Regardless of these assertions they are only infrequently backed up with serious empirical analyses. To be sure, plenty of consulting reports exist, often commissioned by convention and visitor bureaus, yet much of the information provided is in summary form and the utilized methodology only sketchily explained. It appears almost as if we have been bombarded so often concerning tourism's major presence in the economy that everyone believes this to be fact, no questions asked. Judd (1995) has pointed out that in urban areas of the United States, many visitor-oriented projects, such as sports arenas or aquariums are rarely justified through detailed feasibility analyses, including cost-benefit studies. Indeed, many observers take it for granted that such visitor-oriented projects cost far above initial estimates and, in many instances, do not bring in the expected proceeds (Page 1995). Despite this situation, tourism projects have numerous supporters simply because this is a sector that boosts the image of their community and region. So what if the proposed baseball stadium or convention center costs a few tens or hundreds of millions more than originally estimated? In the eyes of their advocates these overpriced projects are constructed primarily to enhance the image of their community or region. If ultimately, the new golf course, convention center, baseball stadium, or aquarium exceeds the initial budget and does not rake in the expected proceeds, civic leaders appear to turn a blind eye to this issue, since they regard these projects as a means of enhancing the popularity of the community for visitors and enticing additional investors and new residents into the area.

This situation is, of course, unfortunate, since it perpetuates an inability to comprehend with a higher degree of accuracy the true measure of the tourism economy. How large is tourism's contribution precisely? How many jobs does it generate both directly and indirectly? What is the sector's economic multiplier? What are tourism's intersectoral linkages? These are just some of the initial questions that continue to puzzle observers. There are, of course, those who may question the importance of such questions and their answers. These persons should be reminded that developing a superior understanding of the economics of tourism is of paramount significance if for no other reason than such an endeavor lends further credibility to the study of this sector, which is perceived by some social scientists as superfluous and without academic merit (Agarwal *et al.* 2000; Ioannides and Debbage 1998).

In this chapter we do not pretend to generate new knowledge regarding the economics of tourism. Rather, much less ambitiously we seek to paint a simple picture of the significance of tourism within the United States at various geographical scales: the national, regional, and local. The analysis is backed up with numbers assembled from a variety of sources, including state agencies, privately commissioned reports, the US Census Bureau (2009b) and the Bureau of Labor Statistics (2009). Following a brief section in which the reader is reminded of the pitfalls involved in understanding what precisely the tourism industry entails, we move on to analyze tourism's performance in certain states and cities, and examine the efficacy of using tourism satellite accounts (TSAs) and the North American Industrial Classification System (NAICS) to understand economic impact and employment.

What is the tourism industry?

For years scholars have debated whether or not tourism can be classified as an industry in a manner similar, for example, to dairy farming, coal mining, automobile manufacturing, or various service activities like banking, insurance, health care, and education (Debbage and Daniels 1998; Ioannides and Debbage 1998; Smith 1998; Debbage and Ioannides 2004; Ioannides 2006; Judd 2006; Leiper 1979). The answer is, of course, far from simple, since travel and tourism cannot be neatly bracketed into a single industrial activity engaged in fundamentally similar production processes aimed at delivering a well-defined commodity (Smith 1998: 35). Rather, this sector includes an array of quite distinct services provided by numerous suppliers that at first glance bear no relationship to one another. Consider that what observers generally believe to be two of the most important components of tourism, namely air travel and hotel accommodation, are fundamentally vastly different sectors, whose products/services are quite distinct; while the former is engaged in shuffling people from one geographical point to another the latter is designed to provide a resting spot in one fixed place (Smith 1998). Despite this fact, however, Smith maintains that the two sectors, as well as many others, "are functionally linked in that they facilitate activities by people temporarily away from their home environment" (Smith 1998: 36). This has led some observers to suggest that because tourism is not a single industry or sector, but rather an amalgamated system of interconnected services and sectors, it should be conceptualized and operationalized as a set of "tourism industries" rather than a singular industry (Edgell *et al.* 2007; Leiper 2008).

Dennis Judd (2006: 323) has added an interesting twist to the whole debate concerning tourism's definitions by insisting that the sector "should be regarded as a production process involving a distinct product and identifiable inputs." For this to be achieved, Judd suggests utilizing the commodity chain concept, a network approach allowing one to visualize how a particular industry is constructed all the way from the primary production of inputs to final consumption. He argues that the various components the tourist consumes before and during the trip are incidental to the primary objective of the journey, which is ultimately to gain novel experiences (see also Urry 1990). In Judd's mind the *experience* is the final product consumed; this experience is a product derived through the combined actions of a multiplicity of players including private companies, individual entrepreneurs, and an ensemble of public entities (Ioannides 2006).

An issue that Smith dismisses and Judd only marginally acknowledges is that since tourism's final product is the experience itself, the consumer must somehow be involved in creating that experience; in other words, the tourist is an active player in the production process, a situation not necessarily occurring in the manufacturing of tangible commodities such as television sets and automobiles, or even when developing financial services. Judd believes that although travelers may frequently engage in non-commodified experiential activities, these are only "interludes between commodified experiences" that have been shaped by various tourism producers. On the other side of the coin, Leiper (1979, 1990, 1993) has been the harshest critic of a purely industrial approach to defining tourism, arguing that tourist activities include a large proportion of non-industrialized activities including sightseeing, cycling, or photography. According to him, since the total experience the tourist derives during the trip incorporates a considerable number of non-industrialized activities, it is impossible to view tourism like any other industry; instead, he argues that tourism is partially industrialized.

Shaw and Williams (2004) have recently come up with a conceptual model that breaks tourism down into goods and services with a distinct market value versus those that merely have an experiential value. Their argument is that "unlike some goods and services, the commodification of tourism is based not only on the labour, capital and natural resources used in production, but also on the 'sign value' or symbolic value of the tourism experience" (2004: 24). In their minds people seek to buy the means to a tourist experience because, to an extent, they are pursuing a certain lifestyle and wish to achieve a particular status among their peers. Shaw and Williams view at least some tourism commodities as "fetishized" meaning their "exchange values . . . may become detached from the actual costs of production" (p. 25).

Their typology includes four classes. The first includes experiences, which are directly commodified, meaning one has to pay an entrance or user fee (as when entering a national park). The second category comprises indirectly commodified experiences, those derived from necessary services geared to serve the visitors like transportation or accommodations. The next type of experiences are those emerging from partly commodified services relating, for example, to situations where visitors rent a car while on holiday or when they use self-catering cottages. In situations like these, the visitors may effectively end up performing a considerable amount of work without remuneration and could incur considerable expenses before obtaining the actual experience; in the case of the cottage they may actually furnish the "fixed capital asset (house)" themselves (Shaw and Williams 2004: 26). The final type of tourist experience, according to Shaw and Williams, is the one that is entirely non-commodified. These experiences result from non-market actions such as staying with friends and relatives and participating in activities including hiking, cycling, or picture-taking, without incurring direct fees. Shaw and Williams (2004: 26) acknowledge that their typology is not rigid but, instead, at any destination a variety of combinations of these four forms of commodification exists and "it is the exact combination of these which, in large part determines place characteristics."

Many years ago Mathieson and Wall (1982) recognized that precisely because tourism, when viewed as an industry includes both tangible products necessary for one's trip (e.g., the airline seat, hotel bed, and restaurant services) and intangible components, for which the user incurs no fee (e.g., the experience derived from sightseeing) it must be described as an "odd" sector (see also Wall and Mathieson 2006). To begin, it should be labeled an "invisible export industry" (Wall and Mathieson 2006: 73), meaning it does not produce tangible goods that can be transported between two or more places; in this manner it resembles sectors like banking or financial services. Other things that make tourism an oddity include the fact that the consumers (tourists) do not wait for the commodity to be delivered within their home environment, but instead must travel to the place where the product is manufactured (the destination). Given that the tourism product cannot be examined prior to departure (other than through promises viewed on websites and in guidebooks) the amount of expenditure incurred can often be perceived as extravagant, especially for what is really an experience and not a tangible good. Like other service sectors, the tourism product is produced and consumed simultaneously and cannot be stored for future use; if unused then the rental opportunity (e.g., airline seat, a hotel night, or a seat at a concert) "is lost and cannot be replaced" (Debbage and Daniels 1998: 23).

The debates considering tourism's definition as an industrial sector are without doubt valuable, and people interested in tourism would do well to familiarize themselves with these. From a more practical standpoint, however, we end up with the following straightforward questions: How should statisticians and policymakers measure tourism? For instance, how many people work in the so-called tourism industry? What proportion of a community's economy does tourism comprise? What is the contribution of tourism to the gross regional product?

Wall and Mathieson (2006) provide a useful overview of techniques for measuring tourism's economic impacts, which can serve as a point of departure for scholars who are interested in this topic. From a practical standpoint an especially valuable database for measuring the labor force by economic sector is the standard classification system of any given country. Yet, neither the International Standard Industrial Classification (variations of which most countries depend on) nor its North American counterpart, the NAICS (North American Industrial Classification System), has a grouping of industries under the heading "tourism" (Roehl 1998; US Census Bureau 2009a). Rather, an examination of the NAICS indicates that the services used by tourists are scattered throughout numerous sectors such as transportation (NAICS codes 48–49), real estate and leasing (code 53), arts, entertainment and recreation (code 71), and accommodation and food services (code 72) (Table 7.1) (Roehl 1998), again giving rise to the concept of tourism industries Additionally, not every sector within each of these classes can be truly thought of as tourism. The arts, entertainment, and recreation sector, for example, includes activities consumed primarily by local residents and cannot, therefore, be described as pure tourism. Similarly, when one examines the accommodation and food services sectors for a particular community, it is obvious that many food facilities cater largely to a local clientele, not just visitors. Additionally, it is worth mentioning that determining whether a particular sector constitutes tourism or not is very much contingent on the nature of the community. For instance, in a mountain ski resort a gas station may derive almost all its income from tourists, while in a major city a similar facility would be almost entirely dependent on local consumption.

The use of the industrial classification system for measuring the contribution of tourism to the economies of particular communities throughout the US is an issue that will be touched upon later in this chapter. First, however, we will provide an overall viewpoint of tourism's contribution to the national, regional, and local levels throughout the United States.

Table 7.1 Selected sectors of the NAICS that can be attributed directly to tourism

NAICS Code	Sector
48-49	Transportation and warehousing
48111	Scheduled air transportation
48521	Interurban and rural bus lines
48711	Scenic and sightseeing transportation, land
48721	Scenic and sightseeing transportation, water
48799	Scenic and sightseeing transportation, other
532111	Passenger car rental
56151	Travel agencies
56152	Tour operators
56159	Other travel arrangements and reservation services
71211	Museums
71212	Historical sites
71213	Zoos and botanical gardens
71219	Nature parks and other similar institutions
71311	Amusement and theme parks
71321	Casinos (except casino hotels)
71392	Skiing facilities
72111	Hotels (except casino hotels) and motels
72112	Casino hotels
72119	Other traveler accommodations

Source: Roehl (1998: pp. 63–4)

Note: This table is not comprehensive but merely reflects key sectors in the NAICS that either directly or indirectly serve tourists. Only sectors that in most communities depend heavily on tourists are shown. Other activities like restaurants, which albeit may in some communities be heavily dependent on visitors, have been left out in this table.

For a more concrete listing, please consult Roehl (1998).

The size of American tourism

In 1996 the Travel Industry Association of America (TIA) produced *A Portrait of Travel Industry Employment in the US Economy*. This report began with a preface by John Marks (1996), the chair of this organization, who was then the President of the San Francisco Convention and Visitors Bureau. Marks challenged many observers' assertion that tourism-related employment is characterized mostly by low-income jobs, offering little chance for upward mobility. He mentioned that "this perception stems from an earlier era when much of our economy and employment centered around [*sic*] manufacturing and production" (1996: v). Marks continued to argue that "employment growth in the travel industry is one of our nation's great success stories of the last decade. Both the rate of growth and the number of jobs created, have contributed materially to the economic well being of the United States." He also stressed that the quality of jobs had improved and that average earnings from tourism-related jobs were on par with all private industry sectors.

To be sure, the TIA is an advocacy group for tourism, so there are suspicions that its data presentation favors the industry. For instance, the 1996 report argued that unemployment in 1995 would have been in the double digits had it not been for the travel sector and maintained that "average hourly earnings in the service sector have grown faster than in all other industries except finance, insurance, and real estate" (TIA 1996: 3). What the report neglected to mention is the likelihood that the earnings in tourism jobs were on average at a much lower level than in other sectors. It is also important to mention that the data presented are highly aggregated and include transportation-related jobs that, especially at that time, were extremely well paid compared to a number of other sectors in tourism.

A more recent report by the same body (TIA 2006) indicates that in 2005, 7.5 million people throughout the US were employed in tourism-related jobs and travel expenditures amounted to $654 billion. These, in turn, created almost $105 billion in taxes for federal, state, and local governments. The jobs in tourism represented approximately 5.6 percent of total non-farm dependent employment nationwide. By far, the largest proportion of tourism-related jobs were in food services (2.4 million in 2004), while the accommodation sector employed a further 1.2 million people in what can be described as tourism-related employment (TIA 2005).

The data provided by the TIA are derived from their proprietary TEIM (Travel Economic Impact Model) originally developed in the mid-1970s for the US Department of the Interior (TIA 2005).

> The domestic component of the TEIM is based on national surveys conducted by TIA and other travel-related data developed by TIA, various federal agencies, and national travel organizations each year. Through the TEIM, TIA is able to measure travel and tourism at the national, state, and local levels.
>
> (TIA 2005: 2)

The TIA (2006) shows that in 2004 California was ranked first in terms of travel-related expenditures, tourism jobs, and tax receipts. Overall, travel expenditures in that state amounted to $77.3 billion, while jobs relating to the sector were estimated at 827,000. Tax revenues for California from various tourism sectors amounted to $12.6 billion.

Other states included in the top ten in terms of travel expenditures were Florida, New York, and Texas, ranked second, third, and fourth respectively. Florida stood first in terms of international traveler spending, a fact that is hardly surprising considering the wealth of international attractions this state has on offer. It is also interesting to note that in Hawaii, Nevada, and Wyoming tourism was the single largest employer, with 28.3 percent, 37.6 percent, and 10.9 percent of total non-farm employment respectively. In Florida, 10 percent of non-farm jobs were in travel and tourism, while in certain other states the sector's contribution was much more modest in percentage terms (e.g., New York with 4.8 percent of the total), reflecting the larger diversity of their economies. Overall, travel and tourism ranked number five "or better in terms of private employment in 19 states during 2004" (TIA 2006: 6). Even the effect on travel and tourism of the September 11 attacks in 2001 has been short-lived. Following a three-year decline from 2001–3, employment in travel and tourism began to grow in 2004 and was expected to continue to increase over the next decade; it is important to mention that at the time of writing (2009), the widespread economic downturn combined with the alarming growth in fuel prices, not to mention the plunge in the value of the dollar, had severely dampened expectations, though it is far from obvious at this stage what the long-term consequences of these events will be. Already, Americans have had to endure skyrocketing airfares, as airlines seek to find ways to reduce their own operational costs. Moreover, other elements of travel are becoming more expensive while consumers also have to contend with rapidly shrinking disposable incomes owing to the increasing prices of various items including food, fuel, and clothing.

California, the leading tourist destination in the United States, received more than 300 million visitors in 2005, reflecting an increase of 6.7 percent from the previous year. In fact, the state accounted for 11.08 percent of total US travel (based on person-stays).

During the same year, Texas and Florida accounted for 6.71 percent and 6.62 percent of total US travel (person-stays based). In California, resident travel within the state amounted to almost 280 million in 2005. Three-quarters of all arrivals in California came for the purpose of leisure (Shifflet and Associates 2006).

Other statistics for California (for the year 2005) indicate average per person per day expenditure amounting to $121.10, including transportation, compared to the national average of $111.40 per person per day. A further breakdown reveals that most of the expenditure, other than for transportation goes for food and, subsequently, shopping. When examining expenditure patterns by county it is not surprising that San Francisco shows the highest per person per day spending, whereas expenditures in rural counties are significantly lower (Shifflet and Associates 2006).

While tourism is a vast economic sector in California, plenty of other states boast the economic significance of their respective tourism industries. A study conducted by the Center for Business and Economic Development at Auburn University (2006) demonstrated the economic effects of tourism in Alabama. Nearly 22 million people visited Alabama in 2005, spending $7.6 billion. The tourist-related expenditures accounted for 3 percent of the Gross State Product (GSP) and more than 159,000 jobs (about 8 percent of the total non-agriculture employment). Not surprisingly, eating and drinking establishments accounted for a large portion of these jobs (almost 50 percent). In all, tourism generated $580 million in tax revenue for the state. Approximately 73 percent of travel-related jobs were concentrated in just seven counties out of a total of 67.

In the state of Washington, tourism is one of the leading export industries, based on its contribution to GSP (Dean Runyan and Associates 2004, 2006). Of course, the presence of Microsoft ensures the leading industry in Washington in terms of economic impact is the software sector, which during 2003 contributed $13.2 billion to GSP. During the same year, the aerospace industry, largely thanks to Boeing, accounted for $5.7 billion, with travel and tourism in third spot, responsible for $4.8 billion. To illustrate further the magnitude of tourism, the state of Washington also stresses the job-creation opportunities within the sector (primarily entry level jobs) and the fact that tourism generates plenty of potential for entrepreneurial activity, especially small business formation. The authors of the Washington report also extol the industry's primary and secondary impacts both in monetary terms and job-creation opportunities. It was estimated that in 2003 the indirect GSP of the travel and tourism sector amounted to $1.7 billion and the induced effect was a further $3.5 billion. This means that combined, the indirect and induced effect of travel was $5.2 billion, which was larger than the direct effect alone. Thus, the multiplier for tourism in Washington was 1.1 (the aerospace sector had a multiplier of 1.5 and the software industry 2.4).

One of the main arguments made in the state of Washington report on tourism is that because the industry is labor intensive it provides an excellent avenue for job creation but is also a sector with limited barriers to entrepreneurial activity, compared to other industries. In other words, just as in many other regions, in Washington the point is made that travel and tourism constitute an excellent chance for the creation and survival of small and medium privately owned businesses. The report also highlights the argument made by countless public officials around the nation that the tax revenue resulting from travel-related sectors as a percentage of GSP is especially high and, importantly, that much of this revenue comes from visitors; effectively, this means that a greater proportion of the cost for public goods and services can be paid for by tourists, thus reducing the burden on local inhabitants. In fact, this is one of the principal reasons numerous cities now charge hotel-motel taxes, while certain communities (e.g., Pittsburgh, Pennsylvania) actually charge higher entrance fees for various venues to non-residents.

Although tourism's magnitude in larger states such as California and Florida is staggering, it is in some of the demographically smaller states that the sector's importance must be highlighted. In a state like Wyoming, the number of arrivals, the amount of revenue, and the jobs generated from tourism are modest. Yet, when these measures are viewed proportionately compared to equivalent measures in other states, it is obvious how dependent Wyoming is on tourism; for instance, travel-dependent employment in this state is higher in percentage terms than in Arizona, Colorado, California, or Oregon (Wyoming Travel and Tourism 2005).

Reports like those for California, Alabama, Washington, and Wyoming paint a rosy picture concerning these states' tourism economies. This is not entirely surprising considering these reports are prepared either by consultants specializing in tourism, or state agencies, including divisions of tourism. By contrast, certain other studies display a more balanced view of tourism's role in a regional economy. For instance, the Buffalo Branch of the Federal Reserve Bank of New York (FRBNY) warns that a regional tourism industry, even in cases where this has been promoted to make up for losses experienced in traditional manufacturing activities, can have serious "drawbacks." "While tourism creates jobs, they are often low-paying and seasonal. The average annual wage in the industry is slightly more than $18,000, well below the national average (although tourism does create job opportunities for low-skilled and part time workers)" (FRBNY 2004: 1–2). Several academic studies have also examined tourism employment more objectively with similar conclusions (Choy 1995; Christensen and Nickerson 1995; Faulkenberry et al. 2000). The FRBNY also highlights certain additional pitfalls associated with tourism including the fact that in tourism-dependent communities, prices of goods and services, not to mention housing, can be significantly inflated while local government expenditures in such places may be significantly higher than elsewhere.

The New York report argues that in most metropolitan areas throughout upstate New York tourism's employment shares are below the national average. Even in the Niagara Falls region the share is 6.2 percent, which is surprisingly low considering the historic reputation of this area as a tourist destination. The FRBNY explains that the reason for this is twofold. On the one hand, Niagara County is actually a very industrialized region because of large amounts of hydroelectric power. On the other hand, the Canadian side of Niagara Falls is a far more successful destination than its US counterpart (Jayawardena et al. 2008; McGreevy 1994; Timothy 2001). From a positive standpoint, it appears that while the tourism industry is relatively small throughout upstate New York, its growth pace exceeds that of every other economic sector in most communities. Finally, the New York report stresses that in rural counties throughout the state, especially in the ones around the Catskills, tourism's employment share is quite high. "These areas are close to New York City, a prime source of regional tourists" (FRBNY 2004: 3).

In a nutshell, many reports, such as those described above, provide descriptions of tourism's economic performance for a particular calendar year. Because, however, there is no straightforward national tourism policy within the United States (a point made in an earlier chapter) there is no actual requirement as to how this information should be collected, analyzed, and reported, and so it remains hard to derive meaningful comparative studies spanning a number of states. To make matters worse, data relating to the supply of tourist accommodations (e.g., number of rooms or bed spaces) per state is sketchy at best and, in fact, rarely reported. Moreover, trying to figure out how many people within a certain community actually work in tourism can be extremely challenging. This, in turn, makes it difficult to estimate with a high degree of accuracy tourism's growth rates in various regions.

Tourism Satellite Accounts (TSAs)

One of the most robust techniques currently available for estimating the magnitude of tourism appears in the shape of Tourism Satellite Accounts, a system advocated more than a decade ago by the Organization of Economic Cooperation and Development (OECD) for calculating tourism's contribution to any country's national accounts (Jones *et al.* 2003). Other organizations that have recommended TSAs include the UNWTO and EUROSTAT (the European Statistical Agency). According to Wall and Mathieson (2006: 100) the principal objectives of a TSA, which have been summarized by EUROSTAT, include a

> provision of macro-economic aggregates to describe the size and economic importance of tourism, such as tourism value-added and tourism GDP [;] provision of detailed data on tourism consumption and how this is made up of domestic supply and imports [;] [and] provision of detailed production accounts on the tourism industries, data on employment, linkages with other production activities and capital formation.

Overall, the positive effect of this methodology is that it leads to estimates of the contribution of goods and services to visitors (both domestic and international) from all sectors of the economy, including travel-related sectors and all other industries (Jones and Munday 2008; Mak 2005; Wall and Mathieson 2006). The TSA approach builds upon the more traditional input–output technique, which fails to indicate clearly how demand for tourism affects industrial output. Jones *et al.* (2003) argue that TSAs can be developed in a step-by-step process whereby the most straightforward information (for which there are readily available data) is built into the model up-front. Subsequently, further steps can be taken to disaggregate tourism demand as additional information becomes available. For example, it may be possible to distinguish between the patterns of demand of residents versus visitors.

In a nutshell,

> the development of the TSA can be of real policy value. For example, a description of how tourism-related value added is divided between profits, earned income and other categories can indicate the level of value added retained locally – particularly important in regions where external control of facilities is significant.
>
> (Jones *et al.* 2003: 2780)

Additionally, TSAs can be used to determine the kinds of tourism with the most significant positive contribution in a host area or to estimate in what manner tourism-related jobs can mitigate unemployment.

A major criticism of the TSA methodology, however, is that it is far from clear what businesses should be targeted for analysis. Seeking to estimate the amounts of tourist expenditures for various goods and services compared to the total can also be an exercise fraught with difficulty. A full-blown TSA analysis can be extremely costly and may take considerable time, since it depends on complicated field work, including the collection of detailed surveys. Furthermore, because there are a number of difficulties in terms of data collection and interpretation, and especially because not every country collects all the required data for a complete TSA, the UNWTO recognizes that comparative studies between various countries are a difficult task.

Most of the early work relating to TSAs occurred in the early 1990s in Canada (Smith 1998). By the mid-2000s almost 25 countries had prepared national TSAs (Wall and Mathieson 2006). Additionally, increasing efforts have been made to undertake regional (sub-national) TSAs in various parts of the world. This, in turn has implications for large countries such as the United States where regional satellite accounts can be developed at the state level (Sacks 2004). Indeed, a number of states, including New Jersey, Virginia, and Hawaii, have already prepared TSAs (McGill 2005).

The Bureau of Economic Analysis (BEA) has produced national TSAs over the last several years. A comparative study for the period 2001–4 (Kuhbach and Herauf 2005) showed that the industry had begun to rebound after the events of 2001, although concern remained about employment growth, which remained weak. An even more recent report issued by the BEA shows that in 2007 tourism was actually up for the sixth consecutive year, the net exports of tourism-related goods and services expanded threefold over the previous year, and the sector's share of the gross domestic product (for 2006) was 2.7 percent, which was larger than that for industries like computer manufacturing, electronic products, and utilities. Overall, tourism accounted for 8.6 million jobs (directly and indirectly), representing a slight increase over the previous year. These numbers closely match the TIA estimates referred to earlier (Kern and Kocis 2007; Mattingly and Griffith 2008). It is interesting to note that by 2006 the number of tourism-related jobs had reached an all-time high, surpassing the previous record, which had been achieved in 2000. This is likely a reflection of the ongoing global and American transformation from manufacturing and extractive primary and secondary economies to tertiary, post-Fordist (service-based) economies (Agarwal *et al.* 2000; Ioannides and Debbage 1997).

According to the BEA's TSA, the largest contributors in the overall increase in tourism output between 2005 and 2006 were the recreation, entertainment, and retailing sectors, which made up 36 percent of this growth. "That contribution was more than twice its 17-percent contribution in 2005" (Kern and Kocis 2007: 15). The prices of tourism goods and services increased by 4.5 percent in 2006 (prices were 15.7 percent higher than in 2000) and much of this price increase was caused by the increase in air fares and gasoline prices. Additionally, the entire output resulting from the travel and tourism sector amounted to $700 billion (direct output) plus another $533 billion (indirect output).

In terms of tourism demand, the balance of trade derived from tourism declined slightly between 2005 and 2006 because the numbers of US citizens traveling abroad (outbound tourism) slightly exceeded the numbers of non-Americans traveling to the US (inbound tourism). The share of inbound tourism as a proportion of internal tourism (domestic and inbound travel) also increased after falling to a post 9/11 low of 11.7 percent of the total in 2003 (Kern and Kocis 2007).

The New Jersey TSA (McGill 2005) indicated that in 2004 the total tourism-related expenditure amounted to $32.3 billion in that state. This included travel expenditures by state residents, in-state business travel, government spending on travel and tourism, tourism-related investment, and spending by out-of-state visitors (both from other parts of the USA and international). The TSA revealed that the tourism sector was the ninth largest in terms of contribution to GSP by private industries and was the third largest employer, accounting for 9 percent of non-farm jobs. The largest portion of spending by visitors went towards their accommodation needs (37 percent), but tourists also incurred expenditures in numerous other sectors including food services, retailing, gas stations, and real estate (including second homes). A further analysis of expenditures by county indicates that Atlantic City (due to its gaming industry) and Cape May and Ocean counties account for two-thirds of the total (McGill 2005).

Local level

The evidence provided from the TSAs and various other analyses demonstrates tourism's importance at both the national and state levels. However, it is also imperative to understand the sector's contribution within local economies. Countless municipalities of varying sizes – from major metropolitan regions down to isolated rural communities with small populations – regard tourism as a major player in their respective economies. Perhaps it is not surprising that some localities have hired consulting firms to undertake economic impact studies of travel and tourism. The main objective of such studies appears to be to estimate tourism's economic and tax effects. The fiscal benefits of tourism have received considerable attention at local and regional levels, particularly as they pertain to special events, such as baseball World Series, World's Fairs, Olympics, and other such periodic or one-off events (Chhabra *et al.* 2003; Tyrrell and Johnston 2001). In these cases, local administrators are interested in understanding the temporary economic implications of events, although general tourism trends are equally important to destinations in the United States. It is worth mentioning, however, that while a lot of emphasis is placed on attempting to play up the economic effects of visitor-based activities the environmental and sociocultural repercussions of tourism development are often swept aside, unless it is too late. Closer Look Case 7.1 provides a good example of a community that has flourished economically through tourism but at a major expense, especially for its environmental resources.

CLOSER LOOK CASE 7.1

Avoiding the straw that breaks the camel's back: balancing tourism's impacts

Branson, Missouri, has regularly featured in the news over the last twenty years or so as a truly astounding phenomenon of tourism growth. This small town nestled in the Ozark Mountains of southwest Missouri was once a quiet resort community popular for people interested in outdoor activities. The creation of a series of dams in the region in the 1950s, most notably Table Rock Lake on the White River, transformed Branson into a popular destination for water enthusiasts who wanted to fish, water ski, or canoe.

By the 1960s Branson itself began to witness several changes. For example, Silver Dollar City, a park based on the theme of a frontier town with real-life actors dressed in period costume, was established and this was soon followed by the Baldknobbers' show, a popular event celebrating, among others, the music of the Ozarks. Both these attractions and a handful of others began drawing visitors in ever-increasing numbers. By the late 1980s and 1990s several additional attractions were developed, most notably a number of music theaters where various famous country and western singers like Wayne Newton, Bobby Vinton, and Andy Williams began performing on a regular basis. What truly placed Branson on the map, however, was a segment in the popular TV series *60 Minutes* in 1991, which claimed that the community had become the live music capital of the whole world. Overnight, this show made Branson an instant star on the tourism scene and visitors began coming in the millions. By the mid-1990s more than 5 million visitors came each year and the number of shows, additional attractions, not to mention supporting facilities like hotels and restaurants expanded impressively. All of a sudden community leaders were praising the visitor industry's contribution to job creation, not to mention the enormous expansion of the tax base.

Unfortunately, however, this impressive growth came with a host of accompanying problems. By 1996 alarm was spreading that the existing sewerage treatment facility, built for a town of under 3,000 residents, could not accommodate the enormous influx of visitors. Similarly, the emergency services (fire, ambulance, and police) were not able to handle a crisis. Much of the development that had taken place had been as a result of the actions of individual entrepreneurs and had not followed a coordinated community development plan.

The transportation consequences resulting from the collective actions of individual developers were never anticipated. Similarly, the housing needs of the new workers who were drawn to the town were not planned for. Existing schools could not handle the influx of children. Moreover, the architectural pollution resulting from shoddy building designs and ill-proportioned neon signs that severely impacted on the natural scenery led to massive criticism from environmental campaigners.

Amid accusations that many of the hotels did not even meet basic building code standards (e.g., they did not have sprinklers installed in each room) the local authority realized that something had to be done to improve the situation. In recent years a planning department has been set up, and the community has at least paid lip service to sustainable development by adopting various regulations, including aesthetic guidelines. Nevertheless, economic priorities continue to overshadow environmental and socio-cultural considerations, and numerous controversial developments keep cropping up around the community. Most importantly, many of the guidelines that have been developed to enable a more sustainable approach to development have not been rigorously enforced. Branson continues to face many problems.

The story of Branson is not unique. Several communities around the United States have witnessed astronomical growth, reflecting their leaders' blind adherence to short-term economic growth objectives without thinking about the long-term consequences of their actions. Importantly, because overall tourism development in most communities often results from the actions of numerous individual actors, the cumulative impacts of these actions are rarely anticipated until it is too late. In other words, while each small tourism business (e.g., hotel) on its own may have but a very minor impact on the community, at some stage, the number of businesses collectively will have an adverse consequence for the host society. This means that eventually the straw breaks the proverbial camel's back and without some form of remedy the tourist destination faces a major crisis.

Consequently, one of the major challenges that communities throughout the United States face on a daily basis is how to become more proactive when it comes to planning for tourism development. Despite the enormous merits of such an approach this is extremely difficult to achieve in a society that views regulations as an impediment to the operations of the free market. In other words, the laissez-faire attitude that continues to prevail in much of the United States when it comes to development is a major obstacle to sustainable development ideology.

Questions

1. It is very common in a community that is seeking to develop tourism to witness battle lines drawn between different groups of stakeholders. At one end of the spectrum, for

instance, may be stakeholders who are primarily concerned about a fast way to make a profit while at the other end one may see groups who are worried about the socio-cultural and/or environmental costs associated with poorly planned and controlled tourism development. Can you think of at least four groups of stakeholders and describe their respective agendas? How would you seek to generate a compromise between all these groups? Try to be as specific as possible.

2. The tourism development witnessed in places like Branson has had an impressive economic impact on the community. There are several other communities around the United States (for example Pigeon Forge, Tennessee) that also have benefited economically from the sector's growth. What do you think lies ahead for such places? Can they maintain their attraction as destinations? And, if so, what do they need to do? Importantly, how can they survive during periods of crisis such as economic recessions? Is it wise for them to put all their eggs into one basket, or should they seek to diversify their economies? What other sectors would be beneficial to such places?

Global Insight, in partnership with D.K. Shifflet and Associates Ltd (2005a), completed a study of tourism's economic effects in Austin, Texas. In this case, the entire economic impact of tourism on the city's economy (direct, indirect and induced) for 2003 amounted to $2.81 billion. Some 47,000 jobs were directly attributed to tourism while a further 14,000 positions were created through indirect or induced effects. A breakdown of tourism-related employment by various industry sectors (based on the NAICS), demonstrates that by far the major proportion of jobs (31.02 percent) was in the food and beverage industry. Arts, entertainment and recreation accounted for 18.53 percent of tourism-related jobs and lodging for a further 11.57 percent. Retail was also an important sector within the tourism economy, accounting for a total of 6,362 jobs (10.43 percent of the total). What is interesting to note is the number of indirect and induced tourism-related jobs in sectors like finance, insurance and real estate (FIRE), health care, construction, and public administration. Overall, travel and tourism was ranked the sixth largest industry in Austin's economy in terms of jobs. The consultants estimated that almost 17 million visitors came to Austin in 2003 and about 8 million of these stayed at least one night. In sum, Austin ranked 43rd in the nation in terms of tourism impact.

The same consulting group prepared a study for the Durham, North Carolina, convention and visitors bureau (Global Insight 2005b). Using an almost identical approach to the one they had applied in Austin, the consultants identified 5.21 million visitors who spent a total of $768 million in 2004 in this community. Approximately 11,400 jobs were attributed directly to tourism, while an additional 3,100 resulted from the sector's indirect and induced effects. These tourism-related jobs made up 6 percent of all employment in Durham. The tax revenue resulting from tourist expenditures brought in $188 million in local, state, and federal tax revenues. Approximately one-third of the local tax revenue was spent on a promotion and marketing campaign to lure more tourists to the area.

Both the Austin and Durham studies utilized NAICS data relating to measures such as employment, value added, and wages. Significantly, in both cases the authors acknowledged that tourism jobs span a number of economic sectors. For instance, they point out that in Durham's case, the retail industry employs 14,800 persons, many of whom are supported by out-of-town visitor spending. Similarly, the food services and drinking sector employs about 9,500 people but only a portion of these can be thought of as tourism-related. One way to interpret the results of the Durham study is that tourism employment accounts for 33 percent of all jobs in the food and beverage sector,

15 percent of jobs in entertainment, 14 percent of jobs in lodging, and 10 percent in retail. The proportion of tourism jobs for the lodging sector is surprisingly low, although it has to be assumed that many such establishments actually serve a considerable number of local residents (e.g., wedding banquets and local meetings).

The Global Insight consultants have also prepared tables for the purposes of benchmarking the top hundred metropolitan areas in the USA. According to their estimates, in terms of total visitor spending, Orlando ranks first, Las Vegas second, New York City third, and Los Angeles fourth (Table 7.2). When it comes to employment dependence, according to Global Insight (2005a), it is mostly smaller metropolitan areas with a significant reputation as destinations that see a substantial proportion of their workforce in tourism. These include the Atlantic City–Cape May metropolitan area where more than 70 percent of the workforce is dependent on tourism in a direct, indirect, or induced manner. Other metropolitan areas with a major percentage of their workforce in tourism include Myrtle Beach, South Carolina; Reno, Nevada; Flagstaff, Arizona; and Panama City, Florida. Only two major metropolitan areas in terms of area size and population are included in this list, namely Las Vegas and Orlando.

Undoubtedly the aforementioned consulting reports are valuable for scholars interested in tourism's performance, especially within urban areas. The Global Insight consultants make use of an input–output approach to derive their calculations. Yet, since companies like this are private entities, their models tend to be proprietary, making it hard for other interested parties to follow the utilized methodology closely, or indeed assess its accuracy and effectiveness. The question then is what approach can researchers and students on limited budgets use to measure tourism's presence in urban areas? Is there a technique that can be relatively simply applied to derive some useful observations?

We suggest using NAICS data, either from the Bureau of Labor Statistics or County Business Patterns. Roehl (1998: 76) has repeatedly argued that through the use of existing industrial classifications one can derive "multiple definitions of tourism . . . depending on the context, anything from a broad to a narrow production system can be defined." Strangely, despite this recommendation it does not seem there have been any significant attempts to use NAICS data to derive observations regarding tourism. Thus, the next section offers a brief glimpse into how such an analysis can take place.

Table 7.2 Rank of top 20 US cities according to visitor spending

Rank	City	Rank	City
1	Orlando, Florida	11	Miami, Florida
2	Las Vegas, Nevada	12	Tampa–St. Petersburg
3	New York City, New York	13	Boston, Massachusetts
4	Los Angeles, California	14	Phoenix–Mesa, Arizona
5	Chicago, Illinois	15	Dallas, Texas
6	Washington, DC	16	Philadelphia, Pennsylvania
7	San Francisco, California	17	New Orleans, Louisiana
8	San Diego, California	18	Houston, Texas
9	Atlantic City–Cape May, New Jersey	19	Orange County, California
10	Atlanta, Georgia	20	Honolulu, Hawaii

Source: Global Insight (2005: 15–16)

Measuring tourism through the NAICS

Earlier in this chapter it was mentioned that there is not a single industry in the NAICS, or indeed any industrial classification that can be clearly defined as tourism. Instead, the tourism sector transcends a number of industrial classes, some more obvious than others, and the determination as to whether or not a specific sector can be labeled "tourism" has much to do with the type of community in which it exists. It is not our purpose in this section to make an elaborate use of portions of multiple industrial classes, as defined by Roehl (1998), to devise a so-called tourism industry. Instead, at this stage we merely aim to demonstrate in a simple way how NAICS data can be used to derive meaningful observations regarding the tourism economy of several places.

The most readily available data at the local level regarding any industry, including tourism-related activities, relates to employment. These data are collected on an annual basis through the US Census Bureau's County Business Patterns. Additionally, every five years the same department administers a detailed economic census. Even though the latest census took place in 2007, the most recent data (at the time of writing) dates back to 2002. Data relating to employment by industry according to the NAICS are also collected and analyzed by the Bureau of Labor Statistics (BLS). These data derive from monthly surveys administered to approximately 150,000 private businesses and government agencies through the Current Employment Statistics program.

A useful tool now available to the BLS website users is the on-line location quotient calculator. The location quotient technique is a simple approach traditionally used in economic base analysis, allowing one to compare a local economy to the national economy. Specifically, one is able to see what proportion of the total local labor force is engaged in a particular activity compared to the labor force in the same industry at the national level. If the local labor force of a given industry constitutes a higher proportion of the total labor force compared to its national counterpart, then it is determined that the locality specializes in that activity; in other words, it produces more than it needs for self sufficiency (Hustedde *et al.* 1984).

Using the BLS online calculator the location quotients for several larger communities were estimated with regard to their respective total aggregated accommodation sector (NAICS 721). Of course, it is recognized that tourism is much more than just a particular community's lodging industry; in this case we are using this sector only as a proxy representing the broader tourism economy. The idea is that those communities that are heavily dependent on tourism will have a sizeable accommodation industry.

The analysis reveals that Las Vegas ranks first in terms of accommodation sector employees (more than 177,500). Significantly, this sector accounts for 22.8 percent of the metropolitan area's employment. More importantly, the location quotient for this sector in Las Vegas is more than 13.0, meaning that this city has 13 times more employees in the accommodation sector than its national counterparts. Other major cities with location quotients exceeding unity include Orlando (3.3), San Diego (1.7), Miami (1.4), and San Francisco (1.15) (Table 7.3).

In simple terms, the high location quotients for both Las Vegas and Orlando are to be expected given the extremely specialized nature of these economies. By the same token when one looks at smaller communities that can be characterized as tourism economies (e.g., Atlantic City, Reno, Myrtle Beach, and Santa Fe) it is evident that they also display high location quotients in accommodation – in the case of Atlantic City it is equal to 20.01 (Table 7.4). Conversely, when one examines the top ten metropolitan areas in terms of population it is hard to find one with a location quotient above unity. New York and Chicago, respectively, have location quotients equal to just about 0.6 (Table 7.3). This latter measure is misleading because even though it reflects a shortfall in these two cities

Table 7.3 Ranked location quotients (LQ) for the accommodation sector (NAICS 721), select large cities (2007)

MSA	Total employment	Employment in accommodation	LQ
Las Vegas	826,050	179,618	13.36
Orlando	915,438	49,018	3.29
San Diego	1,101,128	30,461	1.70
Miami	2,000,475	46,193	1.41
San Francisco	1,743,669	32,634	1.15
Phoenix-Mesa	1,645,479	28,964	1.08
Salt Lake City	535,872	9,119	1.05
Dallas-Fort Worth	2,518,758	30,245	0.74
Chicago	3,829,914	39,438	0.63
New York	7,032,453	69,787	0.61

Source: Bureau of Labor Statistics (BLS) – Quarterly Census of Employment and Wages: Location Quotient Calculator (2007) http://data.bls.gov/LOCATION_QUOTIENT/servlet/lqc.ControllerServlet (accessed February 9, 2009)

Table 7.4 Ranked location quotients (LQ) for the accommodation sector (NAICS 721), cities under 200,000 employees (2007)

MSA	Total employment	Employment in accommodation	LQ
Atlantic City	125,110	40,722	20.01
Reno-Sparks	192,876	20,001	6.37
Myrtle Beach	103,484	9,576	5.68
Santa Fe	47,348	2,503	3.25
Asheville, NC	148,724	4,284	1.77

Source: Bureau of Labor Statistics (BLS) – Quarterly Census of Employment and Wages: Location Quotient Calculator (2007) http://data.bls.gov/LOCATION_QUOTIENT/servlet/lqc.ControllerServlet (accessed February 9, 2009)

Table 7.5 Location quotients for various tourism-related sectors for Las Vegas and Orlando

NAICS	Sector	Las Vegas	Orlando	LQ Vegas	LQ Orlando
	All Industries	826,050	915,438		
48531	Taxi	7,684	ND	33.16	ND
48711	Scenic Transp. (land)	195	16	2.56	0.19
48799	Scenic Transp. (other)	863	8	43.31	0.36
56151	Travel agencies	1,133	1,598	1.48	1.88
56152	Tour operators	481	1,690	2.26	7.15
71113	Musical groups	408	164	1.43	0.52
71213	Zoos/Botanic Gardens	ND	84	ND	0.34
71311	Amusement/Theme Parks	ND	49,175	ND	43.41
71321	Casinos, except casino hotels	4,099	NC	5.75	NC
71329	Other gambling industries	1,996	ND	6.08	ND
71391	Golf courses and country clubs	3,867	3,095	1.54	1.11
72112	Casino hotels	168,738	ND	82.98	ND
72211	Full service restaurants	36,829	46,854	1.12	1.29
72241	Drinking places/alcoholic	6,972	2,206	2.72	0.78

Source: Bureau of Labor Statistics (BLS) – Quarterly Census of Employment and Wages: Location Quotient Calculator (2007) http://data.bls.gov/LOCATION_QUOTIENT/servlet/lqc.ControllerServlet (accessed February 9, 2009)

in terms of their accommodation sector employees compared to the national level, it fails to demonstrate that, in fact, both cities have a sizeable number of people working in these sectors and, indeed, their tourism industry is a significant contributor to their overall economies. However, the highly diversified nature of these cities ensures that tourism accommodation (and tourism overall) does not stand out as a sector of specialization.

Beyond using location quotients to draw comparisons between cities, one can examine one or two metropolitan areas in more depth by calculating location quotients for a variety of travel-related sectors. For instance, Table 7.5 demonstrates location quotients for various sectors in Las Vegas as well as Orlando. It is obvious from these data how specialized these particular cities, especially Las Vegas, are in tourism. In fact, the casino hotel sector (NAICS 72112) in Las Vegas alone has a staggering location quotient of 82.98, reflecting the heavy dependence of this city on the gaming industry. In Orlando, the amusement and theme park sector has a high location quotient (43.41) no doubt reflecting the dominance of venues such as Disney World and Universal Studios.

Conclusions

Tourism is a desirable economic alternative in the United States because of its potential to provide jobs, stimulate entrepreneurial activity, and generate tax revenues and regional income. Tourism provides tens of thousands of jobs and generates billions of dollars in tax revenue throughout the country each year, statistics which are hardly surprising given that the United States has long been at the top of the World Tourism Organization's list of countries earning the most from tourism. Having noted this, however, scale and relativism are important considerations in understanding tourism's economic importance in the USA.

At a national level, tourism is not a hugely important part of the overall GDP or other measures of national economy, as it is in some countries in Europe (e.g., Greece) or the Caribbean (e.g., the Bahamas and Aruba). This means that in an economy as large and diversified as that of the USA, tourism plays a relatively small role compared to agriculture, manufacturing, and construction. For example, some 2.7 percent of the US economy is based directly on the travel industries, and less than 6 percent of the non-farm employment in the USA comprises tourism-related jobs. If agricultural jobs were included in the figure, the ratio of tourism to non-tourism jobs would be even smaller.

At the level of individual states, however, scale and relativism become much more apparent. Some US states are heavily dependent on tourism while others are not; tourism plays a much more important economic role in states like Nevada, Hawaii and Wyoming, as already noted. Conversely, even though California is the most visited state in the USA and tourists spend more money there than anywhere else, tourism plays a proportionately small part in that state's economy (2.5 percent of total state GDP). In Nevada, however, which ranks fifth in arrivals of international visitors and significantly lower in domestic arrivals, tourism comprises approximately 13 percent of the total state GDP and provides 31 percent of the state's employment.

At an even smaller scale, some counties and cities are almost entirely dependent on tourism for their economic well being (Plate 7.1). As noted earlier in the chapter, it is typically the smaller tourism-oriented cities, such as Atlantic City and ski resort towns in Utah and Colorado, which rely more on tourism than the larger, more economically diverse cities. Tourism is an important development tool that many smaller communities and rural areas in the USA are beginning to target as a means of generating jobs and increasing tax revenues, a point we touch on in greater detail later on in this book. This is fairly remarkable in itself, because from public administrators' perspectives, tourism

Plate 7.1 Tourism-dependent community: Calistoga, California
(Dimitri Ioannides)

has often been seen in the past as being the domain of cities, playing only a secondary role in rural economic development, after agriculture. This reorientation is especially noticeable in the economically troubled times of the 2007–9 recession, where so many communities and states are required to make significant budget cuts. Unfortunately, simultaneously, potential visitors are cutting back on their travel budgets, so that spending on pleasure travel has also reached a long-time low.

Several important tools have been developed that assist destinations in understanding the true direct, indirect, and induced measures of tourist spending. TSAs are among the most critical tools in analyzing the economic effects of tourism. These are tenuous economic times, and even TSAs cannot predict the future direction of tourism in the US. If the past is any indication of the future, however, the situation will improve and the public will once again demand the tourism product.

Questions

1. Is it true that some organizations exaggerate the economic impact of tourism? Why do you think they do this?
2. Why do community leaders often avoid undertaking a detailed feasibility study when developing a tourism-related project? What would be their rationale in encouraging the development of a project even though it appears that it may not pay for itself over the long run?

3. Is tourism an industry in the conventional sense in which industries are defined or not? Justify your answer.
4. In what way can the NAICS help one better comprehend the size of the tourism industry in a particular locale? What sectors from the NAICS would you use to define the tourism industry in Atlantic City, New Jersey?

Further reading

Baade, R.A., Baumann, R.W. and Matheson, V.A. (2008) Assessing the economic impact of college football games on local economies. *Journal of Sports Economics*, 9(6): 628–43.

Chhabra, D. (2007) Estimating benefits and costs of casino gambling in Iowa, United States. *Journal of Travel Research*, 46(2): 173–82.

Orens, A. and Seidl, A. (2009) Working lands and winter tourists in the Rocky Mountain west: a travel cost, contingent behaviour and input-output analysis. *Tourism Economics*, 15(1): 215–42.

Hjerpe, E.E. and Kim, Y.S. (2007) Regional economic impacts of Grand Canyon river runners. *Journal of Environmental Management*, 85(1): 137–49.

Long, P.T. and Perdue, R.R. (1990) The economic impact of rural festivals and special events: assessing the spatial distribution of expenditures. *Journal of Travel Research*, 28(4): 10–14.

Marcouiller, D.W. and Xia, X.L. (2008) Distribution of income from tourism-sensitive employment. *Tourism Economics*, 14(3): 545–65.

Nichols, M., Giacopassi, D. and Stitt, B.G. (2002) Casino gambling as a catalyst of economic development: perceptions of residents in new casino jurisdictions. *Tourism Economics*, 8(1): 59–75.

Rivera, M.A., Hara, T. and Kock, G. (2008) Economic impact of cultural events: the case of Zora! Festival. *Journal of Heritage Tourism*, 3(2): 121–37.

Stoddard, J., Dave, D., Evans, M. and Clopton, S.W (2006) Economic impact of the arts in a small US county. *Tourism Economics*, 12(1): 101–21.

Tyrrell, B.J. and Ismail, J.A. (2005) A methodology for estimating the attendance and economic impact of an open-gate festival. *Event Management*, 9(3): 111–18.

Useful Internet resources

Bureau of Labor Statistics: http://www.bls.gov/
International Association for Tourism Economics: http://www.tourism-economics.net/
Travel Industry Association of America: http://www.tia.org/index.html
US Department of Commerce: http://www.commerce.gov/
World Tourism Organization: http://www.unwto.org/index.php
World Travel and Tourism Council: http://www.wttc.org/

8 Urban tourism in the USA

Las Vegas's triumph as a world resort was never assured. Virtually no one in the 1920s would have expected the town to blossom into the metropolis that it is today. Lack of water, fertile land, productive mines, and heavy industry made it an unlikely candidate. But the same forces which forged the new west and lured millions of people to the sunbelt, also boosted Las Vegas. Reclamation projects, New Deal Programs, defense spending, air conditioning, interstate highways, jet travel, right to work laws, low taxes . . . helped Las Vegas.

(Eugene Moehring 2000: 13)

Introduction

For many people, Las Vegas is the ultimate tourist destination. This vast conurbation in the midst of a desert is the nation's fastest growing metropolitan region. It boasts a permanent population of approximately 2 million and each month witnesses the arrival of 5,000–6,000 new residents (Schoenmann 2008). On an annual basis the metropolitan region hosts many times that number of visitors. In 2006 alone, 38.9 million arrivals were recorded compared to 28.6 million in 1995 and the Las Vegas Convention and Visitors Authority projected that 39.3 million would visit in 2007. A total of 137,600 rooms were available in 2006 up from fewer than 90,000 a decade earlier. By 2010 the capacity will have increased to a staggering 171,000 rooms (Parker 1999; *USA Today* 2007; Velotta 2008).

Las Vegas is, in many ways, a peculiar place, one that defies traditional theories of urbanization. It is also, as Gottdiener *et al.* (1999) describe, an "improbable metropolis," a place existing in the midst of what was once nowhere, a desert environment far removed from civilization. Even today the challenges Las Vegas faces are formidable. Water has to constantly be pumped from Lake Mead uphill toward the city. And, almost all the raw materials necessary within the city for its residents and visitors from construction materials to food, clothing, and electronic items must be imported.

The city began its existence in the early 1900s as a humble railroad community in an otherwise barren and inhospitable landscape. Already, for many years during the latter part of the nineteenth century and the beginning of the twentieth this locality had served as a rest stop for people en route to California and most notably, Los Angeles (Moehring 2000). Various key factors have underpinned Las Vegas' phenomenal success over the last seven decades or so, including the development of the Hoover Dam in the 1930s, Nellis Air Force Base during the Second World War, but most of all, legalized gambling (Gottdiener *et al.* 1999; Parker 1999; Wheeler 2008). Today the gaming industry is extremely significant to the local economy since two thirds of jobs in the region depend on this (Velotta 2008).

Nevada's liberal gaming laws, originally introduced during the Depression (in a repeal of restrictions on gambling instituted twenty years earlier), served as fodder for Las Vegas' original boom after the Second World War. Hotel casinos and resorts popped up with increasing frequency during the 1950s and 1960s and soon the city was transformed into the world's largest adult playground. In addition to the gambling establishments, more and more venues offering live entertainment (from rock concerts to Tony Bennett, from amazing circus acts to striptease) opened their doors. This became the place where one can check into an affordable first-class hotel room with a Jacuzzi, marry his or her sweetheart in a drive-through chapel, wander aimlessly for hours through the Strip, gaze at a half-scale Statue of Liberty or the Eiffel Tower and spend a whole evening losing money in one of the thousands of slot machines or attending a heavyweight boxing match.

It is also one of America's leading destinations for business tourists, offering enough convention floor-space for hosting numerous major meetings simultaneously (Parker 1999). In 2006 Las Vegas was America's leading city on *Tradeshow Week's* Top Ten List, which ranks the nation's top convention destinations according to the number of trade shows and events with more than 100 attendees during a single year (Massachusetts Convention Center Authority 2005). A total of 23,825 meetings and conventions were hosted in 2006 and these drew 6.3 million delegates compared to 2.9 million in 1995. The economic impact of convention-based tourism amounted to a staggering $8 billion (Las Vegas Convention and Visitors Authority 2007).

Las Vegas never rests on its laurels, however. The actors shaping the fortunes of its tourism industry are fully aware that to ensure continuous success they must constantly diversify the destination. Thus, Las Vegas has become the locality where perfectly good hotels and resorts are torn down with what seems to be amazing regularity to make place for ever-more grandiose edifices, housing some of the world's most impressive lodging establishments. These are vast structures. Indeed, by the early part of this decade nine of the ten largest hotels in the world were located along the Strip, including the Bellagio and Luxor (Todd 2001). The world's second largest hotel, the MGM Grand, boasts an astounding 5,690 rooms; only the First World Hotel in Malaysia has more rooms (Insider Viewpoint of Las Vegas 2007). Moreover, two new convention facilities have been planned that will add close to 900,000 square feet of meeting space over the next three years (Velotta 2008). Las Vegas also spends millions on advertising campaigns each year never taking for granted that its attractions alone can draw visitors without the aid of a promotional strategy. Take a closer look at one of its most successful advertising campaigns in recent years (see Closer Look Case 8.1).

CLOSER LOOK CASE 8.1

Ask me no questions

Las Vegas has always had an unwholesome reputation. It is inherently associated with such decadent activities as gambling, sex, and drinking, arguably deserving the moniker "sin city" more than any place in the world. Nevada's permissive gambling laws early in its history and legalization of prostitution (albeit heavily regulated and actually illegal inside the city of Las Vegas) a little later reinforced the city's image as a decidedly indulgent and hedonistic destination.

In the 1950s and '60s Las Vegas was the epitome of sexy, licentious elegance. Powerful symbols of the time were the rat pack with their stylish masculinity and the show girls who wore more on their heads than on their bodies. Though the styles and the acts on the Strip changed, the image of Las Vegas remained powerfully sinful throughout the years. It is the ultimate destination for those who want to take a short break from their pedantic lives and leave control and inhibitions behind. Its over-the-top surreal architecture reflects the excess the city demands of its visitors and of itself. It is the archetypal "entertainment machine" (Clark *et al.* 2002) with its commodified American culture and packaged hedonism.

With the exception of a period in the '90s when Las Vegas briefly attempted to portray itself as a family-friendly place, the city has been aware of its nature as an adult destination. In April 2009, the Las Vegas Convention and Visitors Authority (LVCVA) brought back the "what happens here stays here" advertising campaign (Velotta 2009). The campaign has become a popular catchphrase spinning off anything from YouTube videos to condom commercials to a feature film with Cameron Diaz and Ashton Kutcher. It is a campaign consisting of several 30-second spots, seemingly arranged in thematic groups to paint different but complementing strokes of the picture of Las Vegas as a decidedly sinful city:

- *Even ordinary middle-aged balding guys can be wild in Las Vegas.* In this spot, a man fitting this description is willing to pay his landscaper more than double the usual fee for the work performed so that the latter does not reveal what happened during the former's recent Vegas trip. The main character of the spot is obviously an affluent upper-class professional with a large suburban house. The audience for this spot is the older business traveler, middle-aged and affluent who, leaving behind the picket fence and the dog for a few days goes to Vegas for some wild partying. The kind of partying is left to the viewers' imagination – gambling, sex, and alcohol, all of the above or other things; however, deviance is implied. The same message is conveyed through another spot, which opens with a man having a cat-scan performed in a clinic. He is perhaps not as upper class as the man in the landscape spot, and looks younger, rather nerdy and slightly overweight – a professional or maybe a salesman. When the doctor proclaims there is nothing wrong with him, his wife, obviously irritated, wonders how on earth this is the case since he seems to have gotten amnesia and has blacked out the week he was in Las Vegas. Notably the doctor, also a man, gives a sideways supporting look to the "patient," under the fiery gaze of the wife. She is wearing a business pantsuit and definitely appears more masculine than her sheepish husband.
- *Girls (ugly or beautiful, young or old) can have fun, too.* This spot opens with an older Asian woman sitting at a poolside bar writing a postcard. The assumption is that she is writing to her family back home as the postcard is a picture of Las Vegas and the writing is clearly not English. She is writing with a fountain pen, implying propriety, even tradition. The lyrics of the song in the background poignantly declare: "ask me no questions, I'll tell you no lies, ask me no questions, I'll be yours tonight." As she writes the postcard, she seems to decide that she gave too much information and starts to smudge the ink with liquid from her drink. Notably, there is no dialogue in the spot. The only thing the viewer can hear, other than her disapproving noises, is the song: "ask me no questions . . ." Again, the transgression is left to the viewers' imagination, which is not really the case with the spot featuring the business woman in the limo. The scene, reminiscent of the limo scene with Sean Young in *No Way Out,* shows a sexy woman in the back of a limo flirting shamelessly with the driver. By the

time the limo arrives at the airport, the woman has resumed her proper, serious business-like attire and persona and is ready to go home to her regular life.

● ***You can assume any identity in Las Vegas – including no identity.*** One of the spots in this group shows an ordinary man perhaps in his mid-thirties trying to pick up various women claiming a number of rather odd and unusual professions, including neurosurgeon, hand model, big game hunter, and cage fighter. Another shows two good-looking women in their mid-thirties wearing little black dresses swapping wigs in the restroom of a high-end night club, while a third takes place in the baggage claim area of the airport showing numerous taxi and limo drivers all waiting for travelers by the name of Smith. The implication here of course is that, anybody can shed their proper identity and become anybody in Las Vegas. At home you can adhere to the strict protestant ethic and be who you are expected to be; however in Las Vegas you can indulge yourself and be Mr. or Ms. Smith, that is Mr. or Ms. Anybody.

The underlying theme of this campaign is that Las Vegas allows decadence, debauchery, deviance, sex, gambling, self-indulgence, and hedonism. Even in the American puritanical society this is all right because it is not the norm. Las Vegas is portrayed as the larger-than-life city of excess that exists for the pleasure of those who can afford it. It is a necessary fact of life; the naughty closet where tourists can leave their skeletons so they can go on being upstanding citizens, good mothers and wives, and respected fathers and husbands.

Sources

Clark, T.N., Lloyd, R., Weng, K. and Jain, P. (2002) Amenities drive urban growth. *Journal of Urban Affairs*, 24(5): 493–515.

Velotta, R. (2009) R&R gets three-year extension on LVCVA ad contract. *Las Vegas Sun*, April 17, 2009. Available from http://www.lasvegassun.com/news/2009/apr/17/rr-gets-three-year-extension-lvcva-ad-contract/ (accessed September 15, 2009).

Questions

1. Consider the character of Las Vegas as a destination and the economic crisis of the late 2000s. Voices of dissent in the city reflect a concern that the current advertising campaign is not money well spent. If you were a LVCVA official, would you seek to reinforce Las Vegas' image as an adult destination or would you try to revive the idea that it is also a family friendly destination? Justify your approach.
2. Look up the "what happens here stays here" campaign spots online or watch for them on television. Can you find more than the ones listed above? Are any additional themes highlighted? Do you think that the ads' portrayal of Las Vegas is accurate?

Evangelia Petridou

The architectural collage (see Plate 8.1) forming Las Vegas of the twenty-first century marks the pinnacle of place image-making and boosterism, that has become the *leitmotif* of economic strategies for places large and small around the nation. To be sure, no other places exist quite like Las Vegas, the definitive tourism-industrial complex, but certainly the leaders of numerous localities of varying size have recognized the significance of attracting visitors. From New York to San Francisco, from Chicago to Atlanta, and from

Seattle to Miami, billions of dollars have been spent in the last few years to develop the stereotypical infrastructure for tourists (Curry *et al.* 2004; Ioannides 2003; Judd 2003a): stadiums, aquariums, convention centers, festival market places, casinos, and so much more. One would be hard-pressed indeed to find a city where at least some of these elements are not present. In 2003, Austin, Texas, for instance, attracted roughly 17 million visitors, almost half of whom stayed at least one night and spent $2.8 billion. A total of 60,992 jobs were attributed to the industry, including 46,995 direct jobs (Global Insight 2006).

This chapter concentrates on the phenomenon of urban tourism in the United States. First, we discuss the status of urban tourism research in academe, highlighting one useful way of examining this phenomenon, namely through the use of regulation theory (Shaw and Williams 2004; Fainstein *et al.* 2004). Subsequently we focus on the reasons behind tourism's ascendancy into a definitive economic growth strategy among urban policy-makers throughout the nation. We then discuss the different types of tourist cities that exist in the USA and highlight the fact that most can fit the category of "converted cities," that is, places that have sanitized at least some of their old manufacturing or warehouse districts into places to play (Fainstein and Judd 1999). Today, these spaces are remarkably homogeneous and predictable offering a similar assortment of attractions and ancillary facilities. Since they offer a full array of amenities, they are, in fact, spaces designed to contain visitors. Nevertheless, it is becoming clear that as tourists become more sophisticated they seek out other parts of the city – neighborhoods that are not necessarily touristic to begin with, but ones that project an abundance of "quality of life" elements.

Plate 8.1 Finding New York City in Las Vegas?
(Dimitri Ioannides)

The study of urban tourism

Casual observers should, perhaps, be forgiven for not immediately thinking of large metropolitan areas and tourism within the same context. In their minds cities are busy places where people work and the production of goods and services occurs. Cities are often extremely noisy, heavily polluted, and overcrowded with people and vehicles. Tourism, in the opinion of these observers, is associated with more tranquil settings such as those found in national parks, historic battlefields, mountain resort communities, riparian corridors, or along an isolated stretch of seashore.

The reality, of course, is far from this. In any given country cities draw the largest portion of visitors (domestic and international) compared to other destinations. Think about the thousands of visitors who on any given day hang around Times Square in New York, Faneuil Hall in Boston, or Fisherman's Wharf in San Francisco. Each year millions of visitors come to the nation's capital and a large proportion of these congregate within the National Mall and the attractions in and around it. When foreign visitors arrive in the United States, more often than not they fly into one of the busiest airports, all of which happen to be within some of the largest metropolitan regions. It is not unusual for these visitors to spend at least part of their vacation soaking up the various tourist sites these cities have to offer. It should also be stressed that many cities have a fair number of attractions marking key events in the country's history. Philadelphia alone is akin to a living history museum for those interested in the events surrounding the American Revolutionary War. Similarly, Boston's centuries-old neighborhoods, churches, and public buildings have long been popular tourist attractions.

Today, one would be hard pressed to find a single urban area within the United States that does not have some form of tourism promotion strategy. Simply stated, urban policymakers view tourism as an economic panacea, especially in light of the decline of traditional economic sectors, including heavy manufacturing. Tourism reflects the general shift towards an economy based on the production and consumption of experiences and reflects the broader phenomenon of cultural commodification (Ioannides and Debbage 1998; Hoffman *et al.* 2004; O'Dell and Billing 2005).

Yet, despite these facts the study of urban tourism has been largely neglected until recently and most investigations on the topic remain theoretically threadbare. Selby (2004) argues that much of the existing work relating to urban tourism remains based on descriptive case studies "concerned with monitoring and describing patterns of land use and tourist flows" (p. 2), while there have also been a fair number of multiplier studies (see also Page 1995). Back in 1989, one of the pioneers in the field of urban tourism, Gregory Ashworth, argued that the neglect of this topic was especially troublesome since it appeared on two fronts. On the one hand, tourism researchers shied away from studying the phenomenon within an urban context while, on the other hand, academics in fields relating to urban studies (like urban geography and urban sociology) entirely ignored the topic (see also Selby 2004).

A simple explanation for the absence of such a focus in urban literature is that it is hard to disaggregate tourism within the complex fabric that makes up the urban economy. How big is tourism in a certain metropolitan area? How many visitors does a city attract to begin with? How, indeed, does one separate genuine tourists from other visitors, including suburbanites, who come to the city for a few hours and use the same services as their counterparts from further away? Given that answers to such questions are not easy to come by, the measurement of urban tourism is an exercise fraught with difficulty. Additionally, many urban scholars (including urban geographers) have traditionally shunned the study of tourism perhaps because they fail to see how an activity commonly, albeit incorrectly, associated with leisure and pleasure, and one that is notoriously fragmented and heterogeneous, can be theoretically stimulating (Agarwal *et al.* 2000; Ioannides and Debbage 1998; Judd 2006; Selby 2004). Ioannides and Debbage (1998) have also argued in the past that yet another reason for the lack of theoretical rigor associated with the geographical studies of tourism stems partly from the fact that some observers regard "the physical regeneration of localities for the consumption of tourism as an affront to the hard, concrete labor of yesteryear" (1998: 5).

Fortunately, the intellectual inattention towards urban tourism has abated drastically. Over the last decade there has been an explosion of academic writings relating to the political economy of urban tourism, much of it emanating not from tourism researchers but from scholars in urban studies (urban geography, political science, city planning, and public administration). These authors have contributed greatly to the intellectual discourse regarding, among others, the role of tourism in the transformation of urban-scapes. Much of the discussion relating to city-based tourism has also focused on improving our understanding of how local forces play out in the face of marked tendencies toward globalization (Appadurai 1996; Gotham 2005). Among the issues examined have been whether or not the growing force of globalization has "annihilate[d] local differences" (Gotham 2005: 309) as reflected through the seeming standardization of tourism landscapes from city to city or whether, in fact, there are significant variations displaying the importance of local agencies and indigenous cultures in the way tourism plays out in different places.

Fainstein *et al.* (2004) have suggested utilizing regulation theory to examine tourism's dynamics in urban regions. Hoffman (2004) contends that "a regulation framework allows us to address the relation between large-scale external forces and local conditions – the issue of scale. Its focus on institutional structure also helps clarify the complex web of cultural, political, and economic factors which are central to . . . tourism in general" (p. 91). Tourism research is, of course, as Shaw and Williams (2004) point out, no stranger to the use of regulation theory, which allows one to "situate tourism in relation to key elements in individual countries . . ., including the development stage of the country, the role of the public versus the private sector, and institutional and regulatory frameworks" (p. 31).

There certainly has been an explosion of studies since the early 1990s examining shifts in the macro-economy or the regime of accumulation (i.e., the manner in which production, distribution, and consumption within capitalism are organized) and their relationship to tourism. Researchers have focused particularly on how the theorized transformation from Fordist (mass-oriented) to more flexible (niche-oriented) production systems in manufacturing plays out within the travel and tourism sector (Agarwal *et al.* 2000; Britton 1991; Ioannides and Debbage 1998; Torres 2002). Unfortunately, while discussions concerning changes in the regime of accumulation and its effect on tourism have proliferated, the other important aspect of regulation theory, namely shifts in the mode of regulation, has thus far been underplayed in tourism research.

The mode of regulation relates to the institutional framework, including the role of the state. This institutional framework exists in capitalism to deal with various crises/problems that recur, which due to its short-term profit-driven goals the private sector is ill-equipped to deal with. These include a range of collective goods of consumption (e.g., health care, public safety and the education system). According to Shaw and Williams (2004) various foci of regulation exist "including the monetary system, wage relations and working conditions, competition, provisions of collective services (health, education, housing, security, etc.) and international relations" (p. 32). Advocates of regulation theory contend that under Fordism the dominant mode of regulation witnesses a heavy presence of the central state, Keynesian economics, and a welfare state. With the transition of the regime of accumulation to post-Fordism, a trend towards globalization is accompanied by a weakened presence of the state and increasing privatization of various services.

The question, within the context of tourism (and urban tourism in particular) concerns the manner in which regulation theory can be used to explain both the similarities and the differences between places and the way in which tourism evolves. Fainstein *et al.* (2004) suggest that regulation theory helps one understand two concurrently occurring phenomena. On the one hand, the institutions and other regulatory forces that occur within the context of globalization to a certain extent diminish the differences between places (including cities), especially in terms of tourism's development; in effect, many tourism landscapes, especially those found within downtown areas of US cities, display elements of standardization and predictability. The reason for this imposed sameness within so many localities is quite simply that public officials and tourism industry representatives seek to reduce the sense of the unexpected in a concerted effort to make visitors feel safe and secure. On the other hand, however, the fact that there exist certain glaring variations between and also within cities in terms of their tourism product implies, according to Fainstein *et al.*, that the political and cultural climate of each destination do actually matter.

"International flows of capital, multinational corporations, and imitative marketing produce standardization, even while differing local regimes, cultures, and conscious efforts at differentiation produce distinctive tourism locales" (Fainstein *et al.* 2004: 2).

Gotham (2005) vehemently supports the notion that despite the fact that tourism is dominated by global players, the hypothesized imposed repetition of sameness from urban space to urban space does not occur to the extent that some observers have argued. Through a study of New Orleans he shows that localities are not simply submissive pawns of the global tourism industry but instead they have a say as to how the sector's development actually plays out. In other words, geography and also historical contingency do actually matter. For instance, although Mardi Gras has now been exported in a commercialized form from New Orleans to a number of American cities, it is immediately evident that what has evolved in Philadelphia or Seattle cannot replace the "real thing" as found in New Orleans. New Orleans' Mardi Gras has a very long history and has become what it is today because of local forces like neighborhood associations and various social networks that are not found in other places.

Later in this chapter we explore some of the strategies that American cities have adopted to promote tourism and demonstrate there are certainly plenty of elements to fuel the argument that standardization of their visitor-based industry is becoming increasingly commonplace. However, we also demonstrate that some of the most successful tourist venues in contemporary cities are unique districts that have little to do with symbols of global capitalism. To a major extent the success of such venues has to do with the growing dissatisfaction of many people who wish to escape the homogenized spaces that have been dictated by global forces and find out what is truly unique about the place they are visiting. Before we do this, however, we explain why the search for tourists has become such a popular strategy in contemporary cities.

Why cities seek visitors

For decades, the central areas of numerous American cities have found themselves in a downward economic spiral and nowhere is this crisis more pronounced than in the older metropolitan areas of the country's northeast quadrant, the so-called Rustbelt. Urban scholars attribute much of this problem to a combination of ill-conceived public policies, dating back to the Urban Renewal Act of 1949. Effectively, this legislation, dubbed the

"Slum Clearance Program," vastly accelerated the exodus of middle-class, predominantly white Americans who in the post-Second World War era had already begun taking advantage of generous federally guaranteed, low-interest mortgages to purchase brand new "cookie-cutter" suburban homes. In the aftermath of President Eisenhower's Federal Aid Highway Act of 1956 the white flight towards the suburbs speeded up even further and by the early 1960s many inner cities began experiencing serious problems associated with their rapidly diminishing tax base.

It is hardly a stretch of the imagination to underline that during the 1970s urban areas throughout the United States faced a massive fiscal crisis, which was made worse because of the widespread decline of traditional manufacturing activities. A major economic recession, which began during the 1973 oil crisis and accelerated between 1975 and 1977, meant local authorities faced an uphill and losing battle to provide even the most basic services while the finances for encouraging urban rehabilitation rapidly dwindled. Following the election of President Reagan in 1980, the federal government, a long-time economic savior of distressed municipalities, dramatically reduced fiscal assistance for local economic development projects, meaning that communities were very much left on their own to identify ways to survive.

It was, ironically, the Reagan administration that fueled the popularity of tourism as one of various possible solutions leading to economic growth, while other measures included making places more attractive for business investors and households through the provision of lucrative incentives packages (Judd 1999). Further, Fainstein and Stokes (1995) have contended that the economic downturn in the property market during the late 1980s and early 1990s, following a period of speculative over-building of office space in central business districts, provided the extra impetus for public officials to seek the development of visitor-based attractions and facilities, including sports stadiums, which were seen as magnets for further development (also Gladstone and Fainstein 2001; Turner and Rosentraub 2002). By 1995, a total of over 2 billion dollars per year was spent on facilities such as these by local and state governments in the United States (Judd 2003b).

Yet another key force behind tourism's expansion within American cities was the historic preservation efforts that gathered momentum nationwide in the late 1950s, '60s, and '70s. Decades earlier, New Orleans and Charleston, South Carolina, had arguably been pioneers in the urban preservation movement. In New Orleans during the 1920s "preservationists had been forging a consensus favoring protection of the [French] Quarter's appearance" (Souther 2007: 806). In 1937 the Vieux Carré Commission was formed and given the charge of overseeing the historic and architectural preservation of the city's French Quarter. Souther insists that the aim behind the preservation of the French Quarter was to protect local businesses and residences from the threat of tasteless development but, unwittingly, this movement prepped the area to become a tourist hub.

In more recent times, community leaders have come to appreciate the value of restoring various historical edifices or even entire districts, instead of permitting their demolition to make room for brand new real estate. The current thinking is that many people, especially those living in suburban subdivisions – the point of origin for a large portion of visitors to urban areas – have powerful feelings of nostalgia for the inner city neighborhoods and buildings their parents and grandparents left behind four or five decades ago (Beauregard 1998). Quite simply, inner city areas often possess a rich heritage of historical buildings that lack the dull and banal uniformity of modern sub-urban residential developments and strip malls. Additionally, according to Turner and Rosentraub (2002) because downtowns historically were spaces where commercial functions co-existed with cultural activities, their transformation into venues for tourist activities has not been as surprising as one might think. Closer Look Case 8.2 indicates that such a transformation of downtown areas not only happens in large US cities but is also an increasingly common phenomenon in certain mid-sized communities, especially if these have a suitable building stock to enable this transformation to happen in the first place.

CLOSER LOOK CASE 8.2

How can mid-sized cities compete for tourism?

Things get quite glitzy at night downtown. Stretch limos and yellow cabs (a sight up till now rarely spotted in town) line the streets; smartly dressed people go from the restaurant to the night club, or the pub, or even to the gig at the gallery down the street which doubles as an intimate concert space. There is a new branch of the public library at the square, which is connected to the adjacent independent and very green-oriented coffee shop. One can actually lounge on one of the soft red couches in the library drinking the organic coffee that has been bought in the coffee shop. Additionally, one can eat American, Spanish, Mexican, Italian, Middle Eastern, and Japanese before or after catching a movie at one of the two movie theaters located downtown. Part of the university campus is located in the area as well as a state-of-the-art nanotechnology center, a convention facility, and a professional-grade baseball stadium. Some of the consumers of this entertainment cluster live in the area. Loft-living is on the rise with more and more rehabilitated spaces; new construction has also increased and the vacancy rate is only 7 percent. However, most of the visitors do not live downtown. Instead they travel in from the suburbs or from urban neighborhoods located within a few miles. A significant number of them are out-of-towners. Of course, this would be hardly anything to write home about if the downtown belonged to an iconic metropolis, such as New York, Chicago, or Miami.

It doesn't, though. This is Springfield, Missouri, located in southwest Missouri (an otherwise rural area), which is the third largest city in the state after St. Louis and Kansas City. Springfield itself has a population of just over 158,000, while the five-county metropolitan region to which it belongs numbers just over 407,000. The metro area has experienced an average annual growth rate of 2.2 percent since 1990, while unemployment has held steady at under 4.5 percent. The area's economic output has doubled over the past decade, making it one of the top 50 fastest growing areas in the USA.

"Glitzy," "cool," "hip," "lively," "crowded," and "busy," however, were not adjectives that could easily be used to describe downtown Springfield until a few years ago. This had been an area of devastation, urban decay, and boarded-up industrial buildings for decades. It was, in many ways, a poster child of a trend that has characterized numerous American urban cores – large and small – in the years following the end of the Second World War: manufacturing started declining, the white middle class fled to the suburbs, malls opened in suburban and exurban areas, and all that remained downtown were empty boarded-up structures and abandoned lots in the place where historic buildings once stood. Springfield was no exception, even though it is by no means a big city. Its old industrial stock stood vacant and a couple of buildings were used for "Horror Hotels," open only during Halloween for a week or so each year. There were a few bars for the university students and a couple of galleries and studios. Downtown was a place to avoid.

Belying the concrete inertia, however, things were happening, albeit slowly. The '70s and '80s saw the opening of a couple of art galleries. Artists were renting space in the derelict industrial buildings because it was cheap and cool. The aspiring artists of the 1970s and '80s in Springfield, Missouri, had a fantastic connection with the New York loft-living artists of the 1960s and '70s and those, in turn, with the Parisian bohemians of the 1920s. The changing scene in downtown areas in so many larger cities around the United States reached the local government which decided to orchestrate a comprehensive program for the city, called Vision 20/20. The center city area was an important element of the plan:

> If Springfield is to prosper and grow in stature, it will mean that Center City will remain vital, valued, and special. This assertion is based on the fact that nearly every great city has a strong and vibrant central area.
>
> (City of Springfield 1998: p.1–4)

The municipality maintained a "privately led, city supported" stance in the revitalization of its downtown. It directly provided the infrastructure and indirectly supported businesses and the arts through public-private partnerships and non-profit organizations. Private developers finally entered the picture, cautiously in the mid-'90s and more aggressively in the 2000s. Most of the buildings in the area are now rehabilitated and there is new construction as well.

Springfield is not a sexy, promiscuous metropolis; its wholesomeness and manageability is attractive in a different way. In a globalized world where cities become entrepreneurial and compete for residents and visitors, mid-sized cities have to find a niche in order to be competitive and a vibrant core is a key asset. Lacking the resources of a larger area, downtown revitalization is a long, arduous and grassroots process with the artists weaving the cultural cloak for the city, the local government stitching this together, and the private sector selling it to residents and visitors alike.

Sources

City of Springfield (1998) *Vision 20/20: Center city plan element.* Springfield, MO: BRW with InMotion.
Springfield Area Chamber of Commerce Web site: http://springfield4business.com.

Questions

1. One of the features that make a downtown like Springfield's "sexy" is that it does not offer the standard range of stores found at the suburban regional mall. Instead, one finds non-chain restaurants and coffee houses, independent movie theaters and bookstores, and specialized clothing stores. McDonald's, Barnes and Noble, and Gap are kept at bay, at least initially. One thing that may happen is that as downtown becomes more and more successful it may come to the attention of these major companies who may, eventually, seek to infiltrate the area. For some community officials this would be a positive step since it would mark the transformation of the area into a mainstream visitor destination. Still others believe that if this were to happen, it would mean that downtown becomes standardized and no longer possesses its own individual character. What is your opinion? Do you think that chain stores would be good or bad for a revived locality? If you were a person who wanted to preserve the local nature of the downtown how would you campaign against companies like McDonald's and Starbucks?

2. To a large extent what has been going on in the downtown area of Springfield, Missouri mirrors trends in much larger cities throughout the United States but also other countries. How influential is globalization in generating these changes at the local level? Do you think that local forces are also important in determining the transformation of downtown areas or do you think most of the influence is exogenous? Try to justify your answer.

Evangelia Petridou

But what exactly is it that makes tourist-related facilities popular as an economic redevelopment strategy compared to something else? Why is the pursuit of smokestacks, once the leading strategy in American cities, being replaced by the need to attract more visitors (Clark *et al.* 2002)? What precisely is it about tourism that makes cities pit themselves against one another to attract visitors in "a competitive struggle that parallels the railroad wars of more than a century ago" (Judd 2002: 279)?

Certain reasons, of course, are obvious. Economically speaking, tourism is an "export" industry – one that draws externally generated money into the host community. In this manner it is much like the manufacturing sector which creates products for export to other communities. The one fundamental difference between tourism and the production, say of plastic cups or processed cheese, is that in the case of tourism the consumer (i.e., the visitor) has to travel to the site where the tourism experience is manufactured (Debbage and Daniels 1998; Ioannides 2003; Urry 1990). Thus, tourism is an invisible export whose production and consumption are spatially fixed but it also has the same effect as the production and export of a tangible good, since it leads to wealth creation, the generation of jobs, and ultimately the expansion of the host population's living standards. One advantage tourism has over other economic sectors is that the ratio of foreign imports to a unit of generated foreign exchange is usually low and this may mean that "a greater proportion of the foreign exchange earnings of tourism can be used for investment in the development of [other] industries or in reducing the foreign earnings debt" (Mathieson and Wall 1982: 45).

Fainstein and Stokes (1995) maintain that local governments are keen to spend public monies on tourism-related facilities because funded projects like these promise a constant revenue stream compared to other public goods, including schools, parks, and roads. Additionally, the burden of spending on major projects such as a sports stadium or an aquarium is often lifted from local taxpayers since much of the money comes from state and not the local government. By contrast if a community engages in smokestack chasing it almost invariably has to offer manufacturing firms a package of enticing incentives, which place a significant burden on taxpayers (Clark *et al.* 2002). Community leaders will also not shy away from seeking to attract a visitor-based facility compared to a manufacturing plant, since it is easier to replicate something like a hotel or a theme park from place to place instead of a plant geared toward heavy manufacturing. Just because one city has a robust tourism industry does not mean that a neighboring locality should not pursue visitors (Ioannides 2003).

Barriers to entry and the cost of job creation in tourism tend to be much lower than in many other sectors of the economy (Fainstein and Gladstone 1999; Shaw and Williams 1994; Urry 1990). Even if some critics argue that the jobs associated with tourism are predominantly low-skilled and poorly paid (Harrison and Bluestone 1988), one could also make the point that in many instances these jobs are better than no jobs at all.

Judd (1995) reflects that all too often the development of tourist-based facilities within a city is not accompanied by a detailed feasibility study and, indeed, often these structures cost far more than initial estimates indicate. This does not seem to pose a problem for city leaders, however, since much of this investment is the means of boosting the city's image, making it more livable for residents, and attracting additional potential investors and inhabitants (Ioannides 2003). Reflecting on the fact that projects like sports complexes are heavily subsidized and seldom lead to the promised economic growth generation, Turner and Rosentraub (2002) argue that community leaders maintain their unwavering support for these facilities because they see them as a means to entice "residents, businesses, and tourists to downtown areas and create a positive impact on the central city's economy" (p. 489). At the end of the day all that matters to these civic boosters is that the property values will increase in downtown areas.

Types of tourist cities

Three types of tourist cities exist within the US (Judd 2003a; Fainstein and Judd 1999). These include "resort cities" built specifically for tourist-related activities, "tourist historic cities" that possess areas with a rich historic and cultural identity (often in the form of architectural heritage), and "converted cities," "places of production that have had to carve out a tourist space amidst an otherwise hostile environment for visitors" (Judd 2003b: 5). In turn, we examine each type of tourist city and provide examples of localities that fit each respective profile.

Resort cities

Plenty of specialized resort communities exist around the nation, often smaller seaside or ski resorts, and theme-tourism places like Branson, Missouri, and Pigeon Forge, Tennessee, that have re-imaged and market themselves as country music destinations. These communities would certainly not enjoy their marked success if it were not for their visitor-based economy. In contrast to these smaller, specialized tourist communities, resort cities are larger urban areas where tourism has become by far the dominant economic activity but, concurrently, these places have witnessed the development of a whole range of other sectors and, consequently, have experienced explosive growth in population. Historically, cities that have fitted this profile include famous seaside locales like Atlantic City, Miami Beach, or Honolulu. But more recently, and on a far grander scale, the two largest resort cities within the USA are Las Vegas and the Greater Orlando metropolitan region. The latter encompasses the various Disney-based attractions as well as many other theme parks.

Within the Greater Orlando region, the Walt Disney Company has also built its very own city (a resort city within a resort metropolitan region), following the popular planning principles of New Urbanism (Duany et al. 2000). Plans for this new town, which was labeled "Celebration," appeared in the early 1990s and "called for three golf courses, a massive shopping mall, a cultural center, and eight thousand private homes" (Foglesong 1999: 100). This new town is linked to the various parks of the company, by the so-called World Drive. The concept behind Celebration is that it should be a resort where lodging, retail, dining and other activities are clustered, but over time "the success of these tourist venues has stimulated further activity, making them become more than mere tourist destinations" (Fainstein and Judd 1999: 262).

Though Celebration and Las Vegas both fit the mold of "Resort Cities," the manner in which each place was conceived and developed differs dramatically (Fainstein and Judd 1999). Celebration is a planned community, albeit the planning has been performed by a private entity. It is expected that over time with the growth of the community, public entities will take over many functions of the city from Disney (Foglesong 1999). Las Vegas, by contrast, is a city that has resulted from the independent actions of numerous players (both large corporations and smaller businesses). It is not a planned city by any means, indeed it has historically developed in a very haphazard manner. Nevertheless, the key actors in this metropolitan region's tourism industry are the major casinos that represent multinational interests (Fainstein and Judd 1999).

Tourist historic cities

Tourist historic cities exist in numerous parts of Europe and are those steeped in heritage, usually in the form of historical neighborhoods and buildings. Often, they are associated with significant events in a country's history. Venice, Florence, Canterbury, Bruges, and Granada immediately spring to one's mind when thinking of this type of city. Within the United States, given it does not have a long history of urban development to match its European counterparts, it is hard to find places fitting this mold. Notable exceptions unique in terms of their architectural heritage, include Charleston, South Carolina; Savannah, Georgia; and Santa Fe, New Mexico.

In most cases within the USA, unlike Europe where many tourist historic cities have experienced tourism development over a long period of time, historic areas have become popular visitor attractions only after the active involvement of local authorities. For example, the French Quarter in New Orleans became a major tourist attraction following the historic preservation movements of the 1930s (Bosselman *et al.* 1999; City of New Orleans 2009).

Despite being a sizeable metropolitan area, Boston has numerous historical neighborhoods and sites, including Beacon Hill, the North End, and Bunker Hill, all of which have long drawn visitors interested in gazing on a slice of American history. Naturally, it can be argued that when they visit cities like Boston, Philadelphia, New Orleans, or San Francisco, tourists do not view these places in their entirety but, rather, are in the business of wandering around and collecting symbolic markers (e.g., Golden Gate Bridge, street cars, or the North End Church) (Fainstein *et al.* 2004).

The symbols visitors seek out within these historic communities regularly result from the purposeful actions of the various stakeholders who have a vested interest in tourism development. Actions such as these, according to Fainstein *et al.* (2004) reflect "the mode of regulation characterizing any place or era" (p. 9). These players wish to fashion the image of the place into something that is easily identifiable and thus marketable. After all, the first-time visitor does not possess the ability to test the product – in this case the city – before the actual trip takes place. Instead, the visitor relies on his or her mental images of the place, all of which are shaped by city marketers. It is, according to Holcomb (1999), the landmark or set of landmarks that provides a place with its touristic identity.

Converted cities

By far the most popular form of tourism development within American cities arguably belongs to this category. In this case, city officials choose an area that is often severely dilapidated and invest heavily in its transformation into a visitor destination. Such an area is commonly, but not always, located within or around the central business district, but also may be an abandoned industrial or warehouse district, a disused railroad corridor or canal, or even a historic neighborhood in another part of the city. Within larger metropolitan areas there may be multiple such areas scattered throughout the city.

One of the earliest examples of such a re-invention of an urban space, which quickly came to serve as the definitive model that numerous cities of all sizes emulated in later years, occurred during the late 1970s in Baltimore's Inner Harbor. At that time this area had truly become the epitome of urban decay, a place that once had bustled with seaport activities, but now lay in ruins with boarded up and abandoned buildings. The "architect" of this revival was James Rouse, a Maryland-based developer who conceived the idea of Harborplace, a festival market place, anchoring a series of waterfront developments, including the Maryland Science Center and the National Aquarium (Olsen 2004). Simply stated, a festival market place is an area that provides a mix of retailing, eating, and accommodation facilities, serving as the centerpiece of a major redevelopment project specifically aimed at attracting visitors (Plate 8.2). Today, more than 30 million visitors arrive in Harborplace annually, matching the number of visits to Disney World.

Over the last two decades or so numerous urban redevelopment projects have appeared in the guise of a "festival market place," including New York's South Street Seaport, Chicago's Navy Peer, San Francisco's Fisherman Wharf, and Boston's Faneuil Hall (Turner and Rosentraub 2002). An element of predictability characterizes these spaces, with their offerings of higher-end retail establishments, restaurants of varying quality, including chain establishments, and souvenir outlets selling among others memorabilia relating to the host city or, perhaps, its sports franchises. The fact that much of what is on offer is remarkably similar from place to place is not accidental, but results from actions on the part of policymakers and industry representatives which are aimed at making visitors feel they are in familiar surroundings. The idea is that if the environment is familiar, then the tourist will gain a sense of comfort and will, thus, also feel safe.

Plate 8.2 Restoring history for tourists – Beale Street, Memphis
(Dimitri Ioannides)

Enter the "Tourist Bubble"

A distinctive trait of festival market places and other redevelopment projects within converted cities geared toward tourists is that they are often enclaves with well-marked boundaries. Within these spaces, the tourist expects to feel safe and is shielded from surrounding run-down districts, which often are associated with high crime and other social problems. It is no secret that visitors to Baltimore's Harborplace find themselves confined within a fairly small geographical area amounting to just a few city blocks and would never dream of venturing too far from the main tourist attractions, into the surrounding residential neighborhoods, which they perceive as crime-ridden and dangerous. Similarly, Detroit's Greektown has been labeled "an island in a sea of decay" (Judd 1999: 36).

Dennis Judd (1999) uses the term "tourist bubble" to describe these safe tourist spaces. He argues that in cities where there is a perception of crime (whether this is based on fact or media-induced infamy), or in places where a significant amount of the building stock is in such poor shape that it emits an aura of poverty and deprivation, local authorities deliberately strive to engineer tourist environments in a manner that engenders a feeling of safety among visitors. These bubbles are, therefore, spaces witnessing a high degree of regulation through the heavy presence of public safety personnel, numerous security cameras, and the physical removal of perceived unsavory businesses (e.g., sex shops) or undesirable people (e.g., the homeless). Tourist bubbles are more often than not extremely well-lit and offer enough activities and attractions to lure in a significant number of users; the sheer presence of visitors in these bubbles presumably acts as a deterrent to any criminal activity. When visitors roam around a tourist bubble, they rarely come into contact with the residents of surrounding neighborhoods, and they hardly ever witness where these individuals work.

Examples of tourist bubbles are abundant throughout the United States. The festival market places described above certainly fit the description of such spaces. So do other areas that may once have been associated with a city's sordid past, such as abandoned sites of production (e.g., manufacturing plants and warehouses), areas of dilapidated housing, or run-down commercial districts. These places are reproduced to demonstrate a sanitized view of city-living from a bygone era, a city that never really existed but one that has been created in the minds of nostalgia-seeking visitors (Judd 1999; Lowenthal 1985; Turner and Rosentraub 2002).

A key characteristic of a tourist bubble rests in its offering of plenty of things to do and see within a space that has been given an expensive face-lift and now projects the twin qualities of cleanliness and fun. Other than festival market places, among the most popular attractions within these tourist bubbles which are repeated from metropolis to metropolis are convention facilities and their associated accommodation establishments, exhibition centers, sports stadiums, concert halls and theaters, aquariums and museums, and in recent years, casinos. Then, in addition to these features, there often exist within these areas many of the symbols of transnational capital in the form of chain restaurants and hotels, not to mention the seemingly ubiquitous Starbucks and Hard Rock Cafes and "nationally recognized super-venues such as ESPN zone" (Turner and Rosentraub 2002: 490). Turner and Rosentraub describe how these downtown districts "with color coordinated logos, street sweeper uniforms, and trashcans (*sic*)" while "guides are hired to give directions and provide assistance" have been transformed into "theme parks" (p. 491).

Alternative urban tourism venues: neo-Bohemia

Despite the remarkable predictability that characterizes these tourist bubbles, obviously not every single one of these places has met with the same degree of success. In the case of Detroit it has not been readily apparent whether or not the new baseball stadium and casinos "will attract the level of consumer energy and investment necessary to revive downtown" (Turner and Rosentraub 2002: 491).

Perhaps, the most tragic example of the failure of a tourist bubble is that of Flint, Michigan. Back in the 1980s, this city was particularly badly hit after the collapse of its automobile industry. In Michael Moore's documentary *Roger and Me*, Flint is depicted as a city striving to rebound from the major blow of economic downturn by seeking to attract visitors. The most ambitious tourism-related project was Autoworld, a festival market place. However, unlike other festival market places (like South Street Seaport, which happened to be built by the same developer), Autoworld proved a massive disappointment, with most of the businesses within it failing within a year of opening (Judd 1995). A wonderful line in the documentary places this failure in perspective. Maxine Kronick, a Flint city official, is filmed saying that initial ambitious ideas that Flint could evolve like Toronto into an entertainment and arts center with a healthy mix of people were swiftly replaced by the realization that: "You can't make Palm Beach out of the Bowery. If you want to make Palm Beach, you have to go to Palm Beach" (Judd 1995: 186). Clearly this quote signifies that not every place has the built-in traits necessary to give it the cutting edge as a tourist destination. Indeed, it is absolutely evident that whereas many places can combine their unique heritage, including their built environment and their natural setting, with various contingent characteristics to create successful tourist bubbles, others like Flint have struggled to compete.

On a broader level the varying fortunes of many of these touristic enclaves signifies that the prediction that, not only within the USA but worldwide, cities are becoming boring carbon copies of each other is vastly exaggerated. Additionally, Gladstone and Fainstein (2001) have noted in their study of Los Angeles and New York that when it comes to tourism there are differences between the two cities both from a spatial and design perspective. In New York City tourism-related activities are overwhelmingly located within Manhattan whereas "the geography of tourism in Los Angeles is highly dispersed" (Gladstone and Fainstein 2001: 26). In New York tourists are relatively confined in their movement by virtue of the fact that they either have to walk from venue to venue or rely on public transportation. In Los Angeles, by contrast, visitors rely heavily on automobile transportation and find themselves in more dispersed locations like Hollywood or Universal City. Interestingly, despite their high degree of geographic concentration within Manhattan, visitors interact considerably with local residents, while tourists to the Los Angeles region find themselves disconnected from the everyday life of the inhabitants. In other words, despite the geographic concentration of tourists within Manhattan, the high interaction of visitors with locals ensures the tourist bubble is not as evident here as it is in Hollywood or Universal City.

Reversing his original position from the late 1990s, Judd (2004) shares Gladstone and Fainstein's opinion that not all visitors to urban areas remain confined within the predictable, highly regulated and sterile touristic bubbles, which are separate worlds within the urban spectrum. Instead, he now believes that "enclaves inhabited by visitors co-exist with downtown business districts, streets populated with local small businesses and shops, neighborhoods, and public buildings, and public spaces" (p. 30). A growing number of visitors, precisely because they are bored and disillusioned with the standardized uniformity of the festival market place or the spaces surrounding a museum complex or ballpark, seek out alternative venues within the urban realm, venues that emit an aura of originality because they maintain much of their (refurbished) historical urban fabric, and local people of various ethnic backgrounds or socioeconomic levels happen to live, work, and play there.

More often than not these spaces are what has been labeled by the American Planning Association "great neighborhoods" (Hinshaw 2008: 8), ones that meet various criteria including interesting architecture, multimodal transportation opportunities, and a character that is unforgettable. They also frequently happen to be close to the downtown or at least conveniently accessible by transit. These are neighborhoods with a variety of housing types, which also offer shopping and other service opportunities. Residents of these districts tend to be vociferous activists in shaping their future development. For example, they seek, as in the case of Old West Austin in Austin, Texas, to ensure that new developments are not incompatible with their district plan (Hinshaw 2008). An additional characteristic in many of these areas is that they have a range of thriving, independently owned local businesses as opposed to national chain operations. Quite simply these enterprises succeed and stay in business because they possess the necessary critical mass of customers in the shape of local residents and visitors.

Many of the places that visitors seek beyond the tourist bubbles are those that, in the aftermath of urban renewal and the flight to the suburbs, were adopted by marginalized populations (e.g., ethnic minorities) but eventually have reinvented themselves as magnets for talented young professionals who have become active players in their gentrification. And because the gentrification of these neighborhoods has been accompanied by the proliferation of an array of amenities (Clark *et al.* 2002), they are attracting visitors from other parts of the metropolitan region and further afield. Such spaces include gay neighborhoods, like San Francisco's Castro District or San Diego's Hillcrest, which have certainly become popular alternative destinations for tourists and suburbanites wishing to escape the confines of more conventional downtown visitor-based landscapes.

A major part of the excitement one derives from strolling around Westport in Kansas City and Soulard in St. Louis, both run-down neighborhoods albeit ones undergoing major revitalization, or Wicker Park a similarly gritty ex-manufacturing district, just outside Chicago's Loop, is that these areas are unique. Their industrial heritage ensures that they are not areas that are naturally touristic though their growing popularity is rapidly converting them into such (Judd 2004). In fact the major players behind the initial transformation of these neighborhoods are often locals, perhaps artists, musicians, or software designers, representatives of what Richard Florida terms the "creative class" (2002) who are enticed into abandoned warehouses and industrial buildings, partly because these properties were, at least initially cheap to rent, but also suited to their needs. This is how Lloyd (2006: 9–10) describes Wicker Park:

> For the "starving" young artist, the neighborhood offered a range of material advantages, principally inexpensive rents and the kinds of derelict industrial spaces that could be reconfigured as studios and performance spaces. Moreover, the neighborhood is strategically located, proximate to the downtown Loop and the near North Side's sprawling networks of independent theaters and musical performance venues. The Elevated Train's Blue Line bisects the neighborhood, with the Damen Avenue stop depositing travelers near the hub of West Side activity.

Lloyd (2002: 517) uses the term "neo-Bohemia" to describe Wicker Park. His argument is that areas such as this, which due to their industrial heritage are deemed "anachronistic" in a post-industrial era, possess plenty of characteristics giving them a clear advantage for locating certain activities including the production and consumption of cultural amenities. Neo-Bohemias challenge mainstream urban theories that stress, among others, the agglomerative tendencies of tourist-based activities in sanitized "Disneyfied" downtown areas. While the players behind these downtown projects are major developers and city government, neo-Bohemias like Wicker Park remind us that urban areas are not just for visitors; people live, work, and entertain themselves in these places and actively participate in shaping these spaces both for local residents but also a growing number of visitors who wish to avoid the clichéd environment of a tourist bubble.

The upshot of these neo-Bohemias is that it is becoming increasingly harder to distinguish the out-of-town visitor from the suburbanite or, indeed, the local inhabitant who lives in the area. After all, the local inhabitants of these spaces mingle with the visitors, taking advantage of the many amenities in their midst: ethnic restaurants, wine bars, fringe theaters, independent cinemas, and second-hand book stores. Ultimately, the desire of visitors to find themselves in the midst of these neighborhoods is tantamount to the wish to resist the regulatory environment of the "Disneyfied" downtowns (Judd 2004; Clark *et al.* 2002).

It is not that these neo-Bohemias are devoid of regulation. In fact, many historic districts have extremely strict ordinances controlling everything from the color of the buildings to the size of signs and from the type of paving to the roofing material in a conscious effort to retain their character (Hinshaw 2008: 11). Interestingly, such ordinances act as a hindrance to chains, which rely on corporate logos and designs and, thus, effectively serve to keep these corporations at bay. In those cases where the brand name chain wants to infiltrate such neighborhoods, it must mold its appearance to satisfy the local design ordinances.

In the final analysis, neighborhoods beyond the tourist bubble, including the neo-Bohemias, have elements making them appear authentic, or what Hinshaw (2008: 11) terms the "genuine article." Ironically, the question that emerges is whether as more such places appear throughout the nation, given their inevitable popularity, they will become increasingly predictable and ubiquitous through the range of amenities on offer and in terms of the activities that visitors and residents engage in; if this is indeed the case, perhaps the homogeneity of touristic landscapes many people wish to avoid is, in fact, inescapable.

Final thoughts

In 2000 the National League of Cities conducted a survey in which 54 percent of downtown areas reported that sectors relating to the experience economy, such as tourism, entertainment, and the arts, were far more significant for contemporary urban economic growth than manufacturing or retailing (Turner 2002). An earlier study by the same organization (Judd *et al.* 2003) proved that cities invest heavily on tourism-related activities since policymakers are becoming increasingly certain that this is the primary way for their community's flagging economy to rebound and thrive.

If one was in any doubt as to tourism's perceived economic power, then one does not have to search any further than Chicago. According to Clark *et al.* (2002: 504), Chicago's principal industry is "entertainment, which city officials define as including tourism, conventions, restaurants, hotels, and related economic activities." The city's long-term mayor Richard M. Daley has placed primary emphasis on reconfiguring the urban environment and introducing numerous amenities to enhance the city's image. No other mayor has ever planted more vegetation than Daley. In addition to trees, bushes, and flowers, he has also put millions of dollars into public art, street lighting, new sidewalks, and other facilities.

Chicago is a popular destination. It attracts millions of visitors each year including conventioneers and leisure-seekers. It is a major destination for international travelers but also for people from nearby communities. And, Chicago is not alone. Numerous cities throughout the country, regardless of their size, have emerged as major tourist destinations. Tourism's ascendancy within the contemporary urban fabric has much to do with economic restructuring and policymakers' boosterist agendas. It also has to do with the shift from a producer-oriented economy into one based on the production and consumption of experiential goods (O'Dell and Billing 2005).

The definitive personification of tourism within American cities comes in the form of downtown spaces that predictably include at least some of the following elements: national and multinational chain stores, restaurants, hotels, sports stadiums, science centers and museums, and aquariums. These highly standardized and unsurprising spaces, which Judd has aptly labeled "tourist bubbles," are deliberately designed to regulate the activities of their visitors and to convey a sense of comfort, safety, and security. Unfortunately, the uniformity of these places has also meant that American cities appear to be relinquishing any of their remaining vestiges of individuality. On the plus side, however, it is not all bad news. It is increasingly becoming obvious that visitors to urban areas are not all remaining within these tourist bubbles. In increasing numbers they seek out neighborhoods which may not necessarily be associated with tourism, neighborhoods – often with older building stock – where locals actually live, work, and play. These spaces, many of which have been labeled neo-Bohemias, demonstrate that the boundaries between who is a tourist and who a local are becoming increasingly blurred as many of the city's inhabitants are taking advantage of their amenities and, at least for some hours during the day, they do exactly the same thing as their guests. It can also be assumed that when the residents of these neighborhoods travel to another city they likely seek out similar spaces and engage in activities which reflect much of what they do at home.

It remains to be seen if the growth in popularity of such neo-Bohemias will eventually lead us to yet another clichéd urban landscape not too dissimilar to the tourist bubbles many people go to lengths to avoid. To be sure, neo-Bohemias are perhaps devoid of chain stores and Starbucks coffee houses, but the types of facilities they include, namely the regular assemblage of Ethiopian, Italian, and Indian restaurants, the breweries, the bed and breakfasts, and the latte bars certainly are beginning to become more familiar.

Questions

1. Explain in your own words what is meant by the "mode of regulation." How does this apply to tourism in an urban setting? Give an example.
2. What forces led American cities to put increasing effort into attracting visitors? Why is tourism seen as an economic panacea by so many leaders?
3. What are the three different types of tourist cities one can find in the United States? Pick one of these types and explain it in some detail. Give examples of cities that fit this category.
4. What is the difference between a neo-Bohemia and a tourist bubble? Do you think that neo-Bohemias run the risk of also becoming part of the tourist bubble?

Further reading

Boo, S.Y., Koh, Y. and Jones, D. (2008) An exploration of attractiveness of convention cities based on visit behavior. *Journal of Convention and Event Tourism*, 9(4): 239–57.

Che, D. (2008) Sports, music, entertainment and the destination branding of post-Fordist Detroit. *Tourism Recreation Research*, 33(2): 195–206.

Gibson, C. and Connell, J. (2007) Music, tourism and the transformation of Memphis. *Tourism Geographies*, 9(2): 160–90.

Gotham, K.F. (2007) Destination New Orleans: commodification, rationalization, and the rise of urban tourism. *Journal of Consumer Culture*, 7(3): 305–34.

Grodach, C. and Loukaitou-Sideris, A. (2007) Cultural development strategies and urban revitalization: a survey of US cities. *International Journal of Cultural Policy*, 13(4): 349–70.

Iroegbu, H. and Chen, J.S. (2001) Urban residents' reaction toward tourism development: do subgroups exist? *Tourism Analysis*, 6(2): 155–61.

Litvin, S.W. (2005) Streetscape improvements in an historic tourist city: a second visit to King Street, Charleston, South Carolina. *Tourism Management*, 26(3): 421–29.

Rath, J. (ed.) (2007) *Tourism, Ethnic Diversity and the City*. London: Routledge.

Spirou, C. (2006) Cultural policy and urban restructuring in Chicago. In M.K. Smith (ed.), *Tourism, Culture and Regeneration*, pp. 123–31. Wallingford, UK: CAB International.

Williams, K.H. and Chacko, H.E. (2008) The effect of ethnic differences on travel characteristics: an exploration of marginality and ethnicity in urban tourism. *International Journal of Hospitality and Tourism Administration*, 9(2): 147–63.

Useful Internet resources

Baltimore's Inner Harbor: http://baltimore.org/about-baltimore/inner-harbor
Creative Class: http://www.creativeclass.com/
Freedom Trail Foundation: http://www.thefreedomtrail.org/
Las Vegas Convention and Visitors Authority: http://www.lvcva.com/index.jsp
New Orleans French Quarter: http://frenchquarter.com/
Western Association of Convention and Visitors Bureaus: http://www.wacvb.com/
Wicker Park and Bucktown Chamber of Commerce: http://www.wickerparkbucktown.com/live/community_organizations/

⑨ On the road to Small Town, USA

Rural tourism and its significance

> It seems like every town you come to, big or small, has got something unique about it. Something it's best at.
>
> (Tom Bodett 1985: 7)

Introduction

Earlier, we argued that tourism has frequently been the principal tool which over the years has gained increasing significance for regenerating struggling communities. Certainly this has been true in the case of countless American urban areas, following the decline of traditional economic activities such as manufacturing. And, despite a host of problems that are often associated with a visitor-based economy, it is clear that cities constantly use tourism to convert their respective identities as they undergo a meta-morphosis from centers of production into spaces of consumption that can be branded and marketed.

It is not just large cities, however, that look to tourism in an effort to stimulate economic recovery. Throughout the United States countless rural communities, from tiny hamlets to small towns of a few thousand inhabitants, seek to revive their stagnant or declining economies by enticing visitors. Many of these places offer easy access to natural amenities, such as those encountered in national and state parks, which provide plenty of opportunities to participate in recreational activities. Others are situated in scenic coastal or mountainous regions allowing the chance to gaze upon excellent views. There are also historic places in rural America, quaint little communities that still look as they did more than a century ago, or communities that lie adjacent to the site of a famous Revolutionary or Civil War battle, or where a famous person once lived. These commu-nities cater to the growing number of visitors wishing to obtain a sanitized view of the way things were in the past (Lowenthal 1985; Ioannides and Ioannides 2002; Timothy and Boyd 2003).

Related to this is a widespread romanticism in the USA associated with rural living. Willits (1993) argues that a rural lifestyle is viewed as wholesome and desirable. Bunce (1994) reiterates Willits' assertion by suggesting that there is an American "countryside idyll" that stirs "warm feelings and positive images about people, places and things called rural . . . rural is a hallowed element" (Willits 1993: 170). This manifests in tourist demand for rural Americana, which is seen as the "other," distanced by time, symbolism, and space from the frenetic pace of urban living (Hopkins 1998; Park and Coppack 1994; Timothy 2005a).

In addition to the communities that possess the natural, architectural, or historic foun-dation for their tourism industry, there are thousands of places dotting the countryside of the USA that at first glance lack the fundamental ingredients for becoming successful destinations. These may not have a unique historic construction style, or they may not be located adjacent to a national park, a ski slope, or a large lake. Despite such a drawback, however, many of these rural communities soldier on, albeit at varying levels of success, in their quest to become established tourist destinations.

In many cases these localities use predictable strategies, such as promoting their existing festivals to a broader audience and constantly searching for new events to hold (Janiskee and Drews 1998). In other instances they play up on the area's ethnic heritage, as has been the case in countless rural towns such as the Swedish community of Lindsborg, Kansas; the Czech descendants of Wilber, Nebraska; the Dutch communities of Pella, Iowa, and Holland, Michigan; and the Germans of Frankenmuth, Michigan (Che 2004; Schnell 2003; Zeitler 2009). Additionally, if a community cannot clearly trace its origins to its first settlers it may then strive to engineer an artificial image of an ethnic past, which is what Leavenworth, Washington, did when it recreated itself into a Bavarian village during the 1960s (Frenkel *et al.* 2000). Finally, there are scores of places throughout the country that play up some characteristic that in the minds of their residents makes them unique. For example, Barrow, Alaska, claims to be the nation's northernmost destination, while Wickenburg, Arizona, labels itself the oldest town north of Tucson (Ioannides 1999).

Many of these rural places succeed in their efforts to draw in more visitors, and not an insignificant number of them have become sites for second home owners, not to mention new permanent residents. Unfortunately, however, others find it exceedingly hard to market themselves and to entice potential travelers. The reasons for this abound, but include *inter alia* a community's isolation from major metropolitan regions and important interstate highways or the fact that what is on offer in numerous rural places is nothing unique and can be found at several intervening places closer to home. Additionally, large parts of the country, including states like Kansas, Nebraska, and the Dakotas, find it hard to overturn the popular prevailing misconceptions of these regions as large expanses of flat emptiness with little to offer to potential visitors.

In this chapter we explore the theme of rural tourism within the United States. Following a preliminary examination of definitional issues, especially with regard to what constitutes a rural region, we investigate the types of tourism that have evolved in various parts of rural America. We recognize that a number of tourism-based communities have boomed but also note that others struggle to survive. We explore why this has happened. Moreover, we investigate the benefits that rural communities derive from expanding their visitor-based economies while we also describe some of the most serious downsides of the sector for such places.

Rural America today

Most Americans today (just under 80 percent) are classified as urban, meaning they live in metropolitan areas, according to the definition of the US Census Bureau (Long and Lane 2000; Johnson and Beale 2002; Porter *et al.* 2004). The other 20 percent of the population (about 60 million people), those labeled "rural," are scattered throughout major swathes of the country that take up approximately nine-tenths of its land area and include a total of more than 2,000 counties. The present situation contrasts starkly with that during the Civil War in the 1860s, when 80 percent of the country's population lived in rural places. Even as recently as the Second World War, 44 percent of the country's population was still classified as rural, with 25 percent being farm-based (Drabenstott 2001).

But what are rural places in reality? Drabenstott defines them in simple terms as the areas where we grow our food and where we go to play, though we should bear in mind that under 2 percent of the country's population now depends on farming; "much less than that if the definition of farm is limited to full-term farms" (Drabenstott 2001: 5). Another way to look at the decline of farming as an economic mainstay of rural areas is to consider that over the last 50 years or so the number of farm-dependent counties declined from 2000 to just around 500.

The above discussion indicates that definitions for what constitutes "rural" are hardly simple. After all, metropolitan statistical areas more often than not encompass sizeable expanses of open space (uninhabited or farm-based land) stretching far beyond the incorporated built-up areas. To complicate matters further, much development within the borders of metropolitan regions increasingly takes place in green-field sites located on the rural–urban boundary and beyond. The new residential subdivisions that have popped up with increasing regularity on the outskirts of Chicago, St. Louis, Dallas, and Pittsburgh can hardly be labeled rural communities (despite their seemingly rustic location). The people living in these developments rarely, if ever, live off the land; rather, they commute to their jobs, which are located within urban areas, or increasingly, office and industrial parks which have also often cropped up on abandoned agricultural land.

Based on this situation, one can easily make the argument that not all non-built-up areas should be called "rural." The open spaces within counties that are part of metropolitan regions are designated (for the purposes of this chapter) urban. It is the spaces beyond the metropolitan regions that can be described as truly rural. Thus, if we exclude the metropolitan counties out of a total of more than 3,000 counties nationwide, this leaves 2,388 non-metropolitan counties (77 percent of the total) (Johnson and Beale 2002). Using a slightly different definition, Porter *et al.* (2004) estimate some 2,166 rural counties.

One thing clearly distinguishing rural spaces from urban regions is their extremely low population densities. Also, rural regions are "a unit of analysis about which generalizations are possible. While many observers have recognized the existence of differences among rural regions, there is a tendency to see these differences as less important than the *overall* [italics ours] classification of a region as rural" (Porter *et al.* 2004: 5).

Of course, there are evidently numerous types of rural areas. Some continue to depend on primary activities such as logging and mining, while others rely on their amenities to entice a growing number of new residents, including retirees and second home owners (Timothy 2004). Then there are obvious geographic characteristics that can help distinguish between various kinds of rural communities. The heterogeneous nature of rural communities throughout the United States means that several attempts have been made to classify such places (Porter *et al.* 2004). Typologies have been developed for the following: those that explore the relative proximity of rural regions to metropolitan regions; those that are derived from the main economic activity in each rural region; and those that depend on "government policy focus" (Porter *et al.* 2004: 9), for example whether they are in or close to federal lands, retirement- or commuting-focused, or transfer-dependent. The latter typology is one that has been developed by the Economic Research Service (ERS) of the United States Department of Agriculture (USDA) (English *et al.* 2000; Long and Lane 2000).

Definitions of what constitutes "rural," like those offered from the ERS, rely mostly on statistics. By contrast, Long and Lane (2000); see also Gartner (2004) serve up a qualitative definition of "rural," focusing on the way of life one is expected to discover when visiting such areas. Essentially, Long and Lane argue that rural communities can be thought of as safe places where the pace of life is less hectic than in cities, where people are perceived as friendlier and more down-to-earth, and where there is a prevalence of locally owned, small and medium-sized business establishments. Additionally, these places are surrounded by sizeable expanses of open space, often enabling the opportunity for nature-based activities. According to Long and Lane (2000), in many instances, rural communities are likelier than cities to allow the opportunity for one to encounter societies that still practice traditional activities (Gartner 2004).

Regardless of whether we adopt a statistically based definition of rural America or Long and Lane's qualitative approach, it is certainly evident that a major part of the American landmass includes uninhabited lands or places where population densities are exceedingly low. The underlying theme in most writings concerning the rural USA is that such regions almost always compare unfavorably on economic grounds with their metropolitan counterparts. Quigley (2002) has argued that much of rural America, like so many peripheral regions throughout the world, suffers from chronic population decline and increasing poverty, while a growing discrepancy has appeared between the incomes of urban and rural residents. In fact, the proportion of people in rural regions defined as poor is higher than in the MSAs, though Quigley argues that because in rural regions overall average incomes are far lower than in cities, the severity of poverty among the rural poor does not seem as high as that of their urban counterparts. One thing is clear, that rural places are more reliant than cities on "social and other transfer payments," which are driven "by a combination of weak economic performance and an aging population" (Porter *et al.* 2004: 8).

There are also stark contrasts in employment patterns between urban and rural regions. Overall, according to Porter *et al.* (2004) in the early 2000s, the 2,166 rural counties included approximately 16 million workers, representing 14.2 percent of the country's total number of employees. Additionally, although metropolitan regions accounted for an increase of 18 million jobs between 1990 and 2001, during the same period the rural counties witnessed an increase of 2.9 million jobs. On average there was job growth in rural areas during the 1990s, although this growth did not match that witnessed in metropolitan regions.

Not surprisingly, rural regions are places where opportunities for innovative activities and the establishment of knowledge-based industries are limited. Consider that during 2001 almost 94 percent of patents were issued to entrepreneurs in metropolitan regions, meaning "8.3 patents were issued per 10,000 employees, versus 2.92 patents per 10,000 employees in rural regions" (Porter *et al.* 2004: 11). Reasons for low levels of innovation in rural areas are plenty but include the fact that the population tends to be older, especially given the out-migration of younger people, and that most people remaining in rural areas are less educated and less skilled than their counterparts in metropolitan areas (Quigley 2002). Furthermore, companies are reluctant to locate in isolated rural regions since the low population density means that the level of basic services (e.g., infrastructure) and access to a readily available, highly skilled labor pool tend to be poor.

At this point we should remind the reader that primary activities, including agriculture, no longer constitute the linchpin of rural economic development. In fact, Drabenstott (2001: 4) states that "rural no longer means farm – if it ever really did." He stresses that, to be sure, farming remains an important activity but, concurrently, modern policymaking with regard to rural regions has to be far more comprehensive than it has been in the past since agriculture is now just one of many sectors found in such places. In reality, more rural counties depend on manufacturing than on farming. Today, less than 10 percent of the entire rural population lives on farms and less than 7 percent of the total number of rural employees works in farming. Just about 2 percent of total rural income comes from farming (Quigley 2002).

There are also significant variations throughout rural America in terms of the location of farm-based counties. The highest concentration of counties that continue to depend on farming is found in the Great Plains (a region including western North Dakota, western Nebraska, and eastern Montana) which is known as "the nation's breadbasket" since this is where most of the wheat in the country is grown (El Nasser 2007). This is also where several other agricultural commodities are produced, including barley, sorghum, sunflower, and cotton while the region is also still a major cattle-grazing area. And yet, although these counties depend on agriculture, and in some instances the amount of acreage farmed has actually increased, four-fifths of the jobs are not in farming (Porter *et al.* 2004), a reflection to a large extent of wide-scale mechanization in the sector, the tendency to replace smaller family holdings with corporate establishments, but also an overall decline in the importance of farming on the national scene as witnessed through a significant decline in federal subsidies (Drabenstott 2001). In fact, the plains states have been in the midst of a chronic crisis, which over the last few decades has seen large-scale population decline and the near death of several rural communities (Popper and Popper 2006; El Nasser 2007).

Rather than agriculture, it is manufacturing that has been the mainstay for numerous rural economies throughout the country over the last 60 or 70 years. However, these areas have not been immune to the decline that affected their urban counterparts in the face of economic restructuring and growing foreign competition. Porter *et al.* (2004) cite a USDA study indicating that the type of manufacturing that can fare best in rural regions nowadays is one concentrating on non-commodity products where labor does not constitute a major proportion of total costs. They also stress that rural counties where manufacturing continues to make up a major part of the economy are those adjacent to metropolitan areas. Alternatively, numerous rural counties have actually seen a transformation from a manufacturing-based economy towards one that is service-dependent and "interestingly, those rural regions that derive at least 50 percent of their total earned income from service employment have stronger population growth. Their growth has come primarily from services in recreation, tourism, and retirement living" (Porter *et al.* 2004: 21).

The significance of tourism within rural communities is certainly highlighted when one takes into account the occurrence of tourism/hospitality clusters – defined as related industries within a sector with a tendency to locate adjacent to one another – in many non-metropolitan regions. This differs somewhat to major urban areas where the prevailing clusters tend to be in business and financial services (Porter *et al.* 2004). Well-known tourism-based clusters in rural America include Taney County, Missouri, and Tunica County, Mississippi, the former known for its country music scene, while the latter has become a popular casino destination.

The importance of rural tourism

Tourism's economic importance for rural localities is especially evident in several places which offer a wealth of recreational amenities – especially nature-based attributes – thus providing opportunities to gaze upon scenic views and/or participate in various outdoor activities, including hiking, mountain biking, rafting, hunting, fishing, and various winter sports (Drabenstott 2001). More often than not, these places are also attractive for retirees and second home owners and, consequently, they have witnessed a boom. Examples of such places abound in the inter-mountain west, various parts of the Ozarks and southern Appalachia, and along the Atlantic and Pacific coastlines (Groves and Timothy 2001).

However, even though rural communities with an abundance of natural amenities possess an obvious competitive edge as tourist destinations, there are literally thousands of additional less well-situated places scattered throughout the US countryside that have

Plate 9.1 Lighthouse in coastal New England
(Dallen Timothy)

also, in the face of limited opportunities, sought to embrace tourism in an effort to stem decline and diversify their economy. While most of these communities may lack quick and easy access to rugged peaks, lakefronts, national parks, and the recreational activities that are associated with these amenities, many do possess alternative attractions that help draw visitors. In some cases, a rural community plays upon its unique architectural heritage or maybe it lies close to the site where an historic incident took place, like a Civil War battle. It may also be the hometown of a famous person, whose childhood home has been transformed into an attraction. There are plenty of places throughout the country that have preserved or restored their old main streets to resemble a bygone era like, for example, Eureka Springs, Arkansas (see Closer Look Case 2.1 in Chapter 2), and Fort Scott, Kansas. Some places seek to reflect their earlier history by restoring a site of earlier economic activities, like abandoned mines (e.g., Leadville and Silverton, Colorado, and Jerome, Arizona). Other, perhaps innocuous locales, take advantage of their portrayal in a popular movie. For example, Winterset, Iowa, has created its tourism industry based on the successful 1995 movie *The Bridges of Madison County*. In addition to the covered bridges that are profiled in the film, the town now boasts of itself as the hometown of John Wayne (Madison County 2009). Another example is Tombstone, Arizona, which has become well known through the perpetuation of the story of the Shootout at the OK Corral, made popular in western American lore and by several movies in recent years, including *Tombstone*. Closer Look Case 9.1 presents the case of Forks, Washington, a town that has risen from obscurity into a highly sought-out destination because of the book *Twilight* by Stephanie Meyers and a film of the same name.

CLOSER LOOK CASE 9.1

Forks, Washington: Twilight zone

Forks, Washington, is an innocuous small town and one of the rainiest places in the United States: a fact of rather dubious value when it comes to attracting visitors. Located in Washington's Olympic Peninsula, with its population measuring just over 3,200 (city-data.com 2007), Forks is a typical small town, any-town USA, which in recent times had witnessed the downturn of its traditional sector, namely logging. Or such it had been, until the success of Stephenie Meyer's book *Twilight*, the first of a series about a teenage girl moving to Forks and falling in love with a vampire. Forks is now on the map, and loyal readers from Atlanta, Georgia, to the middle of Sweden, to Seoul and beyond know where it is and would like to visit. The local Chamber of Commerce beckons from its website. The banner on the home page reads: "Welcome to Forks and the rest of the Olympic Peninsula." Little doubt is left as to which place is more important as the town of 3,200 trumps the whole peninsula, which has the only rainforest in North America. One user in the city-data.com forum in 2007 summarizes this in a posted question: "Have you noticed the number of young people who have shown up on this forum lately, wanting to move to Forks? Huhhh? [*sic*]." The same user answers this question informing other users of the book series and its growing popularity, sparking replies such as: "Oh My [*sic*]! What a 'Claim to Fame!' Hopefully they will bring their wallets and pick up their trash when they leave. . . ." and "Heh [*sic*]. Tourism is the new timber."

The Chamber of Commerce has seized the opportunity to capitalize on the commercial success of the book and the subsequent movie by identifying the town with everything *Twilight*, vampire, and Stephenie Meyer. There are twilight tours, a twilight literary symposium and a sign featuring the sentence "No vampires beyond this point." There will be a Stephenie Meyer day in September 2009, as well as a celebration for the *Twilight* release in DVD. There is locally roasted coffee called "Twilight brew." The label features two arms holding a cup chipped as if bitten by a vampire. The arms are holding the cup in the exact same way as the arms holding the apple on the cover of the *Twilight* book.

Twilight tourism must be the new timber indeed. In Forks, culture has overtly been commodified replacing the raw materials of an erstwhile industrial era as the town has turned to the experience economy in order to attract visitors and residents. Even though the surrounding landscape is breathtakingly beautiful, what Forks sells is intangible, highly subjective, personal, and in the final analysis, surreal experiences. It sells not a fantastic connection to a not-so remote and real past like Eureka Springs (see Closer Look Case 2.1), but a fantastic connection to fiction. Twilight Forks constitutes a mythical geography that does not correspond to the universally accepted reality. It exists in the mind of its author and its readers; furthermore, it is different for each one of them. Each reader-visitor has his or her own private Forks; perhaps he/she visits the local high school (noted as a point of interest on the Chamber of Commerce web site) in an effort to add a visual stroke to the fantastic painting of the book's storyline. Place and fiction become one; the place the author never visited before she wrote her novel become inseparable. At least until the books lose their popularity and nobody remembers who Bella and the vampire were.

Sources

City-data.com (2003–9) Forks, WA statistics. Available from www.city-data.com/city/
Forks-Washington.html (accessed March 20, 2009).

Forks Chamber of Commerce (2009) Forks, Washington. Available from www.forkswa.
com (accessed March 20, 2009).

Tuan, Y.F. (1977) *Space and Place: The Perspective of Experience.* St Paul: University
of Minnesota Press.

MSNBC (2008) Vampire tourism breathes new life into small town. MSNBC, September
21. Avaiilable from http://today.msnbc.com/id/26811199/ (accessed March 20, 2009).

Questions

1. Have you read the book or seen the movie *Twilight*? What is your opinion of these?
   How do you think the place – Forks, Washington – is treated by the author in the book
   and by the movie's director? Do either of these depictions (or both) inspire you to visit
   Forks? What are some of the positive factors the book and movie promote about the
   locale and what are some of the negatives?
2. The Forks Chamber of Commerce has undoubtedly taken major advantage of *Twilight*.
   What advice would you have for the municipality if you were hired to act as a consultant on their long-term tourism strategy?

Evangelia Petridou

There are also countless towns throughout the country that seek to reflect the ethnic
heritage that can be traced back to their early settlers. Examples include Lindsborg,
Kansas (Swedish heritage); Pella, Iowa, and Holland, Michigan (Dutch heritage);
Solvang, California, and Elk Horn, Iowa (Danish heritage). Very often this heritage is
portrayed through events and festivals designed to flesh out the ethnic background of the
community. Pella, for instance, holds an annual Tulip Festival, as does Holland,
Michigan (Che 2004), and Lindsborg has a Midsummer's Day Festival in June and Saint
Lucia Festival in December, both of which are typical Swedish holidays. Some of these
ethnic towns also seek to project their background by restoring their early buildings and,
in many cases, making their downtowns look more like stereotypical images of the "old
country." Pella, for instance, dictates that its downtown maintains a "Dutch feel" and
every proposal for a new development or a redevelopment must be approved by an
architectural review committee, the so-called Dutch Fronts committee (Ioannides
1999).

In addition to the communities that draw on their ethnic background to develop a
tourism product, there are also communities that turn to "theming" in an effort to attract
visitors. In this case, the heritage of the town is entirely an invention and bears little,
if any, relationship to its past. A wonderful example of such a locality that is deemed
to have been a major success is Leavenworth, Washington, which in the 1960s "went
Bavarian" (Frenkel *et al.* 2000: 1). The main reason the community's leaders decided on
this strategy was to overcome problems associated with the decline of its traditional
economy which had been based on the railroad and the timber industry.

In Leavenworth, an authentic heritage or culture was out of the question because the
town lacked any discernible Bavarian roots or ties. Authentic translated largely as
visual conformity, adhering as closely as possible to the physical design of archetypal

villages in Germany . . . In this sense, authenticity derived its credibility from the quality of the copy.

(Frenkel et al. 2000: 8)

The transformation of Leavenworth and other towns like it into themed communities was very much based on emulating successes that had happened elsewhere. Frenkel *et al.* (2000) argue that Leavenworth made no secret of "borrowing" ideas from Solvang, California, which had been deemed a huge success story. They also maintain that many communities like Leavenworth are inspired to move into tourism through the suggestions offered in a variety of publications and the resources of organizations such as the National Main Street Center. Additionally, Gartner (2004) argues that Land Grant Institutions, which are major state universities around the country, have developed "manuals, workbooks and other resources to help communities understand and manage tourism for their benefit . . . One of the earliest publications dealing with rural tourism development issues is *Tourism USA: Guidelines for Tourism Development*" (Gartner 2004: 157).

As noted in Chapter 5, one common tool for drawing visitors that is used by numerous rural communities, regardless of whether these are theme-based or not, is to stage events like festivals. We have already pointed out that Pella and Lindsborg stage many such events annually, but so do numerous other communities, which on the surface may not have as strong a major drawing power for tourists. Janiskee and Drews (1998) argue that since the 1960s the number of small town festivals in the USA has expanded impressively. They estimated that by 1996 there were more than 10,000 festivals nationwide and that in many cases, towns hold more than one annual festival, some of which last for many days. In most cases, these festivals are not major income earners for the host communities. Indeed, they rarely attract more than a few thousand people over their duration. They are often deemed to be a success if the costs of organizing the event are recouped. What is important about these festivals, however, is that they can help restore civic pride, and may act as an incentive to seek money for redevelopment of downtown areas and aesthetic improvements (e.g., through planting trees and installing new street furniture). Additionally, as Janiskee and Drews (1998) and Groves and Timothy (2001) point out, the festivals allow rural communities to imprint the image of the benefits of rustic living on urban visitors and may persuade some of them to come again for other purposes or even to move there permanently, especially as retirees.

Another important issue that is revealed in the attempts of many rural communities when seeking to promote themselves as visitor destinations is their use of a variety of superlatives or hyperboles to evoke their unique sense of place (Ioannides 1999). It is not unusual for example, when one drives through the rural USA to encounter signposts welcoming you to a particular place which is the home of some apparently unique phenomenon (the world's "largest," the state's "oldest," the south's "best," etc). Iron Mountain, Michigan, claims to have the "largest and only" artificial ski jump in the USA. Wall, South Dakota, claims to be the home to the world's "largest drugstore." Also, Bandera, Texas, and Bardstown, Kentucky, refer to themselves as the world's "cowboy capital" and "bourbon capital" respectively (Plate 9.2).

Regardless of whether they possess natural amenities or human-created attractions, or even a combination of both, it is obvious that tourism is one of the major forces of transformation in contemporary rural America. The benefits from this sector can be significant, but there are also numerous problems associated with rural tourism growth. These issues are examined later in the chapter, but first we look at the dynamics of rural tourism growth over time. The focus here is primarily on one type of rural tourism region, namely the one that depends heavily on natural amenities.

Plate 9.2 Finding the unusual in rural North Dakota – Rugby, the geographic center of North America
(Dimitri Ioannides)

Amenity-based tourism in rural America

In his article published in the *International Journal of Tourism Research* in 2004, William Gartner offered a detailed discussion of rural tourism development in the USA. He pointed out that although many people visit rural areas throughout the United States, most visitors to such places are Americans (domestic travelers) and the vast majority of these come from surrounding communities, more often than not located within the same or neighboring states. Gartner says that the phenomenon of traveling to a rural area within one's state is not restricted to the Midwest but occurs, instead, nationwide given that "the US Travel Survey reveals that over half of all trips, 100 miles or more, originated and ended in the same state" (Gartner 2004: 152). By contrast, foreigners coming to the United States visit major urban areas and their environs and rarely come to rural parts, unless their appeal is amenity-based (e.g., ski resorts or national park gateways).

Unfortunately, most rural destinations are not the easiest places to get to, especially if one has no access to a private car. To be sure, an expansive highway network throughout the United States means one can now drive along fairly good quality roads to virtually the remotest of spots. Nevertheless, access to rural areas by public transportation is either difficult and time-consuming – often involving several changes – or entirely non-existent, especially following the deregulation and associated severe decline or elimination of subsidies experienced by transportation services more than two decades ago (Lapping *et al.* 1989; Porter *et al.* 2004). Matters are not helped by the fact that the vast majority of rural America, as opposed to many parts of Europe, can no longer be reached by passenger rail (Gartner 2004). All this means that travel to rural spots throughout the country can be quite expensive and this explains why most visitors to such areas travel from surrounding regions rather than from further afield.

Unless a rural region offers a truly unique natural or historic site (like a National Park or a famous battleground), or provides the opportunity for far from universally available activities like downhill skiing, mountain climbing, or deep-sea fishing, most people throughout the country are perfectly happy to visit rural areas close to their home towns. This is especially the case if all they wish to do is spend some days participating in routine recreational endeavors like fishing, hiking, cycling, or canoeing, or visiting rural antique stores and a harvest festival. Since there exist multiple opportunities to enjoy these activities in many parts of the USA, when it comes to rural tourism, the majority of people will not travel vast distances to locales offering similar attractions unless there is a compelling reason to combine their trip with another activity like visiting friends and family (Gartner 2004).

Hall and Shelby (1998) have noted that in the case of recreation-oriented trips to wilderness areas there has been a growing trend for people to visit places closer to their hometowns. The overall tendency is for families to take trips more frequently, for instance several long weekends throughout the year rather than a single major vacation further afield. They explain that this may have to do with the overall decline in leisure time in the USA since the 1960s and also because there are more two-income households it is harder for people to coordinate their schedules. Hall and Shelby argue that in the case of Mount Jefferson and Three Sisters wilderness areas, which are located in the Cascades in Oregon, high visitation rates are certainly associated with these areas' proximity to a number of fairly large cities in the Willamette Valley.

Historically, as we have already examined earlier in this book, rural areas became especially popular destinations for Americans following the introduction of the railroad. Certainly, the early success of Yellowstone and Yosemite National Parks had much to do with the rail companies providing lodges for "early nature lovers" (Gartner 2004: 154) (see Closer Look Case 9.2). Gartner also argues that early rural tourism development in

Plate 9.3 The majestic American countryside – The Grand Canyon
(Dimitri Ioannides)

the USA was associated with the availability of public land for recreation through services like the National Park Service and the National Forest Service (Plate 9.3), although
he points out that it was mostly after the Second World War that rural tourism really
began to take off with the advent of downhill skiing and other activities like white-water
rafting and off-road trips by jeep (Siehl 2000).

CLOSER LOOK CASE 9.2

National parks and rural tourism

The global national park movement began in the United States in 1872 with the establishment of the world's first national park, Yellowstone National Park, on the border of
Wyoming and Montana. Because of its natural beauty and symbolism of natural America,
the park was established as a pleasure ground to benefit and provide enjoyment for the
public. This March 1872 event set into motion the move throughout the world to establish
national parks for the protection of the environment and to provide recreational opportunities for the public.

Between 1872 and the turn of the century, other protected areas were established as national parks and monuments under the direction of the Department of the Interior, but there was no single entity to administer the affairs of the growing number of parklands. As a result, in 1916, the federal government created the National Park Service (NPS) under the auspices of the Department of the Interior to oversee the management, conservation, and interpretation of the nation's natural and cultural heritage. The new agency's mandate was to conserve natural scenery, historic artifacts, and wildlife and to provide for the enjoyment of these resources for the public in perpetuity for future generations. The national park system in the USA now includes some 390 areas of over 84 million acres in 49 states, American Samoa, Guam, Puerto Rico, the District of Columbia, the Northern Marianas, and the US Virgin Islands. Today, the NPS sees its role as "guardian of our diverse cultural and recreational resources; environmental advocate; world leader in the parks and preservation community; and pioneer in the drive to protect America's open space."

The very core of the NPS and the earliest park properties espouse the values of rural America. It was no mistake that the first parks and NPS-operated monuments were located in rural areas – areas that were seen as worth preserving in a rapidly urbanizing nation. By their very character, the earliest national parks, and indeed most of them today, were a rural tourism resource, as nature and open space were the reason for their establishment. Today there are many National Park Service sites in urban and suburban areas as well, but the majority remain within the rural domain.

The establishment of national parks has provided a significant economic advantage for rural America. Small towns near park entrances, known as gateway communities, have thrived on visitor traffic. In many cases, the largest numbers of gateway community members are employed in park-based, tourism-related jobs. Likewise, many small gateway towns receive considerable tax revenue from tourist spending, because relatively few national parks provide lodging for tourists, and the dining selections are limited. Those that do offer accommodations in historic park lodges or campgrounds have a limited number of bed spaces. Thus, gateway communities, nearby towns, and rural areas are critical to the provision of visitor services. National park-based tourism employs rural residents and new, often well-educated, émigrés who arrive looking for work and who desire to live near a park property. Many rural communities rely on national park and non-park employees for social capital as well. Many rural activists and community volunteers are drawn to the countryside because of the existence of a national park.

Aside from agriculture-based tourism (agritourism), national parks are one of the most significant resources for rural tourism in the United States. As American society continues to urbanize and modernize, it is likely that more and more urbanites will choose to spend their vacations in the national parks of rural America.

Sources

US National Park Service (2009) *History*. Available from http://www.nps.gov/aboutus/history.htm (accessed April 28, 2009).

Machlis, G.E. and Field, D.R. (eds) (2000) *National Parks and Rural Development: Practice and Policy in the United States*. Washington, DC: Island Press.

Questions

1. What are the primary mandates of the US National Park Service?
2. In what ways does the existence of national parks improve the economies of rural America?

Since the opening in the 1930s of Sun Valley, Idaho, one of the nation's first ski resorts, skiing has become a major component of the tourism and recreation industry. In particular, during the 1960s this recreational pastime witnessed a major growth especially in states like Colorado, and by 1982 there were 735 downhill ski areas throughout the USA (Rivera and de Leon 2004). After the mid-1980s, however, the ski industry entered a period of stagnation leading to "intense competition and significant consolidation among ski areas" (Rivera and de Leon 2004: 418). Thus, during 2002–3 the number of ski resorts had declined to 490 while the annual income from skiing amounted to $4.2 billion. Although there are now several ski resorts in different parts of the country, including the Northeast (e.g., Vermont), the major destinations are in the American West, namely the Rocky Mountains and the Pacific West. In fact, half of all visits to ski facilities during the year are to these destinations, even though they make up only one-third of all ski resorts in the country. Rivera and de Leon (2004) point out that the two states with the largest numbers of ski facilities are California and Colorado respectively. It is particularly interesting to note that nine out of ten ski facilities in the western states are on leased federal land and the communities that have benefited from this activity can almost always be described as rural.

The establishment and growth of ski destinations is only one of various tourism and recreation-related developments to sweep through rural America over the last six decades (Siehl 2000). Indeed, in addition to communities associated with mountain sports we have also witnessed the growth of settlements functioning as gateways to national parks (e.g., Pigeon Forge, Tennessee; Jackson Hole, Wyoming, outside Yellowstone; and Wall, South Dakota, on the fringes of Badlands National Park). Many communities situated along major hiking and cycling trails have also seen an unprecedented growth associated with demand for these resources. These include communities along the Appalachian Trail such as Asheville, North Carolina, and several small towns along the Katy Trail (an abandoned railroad corridor in Missouri), including Rocheport and Augusta, Missouri (The Katy Trail was discussed earlier in Chapter 6 – Closer Look Case 6.1).

The development of recreational activities in many parts of rural America and the associated growth of tourism that has taken place were very much fueled by growing demand from a rapidly expanding middle class with an increasing disposable income during the 1950s and '60s (Siehl 2000). It also had much to do with the enormous expansion of the highway system criss-crossing the country (see Chapter 2), which enabled increasingly affluent and mobile Americans to explore their nation. Siehl (2000) indicates that several federal government measures were passed to encourage recreational activities, including the establishment in 1962 of the Recreation Advisory Council by President Kennedy and the passage of the 1964 Wilderness Act. Other steps included the creation of the Land and Water Conservation Fund, which was meant to enable the acquisition of private land by federal agencies like the National Park Service, with the specific aim of catering to recreation purposes. Steps such as these, which happened during the "Golden Era" of recreation (Siehl 2000: 95) inevitably led to an increase in travel to public recreational areas, which consequently influenced the growth of rural tourism (Gartner 2004).

We have already mentioned that rural regions have not been immune to the restructuring that has gripped urban areas throughout the country. Of course, even as early as the 1920s rural decline had began to affect America, and certainly stories of families being forced to leave the Dustbowl of the Plains during the Great Depression abound, with John Steinbeck's (1939) *Grapes of Wrath* being the poster child of this phenomenon. However, the major period of economic upheaval in rural America began after the 1960s (see Long and Lane 2000) following the decline of extractive activities such as mining and logging and the reduced importance of agriculture in the national economy. In more recent years and certainly since the early 1980s rural manufacturing has also witnessed a major decline in the face of growing competition from abroad. It is the combination of these phenomena then that has provided the green light which enabled the transition from traditional economies to tourist-based economies (Lapping *et al.* 1989; Gartner 2004). Long and Lane (2000: 300) emphasize that one underlying reason for the growing importance of tourism throughout rural America has to do with "our changing mental perceptions of country life." Essentially, they argue, a number of reasons such as the standardization and predictability of urban life have made many Americans long for the "authenticity [and] uniqueness" of rural life, regardless of whether these values are real or not.

Subsequently, although rural tourism development has taken place in thousands of communities throughout the United States, nowhere is the effect of this growth more evident than in the so-called rural recreation counties. These include not only the purely tourism-dependent counties but also those with concentrations of seasonal residents because it is not easy to distinguish between effects of the two groups. After all, "many seasonal residents first came to the area as tourists" and this means it is best to measure the "overall impacts of tourism and recreation combined" (Reeder and Brown 2005: 3).

A series of studies commissioned by the ERS of the USDA has revealed the existence of tourism- and recreation-dependent counties throughout the nation (Beale and Johnson 1998; Johnson and Beale 2002; Reeder and Brown 2005). This research has demonstrated that in non-metropolitan counties where tourism constitutes a significant portion of the economy, population growth has consistently outpaced that of other non-metropolitan counties and that of many metropolitan regions. This population growth has been a result both of net in-migration and natural increase. And, it seems that a main reason for this increase has to do with non-economic migration factors such as the desire to live in or close to areas offering high-quality amenities, including plenty of opportunities for recreation.

Using a composite measure derived from statistical analysis of indicators such as the percentage of employees in tourism-related jobs and the percentage of homes that were seasonal, Beale and Johnson's (1998) study classified 285 rural counties as recreational (see Figure 9.1). Later studies revised this number to 329 (Johnson and Beale 2002; Reeder and Brown 2005). This measure reveals that approximately 15 percent of the non-metropolitan population lives in rural recreational counties, which make up approximately 15 percent of all rural counties. Most of these rural recreational counties are concentrated in the mountains of the West, parts of the northeastern United States, and the Upper Great Lakes. They are also found in parts of the Ozarks, the southern Appalachians, and several non-urbanized parts of the Pacific and Atlantic coastlines (Beale and Johnson 1998; Reeder and Brown 2005).

A significant degree of overlap exists between the recreational counties that have been identified in the aforementioned studies and a natural amenity index, which ranks counties on the basis of various attributes such as their elevation, proximity to water, and their climate (McGranahan 1999, quoted in Johnson and Beale 2002). For instance, the opportunity for mountain sports and proximity to national parks are major assets in the

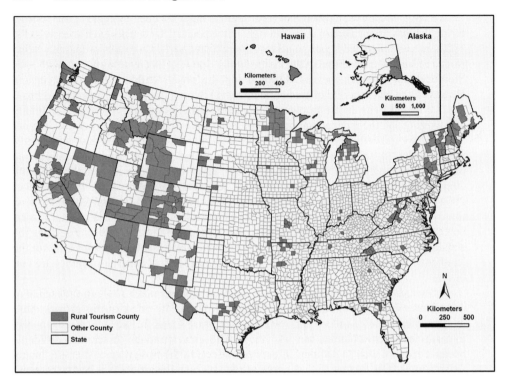

Figure 9.1 Tourism-dependent rural counties
Source: after Beale, C.L. and Johnson, K.M. (1998)

West. In the upper Great Lakes, the high concentration of second homes acts as a draw for visitors. Then, in Nevada the opportunity to gamble draws huge numbers of visitors. It is also worth mentioning that there exist plenty of rural recreation counties scattered around the country which have become popular for visitors and second home owners due to some unique characteristic such as their tie to a historical event. Examples include the area surrounding Gettysburg, the site of one of the most famous Civil War encounters, and the pre-Civil War community of Natchez, Mississippi (Beale and Johnson 1998). On the other side of the coin, these studies have revealed the general absence of rural recreational counties in the Great Plains, the Corn Belt, and much of the southern states like Alabama and Louisiana.

It is evident that recreation-dependent counties in rural America are rapidly increasing. On average, they grew by 20 percent during the 1990s, which was three times as fast as non-recreation/tourism rural counties (Reeder and Brown 2005). Other findings from the ERS studies reveal that overall the economy of recreational counties is more diversified than that of other rural areas. In fact, almost 40 percent of recreational counties depend on just one major industry while 58 percent of other non-metropolitan counties are tied to just a single sector. Additionally, almost a third of recreation counties double up as retirement communities while only 4 percent of other non-metro areas can be classed as retirement settlements.

Differences exist in economic indicators also between recreation- and non-recreation-based rural counties. For instance, 10 percent of recreation counties have high poverty rates compared to 25 percent of non-recreation counties, while the earnings per worker, the incomes per capita, and the median household incomes respectively are all higher in recreation- as opposed to non-recreation-based counties. Finally, the importance of public lands for rural recreational counties is also witnessed in Reeder and Brown's report, since 38 percent of these can be classified as federal land counties (federal counties are those where at least 30 percent of the land belongs to the federal government). By contrast, only 7 percent of the other (non-recreational) rural counties are classed as federally owned.

The effects of rural tourism

Overall, the benefits from tourism often seem to outweigh the problems, especially from an economic standpoint, although the effects of tourism and recreation in rural areas vary from place to place. Reeder and Brown's (2005) study provides a comprehensive image of the positive and negative impacts witnessed in these localities. One thing is clear. In cases where there are tourists as well as seasonal residents, various new businesses are commonly developed. In addition to the obvious lodging facilities and restaurants, a variety of supporting services catering to new residents and workers also emerge, including new retail establishments and amusement facilities as well as expanded school and health care capacity (English *et al.* 2000). Reeder and Brown stress that this situation often leads to "a more diversified economy with more high paying jobs. Even low-paid recreation workers could benefit if better employment became available. Income levels could rise, along with levels of education, health, and other measures of community welfare, and poverty rates could be expected to decline" (Reeder and Brown 2005: iii). Not surprisingly, some of the most affluent rural tourism and recreation communities are the ski resorts, while the tourism/recreation communities that are located adjacent to lakes and reservoirs, including those in the Midwest and southern Appalachia have, by contrast, some of the poorest educated and lowest income people. In counties where casinos have become the major attraction, job growth has been significant while earnings have also grown, especially during the 1990s.

Among the most common advantages that tourism and recreation bestow upon a destination region include increased land values, leading to benefits to landowners; further, unemployment and underemployment can be reduced, resulting, in turn, in a reduction in poverty; and the taxes that arise from short-term visitors and seasonal residents can lead to an improvement in infrastructure and other public services. According to English *et al.* (2000: 185–6), the counties that are natural amenity-based have seen the injection of "new dollars into local businesses, supporting local tax bases, and increasing demands for locally available land, labor, and capital. With regard to the recreational use of natural resources, tourist expenditures create local demand for traded goods and services thus creating jobs and income for local residents." English *et al.* argue that approximately 767,000 jobs have resulted from non-resident trips to rural communities, creating $11.8 billion in income for workers and business owners.

There is also no underestimating the importance of seasonal homes in many rural regions (Timothy 2004). In 2002, 45 percent of the more than 30,000 jobs in Eagle County, Colorado, were linked to the second home sector, while 27 percent of these jobs were tied to winter and summer tourism. Moreover, 38 percent of the income in this community came from the spending of the second home owners (compared to 31 percent from short-term tourists) (Johnson 2005).

Despite the obvious benefits that emerge from tourism and recreation in rural areas, there exist significant problems associated with these activities. Referring specifically to second-home areas in resort counties of Colorado, Venturoni *et al.* (2005) reveal that a common problem in such regions is the shortage of housing and the rise in property values. This creates the thorny issue of plenty of tourism communities that lack afford-able housing for their workers. The problem seems to be worse in communities with little room to expand due to their proximity to public lands. For example, in Eagle County, Colorado, which is a significant second home area, 79 percent of the land is publicly held, while additional land is not suitable for development owing to its topography. Thus, there is very little room for expanding the housing stock, which means that property values are high. Venturoni *et al.* (2005) note that in Eagle County, Colorado, the average price for a single family unit in 2003 stood at $785,000 whereas the average value of a multi-family unit was $443,000. These prices, which significantly exceeded the US average of $100,000 for that time, were well above what most tourism-related workers could afford.

Reeder and Brown (2005) reaffirm the high cost of living in rural tourism and recre-ation prices, especially as this relates to housing costs. They established that on average, rents were 23 percent in recreation counties, although median household incomes in these areas were, on average, $3,185 higher. This higher income partially offsets the high rent prices.

The effects relating to crime in rural recreation counties are mixed. Reeder and Brown's (2005: 25) study shows that serious crime rates are higher in such regions than in non-recreation counties and it also revealed a "positive relationship between crime rates and recreation dependency." However, the authors reveal that this statistic can be misleading since the crimes against seasonal residents and tourists are measured in addition to those against full-time residents, but seasonal residents and tourists are not "part of the population base upon which the rate is calculated" (p. 25). Regardless of these misleading statistics, however, it is obvious that recreational counties do require the maintenance of expanded public safety infrastructure (e.g., ambulance, police, and fire).

Several additional threats can arise from the development of tourism-related activities in rural America. Gartner (2004) indicates that this occurs because development in these places is frequently uncoordinated, unplanned, and market-driven. Often, there is a failure to take into account the cumulative effects of tourism developments, perhaps because each individual development on its own has only a minor effect on the overall host society; it is the collective impact of all these developments that can lead to a crisis, a matter which is regularly revealed only after the most serious problems have emerged (Bosselman *et al.* 1999; Ioannides 2008). Additionally, the lack of effective planning mechanisms often has to do with the absence of public agencies dealing with develop-ment controls in many parts of rural America.

In Missouri, for example, so-called third-class counties, which have traditionally been agricultural areas, do not have building regulations and planning controls. If a county like this experiences a shift to a tourism-oriented economy, as was the case with Taney County (which surrounds Branson) almost two decades ago, then this can prove to be a recipe for disaster. More often than not, planning intervention takes place only after the problems associated with uncoordinated tourism development have reared their ugly heads, and in many cases this is too late (Gartner 2004).

Plenty of stories exist of increasing traffic jams and rising air pollution levels, as well as overcrowded schools in communities like Branson, Missouri, and Pigeon Forge, Tennessee. Simultaneously, rapid and uncontrolled tourism development in rural areas can lead to additional pressures, including threats to the very same natural or historical amenities that spurred tourism's growth in the first place. For example, overbuilding in a haphazard manner, without following design and aesthetic guidelines often causes architectural pollution and the loss of scenic views. Too many visitors in a small rural community can place excessive strain on its fresh water supplies and its sewage treatment capacity. Overdevelopment in rural places can also lead to encroachment on wildlife habitats. In numerous rural regions there are ongoing debates between different user groups who wish to use the same site for different purposes. A good example of this is the long-term battle between snowmobile users and other recreational groups (e.g., cross-country skiers) in Yellowstone National Park.

Finally, rural communities that witness an excessive growth rate often become magnets for chain facilities like Holiday Inn and Howard Johnson and so-called "big box retailers" like Wal-Mart and K-mart. Although many may regard the arrival of these establishments as progress since they undoubtedly provide more options, very likely at significantly discounted prices, for residents and visitors, there is also a more sinister side to this story. Effectively, the arrival of these standardized chain establishments threatens the survival of smaller-scale, locally owned mom-and-pop businesses, especially since these lack the economies of scale to remain competitive *vis-à-vis* their large-scale counterparts. Additionally, the design of the big box retail establishments can become a major blemish on a community, especially if it relies heavily on traditional architecture.

Reflections on rural tourism

This chapter has explored the issue of rural tourism development in the United States. Our underlying premise has been that just like many major metropolitan regions, numerous small rural communities in this country's vast hinterland have turned to tourism in an effort to stimulate economic growth and to stem the chronic decline associated with downturns in traditional sectors like farming, mining, logging, and manufacturing. It is not surprising, therefore, that many places within the Great Plains that were once doomed to extinction due to their massive population loss may now have a lifeline in the form of ecotourism (Popper and Popper 2006). Specifically, some cattle ranchers have converted their grazing lands back into prairie, and reintroduced the American buffalo into its natural habitat in the hope they can entice visitors into the region and re-ignite the economy.

Rural America, of course, is far from a homogeneous region. There are many places within the country possessing the locational advantage of their proximity to breathtaking natural settings and these are the ones that evidently offer few obstacles in terms of attracting visitors as well as second home owners and even new permanent residents. Snow-clad mountains are perfect settings for winter sports, and many communities located in such regions have had a lengthy tradition as tourist destinations. By the same token, communities situated close to bodies of water, such as lakes and rivers, or which exist in the vicinity of a major national or state park or land administered by the National Forest Service, lend themselves to a variety of recreational activities and, as such, are in a position to entice large numbers of tourists.

It is hardly surprising that there appears to be a high correlation between non-metropolitan counties which can be labeled amenity-based, and the existence of permanent residents fitting the profile of the creative class – "people in highly creative occupations such as business ownership and top management, science, engineering, architecture, design, arts, and entertainment" (McGranahan and Wojan 2007: 17). These people are drawn to such regions precisely because of the amenities they offer: their climate, opportunity for recreation, scenic vistas, and so on. In turn, evidence suggests the concentration of these creative people leads to additional amenities for a community, including good places to eat and fine entertainment, as well as art collections. These extra amenities, in turn, serve to enhance even further the attraction of such communities for new permanent residents and also visitors and second home owners (Wojan *et al.* 2007).

Nevertheless, not every place in the USA is fortunate enough to be located in the Rockies, Sierras, or close to the Great Lakes. In addition to the thousands of amenity-based communities around rural America there are thousands of localities offering little or nothing too out of the ordinary when it comes to their natural endowments. Some of these communities are fortunate enough to be able to turn to other resources like their historical attractions or their architectural heritage, which they use to entice visitors. But then there is yet another group consisting of literally countless places that on the surface have precious little to offer to the potential visitor. Not an insignificant number of these try but fail to develop some kind of tourism-based economy. The reasons for this failure are many but often include the relative isolation of such communities from major centers of population and the fact that the product they develop cannot always be competitive, especially if there are intervening opportunities for visits to similar destinations closer to home.

Other communities, however, are able to overcome these handicaps and reinvent themselves through a combination of measures such as the development of events and festivals and/or the development of theme-based tourism. Often, the civic leaders in such communities play up the theme of heritage tourism based on the ethnic background of the original settlers. That is why there are now so many localities throughout the country boasting their association to their ethnic roots (for example, Danish, German, Swedish, Dutch, and French). Still other places, like Leavenworth, Washington, which lack a clear-cut ethnic heritage product, transform themselves into theme towns bearing little if any link to their portrayed past. Finally, there are scores of rural towns that try to entice visitors by touting themselves as places offering some unique attraction, which either they inherit or they construct. The poster child of such a community is Cawker City, Kansas, which calls itself the home of the world's largest ball of twine.

Regardless of whether or not rural places are successful in attracting tourists, it is clear that this sector now features as perhaps their only realistic hope for economic revival. Moreover, unlike many urban areas that have economies which are diversified enough to cushion the blow of a drop in tourism demand, the fortunes of many rural communities are inextricably locked into the fate of their visitor sector. Thus, even though there are many economic benefits associated with tourism development, the danger of depending heavily on a "mono-crop" sector cannot be stressed enough. Additional downsides associated with tourism development include inflated land values and cost of housing, social impacts like the increasing resentment of long-term residents towards newcomers, and environmental problems arising from over-development and congestion. Since many rural communities lack a strong tradition of land-use regulations and planning, the emerging development patterns are frequently haphazard and bear little forethought concerning the consequences of the cumulative effects of the actions of individual players.

The apparent high dependence of rural America on a visitor-based economy combined with the real need to protect the very resources that draw the tourists in the first place, necessitate a more proactive stance when it comes to planning. Lessons of poor development from numerous places signify that it would be to the advantage of such communities to implement approaches that manage tourism's growth *ex ante*. Furthermore, the small size of many of these communities and the fact that they often compete for the same type of visitor indicates that it would be to their advantage to form collaborative approaches in terms of marketing to achieve a growth in tourism, and also planning to mitigate the sector's negative effects.

Questions

1. In simple terms how would you define a rural area? What are the necessary ingredients that distinguish such an area from an urban environment?

2. Define in simple terms what is meant by a tourism cluster? Can you think of tourism clusters in various parts of rural America? Give several examples.
3. Can you think of examples where a popular film or book has led to the transformation of a quiet rural community into a major tourist destination? Try to provide several examples.
4. What is meant by an amenity-based rural community? Why have these places been successful in attracting visitors and permanent residents?

Further reading

Carpio, C.E., Wohlgenant, M.K. and Boonsaeng, T. (2008) The demand for agritourism in the United States. *Journal of Agricultural and Resource Economics*, 33(2): 254–69.

Crotts, J.C. and Holland, S.M. (1993) Objective indicators of the impact of rural tourism development in the state of Florida. *Journal of Sustainable Tourism*, 1(2): 112–20.

Huang, Y.H. and Stewart, W.P. (1996) Rural tourism development: shifting basis of community solidarity. *Journal of Travel Research*, 34(4): 26–31.

Lewis, J.B. and Lelisle, L. (2004) Tourism as economic self-development in rural Nebraska: a case study. *Tourism Analysis*, 9(3): 153–66.

Luloff, A.E., Bridger, J.C., Graefe, A.R., Saylor, M., Martin, K. and Gitelson, R.J. (1994) Assessing rural tourism efforts in the United States. *Annals of Tourism Research*, 21: 46–64.

Marcouiller, D.W. (1997) Toward integrative tourism planning in rural America. *Journal of Planning Literature*, 11(3): 337–57.

McGehee, N.G. and Andereck, K.L. (2004) Factors predicting rural residents' support of tourism. *Journal of Travel Research*, 43(2): 131–40.

Petrzelka, P., Krannich, R.S., Brehm, J. and Trentelman, C.K. (2005) Rural tourism and gendered nuances. *Annals of Tourism Research*, 32: 1121–37.

Tweeten, K., Leistritz, L. and Hodur, N. (2008) Growing rural tourism opportunities. *Journal of Extension*, 46(2): 2–22.

Wilson, S., Fesenmaier, D.R., Fesenmaier, J. and van Es, J.C. (2001) Factors for success in rural tourism development. *Journal of Travel Research*, 40(2): 132–38.

Xie, P. (2004) Visitors' perceptions of authenticity at a rural heritage festival: a case study. *Event Management*, 8(3): 151–60.

Useful Internet resources

Buffalo Commons: http://www.gprc.org/buffalocommons.html
City of Aspen, Colorado: http://www.aspenpitkin.com/
Eagle County, Colorado: http://www.eaglecounty.us/
Institute for Rural America: http://www.instituteruralamerica.org/
Leavenworth, Washington: http://www.leavenworth.org/
Little Sweden, USA: http://www.lindsborg.org/
Main Street (National Trust for Historic Preservation): http://www.preservationnation.org/main-street/
Pella, Iowa: http://www.cityofpella.com/
US Department of Agriculture: http://www.ers.usda.gov/Emphases/Rural/

10 Conclusions
Trends and futures of tourism in the USA

On September 10, 2001, the United States was the most open, and some might have said most naïve, country in the world . . . Government scrutiny for the more than 7 million visas granted each year to foreign visitors was cursory, while another 11 million travelers from Europe and nearly 25 million visitors from Canada and Mexico crossed with virtually no scrutiny at all. U.S. policy was explicitly to facilitate and promote travel, believing it could only bring economic, social, and cultural benefits to the country . . . But in the aftermath of the worst terrorist attack on U.S. soil, which had left nearly three thousand people dead and their grieving families behind, the risks suddenly appeared vastly to outweigh the benefits.

(Alden 2008: 4–5)

The preceding chapters of this book have made perfectly clear the complexities of tourism in the United States. The country possesses a rich cultural heritage stemming from its indigenous peoples and European settlers that exudes an extremely attractive appeal to domestic and foreign tourists. The natural heritage of the United States is also remarkable, ranging from permanent mountain glaciers to tropical rainforests, with many different climatic and vegetative zones in between. Its topography is among the most diverse in the world, with high peaks rivaling those in Europe and Asia and flatlands in the agricultural heartland, with thousands of unique and interesting physical features at either extreme and in between.

The vastness of the United States is itself one of the country's primary assets. There is a common perception among many Americans that there is no need to travel abroad, since their own country has everything a person could desire to see and experience. America's size and this commonplace attitude among its people have traditionally resulted in fewer Americans (as per proportion of total population) traveling overseas, compared to other nationalities, and domestic tourism being paramount in the minds of American travelers. While domestic travel remains most popular, there has been a notable increase in outbound travel in recent years (US Department of Commerce 2008c), although the current (2007–9) recession has slowed international travel considerably. Nonetheless, overseas travel by Americans has grown several-fold in only a generation or two, spurred by technological innovations, more affluent societies and individual families, global accessibility, and a growing world awareness.

The aim of this book has been to provide a social scientific overview of tourism and related issues in the United States of America. Aside from the size and diversity of places noted above, the United States is unique in many other respects compared to other countries in the world when it comes to tourism. First, history has been kind to American tourism. The USA has been a trend setter in travel innovations that facilitated higher levels of global accessibility. The advent of steam trains, combustible-engine automobiles, airplanes, recreational vehicles, and interstate highways, many of which were invented and developed in the USA, has been extremely advantageous for tourism's evolution.

Americans have long been extremely independent-minded; in fact, self-determination has formed the ideological foundations of the state since the 1600s and still does so today. Americans are a proud people who value their freedom to travel nearly everywhere in the world. This was manifested especially with the proliferation of the automobile, when families from the eastern states made their way on stony roads and dirt tracks in the early twentieth century to explore the breathtaking landscapes of the west. This was in fact a demonstration of their independent-mindedness; train travel for many would no longer suffice. Americans still pride themselves on being the most mobile people in the world and leaders in the field of travel innovations.

Another of the most notable characteristics of tourism in the USA is the lack of targeted national-level policies and a central organization to deal with tourism promotion, collect comprehensive data, and liaise between the public and private sectors. It is one of the few countries in the world without a national tourism organization, leaving promotion and development to the devices of individual states, counties and municipalities.

Additionally, even though the United States has long been the top earner from tourism among all the world's countries in terms of total dollar amounts, because of the magnitude of America's economy, tourism's role in the overall economy is relatively small compared to the role of other industries. This is perhaps one of the reasons why the federal administration has, unfortunately, not paid the same attention to tourism as it has to other sectors of the economy.

Having said this, however, one would be hard pressed today to find a major city or indeed a small rural community that does not have some sort of visitor promotion strategy. Especially in an era that has witnessed the wide-scale de-industrialization of numerous localities, coupled with massive reductions in federal subsidies for towns and cities, it appears that community leaders have now come to accept that tourism-related initiatives can generate economic growth and diversification as well as create new job opportunities. Perhaps, even more importantly, the promotion of tourism-led developments is a way for communities to boost their image. For instance, policymakers hope that the upfront expenditure for a new convention center, a civic arena, or a public park will be justified since it enhances the image of the city as an enjoyable place to live and, in so doing, it can attract not only temporary visitors but, importantly, new residents and, perhaps, companies.

In addition to the topics highlighted in this book, there are several other issues that have not been examined in depth in the text owing to space constraints. Nonetheless, they are extremely important matters facing the tourism sector in the United States today and merit brief consideration here.

One of the pre-eminent issues of today is safety and security. This is, as the introductory chapter noted, an unavoidable part of the current tourism landscape in the era of "war on terrorism." The US government has taken bold steps to minimize the threat of terrorism and other security risks to the public in general, and to the traveling public in particular. Recent visa and passport regulations are a salient part of this concern. Whereas visa regimes throughout much of the world are loosening with the growth of supranationalism and cross-border cooperation, the United States is simultaneously tightening its visa and immigration policies to reflect heightened vigilance on the part of the federal government to prevent undesirable forces from entering the country. As part of this broad effort, biometric identification technology has been implemented (e.g., eye scans, fingerprinting, and DNA testing) at ports of entry and international airports to document all arriving foreigners (Timothy 2006a). Some travelers entering the US and other observers have complained of humiliation, invasion of privacy, and lack of human rights associated with biometrics at American airports (Prabhakar *et al.* 2003; Sasse 2007). Regardless of what might seem inconvenient or unfair, the US government maintains its position that such steps are necessary to ensure the safety and security of its borders and its population. It is likely that these measures will continue far into the future and will no doubt become even more sophisticated in time.

Related to this broader issue of national security is the tightening of border controls at the country's land boundaries. The weakness of the USA's southern border and the infiltration of illegal immigrants have long been at the forefront of political discussions and debates. However, in recent years, particularly since September 11, 2001, the debate has surged yet again but now includes additional fodder related to the illegal crossing of people who may intend to harm the American public. While the US–Mexico border on both sides has been a popular tourist destination since the early 1900s, recent events related to drug wars and mass murders have reduced the cross-border flows substantially. Efforts are presently under way by the US military and other federal agencies to better seal the border to prevent drug smuggling and to stop other illegal activities from crossing the border northward. All these steps, plus official government warnings that fervently discourage Americans from crossing into Mexico, have a major bearing on tourism, especially since once desirable day-trip destinations for Americans (i.e., Mexican border towns like Nogales, Ciudad Juarez, and Tijuana) have become virtual tourist ghost towns. Other State Department travel warnings, which are regularly issued in the name of securing travel space for US citizens, have also dealt a considerable blow to tourism in numerous countries throughout the world.

Such issues related to security, terrorism, and crime have elucidated the depth and gravity of questions about individual freedom and mobility, not to mention basic human rights. Unfortunately, the world sees these more stringent controls by the USA as an affront, because in many parts of the globe, borders and other ports of entry are increasingly becoming more relaxed and welcoming. Consider, for instance, that once a traveler has entered the Schengen zone in Europe (say through Paris) that person can then travel unimpeded throughout many countries of the EU that are signatories of the agreement. The current steps that have been issued in the name of the "war against terror" and some of its manifestations have upset many of the USA's traditional allies. This displeasure has spilled into tourism, and the country has a great deal of work ahead to rebuild its image abroad as a peaceful, safe, and welcoming tourist destination.

Chapter 3 examined some of the management, planning and policy implications of tourism in the USA. One aspect that should be mentioned further is that of cross-border cooperation between the United States and its neighbors in the form of supranationalism. Supranationalism, often referred to as trading blocs, customs unions, or economic communities, and its effects on tourism are seen at their best in the European Union, where tourism has received a great deal of public and legislative attention. The North American Free Trade Agreement (NAFTA) is North America's most viable supranationalist endeavor. While few of the treaties that formed and expanded the role of NAFTA mention tourism specifically, they do touch directly on tourism-related phenomena, such as environmental protection, cross-border mobility of people, trade in goods and services, and water resources protection. These elements are especially crucial in the modern globalized world, where each individual country can no longer act alone in regard to economic, social, and environmental development. While NAFTA and many of its trinational policies are unpopular with some people in the USA, Canada and Mexico, the treaty does have some positive elements that have a bearing on the future growth and development of tourism in the United States and between the three countries of North America. This is especially true in light of current debates on illegal immigration (many illegal and legal immigrants are employed in the hospitality and tourism sectors) and environmental conservation, since a number of natural and cultural areas important for tourism lie across or adjacent to North America's international boundaries (Timothy 1999a).

Another geopolitical concept is the opening up of new foreign destinations to the US tourist market. Currently the federal government is considering dismantling America's embargo against Cuba, which has been in place since 1962. This is highly controversial, but many observers claim that the embargo has been ineffective, and it is now time to lift the sanctions to allow Americans free access to Cuba as a tourist destination and trading partner. Prior to the 1960s, Cuba was an important American tourist destination in the Caribbean. It remains to be seen if the sanctions will be lifted in the near future. If this occurs, it is very likely that Americans by the millions will flock to the nearby Caribbean island for vacations and business, extending outbound demand even further.

Likewise, North Korea, which has been off-limits to US citizens until very recently, is now cooling its offensive against American tourists. During the past five years the country started issuing a limited number of visas to US passport holders, allowing American access to a country that many consider the most reclusive, and therefore tantalizing, destination in the modern world.

Another critical and futuristic issue is sustainable development. The United States is no different from other parts of the developed world when it comes to sustainable development. A most important issue, which seems to recur from locality to locality, is that it is often exceedingly hard to balance economic growth priorities with environmental and social equity concerns. The predominantly *laissez-faire* land-use planning system that exists in most communities throughout the United States means that it is often hard to regulate development effectively. Since tourism development is more often than not the result of numerous individual actions on behalf of various entrepreneurs, little coordination accompanies this form of growth and, consequently, the cumulative effects of these developments are not well, if at all, anticipated. This means that all too often tourism has caused a whole series of adverse problems in many popular destinations around the country, and these problems are hard to solve after they have taken root. On the plus side, however, there is a small but growing number of communities around the country that have paid heed to the issue of sustainable development and have attempted to introduce measures that lead to more balanced development forms. Clearly, the leaders of localities that are toying with the idea of expanding their visitor-based economy should pay heed to the successful measures that have been adopted in places like Park City, Utah, which in 1992 adopted a "Sensitive Lands" ordinance aimed at protecting "steep slopes, ridge lines, entry corridors, wetlands, and streams" from development associated with the resort town's rapid growth (Bosselman *et al.* 1999: 80).

It is also worth mentioning that there is a strong sustainability and green movement going on in the country's tourism industry because a growing number of consumers are demanding more eco-friendly products and services, while corporations realize that being green translates into good business. This is especially apparent in the lodging, food services, and transportation sectors. There are several interesting trends taking place in this regard (Butler 2008; Stipanuk 1996). The first trend is eco-certification. The Green Restaurant Association based in Boston, for example, certifies restaurants, cafés, bars and other food service providers. Its certification program is based on an establishment's adherence to certain criteria that define it as environmentally sustainable: energy use, water conservation, reduced chemical usage and pollution output, use of local and sustainable food products, and the implementation of sustainable architectural designs and construction materials (Timothy and Teye 2009). A similar program, Green Seal, certifies transportation businesses, food services, and lodging facilities under its Greening

Plate 10.1 Ethnic foods as a tourist attraction: Chinatown, San Francisco
(Dimitri Ioannides)

the Lodging Industry Program. Green Seal's aim is to increase profits while encouraging and rewarding ecologically sustainable management (Timothy and Teye 2009).

The Slow Food Movement is yet another sustainability-related phenomenon that is coming to the forefront of tourism in the United States. The movement combines elements of healthy eating and sustainable living. It developed in Italy in response to the ubiquity of fast food, which is commonly acknowledged as unsustainable and unhealthy. Slow food focuses on producing foods made from organic products, heirloom vegetables, indigenous foods, and cuisines that are important in regional culinary heritage. It also encourages ethical growing and packaging standards, and food products are often bought from small-scale, family-operated farms (Pietrykow 2004). The Slow Food Movement has become very popular in Europe and is now gaining momentum in the United States, and more and more restaurants and cafés have begun offering slow food cuisine alternatives on their menus (Plate 10.1).

A similar sustainability endeavor is the linen reuse program adopted by many American hotels and resorts during the past two decades (Enz and Siguaw 2003; Johnson 2002). This "choose to reuse" program encourages hotel guests to use their towels and bed sheets more than once rather than having them changed daily. Observers suggest that such a program will help save water, energy, and detergent costs; a few initial industry studies have found that nearly three-quarters of hotel guests elect to re-use their towels, saving large hotel companies millions of dollars in linen cleaning costs (Timothy and Teye 2009). In the realm of transportation, there is considerable debate going on in the United States with regard to adopting alternative fuel sources (e.g., nuclear, wind, and solar) and exploiting domestic oil sources rather than depending on overseas imports. This is not only a matter of money and environment, but also national security.

There are many trends in tourism attractions and development, not all of which have been discussed in detail in Chapter 5. For example, there are several important additional heritage issues in the United States. One of the most common is urban gentrification and waterfront development. Baltimore's harbor and redeveloped waterfront (noted in Chapter 8) is among the most often-cited success stories of urban gentrification in the USA. Then there are many other similar urban regeneration projects, including those in various areas of greater New York City, Miami Beach, and Chicago, as well as some smaller cities such as Toledo, Ohio, and Louisville, Kentucky. Even communities whose economy does not focus on tourism, such as Tempe and Mesa, Arizona, have undergone important downtown revitalization projects to appeal to local recreationists and out-of-town visitors. Preserving heritage buildings, constructing shops and restaurants, enhancing the streetscape, landscape improvements, providing more parking spaces, and remodeling structures that might otherwise be torn down are characteristic of townscape and urban gentrification. The National Trust for Historic Preservation's Main Street Program has been particularly instrumental in assisting small towns and urban neighborhoods in revitalizing their infrastructures and economies for local consumption and for tourism.

Similarly, personal heritage was not addressed in Chapter 5, but because of its futuristic aspects it deserves brief mention here from two perspectives: genealogy travel and diaspora-related tourism. Both of these forms of heritage tourism have international and domestic dimensions and are not mutually exclusive. Genealogy is becoming one of the most popular leisure pursuits in the United States today, particularly because Americans need to be rooted in the simpler life of the past when modernization and technological growth were not running rampant and where life was less frenetic but more certain (Lowenthal 1996). Genealogy travel has resulted in an increase in the number of trips to discover one's roots to visit the places associated with one's ancestors, or to conduct family history research in archives and cemeteries. While much of this behavior is international in nature, since Americans travel to the lands of their ancestors, it also is mirrored in domestic travel as Americans desire to visit the settlements and homesteads of their earliest immigrant forebears, immigration museums (e.g., Ellis Island), or genealogical libraries (Timothy 2008).

Diaspora travel is part of the broader notion of personal heritage tourism and entails people of various ethnic groups traveling to their homelands to visit relatives, do genealogy research, or simply experience the landscapes where their ancestors farmed, lived, worshipped, or were enslaved. Scottish-Americans, Chinese-Americans, Irish-Americans, Ukrainian-Americans, and many other "hyphenated" Americans are avid overseas travelers for diasporic or genealogical purposes (Basu 2001, 2005). Nearly all Americans originated from some diasporic movement, so such forms of travel are important in the US context and are becoming even more salient. African-Americans are among the most fervent of these. For many African-Americans the journey to Africa is a personal pilgrimage undertaken in the hope of finding closure to past wrongs, connecting to their ancestral heritage and the spirits of their predecessors, or simply setting foot on the same terra their forebears walked before them (Bruner 1996; Goodrich 1985; Timothy and Teye 2004).

Chapter 9 highlighted some of the various mechanisms used by small towns and rural areas to develop tourism, including festivals and special events. These approaches remain one of the time-proven subjects of tourism in the USA with ever more communities turning to celebrate particular elements of their agricultural or ethnic heritage as a way of drawing people to town. As the population continues to diversify, not least through immigration, there is little doubt that the nature of, and competition between, these festivals and other related events will continue far into the future.

Likewise, as noted in Chapter 8, sports stadiums and other sporting venues are an important part of the urban tourism mix. Sport tourism, while not explicitly examined in the previous chapters, is especially popular in the United States. Simply stated, Americans have a love affair with American football, baseball, and basketball. Other sports, such as golf and NASCAR racing, are topping the charts as well since they become popularized in movies and other media. Mega sporting events have long been an important part of the tourism economy in the US. The annual World Series baseball championship and the Super Bowl draw thousands of spectator devotees every year. The USA has also hosted the summer and winter Olympics on several occasions, bringing millions of visitors from the world over and from across the country to observe this mega sporting event. Even at the city and small town level there are sporting competitions (Little League) that stimulate travel to compete or observe. There is little doubt that the role of sports in tourism in the United States will continue to be strong in the future. In fact, a wider array of sports is gaining a unique following (e.g., volleyball, dirt-biking, tennis, lacrosse, soccer), which will likely create additional demand for sport-related travel.

Tourism in the United States is multidimensional and complex. Draconian immigration procedures, new forms of tourism, increasing demand for domestic and international travel (incoming and outgoing), demographic changes, a keener awareness of the need for more sustainable forms of tourism, and a realization that the world has changed from a security perspective signify that life will no longer be as it was before the new millennium. While these are but a small handful out of a multitude of current and futuristic issues and trends relating to the US tourism sector, they confirm the old adage that the only constant in life is change. In the United States, change is the key to the present and the future of tourism; planning, management, and development must come to that realization. While the future is uncertain, come what may, it is likely that the United States of America will continue to be among the world's leading tourist destinations and a major generator of overseas travel.

Questions

1. Do you feel that the measures being instituted in the name of safety and security have gone too far? Do you think that such measures give the United States a poor image abroad? Pick a position and make an argument as to what you think about these measures.
2. Based on what you have read in this chapter and throughout the book, what is one of the most important trends regarding sustainable development in the United States? What are some of the constraints to sustainable development?
3. Look up online the "Slow Food Movement." In what way can this movement help tourism in a specific American region? Do you believe that a rural region, for example, could benefit from subscribing to the ideas of this movement?

Further reading

Amendah, E. and Park, J.K. (2008) Consumer involvement and psychological antecedents on eco-friendly destinations: willingness to pay more. *Journal of Hospitality and Leisure Marketing*, 17(3/4): 262–83.

Blalock, G., Kadiyali, V. and Simon, D.H. (2007) The impact of post-9/11 airport security measures on the demand for air travel. *Journal of Law and Economics*, 50(4): 731–56.

Hritz, N. and Cecil, A.K. (2008) Investigating the sustainability of cruise tourism: a case study of Key West. *Journal of Sustainable Tourism*, 16(2): 168–81.

Useful Internet resources

Arizona Tourism Safety and Security Conference: http://www.aztourismsafety.com/displayconvention.cfm

Green Hotels Association: http://www.greenhotels.com/media.htm

Green Restaurant Association: http://www.dinegreen.com/

International Ecotourism Society: http://www.ecotourism.org

NAFTA Secretariat: http://www.nafta-sec-alena.org/

Park City, Utah (land management code): http://www.parkcity.org/government/codesandpolicies/title_15_c_2_21.html

Slow Food Movement: http://www.slowfood.com/

Slow Food New York: http://www.slowfoodnyc.org/

Slow Food USA: http://www.slowfoodusa.org/index.php/slow_food/

U.S. Green Building Council: http://www.usgbc.org/DisplayPage.aspx?CategoryID=19

References

Adams, J.A. (1991) *The American Amusement Park Industry: A History of Technology and Thrills*. Boston: Twayne Publishers.

Agarwal, S., Ball, R., Shaw, G. and Williams, A.M. (2000) The geography of tourism production: uneven disciplinary development? *Tourism Geographies* 2(3): 241–63.

Air Transport Association (2008) Annual Reports of the U.S. Airline Industry. Available from http://www.airlines.org/economics/review_and_outlook/annual+reports.htm (accessed January 7, 2008).

Alban, D. (2008) Staycations: Alternative to pricey, stressful travel. *CNN.com*, June 12. Available from http://www.cnn.com/2008/LIVING/worklife/06/12/balance.staycation/index.html (accessed April 13, 2009).

Alden, E. (2008) *The Closing of the American Border: Terrorism, Immigration and Security Since 9/11*. New York: HarperCollins.

Aldred, L. (2000) Plastic shamans and Astroturf sun dances: New Age commercialization of Native American spirituality, *American Indian Quarterly* 24(3): 329–52.

Alfrey, J. and Putnam, T. (1992) *The Industrial Heritage: Managing Resources and Uses*. London: Routledge.

Allen, F. (1999) History happened here: the new old west, *American Heritage* 50(5): 30–3.

Allen R.A. (2003) Does the rails-to-trails act affect a taking of property? *Transportation Law Journal* 31(1): 35–68.

American Resort Development Association (2008) State of the Vacation Timeshare Industry. Available from http://www.arda.org/AM/Template.cfm?Section=State_of_the_Industry (accessed December 1, 2008).

Amtrak (2008) National Fact Sheet. Available at http://www.amtrak.com/pdf/Amtrak BackgroundInformationFacts-020409.pdf (accessed January 15, 2009).

Andersen, M.S. and Miller, M.L. (2005) Onboard marine environmental education: whale watching in the San Juan Islands, Washington, *Tourism in Marine Environments* 2(2): 111–18.

Appadurai, A. (1996) *Modernity at Large: Cultural Dimensions of Globalization*. Minneapolis: University of Minnesota Press.

Ashworth, G.J. (1989) Urban tourism: an imbalance in attention, in C.P. Cooper (ed.) *Progress in Tourism, Recreation and Hospitality Management* Vol. 1, pp. 33–54. London: Belhaven.

Ashworth, G.J. and Voogd, H. (1990) *Selling the City: Marketing Approaches in Public Sector Urban Planning*. London: Belhaven.

Attix, S.A. (2002) New Age-oriented special interest travel: an exploratory study, *Tourism Recreation Research* 27(2): 51–8.

Baron, D.P. (1990) Distributive politics and the persistence of Amtrak, *Journal of Politics* 52(3): 883–913.

Baron, E. (1998) Casino gambling and the polarization of American Indian reservations, in A.A. Lew and G.A. van Otten (eds) *Tourism and Gaming on American Indian Lands*, pp. 163–71. New York: Cognizant.

Bartlett, T. (2001) Virginia develops African-American tourism sites, *Travel Weekly* 4 June: 16.

Basu, P. (2001) Hunting down home: reflections on homeland and the search for identity in the Scottish diaspora, in B. Bender and M. Winter (eds) *Contested Landscapes: Movement, Exile and Place*, pp. 333–48. Oxford: Berg.

Basu, P. (2005) Pilgrims to a far country: North American "roots-tourists" in the Scottish Highlands and Islands, in C. Ray (ed.) *Transatlantic Scots*, pp. 286–317. Tuscaloosa: University of Alabama Press.

Beale, C.L. and Johnson, K.M. (1998) The identification of recreational counties in nonmetropolitan areas in the USA. *Population Research and Policy Review* 17: 37–53.

Beauregard, R. (1998) Tourism and economic development policy in US urban areas, in D. Ioannides and K. Debbage (eds) *The Economic Geography of the Tourist Industry: A Supply-side Analysis*, pp. 220–34. London: Routledge.

Behan, J.R., Richards, M.T. and Lee, M.E. (2001) Effects of tour jeeps in a wildland setting on non-motorized recreationists' benefits, *Journal of Park and Recreation Administration* 19(2): 1–19.

Belasco, W.J. (1979) *Americans on the Road: From Autocamp to Motel*, Cambridge: MIT Press.

Belhassen, Y. and Santos, C.A. (2006) An American evangelical pilgrimage to Israel: a case study on politics and triangulation, *Journal of Travel Research* 44(4): 431–41.

Berton, P. (1997) *Niagara: A History of the Falls*. Palo Alto, CA: Kodansha.

Bocock, R. (1993) *Consumption (Key Ideas)*. London: Routledge.

Bodett, T. (1985) *As Far as You Can Go Without a Passport: The View from the End of the Road*, New York: Da Capo Press.

Bold, C. (1999) *The WPA Guides: Mapping America*. Jackson: University Press of Mississippi.

Bolotin, N. and Laing, C. (2002) *The World's Columbian Exposition: The Chicago World's Fair of 1893*. Champaign: University of Illinois Press.

Boniface, P. and Fowler, P.J. (1993) *Heritage and Tourism in "The Global Village."* London: Routledge.

Bosselman, F.P., Peterson, C.A. and McCarthy, C. (1999) *Managing Tourism Growth: Issues and Applications*. Washington, DC: Island Press.

Bowen, J. (2002) Network change, deregulation, and access in the global airline industry, *Economic Geography* 78(4): 425–39.

Bram, J. (1995) Tourism and New York City's economy, *Current Issues in Economics and Finance* 1(7): 1–6.

Braunlich, C.G. (1996) Lessons from the Atlantic City casino experience, *Journal of Travel Research* 34(3): 46–56.

Brewton, C. and Withiam, G. (1998) United States tourism policy: alive but not well, *Cornell Hotel and Restaurant Administration Quarterly* 39(1): 50–9.

Britton, S. (1991) Tourism, capital and place: towards a critical geography of tourism, *Environment and Planning D: Society and Space* 9(4): 451–78.

Brown, D. (1995) *Inventing New England: Regional Tourism in the 19th Century*, Washington, DC: Smithsonian Institution Press.

Brown, D.M. (1998) When rural communities lose passenger rail service, *Rural Development Perspectives* 12(2): 13–18.

Brown, D.M. (1999) Rail freight consolidation and rural America, *Rural Development Perspectives* 13(2): 19–23.

Bruner, E.M. (1996) Tourism in Ghana: the representation of slavery and the return of the Black diaspora, *American Anthropologist* 98(2): 290–304.

Bryman, A. (1995) *Disney and His Worlds*. London: Routledge.

Budruk, M., White, D.D., Wodrich, J.A. and van Riper, C.J. (2008) Connecting visitors to people and place: visitors' perceptions of authenticity at Canyon de Chelly National Monument, Arizona, *Journal of Heritage Tourism* 3(3): 185–202.

Bunce, M. (1994) *The Countryside Ideal: Anglo-American Images of Landscape*. London: Routledge.

Bureau of Labor Statistics (2009) *Occupational Outlook Handbook, 2008–09 Edition*. Available from http://www.bls.gov/oco/ocos124.htm (accessed March 19, 2009).

Bureau of Transportation Statistics (2008) *National Transportation Statistics 2008*. Washington, DC: US Department of Transportation, Bureau of Transportation Statistics.

Butler, J. (2008) The compelling "hard case" for "green" hotel development, *Cornell Hospitality Quarterly* 49(3): 234–44.

California Travel and Tourism Commission (2007) *2007–2013 Strategic Marketing Plan*. Sacramento: California Travel and Tourism Commission.

California Travel and Tourism Commission (2009) *Bylaws/History*. Available from http://industry.visitcalifornia.com/Industry/TravelIndustry/ByLawsHistory/ (accessed February 15, 2009).

Campbell, S. (1996) Green cities, growing cities, just cities? Urban planning and the contradictions of sustainable development, *Journal of the American Planning Association* 62(3): 296–312.

Carmichael, B.A. and Jones, J.L. (2007) Indigenous owned casinos and perceived local community impacts: Mohegan Sun in South East Connecticut, USA, in R. Butler and T. Hinch (eds) *Tourism and Indigenous Peoples: Issues and Implications*, pp. 95–111. Oxford: Butterworth-Heinemann.

Carmichael, B.A. and Peppard, D.M. (1998) The impacts of Foxwoods Resort Casino on its dual host community: southeastern Connecticut and the Mashantucket Pequot tribe, in A.A. Lew and G.A. van Otten (eds) *Tourism and Gaming on American Indian Lands*, pp. 128–44. New York: Cognizant.

Catholicshrines.net (2009) *Catholic Shrines USA*. Available from http://www.catholicshrines.net/ (accessed March 10, 2009).

Center for Business and Economic Development (2006) *Economic Impact: Alabama Travel Industry 2005*. Montgomery: Center for Business and Economic Development, Auburn University.

Central Intelligence Agency (2009) *World Factbook*. Available from https://www.cia.gov/library/publications/the-world-factbook/rankorder/2053rank.html (accessed February 23, 2009).

Chadee, D. and Mieczkowski, Z. (1987) An empirical analysis of the effects of the exchange rate on Canadian tourism, *Journal of Travel Research* 26(1): 13–17.

Chazan, B. (1991) What is informal Jewish education? *Journal of Jewish Communal Service* 67(4): 300–8.

Che, D. (2004) Reinventing Tulip Time: evolving diasporic Dutch heritage celebration in Holland (Michigan), in T. Coles and D.J. Timothy (eds) *Tourism, Diasporas and Space*, pp. 261–78. London: Routledge.

Che, D. (2006) Developing ecotourism in First World, resource-dependent areas, *Geoforum* 37(2): 212–26.

Chhabra, D. (2007) Exploring social exchange theory dynamics in Native American casino settings, *UNLV Gaming Research & Review Journal* 11(2): 31–48.

Chhabra, D., Sills, E. and Dubbage, F.W. (2003) The significance of festivals to rural economies: estimating the economic impacts of Scottish Highlands Games in North Carolina, *Journal of Travel Research* 41(4): 421–7.

Chicago Convention and Tourism Bureau (2009) *Monthly Occupancy.* Available from http://www.choosechicago.com/media/statistics/hotel_industry/Pages/monthly_occupancy.aspx (accessed February 1, 2009).

Choy, D.J.L. (1995) The quality of tourism employment, *Tourism Management* 16(2): 129–37.

Christensen, N.A. and Nickerson, N.P. (1995) *Jobs & Wages: The Tourism Industry Dilemma.* Missoula, MT: University of Montana, Institute for Tourism and Recreation Research.

Christiansen, E.M. (1998) Gambling and the American economy, *Annals of the American Academy of Political and Social Science* 556: 36–52.

City of New Orleans (2009) *Vieux Carré Commission History.* Available from http://www.cityofno.com/portal.aspx?portal=59&tabid=14 (accessed February 23, 2009).

Clark, J. (2006) Americans like what they like for travel spots. *USA Today* (December 28, 2006). Available from http://www.usatoday.com/travel/destinations/2006-12-28-travel-trends_x.htm (accessed February 23, 2009).

Clark, T.N., Lloyd, R., Wong, K. and Jain, P. (2002) Amenities drive urban growth, *Journal of Urban Affairs* 24(5): 493–515.

Clausing, K.A. (2001) Trade creation and trade diversion in the Canada-United States Free Trade Agreement, *Canadian Journal of Economics* 34(3): 677–96.

Clavé, S.A. (2007) *The Global Theme Park Industry.* Wallingford, UK: CAB International.

CLIA (2008a) CLIA Cruise Market Overview – Statistical Cruise Industry Data Through 2007. Available from http://www.cruising.org/press/overview2008/ (accessed February 28, 2009).

CLIA (2008b) *The Contribution of the North American Cruise Industry to the U.S. Economy in 2007.* Fort Lauderdale, FL: Cruise Lines International Association.

CLIA (2009) The state of the cruise industry in 2009: Well-positioned for challenging times, *Cruise News*, 14 January. Available from http://www.cruising.org/cruisenews/news.cfm?nid=384 (accessed March 3, 2009).

Cocks, C. (2001) *Doing the Town: The Rise of Urban Tourism in the United States, 1850–1915.* Berkeley: University of California Press.

Cohen, E.H. (2006) Religious tourism as an educational experience, in D.J. Timothy and D.H. Olsen (eds) *Tourism, Religion and Spiritual Journeys*, pp. 78–93. London: Routledge.

Cohen Ioannides, M. and Ioannides, D. (2006) Global Jewish tourism: pilgrimages and remembrances, in D.J. Timothy and D.H. Olsen (eds) *Tourism, Religion and Spiritual Journeys*, pp. 156–71. London: Routledge.

Coles, T. (2003) Urban tourism, place promotion and economic restructuring: the case of post-socialist Leipzig, *Tourism Geographies* 5(2): 190–219.

Collins-Kreiner, N., Kliot, N., Mansfeld, Y. and Sagi, K. (2006) *Christian Tourism to the Holy Land: Pilgrimage During Security Crisis.* Aldershot: Ashgate.

Conforti, J.M. (1996) Ghettos as tourism attractions, *Annals of Tourism Research* 23: 830–42.

Corbett, T. (2001) *The Making of American Resorts: Saratoga Springs, Ballston Spa, Lake George.* New Brunswick, NJ: Rutgers University Press.

Crompton, J. (2004) Beyond economic impact: an alternative rationale for the public subsidy of major league sports facilities, *Journal of Sport Management* 18(1): 40–58.

Cullingworth, B. (2007) *Planning in the USA: Policies, Issues, and Processes.* New York: Taylor & Francis.

Curry, T.J., Schwirian, K., and Woldoff, R.A. (2004) *High Stakes: Big Time Sports and Downtown Redevelopment.* Columbus: The Ohio State University Press.

Davis, J.A. and Hudman, L.E. (1998) The history of Indian gaming law and casino development in the western United States, in A.A. Lew and G.A. van Otten (eds) *Tourism and Gaming on American Indian Lands*, pp. 82–92. New York: Cognizant.

Davis, S.G. (1999) Landscapes of imagination: tourism in southern California, *The Pacific Historical Review* 68(2): 173–91.

Dean Runyan Associates (2004) *The Economic Significance of the Washington State Travel Industry.* Olympia: State of Washington, Department of Community, Trade and Economic Development.

Dean Runyan Associates (2006) *Washington State Statewide Travel Impacts and Visitor Volume 1991–2006.* Olympia: State of Washington, Department of Community, Trade and Economic Development.

Debbage, K.G. (1990) Oligopoly and the resort cycle in the Bahamas, *Annals of Tourism Research* 17: 513–27.

Debbage, K.G. (2002) Airport runway slots: limits to growth, *Annals of Tourism Research* 29: 933–51.

Debbage. K.G. and Daniels, S. (1998) The tourist industry and economic geography: missed opportunities?, in D. Ioannides and K.G. Debbage (eds) *The Economic Geography of the Tourist Industry: A Supply Side Analysis*, pp. 17–30. London: Routledge.

Debbage, K.G. and Ioannides, D. (2004) The cultural turn? Towards a more critical economic geography of tourism, in A.A. Lew, C.M. Hall and A.M. Williams (eds) *A Companion to Tourism*, pp. 99–109. Oxford: Blackwell.

Dehghani, Y., Saranathan, K. and Gihring, C. (1997) Comprehensive planning model for ferry ridership forecasting analysis in the Puget Sound region, *Transportation Research Record* 1608: 30–9.

Dense, J. and Barrow, C.W. (2003) Estimating casino expenditures by out-of-state patrons: Native American gaming in Connecticut, *Journal of Travel Research* 41(4): 410–15.

Denver Metro Convention and Visitors Bureau (2008) On-line visitors' guide. Available from http://www.denver.org (accessed February 15, 2009).

Destler, I.M. (2005) *American Trade Politics.* Washington, DC: Institute for International Economics.

Di Matteo, L. and Di Matteo, R. (1996) An analysis of Canadian cross-border travel, *Annals of Tourism Research* 23: 103–22.

Diehl, P.N. (1983) The effects of the peso devaluation on Texas border cities, *Texas Business Review* 57: 120–5.

Dimanche, F. and Speyrer, J.F. (1996) Report on a comprehensive five-year gambling impact research plan in New Orleans, *Journal of Travel Research* 34(3): 97–100.

Dingell, J.D. (1996) HR 2579, US National Tourism Organization Act of 1996: Dissenting Views. Available from http://energycommerce.house.gov/comdem/legviews/mv2579.htm (accessed December 15, 2008).

Douglas, N. and Douglas, N. (1991) Where the tiki are wired for sound and poi glow in the dark: a day at the Polynesian Cultural Center, *Islands Business Pacific* 17(12): 60–4.

Douglas, N. and Douglas, N. (2001) The cruise experience, in N. Douglas, N. Douglas and R. Derrett (eds) *Special Interest Tourism: Context and Cases*, pp. 330–54. Brisbane: Wiley.

Drabenstott, M. (2001) New policies for a new rural America, *International Regional Science Review* 24(1): 3–15.

Duany, A., Plater-Zyberk, E. and Speck, J. (2000) *Suburban Nation: The Rise of Sprawl and the Decline of the American Dream*. New York: North Point Press.

Dumych, D.M. (1996) *Niagara Falls*. Chicago, IL: Arcadia.

Duval, D.T. (2007) *Tourism and Transport: Modes, Networks and Flows*. Clevedon, UK: Channel View.

Eco, U. (1986) *Travels in Hyperreality*. Orlando, FL: Harcourt.

Edgell, D.L., Delmastro Allen, M., Smith, G. and Swanson, J.R. (2007) *Tourism Policy and Planning: Yesterday, Today and Tomorrow*. Oxford: Butterworth-Heinemann.

El Nasser, H. (2007) Life on the Great Plains is anything but plain, simple. *USA Today* (December 12). Available from http://www.usatoday.com/news/nation/2007-08-12-great-plains_N.htm (accessed December 5, 2008).

Eltis, D. (2000) *The Rise of African Slavery in the Americas*. Cambridge: Cambridge University Press.

English, D.B.K., Marcouiller, D.W. and Cordell, H.K. (2000) Tourism dependence in rural America: estimates and effects, *Society and Natural Resources* 13: 185–202.

Enz, C.A. and Siguaw, J.A. (2003) Revisiting the best of the best: innovations in hotel practice, *Cornell Hotel and Restaurant Administration Quarterly* 44(5/6): 115–23.

Ewald, R.J. (2003) *Technology and Transportation: 1790–1870 Tourism and Recreation*. Available from http://www.flowofhistory.org/themes/technology_transportation/tourism.php (accessed March 12, 2008).

Fainstein, S.S. and Gladstone, D. (1999) Evaluating urban tourism, in D.R. Judd and S.S. Fainstein (eds) *The Tourist City*, pp. 21–34. New Haven: Yale University Press.

Fainstein, S.S. and Judd, D.R. (1999) Cities as places to play, in D.R. Judd and S.S. Fainstein (eds) *The Tourist City*, pp. 261–72. New Haven: Yale University Press.

Fainstein, S.S., Hoffman, L.M. and Judd, D.R. (2004) Introduction. In L.M. Hoffman, S.S. Fainstein and D.R. Judd (eds) *Cities and Visitors: Regulating People, Markets, and City Space*, pp. 1–19. Oxford: Blackwell.

Fainstein, S.S. and Stokes, R. (1995) Spaces for play: the impacts of entertainment development in New York City. Paper presented at the annual meeting of the Association of Collegiate Schools of Planning, Detroit, Michigan, 18–22 October.

Farrell, B.H. (1982) *Hawaii, The Legend that Sells*. Honolulu: University Press of Hawaii.

Faulkenberry, L.V., Coggeshall, J.M., Backman, K. and Backman, S. (2000) A culture of servitude: the impact of tourism and development on South Carolina's coast, *Human Organization* 59(1): 86–95.

Federal Reserve Bank of New York (2004) *The Regional Economy of Upstate New York: Tourism's Role in the Upstate New York Economy*. Buffalo, NY: The Buffalo Branch, Federal Reserve Bank of New York.

Fennell, D. (ed.) (2006) *North America: A Tourism Handbook*. Clevedon, UK: Channel View.

Fennell, D. (2008) *Ecotourism* (3rd edn). London: Routledge.

Findley, J.A. and Bing, M. (1998) Touring Florida through the Federal Writers' Project, *The Journal of Decorative and Propaganda Arts* 23 (Florida Theme Issues). Available from http://www.broward.org/library/bienes/lii10213.htm (accessed March 12, 2008).

Florida, R. (2002) *The Rise of the Creative Class*. New York: Basic Books.

Floyd, M., Gibson, H., Pennington-Gray, L. and Thapa, B. (2003) The effect of risk perceptions on intentions to travel in the aftermath of September 11, 2001, in C.M. Hall, D.J. Timothy and D.T. Duval (eds) *Safety and Security in Tourism: Relationships, Management, and Marketing*, pp. 19–38. New York: Haworth.

Foglesong, R. (1999) Walt Disney World and Orlando deregulation as a strategy for tourism, in D. Judd and S. Fainstein (eds) *The Tourist City*, pp. 89–106. New Haven: Yale University Press.

Fox, D.M. (1961) The achievement of the Federal Writers' Project, *American Quarterly* 13(1): 3–19.

Frenkel, S., Walton, J. and Andersen, D. (2000) Bavarian Leavenworth and the symbolic economy of the theme town, *Geographical Review* 90(4): 559–85.

Fritsch, A. and Johannsen, K. (2004) *Ecotourism in Appalachia: Marketing the Mountains.* Lexington, KY: University Press of Kentucky.

Gartner, W.C. (2004) Rural tourism development in the USA, *International Journal of Tourism Research* 6(3): 151–64.

Gassan, R. (2005) The first American tourist guidebooks: authorship and the print culture of the 1820s, *Book History* 8: 51–74.

Gibbons, J.D. and Fish, M. (1987) Market sensitivity of U.S. and Mexican border travel, *Journal of Travel Research* 26(1): 2–6.

Gladstone, D. and Fainstein, S. (2001) Tourism in US global cities: a comparison of New York and Los Angeles, *Journal of Urban Affairs* 23(1): 23–40.

Glaeser, E.L., Kahn, M.E. and Rappaport, J. (2008) Why do the poor live in cities? The role of public transportation, *Journal of Urban Economics* 63(1): 1–24.

Global Insight (2005a) *City Tourism Impact: The Economic Impact of Travel and Tourism in Austin, Texas: A Comprehensive Analysis.* Austin: Austin Convention and Visitors Bureau (with Shifflet and Associates Ltd.).

Global Insight (2005b) *The Economic Impact of Visitors to Durham, North Carolina: A Comprehensive Analysis.* Durham: Durham Convention and Visitors Bureau.

Global Insight (2006) *City Tourism Impact: The Economic Impacts of Travel and Tourism in Travis County, Texas.* Austin: Austin Convention and Visitors Bureau.

Go, F.G. and Pine, R. (1995) *Globalization Strategy in the Hotel Industry.* London: Routledge.

Goeldner, C.R and Ritchie, J.R. (2006) *Tourism: Principles, Practices, Philosophies.* Hoboken, NJ: Wiley.

Goetz, A. and Sutton, C. (1997) The geography of deregulation in the US airline industry, *Annals of the Association of American Geographers* 87(2): 238–63.

Goodrich, J.N. (1985) Black American tourists: some research findings, *Journal of Travel Research* 24(2): 27–8.

Goodrich, J.N. (2002) September 11, 2001 attack on America: a record of the immediate impacts and reactions in the USA travel and tourism industry, *Tourism Management* 23: 573–80.

Gotham, K.F. (2005). Tourism from above and below: globalization, localization and New Orleans's Mardi Gras, *International Journal of Urban and Regional Research* 29(2): 309–26.

Gottdiener, M., Collins, C. and Dickens, D. (1999) *Las Vegas: The Social Production of an All American City.* Malden, MA: Blackwell.

Graham, B., Ashworth, G.J. and Tunbridge, J. (2000) *A Geography of Heritage: Power, Culture and Economy.* London: Arnold.

Grand Canyon Railway (2009) *Grand Canyon Railway History.* Available from http://www.thetrain.com/history/ (accessed February 20, 2009).

Green, C.G., Bartholomew, P. and Murrmann, S. (2003) New York restaurant industry: strategic responses to September 11, 2001, in C.M. Hall, D.J. Timothy and D.T. Duval (eds) *Safety and Security in Tourism: Relationships, Management, and Marketing,* pp. 63–80. New York: Haworth.

Groves, D.L. and Timothy, D.J. (2001) Festivals, migration, and long-term residency, *Téoros International: Revue de Recherche en Tourisme* 20(1): 56–62.

Gunn, C.A. (2004) *Western Tourism: Can Paradise be Reclaimed?* New York: Cognizant.

Hall, C.M. (1994) *Tourism and Politics: Policy, Power, and Place*. Chichester: Wiley.

Hall, C.M. (1998a) Historical antecedents of sustainable development and ecotourism: new labels on old bottles, in C.M. Hall and A. Lew (eds) *Sustainable Tourism Development: A Geographical Perspective*, pp. 13–24. London: Longman.

Hall, C.M. (1998b) The institutional setting: tourism and the state, in D. Ioannides and K. Debbage (eds) *The Economic Geography of the Tourist Industry: A Supply-Side Analysis*, pp. 199–219. London: Routledge.

Hall, C.M. (2008) *Tourism Planning: Policies, Processes and Relationships*. London: Pearson-Prentice Hall.

Hall, C.M. and Jenkins, J.M. (1995) *Tourism and Public Policy*. London: Routledge.

Hall, T.E. and Shelby, B. (1998) Changes in use of three Oregon, USA, wildernesses, *Environmental Management* 22(1): 89–98.

Hanegraaff, W.J. (1998) Reflections on New Age and the secularization of nature, in J. Pearson, R. Roberts and G. Samuel (eds) *Nature Religion Today: The Pagan Alternative in the Modern World*, pp. 22–32. Edinburgh: Edinburgh University Press.

Harreld, H. (1996) US tourism office quietly revived at Commerce Dept. Washington, *Business Journal* (Friday, June 14th). Available from http://www.bizjournals.com/washington/stories/1996/06/17/story7.html (accessed October 2008).

Harris, A.W. (2006) Secure borders, open doors. *The American Tourism Society Press Releases*. Available from http://www.americantourismsociety.org/about/press-050806.html (accessed October 20, 2008).

Harrison, B. and Bluestone, B. (1988) *The Great U-Turn*. New York: Basic Books.

Hawaii Tourism Authority (2005) *Hawaii Tourism Strategic Plan 2005–2015*. Honolulu: Hawaii Tourism Authority.

Hayes, B.J. (1997) Claiming our heritage is a booming industry, *American Visions* 12(5): 43–8.

Hedrich, M.P. (2008) Section 7209 of the Intelligence Reform and Terrorism Prevention Act of 2004: Balancing the western hemisphere travel initiative with international homeland security, *Northwestern Journal of International Law and Business* 28: 341–70.

Herzenberg, S.A., Alic, J.A. and Wial, H. (1998) *New Rules for a New Economy: Employment and Opportunity in Postindustrial America*. Ithaca, NY: Cornell University Press.

Heppenheimer, T. (1995) *Turbulent Skies: the History of Commercial Aviation*. New York: Wiley.

Hinshaw, M. (2008). Great neighborhoods, *Planning* 74(1): 6–11.

Hobson, J.S.P. (1993) Analysis of the US cruise line industry, *Tourism Management* 14(6): 453–62.

Hoffman, L.M. (2004) Revalorizing the inner city: tourism and regulation in Harlem, in L.M. Hoffman, S.S. Fainstein and D.R. Judd (eds) *Cities and Visitors: Regulating People, Markets, and City Space*, pp. 91–112. Oxford: Blackwell.

Hoffman, L.M., Fainstein, S.S. and Judd, D.R. (eds) (2004) *Cities and Visitors: Regulating People, Markets, and City Space*. Oxford: Blackwell.

Holcomb, B. (1999) Marketing cities for tourism, in D.R. Judd and S.S. Fainstein (eds) *The Tourist City*, pp. 54–70. New Haven: Yale University Press.

Hollinshead, K. (1992) "White" gaze, "red" people – shadow visions: the disidentification of "Indians" in cultural tourism, *Leisure Studies* 11: 43–64.

Holloway, J.C. and Taylor, N. (2006) *The Business of Tourism* (7th edn). Harlow: Prentice Hall.

Hopkins, J. (1998) Signs of the post-rural: marketing myths of a symbolic countryside, *Geografiska Annaler B: Human Geography* 80(2): 65–81.

Horton, L.E. (2006) *Slavery and the Making of America*. Oxford: Oxford University Press.

Hotel News Resource (2008) US House of Representatives Passes "Travel Promotion Act of 2008," *Hotel News Resource*. Available from http://www.hotelnewsresource.com/article34798.html (accessed December 10, 2008).

Howder's Site (2009) *United States Domestic Ferries*. Available from http://www.howderfamily.com/travel/united_states_ferry_map.html (accessed February 20, 2009).

Hsu, C.H.C. (1999) History, development, and legislation of riverboat and land-based non-Native American casino gaming, in C.H.C. Hsu (ed.) *Legalized Casino Gaming in the United States: the Economic and Social Impact*, pp. 63–90. New York: Haworth.

Hudman, L.E. and Jackson, R.H. (1992) Mormon pilgrimage and tourism, *Annals of Tourism Research* 19: 107–21.

Hustedde, R.J., Shaffer, R. and Pulver G. (1984) *Community Economic Analysis: A How to Manual*. Ames, Iowa: North Central Regional Center for Rural Development, Iowa State University.

Insider Viewpoint of Las Vegas (2007) *Insider Viewpoint.com*. Available from http://InsiderVLV.COM (accessed June 2, 2008).

Inskeep, E. (1991) *Tourism Planning: An Integrated and Sustainable Development Approach*. New York: Van Nostrand Reinhold.

International Association of Amusement Parks and Attractions (2009) *Amusement Park and Attractions Industry Statistics*. Available from http://www.iaapa.org/pressroom/Amusement_Park_Industry_Statistics.asp (accessed March 10, 2009).

Ioannides, D. (1998) Tour operators: the gatekeepers of tourism, in D. Ioannides and K. Debbage (eds) *The Economic Geography of the Tourist Industry: A Supply-side Analysis*, pp. 139–58. London: Routledge.

Ioannides, D. (1999) Assessing the globalization and localization of dynamics of tourism development: the case of small towns in rural USA. Unpublished working paper, Department of Geography, Geology, and Planning, Missouri State University.

Ioannides, D. (2003) The economics of tourism in host communities, in S. Singh, D.J. Timothy and R.K. Dowling (eds) *Tourism in Destination Communities*, pp. 37–54. Wallingford, UK: CAB International.

Ioannides, D. (2006) Commentary, the economic geography of the tourist industry: ten years of progress in research and an agenda for the future, *Tourism Geographies* 8(1): 76–86.

Ioannides, D. (2008) Hypothesizing the shifting mosaic of attitudes through time: a dynamic framework for sustainable tourism development on a "Mediterranean Isle," in S. McCool and R. Moisey (eds) *Tourism, Recreation and Sustainability* (2nd edn), pp. 51–75. Wallingford, UK: CAB International.

Ioannides, D. and Cohen Ioannides, M. (2002) Pilgrimages of nostalgia: patterns of Jewish travel in the US, *Tourism Recreation Research* 27(2): 17–25.

Ioannides, D. and Cohen Ioannides, M. (2004) Jewish past as a "foreign country": the travel experiences of American Jews, in T. Coles and D.J. Timothy (eds) *Tourism, Diasporas and Space*, pp. 95–110. London: Routledge.

Ioannides, D. and Daughtrey, E. (2006) Competition in the travel distribution system: the US travel retail sector, in A. Papatheodorou (ed.) *Corporate Rivalry and Market Power: Competition Issues in the Tourism Industry*, pp. 124–42. London: IB Tauris.

Ioannides, D. and Debbage, K. (1997) Post-Fordism and flexibility: the travel industry polyglot, *Tourism Management* 18(4): 229–41.

Ioannides, D. and Debbage, K. (eds) (1998) *The Economic Geography of the Tourist Industry: A Supply Side Analysis*. London: Routledge.

Ivakhiv, A. (1997) Red rocks, "vortexes" and the selling of Sedona: environmental politics in the new age, *Social Compass* 44(3): 367–84.

Ivakhiv, A. (2003) Nature and self in New Age pilgrimage, *Culture and Religion* 4(1): 93–118.

Jakle, J.A., Keith A.S. and Jefferson S.R. (1996) *The Motel in America.* Baltimore, MD: Johns Hopkins University Press.

Jakle, J.A. and Sculle, K.A. (2008) *Motoring: The Highway Experience in America.* Athens, GA: University of Georgia Press.

Janes, P.L. and Collison, J. (2004) Community leader perceptions of the social and economic impacts of Indian gaming, *UNLV Gaming Research & Review Journal* 8(1): 13–30.

Janiskee, R.L. and Drews, P.L. (1998) Rural festivals and community reimaging, in R.W. Butler, C.M. Hall, and J. Jenkins (eds) *Tourism and Recreation in Rural Areas*, pp. 157–75. Chichester: Wiley.

Jayawardena, C., White, A. and Carmichael, B.A. (2008) Binational tourism in Niagara: insights, challenges, and the future, *International Journal of Contemporary Hospitality Management* 20(3): 347–59.

Jeffries, D. (2001) *Governments and Tourism.* Oxford: Butterworth-Heinemann.

Jenkins, L., Dongoske, K.E. and Ferguson, T.J. (1996) Managing Hopi sacred sites to protect religious freedom, *Cultural Survival Quarterly* 21(1): 36–8.

Jenks, L.H. (1944) Railroads as an economic force in American development, *The Journal of Economic History* 4(1): 1–20.

Jensen, O. (1993) *The American Heritage History of Railroads in America.* New York: Random House.

Jett, S.C. (1990) Culture and tourism in the Navajo country, *Journal of Cultural Geography* 11(1): 85–107.

Johnson, C. (2002) Sustainable development in the hotel industry, *Travel and Tourism Analyst* 5: 3.1–3.24.

Johnson, D.M. (1981) Disney World as structure and symbol: re-creation of the American experience, *Journal of Popular Culture* 15(1): 157–65.

Johnson, K. (2005) Second homes remake the West's resorts, *The New York Times*, (May 8). Available from http://www.nytimes.com/2005/05/08/national/08colorado. html?ragewanted=print&oref=login (accessed November 8, 2008).

Johnson, K.M. and Beale, C.L. (2002) Non-metro recreation counties: their identification and rapid growth, *Rural America* 17(4): 12–19.

Johnston, A.M. (2006) *Is the Sacred for Sale? Tourism and Indigenous Peoples.* London: Earthscan.

Jones, C. and Munday, M. (2008) Tourism satellite accounts and impact assessments: some considerations, *Tourism Analysis* 13(1): 53–69.

Jones, C., Munday, M. and Roberts, A. (2003) Regional tourism satellite accounts: a useful policy tool? *Urban Studies* 40(13): 2777–94.

Jones, W. and Rice, M.F. (1979) Race, social class, and attitudes toward urban transportation: a comparative study of four cities, *Western Journal of Black Studies* 3(1): 39–42.

Judd, D.R. (1995) Promoting tourism in US cities, *Tourism Management* 16(3): 175–87.

Judd, D.R. (1999) Constructing the tourist bubble, in D.R. Judd and S.S. Fainstein (eds) *The Tourist City*, pp. 35–53. New Haven: Yale University Press.

Judd, D.R. (2002) Promoting tourism in US cities, in S.S. Fainstein and S. Campbell (eds) *Readings in Urban Theory* (2nd edn), pp. 278–99. Oxford: Blackwell.

Judd, D.R. (2003a) *The Infrastructure of Play: Building the Tourist City.* London: M.E. Sharpe.

Judd, D.R. (ed.) (2003b) Building the tourist city: editor's introduction, in D.R. Judd (ed.) *The Infrastructure of Play: Building the Tourist City*, pp. 3–16. London: M.E. Sharpe.

Judd, D.R. (2004) Visitors and the spatial ecology of the city, in L.M. Hoffman, S.S. Fainstein, and D.R. Judd (eds) *Cities and Visitors: Regulating People, Markets, and City Space*, pp. 23–38. Oxford: Blackwell.

Judd, D.R. (2006) Commentary: tracing the commodity chain of global tourism, *Tourism Geographies* 8(4): 323–36.

Judd, D.R. and Fainstein S.S. (eds) (1999) *The Tourist City*. New Haven: Yale University Press.

Judd, D.R., Winter, W., Barnes, W. and Stern, E. (2003) Tourism and entertainment as local economic development: a national survey, in D.R. Judd (ed.) *The Infrastructure of Play: Building the Tourist City* 50–74. London: M.E. Sharpe.

Kahn, A.E. (1988) Surprises of airline deregulation, *American Economic Review* 78(2): 316–22.

Kehoe, A.B. (1990) "In fourteen hundred and ninety-two, Columbus sailed . . .": the primacy of the national myth in US schools, in P. Stone and R. MacKenzie (eds) *The Excluded Past: Archaeology in Education*, pp. 201–16. London: Unwin Hyman.

Kennedy, F.H. (1998) *The Civil War Battlefield Guide*. New York: Houghton Mifflin.

Kern, P.V. and Kocis, E.A. (2007) *US Travel and Tourism Satellite Accounts for 1998–2006.* Survey of Current Business (June 2007) Bureau of Economic Analysis. Available from www.bea.gov/scb/pdf/2007/06%20June/0607_Travel.pdf (accessed February 11, 2009).

Kerstetter, D., Confer, J. and Bricker, K. (1998) Industrial heritage attractions: types and tourists, *Journal of Travel and Tourism Marketing* 72(2): 91–104.

King, A. (2003) Over a century of explorations at Etowah, *Journal of Archaeological Research* 11(4): 279–306.

King, M.J. (1981a) Disneyland and Walt Disney World: traditional values in futuristic form, *Journal of Popular Culture* 15(1): 116–40.

King, M.J. (1981b) The new American muse: notes on the amusement/theme park, *Journal of Popular Culture* 15(1): 56–62.

Kole, S.R. and Lehn, K.M. (1999) Deregulation and the adaptation of governance structure: the case of the U.S. airline industry, *Journal of Financial Economics* 52(1): 79–117.

Kreck, L.A. (1985) The effect of the across-the-border commerce of Canadian tourists on the city of Spokane, *Journal of Travel Research* 24(1): 27–31.

Kuhbach, P. and Herauf, B. (2005) *US Travel and Tourism Satellite Accounts for 2001–2004.* Bureau of Economic Analysis. Available from http://www.bea.gov/scb/pdf/2005/06June/0605_Travel.pdf (accessed August 12, 2009).

Kuhbach, P. and Herauf, B. (2006) *US Travel and Tourism Satellite Accounts for 2002–2005.* Survey of Current Business (June 2006) Bureau of Economic Analysis. Available from http://www.bea.gov/scb/pdf/2007/06%20June/0607_Travel.pdf (accessed February 11, 2009).

Kummer, P.K. (2003) *Washington, D.C.* Mankato, MN: Capstone Books.

Lapping, M.B., Daniels, T. and Keller, J.W. (1989) *Rural Planning and Development in the United States*. New York: Guilford Press.

Las Vegas Convention and Visitors Authority (2007) *LVCVA Executive Summary.* Available from http://www.lvcva.com/getfile/ES-Dec2007%20Final.pdf?fileID=37 (accessed March 5, 2008).

Laxson, J.D. (1991) How "we" see "them": tourism and Native Americans, *Annals of Tourism Research* 18: 365–91.

Leary, T.E. and Sholes, E.C. (2000) Authenticity of place and voice: examples of industrial heritage preservation and interpretation in the U.S. and Europe, *The Public Historian* 22(3): 49–66.

Leiper, N. (1979) The framework of tourism: towards a definition of tourism, tourist, and the tourist industry, *Annals of Tourism Research* 6: 390–407.

Leiper, N. (1990) Partial industrialization of tourism systems, *Annals of Tourism Research* 17: 600–5.

Leiper, N. (1993) Industrial entropy in tourism systems, *Annals of Tourism Research* 20: 221–5.

Leiper, N. (2008) Why "the tourism industry" is misleading as a generic expression: the case for the plural variation "tourism industries," *Tourism Management* 29(2): 237–51.

Lengfelder, J.R. and Timothy, D.J. (2000) Leisure time in the 1990s and beyond: cherished friend or incessant foe? *Visions in Leisure and Business* 19(1): 13–26.

Lenhart, M. (2004) Dynamic packaging: the next big thing, *Travel Professional: The Official Journal of the Travel Institute* (August/September): 19–27.

Lew, A.A. (1996) Tourism management on American Indian lands in the USA, *Tourism Management* 17(5): 355–65.

Lew, A.A. and Kennedy, C.B. (2002) Tourism and culture clash in Indian country, in S. Krakover and Y. Gradus (eds) *Tourism in Frontier Areas*, pp. 259–82. Lanham, MD: Lexington Books.

Lew, A.A. and van Otten, G.A. (eds) (1998) *Tourism and Gaming on American Indian Lands*. New York: Cognizant.

Lewis, T. (1999) *Divided Highways: Building the Interstate Highways, Transforming American Life*. New York: Penguin Books.

Li, Q. and Brewer, M.B. (2004) What does it mean to be an American? Patriotism, nationalism and American identity after 9/11, *Political Psychology* 25(5): 727–39.

Light, I. (1974) From vice district to tourist attraction: the moral career of American Chinatowns, 1880–1940, *The Pacific Historical Review* 43(3): 367–94.

Limerick, J.W. (1975) The grand resort hotels of America, *Perspecta* 15: 87–108.

Litvin, S.W. and Alderson, L.L. (2003) How Charleston got her groove back: A convention and visitors bureau's response to 9/11, *Journal of Vacation Marketing* 9(2): 188–97.

Liu, J.C. and Var, T. (1986) Resident attitudes toward tourism impacts in Hawaii, *Annals of Tourism Research* 13: 193–214.

Liu, Z. and Lynk, E.L. (1999) Evidence on market structure of the deregulated US airline industry, *Applied Economics* 31(9): 1083–92.

Lloyd, R. (2002) Neo-Bohemia: art and neighborhood redevelopment in Chicago, *Journal of Urban Affairs* 24(5): 517–32.

Lloyd, R. (2006) *New Bohemia: Art and Commerce in the Post-Industrial City*. New York: Routledge.

Löfgren. O. (1999) *On Holiday: A History of Vacationing*. Berkeley: University of California Press.

Long, P. and Lane, B. (2000) Rural tourism development, in W.C. Gartner and D.W. Lime (eds) *Trends in Recreation, Leisure and Tourism*, pp. 299–308. Wallingford, UK: CAB International.

Lowenthal, D. (1985) *The Past is a Foreign Country*. Cambridge: Cambridge University Press.

Lowenthal, D. (1996) *Possessed by the Past: The Heritage Crusade and the Spoils of History*. New York: Free Press.

Lujan, C.C. (1993) A sociological view of tourism in an American Indian community:

maintaining cultural integrity at Taos Pueblo, *American Indian Culture and Research Journal* 17(3): 101–20.

Madison County (2009) *Greetings from Madison County, Iowa*. Available from http://www.madisoncounty.com/ (accessed February 22, 2009).

Maitland, R. and Ritchie, B.W. (2007) Special issue: marketing national capital cities, *Journal of Travel and Tourism Marketing* 22(3/4): 1–5.

Mallari, A.A. and Enote, J.E. (1996) Maintaining control: culture and tourism in the Pueblo of Zuni, in M.F. Price (ed.) *People and Tourism in Fragile Environments*, pp. 19–31. Chichester: Wiley.

Mak, J. (2005) Tourism demand and output in the U.S. tourism satellite accounts: 1998–2003, *Journal of Travel Research* 44(1): 4–5.

Marks, J. (1996) Preface, in Travel Industry Association of America (ed.) *A Portrait of Travel Industry Employment in the US Economy*, p. vi. Washington, DC: Travel Industry Association of America Foundation.

Marti, B.E. (2007) Trends in Alaskan cruising, *Tourism Analysis* 12(4): 327–34.

Massachusetts Convention Center Authority (2005) *Boston #7 on Tradeshow Week's Top Ten List of Leading Cities*. Available from http://www.mccahome.com/download/newsletter/MCCA_newsletter_winter05_06.pdf (accessed March 5, 2008).

Mathieson, A.R. and Wall, G. (1982) *Tourism: Economic, Physical and Social Impacts*. Harlow: Longman.

Mattingly, S.R. and Griffith E.S. (2008) *US Travel and Tourism Satellite Accounts for 2004–2007*. Survey of Current Business (June 2008). Bureau of Economic Analysis. Available from http://www.bea.gov/scb/pdf/2008/06%20June/0608_travel.pdf (accessed February 18, 2008).

McGill, K. (2005) *The New Jersey Tourism Satellite Account: A Comprehensive Understanding of the Economic Contribution of Travel and Tourism in the State of New Jersey*. Lexington, MA: Global Insight Inc.

McGranahan, D.A. (1999) *Natural Amenities Drive Rural Population Change*. Washington, DC: US Department of Agriculture.

McGranahan, D. and Wojan, T. (2007) Recasting the creative class to examine growth processes in rural and urban counties, *Regional Studies* 41: 197–216.

McGreevy, P.V. (1994) *Imagining Niagara: The Meaning and Making of Niagara Falls*. Amherst: University of Massachusetts Press.

McHugh, K.E. (2006) Citadels in the sun, in N. McIntyre, D.R. Williams and K.E. McHugh (eds) *Multiple Dwelling and Tourism: Negotiating Place, Home and Identity*, pp. 262–77. Wallingford, UK: CAB International.

McHugh, K. and Mings, R. (1992) Canadian snowbirds in Arizona, *Journal of Applied Recreation Research* 17(3): 255–77.

Meyer-Arendt, K. and Hartmann, R. (1998) *Casino Gambling in America: Origins, Trends and Impacts*. New York: Cognizant.

Miller, A.R. and Grazer, W.F. (2006) Cruising and the North American market, in R.K. Dowling (ed.) *Cruise Ship Tourism*, pp. 74–85. Wallingford, UK: CAB International.

Mings, R. and McHugh, K. (1995) Wintering in the American Sunbelt: linking place and behaviour, *Journal of Tourism Studies* 6(2): 56–61.

Missouri Division of Tourism (no date) *Missouri's Funding for Tourism Promotion* (information sheet). Available from http://www.missouritourism.org (accessed November 10, 2008).

Missouri Division of Tourism (2007) *Annual Report FY 07*. Jefferson City, MO: Missouri Division of Tourism.

Moehring, E. (2000) *Resort City in the Sunbelt: Las Vegas, 1930–70* (2nd edn). Reno: University of Nevada Press.

Montag, J.M., Patterson, M.E. and Freimund, W.A. (2005) The wolf viewing experience in the Lamar Valley of Yellowstone National Park, *Human Dimensions of Wildlife* 10(4): 273–84.

Morrison, A.M., Bruen, S.M. and Anderson, D.J. (1998) Convention and visitor bureaus in the USA: a profile of bureaus, bureau executives, and budgets, *Journal of Travel and Tourism Marketing* 7(1): 1–19.

Moufakkir, O. (2005) An assessment of crime volume following casino gaming development in the city of Detroit, *UNLV Gaming Research & Review Journal* 9(1): 15–28.

Munro, J.M. and Gill, W.G. (2006) The Alaska cruise industry, in R.K. Dowling (ed.) *Cruise Ship Tourism*, pp. 145–59. Wallingford, UK: CAB International.

Nabokov, P. and Easton, R. (1989) *Native American Architecture*. Oxford: Oxford University Press.

National Conference of Catholic Bishops (1998) *Catholic Shrines and Places of Pilgrimage in the United States*. Washington, DC: United States Catholic Conference.

National Park Service (2009) *National Park Type Report for 2008*. Available from http://www.nature.nps.gov/stats/viewReport.cfm (accessed March 10, 2009).

National Sporting Goods Association (2008) *Ten-Year History of Sports Participation*. Available from http://www.nsga.org/files/public/10yr.SportsParticipation_4web_ 2007 – 080904.pdf (accessed March 10, 2009).

Nelson, J.G. (2000) Tourism and national parks in North America: an overview, in R.W. Butler and S.W. Boyd (eds) *Tourism and National Parks: Issues and Implications*, pp. 303–21. Chichester: Wiley.

Nwanna, G.I. (2004) *Americans Traveling Abroad: What You Should Know before You Go*. Baltimore, MD: Frontline.

Nyaupane, G.P., White, D.D. and Budruk, M. (2006) Motive-based tourist market segmentation: an application to Native American cultural heritage sites in Arizona, USA, *Journal of Heritage Tourism* 1(2): 81–99.

O'Dell, T. and Billing, P. (eds) (2005) *Experience-Scapes: Tourism, Culture, and Economy*. Koge, Denmark: Copenhagen Business School Press.

Office of Travel and Tourism Industries (2009) *Welcome to OTTI*. Available from http://tinet.ita.doc.gov/ (accessed February 15, 2009).

O'Leary, C.E. (1999) *To Die For: The Paradox of American Patriotism*. Princeton, NJ: Princeton University Press.

Olsen, D.H. (2006) Tourism and informal pilgrimage among the Latter-day Saints, in D.J. Timothy and D.H. Olsen (eds) *Tourism, Religion and Spiritual Journeys*, pp. 254–70. London: Routledge.

Olsen, D.H. (2008) *Contesting Identity, Space and Sacred Site Management at Temple Square in Salt Lake City, Utah*. PhD Dissertation, University of Waterloo, Canada.

Olsen, J. (2004) *Better Places, Better Lives: A Biography of James Rouse*. Washington, DC: Urban Land Institute.

O'Neil, D.J. (2001) The New Age movement and its societal implications, *International Journal of Social Economics* 28(5): 456–75.

Oregon Tourism Commission (2005) *Travel Oregon: Strategic marketing plan and budget 2005–2007*. Salem, OR: Oregon Tourism Commission.

Otterstrom, S.M. (2008) Genealogy as religious ritual: the doctrine and practice of family history in the Church of Jesus Christ of Latter-day Saints, in D.J. Timothy and J. Kay Guelke (eds) *Geography and Genealogy: Locating Personal Pasts*, pp. 137–51. Aldershot, UK: Ashgate.

Page, S.J. (1995) *Urban Tourism*. London: Routledge.

Page, S.J. (2005) *Transport and Tourism: Global Perspectives*. Harlow, UK: Pearson.

Park, D.C. and Coppack, P.M. (1994) The role of rural sentiment and vernacular landscapes in contriving sense of place in the city's countryside, *Geografiska Annaler B: Human Geography* 76(3): 161–72.

Parker, R. (1999). Las Vegas: casino gambling and local culture, in D.R. Judd and S.S. Fainstein (eds) *The Tourist City*, pp. 107–23. New Haven: Yale University Press.

Pearce, D. (1989) *Tourism Development*. Harlow: Longman.

Peisley, A. (2004) Cruises: North America and the Caribbean, *Travel and Tourism Analyst* 9: 1–42.

Pennington-Gray, L. (2006) Florida's day cruise industry: A significant contributor to Florida's economy, in Ross Dowling (ed.), *Cruise Ship Tourism*, pp. 290–8. Wallingford, UK: CAB International.

Pfaffenberg, C.J. and Costello, C. (2001) Items of importance to patrons of Indian and riverboat casinos, *UNLV Gaming Research & Review Journal* 6(1): 33–41.

Picolli, G., O'Connor, P., Capaciolli, C. and Alvarez, R. (2003) Customer relationship management: a driver for change in the structure of the US lodging industry, *Cornell Hotel and Restaurant Administration Quarterly* 44(4): 61–73.

Pietrykow, B. (2004) You are what you eat: the social economy of the Slow Food Movement, *Review of Social Economy* 62(3): 307–21.

Polzin, S.F, Chu, X. and Rey, J.R. (1999) *Mobility and Mode Choice of People of Color for Non-Work Travel*. Washington, DC: Transportation Research Board.

Poor, H.V. (1970) *History of the Railroads and Canals of the United States of America: Exhibiting Their Progress, Cost, Revenues, Expenditures and Present Condition*. Ann Arbor: University of Michigan.

Popper, D.E. and Popper, F.J. (2006) The onset of the Buffalo Commons, *Journal of the West* 45(2): 29–34.

Porter, M.E., Ketels, C.H.M., Miller, K. and Bryden, R.T. (2004) *Competitiveness in Rural US Regions: Learning and Research Agenda*. Cambridge, MA: Institute for Strategy and Competitiveness, Harvard Business School.

Prabhakar, S., Pankanti, S. and Jain, A.K. (2003) Biometric recognition: security and privacy concerns, *Security and Privacy* 1(2): 33–42.

Pucher, J., Ioannides, D. and Hirschman, I. (1993) Passenger transport in the United States and Europe: a comparative analysis of public sector involvement, in D. Banister and J. Berechman (eds) *Transport in a Unified Europe: Policies and Challenges*, pp. 369–414. Amsterdam: Elsevier.

Quigley, J. (2002) *Rural Policy and the New Regional Economics: Implications for Rural America*. Berkeley: University of California.

Randall, E.O. (2003) *Serpent Mound, Adams County, Ohio*. Whitefish, MT: Kessinger Publishing.

Reeder, R.J. and Brown, D.M. (2005) *Recreation, Tourism, and Rural Well-Being. A Report from the Economic Research Service*. Washington, DC: United States Department of Agriculture.

Regional Airline Association (2009) *Airline Member Listings*. Available from http://www.raa.org/airlines/ (accessed February 10, 2009).

Relph, E.C. (1979) *Place and Placelessness*. London: Pion.

Ringer, G. (2006) Cruising north to Alaska: the new "Gold Rush," in R.K. Dowling (ed.) *Cruise Ship Tourism*, pp. 270–9. Wallingford, UK: CAB International.

Rinschede, G. (1990) Catholic pilgrimage places in the United States, in G. Rinschede and S.M. Bhardwaj (eds) *Pilgrimage in the United States*, pp. 63–147. Berlin: Dietrich Reimer Verlag.

Ritzer, G. and Liska, A. (1997) "McDisneyization" and "Post-tourism," in C. Rojek and J. Urry (eds) *Touring Cultures: Transformations of Travel and Theory*, pp. 96–109. London: Routledge.

Rivera, J. and de Leon, P. (2004) Is greener whiter? Voluntary environmental performance of western ski areas, *The Policy Studies Journal* 32(3): 417–37.

Roehl, W. (1998) The tourism production system: the logic of industrial classification, in D. Ioannides and K.G. Debbage (eds) *The Economic Geography of the Tourist Industry: A Supply Side Analysis*, pp. 53–76. London: Routledge.

Rogers, P. (1995) *The Mumbles Train – World's First Railway Service*. Available from http://www.welshwales.co.uk/mumbles_railway_swansea.htm (accessed February 20, 2009).

Rothman, H.K. (1998) *Devil's Bargains: Tourism in the Twentieth-Century American West*. Lawrence, KS: University Press of Kansas.

Rountree, K. (2002) Goddess pilgrims as tourists: inscribing the body through sacred travel, *Sociology of Religion* 63(4): 475–96.

Rowntree, L., Lewis, M., Price, M. and Wyckoff, W. (2006) *Diversity amid Globalization: World Regions, Environment, Development*. Upper Saddle River, NJ: Pearson–Prentice Hall.

Rubenstein, J. (1984) Casino gambling in Atlantic City: issues of development and redevelopment, *Annals of the American Academy of Political and Social Science* 474: 61–71.

Rudd, M.A. and Davis, J.A. (1998) Industrial heritage tourism at the Bingham Canyon Copper Mine, *Journal of Travel Research* 36(3): 85–9.

Sacks, A. (2004) *The New Jersey Tourism Satellite Account: A Comprehensive Understanding of the Economic Contribution of Travel and Tourism in the State of New Jersey*. Lexington, MA: Global Insight Inc.

Saint Louis Convention and Visitors Commission (2009) *St Louis: The Perfect Getaway . . . All Within Reach*. Available from http://www.explorestlouis.com/visitors/index.asp (accessed February 15, 2009).

Samuelson, D. and Yegoiants, W. (2001) *The American Amusement Park*. St. Paul, MN: MBI Publishing.

San Diego Convention and Visitors Bureau (2008) *San Diego County Visitor Industry Summary*. Available from http://www.sandiego.org/downloads/1233876886.93243800_2c5f54d378/VIS_2005-7.pdf (accessed February 3, 2009).

Sasse, M.A. (2007) Red-eye blink, bendy shuffle, and the yuck factor: a user experience of biometric airport systems, *Security and Privacy* 5(3): 78–81.

Schnell, S.M. (2003) Creating narratives of place and identity in "Little Sweden, USA," *Geographical Review* 93(1): 1–29.

Schoenmann, J. (2008) What is Las Vegas? For tourists it is the strip; for residents it's home, *Planning* 74(2): 6–13.

Schott, J.J. (2004) *Free Trade Agreements: US Strategies and Priorities*, Washington, DC: Institute for International Economics.

Scottsdale Convention and Visitors Bureau (2009) *Research and Resources*. Available from http://www.scottsdalecvb.com/docs/Tourism-Industry-Measurements-Jan-091.pdf (accessed February 3, 2009).

Sears, J.F. (1998) *Sacred Places: American Tourist Attractions in the 19th Century*. Amherst: University of Massachusetts Press.

Selby, M. (2004) *Understanding Urban Tourism: Image, Culture and Experience*. London: I.B. Tauris.

Shaffer, M.S. (2001) *See America First: Tourism and National Identity, 1880–1940*. Washington, DC: Smithsonian Institution Press.

Shaw, D.V. (1986) Making leisure pay: street railway owned amusement parks in the United States, 1900–1925, *Journal of Cultural Economics* 10(2): 67–80.

Shaw, G. and Williams, A. (1994) *Critical Issues in Tourism: A Geographical Perspective*. Oxford: Blackwell.

Shaw, G. and Williams, A. (2004) *Tourism and Tourism Spaces*. London: Sage.

Sheldon, P., Knox, J.M., and Lowry, K. (2005) Sustainability in a mature mass tourism destination: the case of Hawaii, *Tourism Review International* 9(1): 47–59.

Shifflet and Associates (2006) *California Domestic Travel Report, 2005: From the Destination Performance/ Monitor*. McLean, VA: D.K. Shifflet and Associates Ltd.

Siehl, G.H. (2000) US recreation policies since World War II, in W.C. Gartner (ed.) *Trends in Outdoor Recreation, Leisure and Tourism*, pp. 91–101. Wallingford, UK: CAB International.

Smith, L. (2000) Slave cabin opens at Virginia plantation, *Washington Post*, 8 October: 16.

Smith, M.K. and House, M. (2006) Snowbirds, sunbirds, and stayers: seasonal migration of elderly adults in Florida, *Journal of Gerontology B: Social Sciences* 61(5): 232–9.

Smith, S.L.J. (1998) Tourism as an industry: Debates and concepts, in D. Ioannides and K.G. Debbage (eds) *The Economic Geography of the Tourist Industry: A Supply Side Analysis*, pp. 31–52. London: Routledge.

Smith, S.L.J. and Timothy, D.J. (2006) Demand for tourism in North America, in D. Fennell (ed.) *North America: A Tourism Handbook*, pp. 32–52. Clevedon, UK: Channel View.

Smith, V.L. (2006) Adventure cruising: an ethnography of small ship travel, in R.K. Dowling (ed.) *Cruise Ship Tourism*, pp. 240–50. Wallingford, UK: CAB International.

Sobek, D. and Braithwaite, A. (2005) Victim of success: American dominance and terrorism, *Conflict Management and Peace Science* 22(2): 135–48.

Solomon, B.D., Corey-Luse, C.M. and Halvorsen, K.E. (2004) The Florida manatee and eco-tourism: toward a safe minimum standard, *Ecological Economics* 50(1/2): 101–15.

Sönmez, S. (1998) Tourism, terrorism and political instability, *Annals of Tourism Research* 25: 416–56.

Souther, J.M. (2007) The Disneyfication of New Orleans: the French Quarter as façade in a divided city, *Journal of American History* 94: 804–11.

Springfield Missouri Convention and Visitors Bureau (2007) *Annual Report*. Available from http://www.springfieldmo.org/final/newsite/pdf/2007_annual_rpt.pdf (accessed June 11, 2008).

Stansfield, C.A. (1977) Changes in the geography of passenger liner ports: the rise of the southeastern Florida ports, *Southeastern Geographer* 17(1): 25–32.

Stansfield, C.A. (1978) Atlantic City and the resort cycle: a background to the legalization of gambling, *Annals of Tourism Research* 5: 238–51.

Stansfield, C.A. (2004) *Vacationing on the Jersey Shore: Guide to the Beach Resorts Past and Present*. Mechanicsburg, PA: Stackpole Books.

Stansfield, C.A. and Rickert, J.E. (1970) The recreational business district, *Annals of Tourism Research* 4: 213–25.

State of New Jersey Division of Travel and Tourism (2009) *New Jersey: Great Destinations in Any Direction*. Available from http://www.state.nj.us/travel/ (accessed February 15, 2009).

Steel, B.S. (1996) Thinking globally and acting locally? Environmental attitudes, behaviour and activism, *Journal of Environmental Management* 47(1): 27–36.

Steinbeck, J. (1939) *Grapes of Wrath*. New York: The Viking Press.

Sterngass, J. (2001) *First Resorts: Pursuing Pleasure at Saratoga Springs, Newport and Coney Island*. Baltimore, MD: Johns Hopkins University Press.

Stipanuk, D.M. (1996) The US lodging industry and the environment, *Cornell Hotel and Restaurant Administration Quarterly* 37(5): 39–45.

Stitt, G., Nichols, M. and Giacopassi, D. (2005) Perception of casinos as disruptive influences in USA communities, *International Journal of Tourism Research* 7: 187–200.

Stover, J.F. (1997) *American Railroads*. Chicago: University of Chicago Press.

Sweet, J.D. (2007) "Let 'em loose": Pueblo Indian management of tourism, *American Indian Culture and Research Journal* 15(4): 59–74.

Takaki, R. (1994) *Ethnic Islands: the Emergence of Urban Chinese America*. New York: Chelsea House.

Tapia, E.S. (2002) Earth spirituality and the people's struggle for life: reflection from the perspective of indigenous peoples, *Ecumenical Review* 54(3): 219–27.

Thapa, B. (2003) Tourism in Nepal: Shangri-La's troubled times, *Journal of Travel and Tourism Marketing* 15(2/3): 117–38.

Themed Entertainment Association (2008) *Themed Entertainment Association/Economic Research Associates' Attraction Attendance Report*. Burbank, CA: Themed Entertainment Asociation.

Theobald, W.F. (2005) The meaning, scope and measurement of travel and tourism, in W.F. Theobald (ed.) *Global Tourism* (3rd edn), pp. 5–24. Oxford: Butterworth-Heinemann.

Thomopoulos, E.C. (2005) *Resorts of Berrien County*. Chicago, IL: Arcadia.

Timothy, D.J. (1999a) Cross-border partnership in tourism resource management: international parks along the US–Canada border, *Journal of Sustainable Tourism* 7(3/4): 182–205.

Timothy, D.J. (1999b) Cross-border shopping: tourism in the Canada-United States borderlands, *Visions in Leisure and Business* 17(4): 4–18.

Timothy, D.J. (2001) *Tourism and Political Boundaries*. London: Routledge.

Timothy, D.J. (2002) Tourism and the growth of urban ethnic islands, in C.M. Hall and A.M. Williams (eds) *Tourism and Migration: New Relationships between Production and Consumption*, pp. 135–52. Dordrecht: Kluwer.

Timothy, D.J. (2004) Recreational second homes in the United States: development issues and contemporary patterns, in C.M. Hall and D. Müller (eds) *Tourism, Mobility and Second Homes: Between Elite Landscape and Common Ground*, pp. 133–48. Clevedon, UK: Channel View.

Timothy, D.J. (2005a) Rural tourism business: a North American overview, in D. Hall, I. Kirkpatrick, and M. Mitchell (eds) *Rural Tourism and Sustainable Business*, pp. 41–62. Clevedon, UK: Channel View.

Timothy, D.J. (2005b) *Shopping Tourism, Retailing and Leisure*. Clevedon, UK: Channel View.

Timothy, D.J. (2006a) Safety and security issues in tourism, in D. Buhalis and C. Costa (eds) *Tourism Management Dynamics: Trends, Management and Tools*, pp. 19–27. Oxford: Butterworth-Heinemann.

Timothy, D.J. (2006b) Supply and organization of tourism in North America, in D. Fennell (ed.) *North America: A Tourism Handbook*, pp. 53–81. Clevedon, UK: Channel View.

Timothy, D.J. (2008) Genealogical mobility: tourism and the search for a personal past, in D.J. Timothy and J.K. Guelke (eds) *Geography and Genealogy: Locating Personal Pasts*, pp. 115–35. Aldershot: Ashgate.

Timothy, D.J. (2009) River-based tourism in the United States: tourism and recreation on the Colorado and Mississippi Rivers, in B. Prideaux and M. Cooper (eds) *River Tourism*, pp. 41–54. Wallingford, UK: CAB International.

Timothy, D.J. and Boyd, S.W. (2003) *Heritage Tourism*. Harlow: Prentice Hall.

Timothy, D.J. and Boyd, S.W. (2006a) Heritage tourism in the 21st century: valued traditions and new perspectives, *Journal of Heritage Tourism* 1(1): 1–17.

Timothy, D.J. and Boyd, S.W. (2006b) World Heritage Sites in the Americas, in A. Leask and A. Fyall (eds) *Managing World Heritage Sites*, pp. 235–45. Oxford: Butterworth-Heinemann.

Timothy, D.J. and Butler, R.W. (1995) Cross-border shopping: a North American perspective, *Annals of Tourism Research* 22: 16–34.

Timothy, D.J. and Canally, C. (2008) The role of the US-Mexico border as a destination: student traveler perceptions, *Tourism Analysis* 13(3): 259–69.

Timothy, D.J. and Conover, P.J. (2006) Nature religion, self spirituality and New Age tourism, in D.J. Timothy and D.H. Olsen (eds) *Tourism, Religion and Spiritual Journeys*, pp. 139–55. London: Routledge.

Timothy, D.J. and Teye, V.B. (2004) American children of the African diaspora: journeys to the motherland, in T. Coles and D.J. Timothy (eds) *Tourism, Diasporas and Space*, pp. 111–23. London: Routledge.

Timothy, D.J. and Teye, V.B. (2009) *Tourism and the Lodging Sector*. Oxford: Butterworth-Heinemann.

Todd, R. (2001) "Las Vegas, 'Tis of thee." *The Atlantic* vol. 287(2). Available from http://www.theatlantic.com/doc/200102/todd (accessed February 15, 2008).

Torres, R.M. (2002) Cancun's tourism development from a Fordist spectrum of analysis, *Tourist Studies* 2(1): 87–116.

Torres, R.M. and Momsen, J.D. (2005) Gringolandia: the construction of a new tourist space in Mexico, *Annals of the Association of American Geographers* 95: 314–35.

Travel Industry Association of America (TIA) (1996) *A Portrait of Travel Industry Employment in the US Economy*. Washington, DC: Travel Industry Association of America.

Travel Industry Association of America (TIA) (2005) *Impact of Travel and Tourism on the US and State Economies: Executive Summary*. Washington, DC: Travel Industry Association of America and US Chamber of Commerce.

Travel Industry Association of America (TIA) (2006) *Travel and Tourism Works for America: The Economic Impact of Travel on States and Congressional Districts (2006 Research Report)*. Washington, DC: Travel Industry Association of America.

Travel Industry Association of America (TIA) (2007) *Domestic Travel Market Report, 2007*. Washington, DC: Travel Industry Association of America.

Truitt, L.J. (1996) Casino gambling in Illinois: riverboats, revenues, and economic development. *Journal of Travel Research*, 34(3): 89–96.

Turco, D.M. (1999) Ya' 'at 'eeh: a profile of tourists to Navajo Nation, *Journal of Tourism Studies* 10(2): 57–61.

Turner, R.S. (2002) Design and development in the postmodern downtown, *Journal of Urban Affairs* 24(5): 533–48.

Turner, R.S. and Rosentraub, M.S. (2002) Tourism, sports and centrality of cities, *Journal of Urban Affairs* 24(5): 487–92.

Tyrrell, T.J. and Johnston, R.J. (2001) A framework for assessing direct economic impacts of tourist events: distinguishing origins, destinations, and causes of expenditures, *Journal of Travel Research* 49(1): 94–100.

United States Tour Operators Association (n.d.) Americans like making their own travel plans despite packaged travel savings: baby boomers most likely to choose independent touring. Available from http://www.ustoa.com/pressroom/newsreleases/travel typesurvey. pdf (website accessed February 23, 2009).

Urry, J. (1990) *The Tourist Gaze: Leisure and Travel in Contemporary Societies*. London: Sage.

US Census Bureau (2004) *County Business Patterns*. Available from http://www.census.gov (accessed January 15, 2005).

US Census Bureau (2008) Housing Vacancies and Ownership. Available from http://www.census.gov/hhes/www/housing/hvs/annual07/ann07t9.html (accessed December 5, 2008).

US Census Bureau (2009a) North American Industrial Classification System (NAICS). US Census Bureau. Available from http://www.census.gov/eos/www/naics/ (accessed February 12, 2009).

US Census Bureau (2009b) US Census Bureau Website. Available from http://www.census.gov (United States Department of Commerce) (accessed February 2009).

US Congress (2008) *Travel Promotion Act of 2008 (H.R. 3232)*. Washington, DC: US Congress.

US Department of Commerce (2008a) *2007 International Arrivals to the United States*. Washington, DC: Department of Commerce, International Trade Administration.

US Department of Commerce (2008b) *Overseas Visitation Estimates for U.S. States, Cities, and Census Regions: 2007*. Washington, DC: Department of Commerce, International Trade Administration.

US Department of Commerce (2008c) *2007 United States Resident Travel Abroad*. Washington, DC: Department of Commerce, International Trade Administration.

US Department of Commerce (2009) *Total Arrivals, Canada, Mexico, Total Overseas, Western Europe Non-Resident Arrivals to the U.S. by World Region/Country of Residence 2008*. Washington, DC: Department of Commerce, International Trade Administration.

US Department of Transportation (2008a) *Fact Sheet for the National Scenic Byways Program*. Washington, DC: Federal Highway Administration, US Department of Transportation.

US Department of Transportation (2008b) *History of the Interstate Highway System*. Washington, DC: USDOT, Federal Highway Administration. Available from http://www.fhwa.dot. gov/interstate/history.htm (accessed March 12, 2008).

US National Park Service (2009) *NPS Stats*. Available from http://www.nature.nps.gov/stats/ (accessed March 5, 2009).

US Tour Operators' Association (USTOA) (2009) Official Website. http://www.ustoa.com/missionandgoals.cfm (accessed March 18, 2009)

US Travel and Tourism Advisory Board (2006) *Restoring America's Brand: National Strategy to Compete for International Visitors: recommendations to the US Secretary of Commerce*. Washington, DC: USTTAB.

USA Today (2007) It's crunch time for all those Vegas tourists. (5/17/2007). Available from http:// www.usatoday.com/travel/destinations/2007-05-17-vegas-congestion_N.htm (accessed March 5, 2008).

Velotta, R.N. (2008) "The G word," *Planning* 74(2): 26–32.

Velotta, R.N. (2009) Tourism industry can close book on dismal '08 figures. *Las Vegas Sun* (February 20). Available from http://www.lasvegassun.com/news/2009/feb/20/tourism-industry-can-close-book-dismal-08-figures/ (accessed April 13, 2009).

Venturoni, L., Long, P. and Perdue, R. (2005) The economic and social impacts of second homes in four mountain resort counties of Colorado. Paper presented at the 2005 Annual Meeting of the Association of American Geographers, April 7, Denver, Colorado.

Wall, G. and Mathieson, A. (2006) *Tourism: Change, Impacts and Opportunities*. Harlow, UK: Pearson.

Wang, Y. and Fesenmaier D. (2006) Identifying the success factors of web-based marketing strategy: An investigation of convention and visitors bureaus in the United States, *Journal of Travel Research* 44(3): 239–49.

Watkins, E. (2005) *Growth Leaders. Lodging Hospitality: Ideas for Hotel Developers and Operators*. Available from http://ihonline.com/mag/growth_leaders (accessed March 18, 2009).

Weaver, D.B. (1998) *Ecotourism in the Less Developed Word*. Wallingford, UK: CAB International.

Weber, K. (2001) Meeting planners' use and evaluation of convention and visitor bureaus, *Tourism Management* 22: 599–606.

Weigle, M. (1989) From desert to Disney World: the Santa Fe Railway and the Fred Harvey Company display the Indian southwest, *Journal of Anthropological Research* 45(1): 115–37.

Weisbrod, R.E. and Lawson, C.T. (2003) Ferry systems: planning for the revitalization of U.S. cities, *Journal of Urban Technology* 10(2): 47–68.

Wheatcroft, S. (1998) The airline industry and tourism, in D. Ioannides and K. Debbage (eds) *The Economic Geography of the Tourist Industry: A Supply-side Analysis*, pp. 159–79. London: Routledge.

Wheeler, M. (2008) "Why here? A short history of Las Vegas," *Planning* 74(2): 18–19.

White, D.D., Virden, R.J. and Cahill, K.L. (2005) Visitor experiences in national park service cultural sites in Arizona: implications for interpretive planning and management, *Journal of Park and Recreation Administration* 23(3): 63–81.

Williams, J.H. (1996) *A Great and Shining Road: The Epic Story of the Transcontinental Railroad*. Lincoln: University of Nebraska Press.

Williams, M. (1990) *The Mexican American Family: Tradition and Change*. Walnut Creek, CA: AltaMira Press.

Willits, F.K. (1993) The rural mystique and tourism development: data from Pennsylvania, *Journal of the Community Development Society* 24(2): 159–74.

Wojan, T.R., Lambert, D.M. and McGranahan, D.A. (2007) Emoting with their feet: Bohemian attraction to creative milieu. *Journal of Economic Geography* 7: 711–36.

World Tourism Organization (2009) *World Tourism Barometer*. Madrid: UNWTO.

World Travel and Tourism Council (2003) *Blueprint for New Tourism*. London: WTTC.

Wyoming Travel and Tourism (2005) *Wyoming Travel Industry: 2005 Impact Report. Wyoming Travel and Tourism*. Cheyenne: Wyoming Travel and Tourism.

Xie, P.F. (2006) Developing industrial heritage tourism: a case study of the proposed Jeep museum in Toledo, Ohio, *Tourism Management* 27(6): 1321–30.

York, M. (2001) New Age commodification and appropriation of spirituality, *Journal of Contemporary Religion* 16(3): 361–72.

Yuan, Y.L., Gretzel, U. and Fesenmaier D. (2003) Internet technology use by American convention and visitors' bureaus, *Journal of Travel Research* 41(3): 240–55.

Zeitler, E. (2009) Creating America's "Czech Capital": ethnic identity and heritage tourism in Wilber, Nebraska, *Journal of Heritage Tourism* 4(1): 73–85.

Index

accessibility 10, 27, 28, 102–105, 161, 175, 186
accommodations 25, 40, 44, 50, 58, 60, 73, 93–96, 99–100, 119, 126, 128, 130, 132, 134, 138, 139, 141, 158, 159, 177, 181, 189; *see also* bed and breakfasts; hotels; resorts
adventure tourism 21, 67, 121, 122
affluence 12, 27, 146, 181, 186
Africa 58, 63, 65, 67, 83, 102, 191
African-Americans 7, 67, 81, 191
agriculture 19, 80–81, 86, 141, 142, 167, 168–169, 177, 179, 183, 191
agritourism 177
air travel 4, 9, 28–29, 54, 55, 56, 59–60, 96, 102, 103, 104, 105, 111–118, 119, 126
airline deregulation 13, 28, 112, 116
airlines 1, 3, 28, 34, 96, 98, 99, 116, 117–118, 120, 127; discount airlines 114, 116–117; *see also* regional carriers
airplanes 28, 111–112, 186
airports 3, 12, 29, 38, 54, 57, 65, 112–114, 147, 149, 187–188
Alabama 79, 89, 103, 131, 132, 180
Alaska 5, 6, 7, 47–48, 72, 80, 89, 96, 120–122, 166
alternative fuels 190
amenity migration 179, 184; *see also* seasonal migration
American Automobile Association (AAA) 25
American Resort Development Association 95
American Samoa 177
Americanization 2
Amtrak 104–105, 107
amusement parks 22, 24, 29, 54, 56, 70, 72, 73, 87–88, 94, 95, 141, 155, 159
Appalachia/Appalachian Mountains 5, 169, 179, 181
Appalachian Trail 178
aquariums 29, 125, 148, 155, 159, 163
archeological sites *see* heritage sites
Arctic Ocean 5
Arizona 4, 7, 21, 46, 56, 58, 67, 68, 73, 74, 75–76, 79, 80, 82, 83, 89, 91–92, 95, 132, 166, 170, 191; *see also* Phoenix; Scottsdale; Sedona

Arkansas 16, 46, 79, 170
Arlington National Cemetery 79
Asia 38, 42, 58, 65, 80, 83, 102
Asian-Americans 7
Atlanta 147, 171
Atlantic City 28, 85, 88, 103, 111, 134, 138, 139, 141, 156
Atlantic Ocean/coast 5, 6, 119, 122, 169, 179
Austin 137, 148, 161
Australia 38
attractions 5, 33, 40, 42, 50, 72, 73, 93, 102, 136, 148, 149, 152, 157, 159, 170, 184, 191
authenticity 16, 75, 87, 88, 162, 166, 172
automobiles 4, 8, 9, 12, 13, 21, 23, 25, 27–28, 29, 36, 59, 70, 83, 85, 93, 99, 102–103, 105, 108–110, 111, 122, 127, 160, 175, 186–187
Aztec Ruins National Monument 73

Badlands National Park 178
balance of trade 134
Baltimore 103, 105, 158, 159, 191
bankruptcies 28, 65, 116
barriers to travel 43
battlegrounds 6, 12, 18, 29, 73, 79, 82, 149, 165, 170, 175
beaches 22, 54, 61, 67, 70, 72; *see also* resorts
bed and breakfasts 17, 25, 60, 93, 107, 163; *see also* accommodations; hotels; resorts
bird watching 83
boosterism 29, 30, 163
border crossings 54, 56, 65, 187
borders 55, 56, 58, 167, 187–189
Boston 7, 18, 28, 76, 99, 105, 111, 149, 157, 158, 189
Branson (Missouri) 17, 135–137, 156, 182
Brazil 17, 102
British tourists 99
Bureau of Land Management 42, 82
Bureau of Labor Statistics 97, 126, 138, 139
business travel 59–60, 61, 64, 99, 134, 145, 189

California 5, 6, 8, 22, 23, 28, 45, 46, 56, 57, 58, 59, 67, 68, 72, 80, 83, 87–88, 89, 94, 95, 103, 117, 119, 120, 125, 130, 132, 141,

142, 144, 173; *see also* Disneyland; Los
Angeles; San Diego; San Francisco
California Tourism and Travel Commission 50
campgrounds 60, 177
camping 21–23, 68, 82–83
Canada 5, 7, 42–43, 55, 56, 61, 63, 65, 68, 70,
95, 102, 120–122, 132, 133, 186, 188
Canada–US Free Trade Agreement 55
Canadian tourists 7, 55, 65, 99, 119
Canyon de Chelly National Monument 73
Cape May (New Jersey) 15, 134, 138
Caribbean 4, 38, 58, 64, 111, 117, 120–121,
141, 189
car travel *see* automobiles
cars *see* automobiles
casinos *see* gambling
cathedrals *see* churches
Catholics 64, 89
cemeteries 73, 191
Charleston 152, 157
Charlotte 115
Chicago 4, 22, 24, 30, 54, 67, 99, 104,
114–115, 118, 139, 147, 153, 158, 161,
162–163, 167, 191
China 5, 34, 35, 54, 57, 111, 123; approved
destination status 57
Chinatown 7, 25, 72
Christians 90; *see also* Catholics; Evangelical
Christians; Mormons
Church of Jesus Christ of Latter-day Saints
90–91; *see also* Christians
churches 77, 89, 149
Cincinnati 115
Civil Aeronautics Board 111
Civil War 12, 14, 18, 30, 79, 81, 165, 166,
170, 180
cities 6, 10, 23–24, 26, 28, 57, 70, 81, 88, 99,
102, 122, 135, 138–139, 141, 142,
144–163, 165, 167, 177, 184, 187;
converted cities 148, 157–158; resort cities
156–157; tourist cities 156–158; tourist
historic cities 157; *see also* urban tourism
climate 5, 186
"collective amnesia" 81
colonial heritage 6, 76–79
Colonial Williamsburg 77–78
Colorado 68, 72, 73, 78, 80, 89, 95, 132, 141,
178, 181–182
Colorado River 21
commodification of culture/experiences 88,
127, 149
commodity chain 126
commuter airlines *see* regional carriers
Coney Island 24, 87
conference centers *see* convention centers
conferences *see* conventions
Connecticut 78, 86, 89
conservation 32, 176, 177, 188–189
cost–benefit analysis 125

consumer culture 13
convention and visitors bureaus 46–49, 51,
125, 129
convention centers 3, 29, 38, 95, 125, 148,
153, 187
conventions 59, 64, 99, 145, 162
"countryside idyll" 165
crime 65, 66, 86, 88, 159, 182, 188
crises 1, 136, 150, 152, 182
Cruise Lines International Association 120
cruises 8, 9, 12, 61, 72, 97, 103, 119–122
cruises to nowhere 8, 86, 122–123
nostalgia cruises 121
Cuba 34, 111, 189
cuisine 7, 74, 80, 190
cultural arrogance 63
cultural diversity *see* multiculturalism
cultural landscapes 72, 73, 80
cultural resources 42, 44, 54, 83, 102, 105,
161, 165, 173, 177, 179, 182
cultural sites *see* heritage sites
cultural tourism *see* heritage tourism

Dallas 42, 114, 115, 118, 167
day-trippers 7, 56, 69, 188
Death Valley 6
Declaration of Independence 77
demand for tourism 54–70
demand shifters 64–67, 70
demographics 54, 64, 67, 70, 168, 192
Denver 48
Department of Commerce 8, 39–41, 65
Department of Homeland Security 39, 42
Department of the Interior 84, 130
dependence *see* overdependence on tourism
deserts 29, 83, 144
destination management organizations
(DMOs) 3, 34, 38, 52
destinations 6, 13, 67, 132, 135, 136, 160, 166,
169, 173, 183, 189, 192
Detroit 46, 115, 159–160
development of tourism 33–34, 47–48, 52, 75,
136–137, 151, 187, 192; *see also*
sustainability
Disney Company 35–7, 72, 95, 156–157
Disney World 7, 8, 12, 29, 36–37, 58, 87, 99,
141, 158
"Disneyfication" 87, 162
Disneyland 58, 87
disposable income *see* affluence
distribution channels 120
domestic tourism 28, 30, 54–55, 58–60, 70,
99, 117, 133, 134, 141, 149, 186, 191,
192
downtown revitalization *see* gentrification

eco-certification 189
economic development 30, 38, 39, 41, 44,
47–48, 50–52, 83, 134, 136, 142, 168, 183

economic impact of tourism 3, 46, 86, 125–142, 131, 181
economic multiplier 126, 131, 149
economics 1, 9, 125–142, 165, 181
economy of scale 55, 183
ecotourism 67, 82–83, 120, 168, 169
educational travel 67
El Morro National Monument 73
embassies 79
employment 3, 32, 86, 126, 130–133, 136, 137, 139, 141, 155, 167, 168, 177, 181, 187
empowerment of communities 75
England 13, 76, 111
entertainment 12, 58, 72, 93, 119, 128, 134, 137–138, 145, 162, 183
entrepreneurialism 127, 131, 136, 141, 168, 181, 189
environmental impacts 16, 51, 83, 135–136, 181–182, 184
environmental protection *see* conservation
Environmental Protection Agency 42
Erie Canal 14–16
ethnic heritage 7, 25, 50, 80–81, 166, 172, 184, 191
ethnic minorities 25, 161, 172; *see also* immigration
ethnic villages 7, 172
Etowah Indian Mounds 74
Eureka Springs (Arkansas) 16–17, 170
Europe 4, 13, 14, 30, 42, 56, 63, 64, 65, 70, 77, 81, 91, 96, 102, 103, 111, 120, 157, 175, 190
European tourists 13, 96
European Union 5, 188
evangelical Christians 17, 61
events 22, 49, 64, 80, 135, 149, 157, 172, 180, 191–192
exchange rates 55, 61, 65
expenditures 128, 130, 133, 137, 142; indirect 137–138; induced 137–138

factories 24, 56, 81–82
Fashionable Tour 14–16
feasibility studies 155
Federal Aviation Administration (FAA) 112
Federal Aid Highway Act 20, 26, 27, 109, 152
festival market places 148, 158–160
festivals 69, 74, 80–81, 166, 172–173, 175, 191–192
financial crisis *see* recession
fishing 82–83, 135, 169, 175
Flagstaff (Arizona) 105, 138
Florida 4, 5, 8, 13, 28, 29, 35, 44, 55, 56, 58, 59, 68, 72, 79, 83, 87–88, 89, 95, 108, 111, 119, 120–121, 130, 131, 132, 138; *see also* Disney World; Miami; Orlando
Florida Everglades 6
folk museums *see* museums
folklore 80

food *see* cuisine
foreign tourists *see* international tourism
France 8, 34, 80, 89, 123
Freedom Trail (Boston) 7, 76–77
frequent flyer programs 116
frontier settlement 4, 79–80
fuel prices 130, 134
future of tourism 186–192

gambling 1, 58, 73, 85–86, 94, 134, 144–147, 157, 169
gambling cruises *see* cruises
gaming *see* gambling
gas stations 128, 134
gateways 114–115, 175, 177
genealogy-based tourism 91, 191; *see also* heritage tourism
gentrification 151, 154, 161, 165, 173, 191
geography 14, 149–150, 151, 160
Georgia 58, 74, 78, 79, 89, 122, 157, 171; *see also* Atlanta
Germany 8, 56, 61, 123, 173
global capital 151
globalization 1, 9, 150–151, 157, 163, 186
Global Distribution Systems 96, 98, 117
Gold Rush 80
Golden Gate Bridge 2, 157
golf 35, 72, 94, 125
government, role of 32–40, 125
Grand Canyon 2, 6, 19, 20, 21–22, 25, 58, 105, 176
Grand Canyon Railway 105–106
Grand Tour 13, 22
Great Depression 16, 26–27, 145, 179
Great Lakes 6, 118, 122, 179, 180, 183
Great Serpent Mound 74
green movement *see* sustainability
Green Restaurant Association 189
greenways 106
gross domestic product (GDP) 133–134, 141
gross regional product (GRP) 125, 128
gross state product (GSP) 131
Guam 57, 58, 177
guidebooks 18, 24, 26, 29, 128

handicrafts *see* Indian art
Hawaii 4, 5, 13, 28, 38, 45, 50, 57, 58, 72, 83, 88, 95, 96, 117, 120–121, 122, 130, 134, 141; *see also* Honolulu
Hawaii Tourism Authority 50
Henry Ford 25
heritage sites 12, 14, 25, 27, 33, 54, 56, 70, 73–82, 83, 102, 149, 153, 157, 160, 175, 184, 191; interpretation 74, 81, 177; protection 74, 81; *see also* industrial heritage; Native Americans
heritage tourism 6, 61, 67, 70, 73–82, 88, 99, 121, 122, 186, 191; definition 73; political heritage 79

highways *see* interstate highways
hiking 6, 21, 68–69, 82–83, 169, 175, 178
Hispanic-Americans 7
historic buildings *see* heritage sites
historic routes *see* trails
historic theme parks *see* museums
history of tourism in the USA 13–21
Hollywood 2, 4, 58, 70, 160
Holy Land 61, 89, 90–91
Honolulu 156
Hoover Dam 8, 29
hot springs *see* spa resorts
hotels 13, 14, 16–17, 19, 24, 33, 36, 41, 49,
    60, 72, 83, 87, 88, 93, 96, 98, 119, 120,
    126, 127, 131, 136, 145, 153, 155, 162,
    163, 183, 190
Hovenweep National Monument 74
hub-and-spoke system 28, 112–114, 122
human rights 81
hunting 82–83, 169
hyperreality 7

Idaho 68, 95, 178
identity 157
Illinois 58, 59, 78, 86, 89, 90; *see also*
    Chicago
image 3, 125, 156, 187
immigrant heritage 80–81, 186
immigrants *see* immigration
immigration 6, 22, 58, 65, 72, 81, 188, 192;
    illegal 67, 188
Independence Hall 77
India 54, 89
Indian art 7, 75; *see also* Native Americans
Indian casinos 86
see also gambling
Indian Gaming Regulatory Act 86
Indiana 78, 79, 86, 89
indigenous peoples *see* Native Americans
industrial heritage 81–82, 148, 157, 161; *see
    also* factories; railroads
Industrial Revolution 14, 77, 82
inflation 65, 132
infrastructure 14, 24, 26, 27, 28, 29, 50, 148,
    168, 181
inns *see* bed and breakfasts
input–output techniques 133
insurance 129, 137
international relations *see* globalization;
    supranationalism
International Standard Industrial Classification
    128
international tourism 7, 9, 28, 40, 45, 55–58,
    59, 70, 99, 111, 117, 133, 134, 141, 149,
    175, 186, 191, 192
intersectoral linkages 126
Internet 39, 44, 96, 97, 100, 128, 139
interstate highways 4, 8, 13, 20, 26–28, 38, 88,
    93, 103, 109–110, 175, 178, 186

institutional setting 8, 32–52; *see also* policies
invisible export industry 128, 155
Iowa 68, 86, 89, 166, 170, 172
Israel 64, 89
Italy 7, 61, 89, 190

Japan 8, 61, 91, 123
Japanese tourists 56–57, 96, 99
Jews 80, 91
jobs *see* employment

Kansas 5, 46, 80, 89, 166, 170, 172, 184
Kansas City (Missouri) 153, 161
Katy Trail 178
Kentucky 78, 79, 89, 191
Keynesian economics 150
Knott's Berry Farm 58, 87
Korea 34–35

lakes 10, 14, 17, 18, 96, 166, 170, 183
land-use planning *see* planning
land values 181
Las Vegas 1, 7, 8, 21, 28, 29, 44, 49, 58, 85,
    138, 139–140, 141, 144–147, 156–157
Las Vegas Convention and Visitors Authority
    1, 44, 144, 146
Latin America 42, 43, 58, 65, 80, 81, 83, 102,
    117
Leavenworth (Washington) 166, 172–173, 184
legislation 38, 51, 86
leisure 12–13, 82, 175
leisure travel 57, 59–60, 61, 64, 116, 131, 163,
    189
Lewis and Clark 6
Liberty Bell 77
Little Havana 7
Little Italy 7, 72
living museums *see* museums
lodging *see* accommodations
location quotients 139–141
Los Angeles 25, 28, 42, 115, 120, 138, 144,
    160
lotteries 85–86
Louisiana 7, 79, 86, 89, 180; *see also* New
    Orleans

Main Street Program 191
Maine 55
Mall of America 99
malls 4, 99, 152
Manifest Destiny 76
manufacturing 86, 150, 152, 159, 162, 169,
    179, 183
marinas 38
marketing 8, 33, 39, 45, 46, 51, 61, 137, 145,
    149, 165, 166, 187; budgets 45, 49
markets *see* tourist markets
Maryland 46, 79, 88, 89, 103, 158; *see also*
    Baltimore; Ocean City

mass tourism 18, 49
Massachusetts 18, 58, 78, 89, 122
"McDisneyization" 87
Memphis 115, 158
Mesa Verde National Park 73
metropolitan areas *see* cities
Mexican tourists 8, 55, 65
Mexico 34, 35, 42, 43, 55, 56, 61, 67, 70, 117, 120–121, 186, 188
Miami 8, 42, 115, 123, 139, 148, 153, 156, 191
Michigan 55, 59, 68, 89, 96, 160, 166, 172, 173
Middle East 63, 64–65
mines 80–81, 83, 103, 105, 144, 170
mining 80, 86, 105, 126, 179, 183
Minneapolis 4, 99, 115
Minnesota 68, 89; *see also* Minneapolis
Mississippi 79, 86, 169, 180
Mississippi River 79–80, 86, 118, 121
Missouri 16–17, 44, 45, 46, 48, 59, 79, 86, 89, 90, 106, 107–108, 135–136, 153–155, 156, 169, 178, 182; *see also* Kansas City; Springfield; St. Louis
Missouri Division of Tourism 44–45
mobility 4–5, 187–188
modernization 82, 177, 191
Montana 55, 68, 72, 80, 95, 169, 176
Montezuma Castle National Monument 73
Mormons *see* Church of Jesus Christ of Latter-day Saints
motels *see* hotels
motivations for travel *see* demand
mountains 10, 14, 15, 16, 18, 29, 83, 94, 149, 165, 169, 178, 179, 183, 186; *see also* natural amenities
movie-induced tourism 170–172, 192
multiculturalism 37, 80
multinationalism *see* globalization
museums 3, 29, 73, 77–79, 81, 82, 93, 149, 159, 160, 163, 191
music 73, 74, 80–81, 92, 156
Myrtle Beach (South Carolina) 88, 138, 139
Mystic Seaport 78

National Forest Service 92, 176, 183
National Historic Landmarks 21
national icons 18
National League of Cities 162
National Park Service 17, 20, 21–22, 29, 42, 76–77, 79, 82–83, 110, 176–177, 178
national parks 8, 12, 16, 19, 23, 29, 32, 54, 83–84, 93, 103, 122, 127, 149, 165, 166, 170, 175–178, 177, 179, 183
National Register of Historic Places 16–17, 21, 82
National Sporting Goods Association 82
national tourism organization 32–33, 38, 39–44

National Trust for Historic Preservation 17, 82, 191
Native Americans 7, 20, 21, 72, 74–75, 76, 80, 81, 86, 92, 118, 120; casinos *see* Indian casinos; Hopis 74, 75–76; Taos Pueblo 74, 75; Zuni Pueblo 74
natural amenities 5, 14, 16, 19, 29, 33, 42, 54, 61, 70, 72, 82, 83, 99, 102, 105, 120, 136, 165, 169, 170, 173, 177, 179, 181, 182, 184
natural disasters 64
nature *see* natural amenities
nature-based tourism *see* ecotourism
Nebraska 5, 90, 166, 169
neo-Bohemia 160–163
neocolonialism 3, 86
Netherlands 80
Nevada 44, 45, 56, 58, 68, 83, 85, 130, 141, 144–145, 180
new age spirituality 91–92
New England 25, 78, 95, 120, 170
New Hampshire 15, 18, 19, 68, 90, 95
New Jersey 15, 28, 57, 58, 78, 88, 90, 103, 111, 134; see also Atlantic City; Cape May
New Jersey Division of Tourism 44
New Mexico 7, 67, 73, 74, 75, 79–80, 90, 157
New Orleans 8, 151, 152, 157
new urbanism 156
New York 13, 14–16, 18, 55, 57–58, 59, 79, 90, 103, 111, 113, 130, 132; *see also* New York City; Niagara Falls
New York City 4, 24, 25, 25, 28, 57, 99, 105, 111, 115, 119, 120–121, 138, 139, 147, 149, 153, 154, 158, 160, 191
Newport (Rhode Island) 15, 18
Niagara Falls 6, 14–16, 43, 61
non-profit organizations 42, 154
North American Free Trade Agreement (NAFTA) 55, 188
North American Industrial Classification System (NAICS) 121, 126, 128–129, 137–138, 139–141
North Carolina 58, 59, 78, 79, 137, 178
North Dakota 166, 169, 174
North Korea 189
Northern Marianas 177
nostalgia 121, 152, 159

occupancy rates 1
Ocean City (Maryland) 88, 103
Office of Travel and Tourism Industries 41
Ohio 59, 74, 78, 79, 88, 90, 191
Oklahoma 46, 80, 90
Old Sturbridge Village 78
Olympics 7, 135, 192
Oregon 4, 44, 46, 80, 90, 95, 175
Oregon Tourism Commission 44, 50
Orlando 29, 36–37, 138, 139–140, 141, 156
outbound travel 60–64, 134, 186, 189; *see also* international tourism

overdependence on tourism 33, 132, 141, 180
Ozark Mountains 16–17, 169, 179

Pacific Ocean/coast 179
passports 42–43, 60, 63, 65, 70, 187
patriotism 76
Pennsylvania 58, 59, 79, 90, 103, 131; *see also* Philadelphia; Pittsburgh
Philadelphia 76, 103, 105, 111, 115, 149, 151, 157
Phoenix 21, 25, 28, 58, 115
photography 127
pilgrimage *see* religious tourism
Pittsburgh 131, 167
planning 34, 38–39, 49–51, 52, 136, 150, 156–157, 182, 188, 189, 192
Plimouth Plantation 78
policies 8, 13, 32, 40, 42, 148, 162, 167, 188; lack of 8, 39–43, 132, 187
political economy 3, 150
political instability 64
political science 150
Portland 4
ports 54, 65, 158
Portugal 89
post-Fordism 81, 86, 134, 150, 169
poverty 159, 168, 181
preservation *see* conservation
prisons 18, 24
private sector 46
product development 50; *see also* development of tourism
promotion of tourism *see* marketing
prostitution *see* sex tourism
public administration 150
public-private partnerships 37, 38–39, 187
Puerto Rico 120, 177

quality of life 148

rail travel 13, 59, 87, 102, 103–108, 111, 123
railroads 12, 18, 19–20, 21, 23, 25, 29, 81, 87, 88, 93, 103–108, 123, 155, 157, 175; heritage railroads 105
rails-to-trails 106–109, 178
real estate 128, 129, 134, 137, 152
recession 1, 2, 54, 60, 65, 109, 142, 152, 179
recreation 82, 105–106, 119, 128, 134, 137, 165, 169, 175, 176, 178, 181–182, 191
recreational vehicles (RVs) 186
regional carriers 28, 112
religious tourism 61, 64, 73, 88–92, 191
religious traditions 73, 76, 80, 89
Reno 44, 58, 138, 139
resorts 13, 18, 20, 36, 54, 58, 61, 72, 73, 88, 94–95, 145, 149, 156, 189, 190; beach resorts 88, 149, 156; ski resorts 68–69, 94–95, 128, 141, 156, 166, 175, 178, 181; types of 94–95

restaurants 40, 47, 87, 93, 94, 107, 127, 136, 153, 158, 159, 162, 163, 181, 189, 190, 191
retailing *see* shopping
retirees 35, 169, 173; *see also* seasonal migration; snowbirds
retirement migration 95, 169, 180; *see also* seasonal migration
Revolutionary War 13, 149, 165
Rhode Island 15, 18, 90; *see also* Newport
rituals 75–76
riverboats 86; *see also* gambling
rivers 6, 9, 118, 183; *see also* natural amenities
road-based travel *see* automobiles
Rocky Mountains 5, 72, 95, 178, 183
Route 66 6, 26, 28
rural America 10, 80, 132, 141, 165–184
rural tourism *see* rural America
Russia 5

sacred space 75
safety and security 1, 38, 40, 50, 64, 70, 150, 151, 159, 182, 187–188, 191–192
Saint Louis Gateway Arch 2
Salt Lake City 69, 90–91
San Diego 67, 120, 139, 161
San Francisco 2, 19, 22, 25, 28, 36, 99, 118, 120, 129, 131, 139, 147, 149, 157, 158, 161
Santa Fe 139, 157
Saratoga Springs 15
Saudi Arabia 89
scale 6, 49, 51, 70, 126, 128, 130, 135, 141, 150, 183
scenic byways 46, 110
scenic highways 6, 26, 110
scenic routes *see* scenic highways
Schengen Agreement 43, 188
Scottsdale (Arizona) 95
Sea World 58
seaside resorts *see* resorts
seasonal migration 95–96, 179, 181; *see also* snowbirds
seasonality 67–69
Seattle 4, 120, 148, 151
second homes 22, 35, 60, 61, 95–96, 134, 166, 167, 169, 180, 181, 183; *see also* timeshares
security *see* safety and security
Sedona (Arizona) 91–92
September 11, 2001 tragedy 1, 28, 40, 43, 51, 60, 64–65, 70, 116, 130, 134, 188
sex tourism 145–147, 159
shopping 8, 16, 28, 36, 40, 54, 55, 56, 57, 58, 61, 99, 131, 134, 137, 158, 161, 181
shopping centers *see* malls
short break trips *see* weekend trips
shrines 89–90; *see also* heritage sites; religious tourism
sightseeing 55, 127–128

Six Flags 87
skiing 8, 10, 82–83, 106, 173, 176, 178; water skiing 135; *see also* resorts
slavery 81, 191
Slow Food Movement 190
snowbirds 68, 95–96
social impacts 51, 88, 135–136, 181
South Carolina 79, 88, 95, 138, 157; *see also* Charleston; Myrtle Beach
South Dakota 90, 166, 173, 178
Soviet Union 34
spa resorts 13, 16–17, 18, 22, 72
Spain 33, 80, 89
special events *see* events
sports 12, 39, 82, 94, 99, 125, 152, 156, 158, 178, 179, 183, 192
Springfield (Missouri) 17, 48, 153–155
St. Louis 49, 93, 153, 161, 167
stadiums 3, 29, 125, 148, 152, 153, 155, 159, 163
state parks 29, 79, 82, 165, 183
Statue of Liberty 145
staycations 1
steamboats 18, 121
summer cottages *see* second homes
Super Bowl 7, 99, 192; *see also* sports
supranationalism 187–188; *see also* European Union; North American Free Trade Agreement
sustainability 136, 189–190, 192
sustainable development *see* sustainability
synagogues 91

taxes 39, 49, 65, 86, 95, 130, 131, 135, 137, 141, 144, 152, 181
technology 8, 14, 49, 59, 96, 111, 122, 153, 186–187, 191
Tennessee 79, 90, 137, 156, 178
terrorism 1, 28, 54, 60, 64–65, 186, 187–188; *see also* September 11, 2001 tragedy
Terrorism Prevention Act 42–43
Texas 44, 56, 58, 59, 67, 68, 90, 95, 113, 122, 130, 131, 137, 148, 161; *see also* Austin; Dallas
theme parks *see* amusement parks
themed destinations 156, 157, 172–173, 184
timeshares 60, 95–96
tour operators 120; *see also* travel agents
tourism, definition of 126
tourism information offices 24
tourism landscapes 65, 72, 76, 150, 161, 162, 187
tourism of vice 86, 145, 147
tourism leisure cities 34–35
tourism satellite accounts (TSAs) 126, 133–138
"tourist bubble" 159–163
tourist markets 8, 14, 45, 70, 87, 93, 98, 100, 120

tours 96–97
trails 6, 80, 105, 107–108, 121, 178; *see also* scenic byways
train travel *see* rail travel
transportation 4–5, 9, 12, 13, 15, 18, 20, 25, 29, 38, 44, 47, 49, 50, 102–123, 128, 130, 131, 136, 160, 161, 175, 189, 190; *see also* infrastructure
Transportation Security Administration 1
travel agents 3, 96–99, 120
Travel Industry Association of America 40–41, 129, 134
travel intermediaries 73, 96–100
Travel Promotion Act 39, 40
travel warnings 65–66, 188
Tuzigoot National Monument 73

ugly Americans 61, 63
unemployment 65, 133, 181
UNESCO World Heritage Sites 77
United Kingdom 8, 45, 56, 61, 63, 80, 91, 103
United States Tour Operators' Association 96
United States Travel and Tourism Administration 40
Universal Studios 58, 87
urban areas *see* cities
urban geography 149
urban renewal *see* gentrification; waterfront development
urban sociology 149
urban tourism 23–24, 80, 144–163, 192; *see also* cities
US Census Bureau 126, 139, 166
US Travel and Tourism Advisory Board 42
US Virgin Islands 120, 177
Utah 68–69, 73, 78, 80, 85, 90, 95, 103, 141, 189; *see also* Salt Lake City

vacation travel *see* leisure travel
Vermont 55, 68, 90, 95, 178
Virginia 59, 78, 79, 88, 134
Visa Waiver program 40, 43, 65
visas 38, 42, 65, 70, 187
visiting friends and relatives (VFR) 4, 54, 55–56, 60, 61, 64, 67, 70, 99, 175, 191

War of Independence *see* Revolutionary War
war on terror 1, 187–188
Washington 4, 44, 46, 55, 58, 80, 88, 95, 131, 132, 166, 170–172, 184; *see also* Leavenworth; Seattle
Washington, DC 79, 89, 103, 105
water-based travel 118–119; *see also* cruises
waterfalls 14
waterfront development 191; *see also* gentrification
websites *see* Internet
weekend trips 8, 24, 175
welcome centers 46

West Virginia 79
Western Hemisphere Travel Initiative 42
whale watching 83
white-water rafting 6
White Mountains 15, 18, 19, 95
wine/wineries 69, 107, 162
Wisconsin 68, 78, 90
World Series 135, 192
World Tourism Barometer 1
World Tourism Organization (UNWTO) 1, 7, 54, 55, 58, 133, 141

World Travel and Tourism Council 58, 125
World War One 30, 111
World War Two 16, 27, 104, 111, 144–145, 152, 153, 166, 176
World's Fairs 24, 30, 87, 135
Wyoming 80, 90, 95, 130, 132, 141, 176, 178

Yellowstone National Park 6, 18–20, 22, 29, 83–84, 175, 178, 183
Yosemite National Park 18–19, 22, 175